Unpaid Work and the Economy

Unpaid Work and the Economy

Gender, Time Use and Poverty in Developing Countries

Edited by

Rania Antonopoulos

and

Indira Hirway

First published 2010 by
PALGRAVE MACMILLAN

Palgrave Macmillan in the UK is an imprint of Macmillan Publishers Limited,
registered in England, company number 785998, of Houndmills, Basingstoke,
Hampshire RG21 6XS.

Palgrave Macmillan in the US is a division of St Martin's Press LLC,
175 Fifth Avenue, New York, NY 10010.

Palgrave Macmillan is the global academic imprint of the above companies
and has companies and representatives throughout the world.

Palgrave® and Macmillan® are registered trademarks in the United States,
the United Kingdom, Europe and other countries.

ISBN 978–0–230–21730–0   hardback

This book is printed on paper suitable for recycling and made from fully
managed and sustained forest sources. Logging, pulping and manufacturing
processes are expected to conform to the environment regulations of the
country of origin.

A catalogue record for this book is available from the British Library.

A catalogue record for this book is available from the Library of Congress.

10 9 8 7 6 5 4 3 2 1
19 18 17 16 15 14 13 12 11 10

Printed and bound in Great Britain by
CPI Antony Rowe, Chippenham and Eastbourne

Contents

The Levy Economics Institute
of Bard College

Founded in 1986, The Levy Economics Institute of Bard College is an autonomous nonprofit public policy research organization. It is non-partisan, open to the examination of diverse points of view and dedicated to public service.

The Institute believes in the potential for economic study to improve the human condition. Its purpose is to generate viable, effective public policy responses to important economic problems. It is concerned with issues that profoundly affect the quality of life in the USA, in other highly industrialized nations and in countries with developing economies.

The Institute's present research programs include such issues as financial instability, economic growth and employment, international trade, problems associated with the distribution of income and wealth, the measurement of economic well-being, and gender, globalization and poverty.

The opinions expressed in this volume are those of the authors and do not necessarily represent those of the Institute, its Board of Governors or the Trustees of Bard College.

List of Tables

List of Figures

Preface

Dimitri B. Papadimitriou

The publication of this collection of essays is the product of a project undertaken by The Levy Economics Institute of Bard College in collaboration with members of the International Working Group on Gender, Macroeconomics and International Economics (GEM-IWG) network to analyze the many economic implications of nonmarket activities disproportionately carried out by the world's women, willingly or not.

During the past decade or so, time allocated to unpaid work has received increased attention and, as a result, several countries have committed to conduct ongoing TUS collecting data and developing satellite accounts that could inform policy-making about social and economic issues. Data on how households allocate time for unpaid home production burdens could be used to better analyze and determine each household member's well-being. Various studies on time-use measurement, together with real-life experiences, especially from the developing world, show the dramatic maldistribution of unpaid work and unpaid care work being unfavorable to women. In most developing countries, efforts to reduce poverty, the overarching task for achieving the UN Millennium Development Goals, offer a unique opportunity to recognize women's contribution of unpaid work and to redress implied inequities.

The chapters of this volume assess the already established measures of time use, propose new ones and analyze and compare possible alternates. Conceptual or empirical studies that identify key issues related to measurement and evaluation of time distribution are also included, as are estimates and their significance. While one may not agree with every argument and proposal made or embrace every conclusion drawn, the essays in this collection are thoughtful and perhaps some of them are provocative. They need to be read and discussed, and their implications considered. The gender gaps persist not only in unpaid work, but also in education, health, wages and political participation. The Chinese saying that 'women hold up half the sky' should not be an aspiration, but a fact.

I would like to thank our research scholar Rania Antonopoulos, who directs the Institute's research on 'Gender Equality and the Economy,' and who along with research associate Indira Hirway, the director of the Center for Development Alternatives, took on the task of selecting and editing the papers in this volume. I am grateful to the contributors for their cooperation in carrying out revisions, to Elizabeth Dunn for copy-editing large parts of this volume, managing final details of collating the changes by authors and overseeing all tasks of proofreading. I would be remiss if I did not extend a special thank you to Nilüfer Çağatay of the GEM-IWG network for supporting this endeavor. Finally, my sincere thanks to the trustees of Bard College for supporting the Institute's programs.

Acknowledgements

The seeds for this volume were planted back in October 2005, in the aftermath of a conference on 'Unpaid Work and the Economy: Gender, Poverty, and the Millennium Development Goals,' which was organized by the Levy Economics Institute of Bard College in partnership with GEM-IWG, the International Working Group on Gender, Macroeconomics and International Economics and the United Nations Development Program's Bureau for Development Policy, Gender Team. The promise of bearing fruit was renewed in late 2007–early 2008 when we decided to revamp our commitment and publish newly produced work that had its origins, for the most part, in that conference. In addition to feedback individual authors sought on earlier versions of their work, the selected chapters included here have received the benefit of comments provided by Nilüfer Çağatay, Nancy Folbre, Irwin Friedman, Duncan Ironmonger, Dimitri Papadimitriou, Rathin Roy and Ajit Zacharias. We are grateful to them for their feedback and to the authors for their cooperation in carrying out revisions. Above all, we are indebted to Elizabeth Dunn whose able assistance in all matters, including editing, proofreading and communicating with the authors, was invaluable. To her, our warm and sincere thanks.

Rania Antonopoulos and Indira Hirway

Notes on Contributors

Olagoke Akintola is a Senior Lecturer in the School of Psychology at the University of KwaZulu-Natal, South Africa. His research interests include gender and informal/unpaid care for people living with HIV/AIDS; the general impact of HIV/AIDS on communities, households/families and on the private/public sector; and gender and health risk behavior.

Rania Antonopoulos is a Research Scholar and the Director of the 'Gender Equality and the Economy' program at The Levy Economics Institute of Bard College. Her current research focuses on the macroeconomics of full employment policies and on gender-aware economic modelling.

Lekha S. Chakraborty is a Senior Economist at the National Institute of Public Finance and Policy, India and Research Associate at The Levy Economics Institute of Bard College. Her research interests include macroeconomic issues in public finance, fiscal decentralization, gender budgeting, microfinance, subnational public finance and human development.

Jacques Charmes is an Economist, and the Director of the Department Health and Societies at the *Institut de Recherche pour le Développement* (IRD, Paris). His research focuses on the informal sector, employment, labor income and gender.

Solita Collas-Monsod, popularly known as Mareng Winnie, is a Filipino broadcaster, economist, professor and writer. Dr Monsod has been teaching in the University of the Philippines School of Economics since 1963.

Joana Costa is a Researcher at the UNDP International Poverty Center in Brasilia. Her areas of interest include education, inequality and social policies.

Valeria Esquivel is a Researcher and Assistant Professor of Economics at Universidad Nacional de General Sarmiento, Province of Buenos Aires, Argentina and Research Associate at The Levy Economics Institute of Bard College. Her current research focuses on the tensions between paid and unpaid care work based on time-use results with a strong public policy focus.

Indira Hirway is the Director of the Center for Development Alternatives, India and Research Associate at The Levy Economics Institute of Bard College. The areas of her research interests include poverty and human development, labor and employment, gender development, environment and development, environmental accounting and time-use studies.

Marcelo Medeiros is a Researcher at IPEA, the Institute of Applied Economic Research in Brazil and Associate Researcher at the University of Cambridge, UK. His works are in the fields of poverty, social inequality and mobility, health, education and theories of development and social protection.

Emel Memis is an Assistant Professor of economics at Ankara University in Turkey and Research Associate at The Levy Economics Institute of Bard College. Her research interests include macroeconomics, feminist economics and economic development.

Rafael G. Osório is a Researcher at the UNDP International Poverty Center in Brasilia. His areas of research include social mobility, gender and ethnic/racial inequalities and social policies.

Dimitri B. Papadimitriou is President of The Levy Economics Institute of Bard College and Jerome Levy Professor of Economics at Bard College. An editor and contributor to over 10 books he is a graduate of Columbia University and received a PhD in economics from the New School for Social Research. Dr Papadimitriou has served as the Vice Chairman of the Trade Deficit Review Commission of the US Congress and has testified on a number of occasions in hearings of Senate and House of Representatives Committees of the US Congress.

List of Abbreviations and Acronyms

ACGD	African Center for Gender and Development
ADL	activities of daily living
ARV	anti-retroviral
ATUS	American Time-Use Survey
BIA	benefit incidence analysis
CEDAW	Committee on the Elimination of Discrimination against Women
CSO	central statistics office
CSW	Commission on the Status of Women
CTUR	Center for Time-Use Research
CV	coefficient of variation
DAW	Division for the Advancement of Women
DGEyC	*Dirección General de Estadísticas y Censos*
ECA	Economic Commission for Africa
ECD	early childhood development
ECLAC	Economic Commission for Latin American and the Carribean
EGM	expert group meeting
EGP	employment guarantee program
ELR	employer of last resort
EPH	Encuesta Permanente de Hogars
EPWP	Expanded Public Works Program (South Africa)
ESCAP	United Nations Economic and Social Commission for Asia and the Pacific
EUROSTAT	Statistical Office of the European Communities
FAO	Food and Agriculture Organization of the United Nations
F/M	female/male
GDI	gross domestic income
GDP	gross domestic product
GEM	gender empowerment measure
GET	General Education and Training Certificate
GNP	gross national product
HDI	human development index
HCBC	home- and community-based care

HDR	human development report
HH	household
HS	household survey
IADL	instrumental activities of daily living
IATUR	International Association for Time Use Research
ICATUS	international classification of activities for time-use statistics
ILO	International Labour Organisation
INDEC	Instituto Nacional de Estadísticas y Censos
INE	Instituto Nacional de Estadística
INSTRAW	United Nations Research and Training Institute for the Advancement of Women
LFS	labor-force survey
LSMS	Living Standards Measurement Survey
MECOVI	Encuesta de Mejoramiento de Condiciones de Vida
MDG	Millennium Development Goal
MPCE	monthly per capita expenditures
NCRFW	National Commission on the Role of Filipino Women
NGO	Non-governmental Organization
Non-SNA	Not in the System of National Accounts
NQF	National Qualifications Framework
NREGA	National Rural Employment Guarantee Act (India)
NSCB	National Statistical Coordination Board
NSO	National Statistics Office
NSOT	National Statistics Office, Thailand
OECD	Organization for Economic Cooperation and Development
PDPW	Philippine Development Plan for Women
PEM	Minimum Employment Program (Chile)
PFA	Beijing Declaration and Platform for Action
PPGD	Philippine Plan for Gender Responsive Development
R	Rand (South Africa)
RNTU	Research Network on Time Use
R + U	Rural + Urban
SAM-SA	Social Accounting Matrix–South Africa
SAP	structural adjustment policies
SAQA	South African Qualification Authority
SDP	state domestic product
SNA	system of national accounts
Stats SA	Statistics South Africa
TB	tuberculosis
TURP	St Mary's University Time-Use Research Program

TUS	time-use surveys
TUS SA	time-use survey, South Africa
UHW	unpaid housework
UN	The United Nations
UNDP	United Nations Development Programme
UN ECOSOC	United Nations Economic and Social Council
UNECA	United Nations Economic Commission for Africa
UNIFEM	United Nations Development Fund for Women
UNRISD	United Nations Research Institute for Social Development
UNSD	United Nations Statistics Division
UN-SNA	United Nations System of National Accounts
USBLS	United States Bureau of Labor Statistics
USSR	United Soviet Socialist Republic
VIF	variance inflation factor
WPR	workforce participation rate

Introduction

Rania Antonopoulos and Indira Hirway

Unpaid work is increasingly recognized as an organic component of the economic system. Especially in the context of developing economies, which are the subject matter of this book, much of the provisioning of basic needs and other conveniences of life occur beyond the boundaries of market transactions. To give some examples, time devoted to activities taking place outside the sphere of remunerated activities include unpaid family work, subsistence production, collection of water, fuel wood and other free goods, sanitation and household maintenance work, food processing and meal preparation, and volunteer and unpaid care work. This work still remains unrecognized, undervalued and undercounted.

Despite lack of consistent data, it is well established that across time, geographic location and traditions, gender-based inequalities in the world of unpaid work show extraordinary persistence. Furthermore, and beyond gender differences, existing patterns of unpaid work between developed and developing countries, the poor and non-poor, the employed and the unemployed and among women that are better off and those that are struggling to make ends meet, manifest deeply rooted inequities. Consequently, it is well understood that from a distributional vantage point, the division of labor in the realm of unpaid work disadvantages some groups of people in that it imposes additional burdens on their time, which, in turn, restricts their access to opportunities to improve their lives.

These differences are not immutable and much change can indeed take place in the near future. The urgency of transforming unpaid work inequalities within households notwithstanding, it is important to understand that within a development context it is of some urgency to go beyond gender-based intrahousehold inequalities. The burden of unpaid work is largely ignored due to a lack of understanding of how unpaid work is linked to the rest of the economy. Entering policy spaces and envisioning interventions to reduce such forms of inequity is crucially based on making evident the connections between household production, market production and public sector policy.

Such recognition entails a two-pronged process. First we need time-use allocation data to be collected and to be made widely available.

Second, we must make use of existing data to make evident the linkages between unpaid work and a variety of social and economic policy challenges. In fact, the second item (concrete analysis) highlights the need for, and points out the importance of, national time-use data collection. This present collection of essays joins previous efforts that have contributed towards this end. The chapters that follow are written in the hope that adding visibility to the relationship between unpaid work and the economy, as well as highlighting connections between gender and poverty will provide further testimony to urgently needed remediation. If progress is to be made in reaching developmental goals, *inequalities in unpaid work* must become part of the development discourse.

The book combines methodological, theoretical, technical and policy-oriented discussion in the context of developing countries. It is written with a wide range of audiences in mind, from newcomers into this field of study to graduate students, as well as the more experienced researchers. It also speaks in many different 'voices.' The methodological chapters build upon the existing literature and synthesize diverse strands of research. Other chapters report on new and old surveys and findings, while pointing out critical issues for future data collection. Individual contributions span research from Africa, Latin America and Asia, and report on qualitative and quantitative analysis of data and information. In addition, a comprehensive overview of TUS from the Global South is provided; although this chapter is placed as the very last of the book, it is advisable for readers newly introduced to the topic to give it some priority. Finally, several among the individual contributions add new knowledge, analytically and empirically, by employing time-use data to empirically investigate linkages to poverty and gender issues. Below we provide a summary of each chapter.

Chapter 1, 'Unpaid Work and the Economy,' is written at an introductory level and serves to contextualize, for those less familiar with this field of work, issues that emerge later on in the contributed chapters. It begins with a purview of the concept of unpaid work so as to clarify terms used in this book, such as paid and unpaid work, system of national accounts (SNA) and non-SNA work and so on. It then proceeds to establish some important linkages of unpaid work and the economy. Analytically speaking, it goes beyond an explication of intrahousehold inequalities and points out that unpaid work bestows the fruits of 'extracted' unpaid labor as gifts, so to speak, to the institutions of the market and the state. It unequivocally argues that these 'externalities' are manifestations of a structural system that is exploitative and invites thinking about ways to reduce this systemic inequality. Next, it briefly introduces the issue of 'counting,' (namely measuring) unpaid work through TUS data and discusses some methodological and analytical issues. Finally it puts forwards some thoughts regarding dimensions of unpaid work that are important in the context of development strategies for countries of the Global South.

Chapters 2, 3 and 4 employ existing TUS data to explore empirically the intersections of poverty, gender and unpaid work in India, Bolivia and South Africa.

Chapter 2, 'Understanding Poverty: Insights Emerging from Time Use of the Poor,' by Indira Hirway, uses statistical information of the first (pilot) TUS in India (1998–99) to analyze the time-use patterns of the poor at the bottom (the ultra-poor) and the non-poor in India. The analysis shows that the poor at the bottom are constrained by the way they are forced to use their time to access some of their basic needs and to manage their livelihoods. They seem to be trapped in the vicious circle of unpaid work and poverty, and unless they are helped in getting out of this unpaid SNA and non-SNA work (which is usually drudgery), it will be difficult to bring them out of poverty. The chapter underscores the importance of the provision of basic services and infrastructure, public provisioning of universal services for improved early childhood development and health services and bringing unpaid domestic work under the realm of technological upgradation to reduce drudgery of household work. In addition, the paper also argues that macro-policies will have to pay attention to natural resource management (for example, the regeneration of natural resources) to enable the poor at the bottom to get out of the subsistence mode of production and be able to produce goods for the market at a higher and more stable level of productivity. Finally, the paper shows that women in non-poor households are not necessarily out of poverty, as they are under tremendous time stress on the one hand and constrained by a highly unfavorable pattern of time use on the other. The former tends to deplete their well-being, as well as their human capital, while the latter restricts their access to developmental opportunities, including productive employment. It is clear that women's poverty needs a special focus.

Chapter 3, 'Gender Inequalities in Allocating Time to Paid and Unpaid Work: Evidence from Bolivia,' by Marcelo Medeiros, Rafael Guerreiro Osório and Joana Costa, discusses gender inequalities in allocating time to paid and unpaid work among urban adults in Bolivia using time-use data from a 2001 household survey. It identifies a gender-based division of labor characterized not so much by who does which type of work, but by how much work of each type they do. The findings point out several interesting results. There is, as expected, a trade-off between paid and unpaid work, but such a substitution is only partial; as paid work combines with unpaid work contributions, women's entry into the labor market tends to result in a 'double day.' It also reports very high levels of within-group inequality in the distributions of paid and unpaid work-time for men and women, a sign that beyond the sexual division of labor, subgroup differentiation is also important. Using decompositions of the inequality in the distribution of total time spent at work, it econometrically shows that gender is an important variable to explain how much paid and unpaid work is done by individuals, but less important in fully accounting for why some people have a higher total workload than others.

The next chapter, Chapter 4, 'Unpaid Work, Poverty and Unemployment: A Gender Perspective from South Africa,' by Emel Memis and Rania Antonopoulos, focuses on South Africa. Widespread income poverty and unemployment have remained serious challenges in post-apartheid South Africa, but some population groups have been disproportionately affected. A less discussed form of inequality that is equally challenging pertains to unpaid work. Much like poverty and unemployment, time-use patterns in South Africa continue to have gender, racial and spatial characteristics. Making use of the 2000 South African TUS data, this study explores how gender, poverty, unemployment and location act as stratifiers that impact the overall amount of unpaid work burdens. Their empirical investigation is based on a Tobit estimation. The study shows that, in the context of poverty, unemployment and geographic location of households, if and when more unpaid inputs are observed (or required), the supply of unpaid labor response is highly gendered.

The next three chapters, 5, 6 and 7, concentrate on policy issues. All of these contributions carry a common message. To ameliorate burdens of unpaid work, public investment in physical and social infrastructure is a prerequisite. Chapter 5, 'Unpaid HIV/AIDS Care, Gender and Poverty: Exploring the Links,' by Olagoke Akintola, explores the linkages of unpaid HIV/AIDS care, gender and poverty. Although recent studies have focused on women's role in the care of people living with AIDS, showing evidence of an increase in the amount of care work carried out by women, little is to be found in the way of comprehensive information on the extent and forms of care provided and how these contribute to women's time burdens or impact on poverty in HIV/AIDS-affected households and communities. This chapter argues that the home-based care results in a dramatic increase in women's care work and is contributing to the feminization of poverty. It highlights the dearth of data on the impoverishing impact of home-based care on caregivers and points out the need for new time-use data collection to shed further light on the interplay between women's caring for patients and the corresponding reductions in paid and subsistence production. The fact that caring work increases caregivers' time burdens underscores the importance of respite care so that caregivers have more time to participate in the labor force. Respite care will need to be carried out within the framework of well-funded and well-resourced community-based care programs. The study also reveals the need for policies that aim to protect children from experiencing the adverse effects of providing care, as well as to keep them protected from being removed from school to provide care. Such policies, it is argued, should include interventions that target poor families and guarantee education for all children, particularly those in poor and HIV/AIDS-affected families, who cannot afford education.

Chapter 6, 'Public Investment and Unpaid Work in India: Selective Evidence from Time-Use Data,' is written by Lekha S. Chakraborty. It focuses on public investment in water delivery and sanitation and unpaid work in India. It begins by pointing out that the theory and data on time allocation has revealed that, historically, market-time has never consistently been greater than non-market time and therefore the allocation and efficiency of latter may be equally important, if not more so, to economic growth than that of former. This is particularly important in the context of developing countries, where public infrastructure deficit induces locking of time in unpaid work. Against this backdrop, this chapter examines the link between public infrastructure investment and time allocation across gender in the context of selected states in India. In particular, time-use statistics of water collection show that it is significantly higher for girls in both rural and urban areas, which, in turn, points to the deficiencies in infrastructure for water delivery and sanitation. The results from an illustrative gender-disaggregated benefit incidence analysis carried out for the water sector revealed that public infrastructure investment in water can significantly benefit women (more so than men) whereby unpaid work inequalities are ameliorated. But the study is careful to also note that even with improvements to infrastraucture, there is no evidence that the release of time previously locked up in unpaid SNA work is substituted with market work. This, in turn, implies that though infrastructure investment lessens the time stress in unpaid SNA activity, to reduce household poverty complementary employment policies are also required so as to ensure that freed-up time does not translate to forced leisure but, instead, to market work.

Chapter 7, 'Unpaid Work and Unemployment: Engendering Public Job Creation,' by Rania Antonopoulos, combines the concerns picked up in the two previous contributions and adds to them a key challenge of macroeconomic policy, that is, unemployment. It begins by pointing out the irony of the dynamics of market economies, which end up producing a paradox of too much unemployment on the one hand and too much work performed under unpaid conditions on the other. While the first chapter of this book discussed, among other issues, the disadvantages women face in allocating time disproportionately on unpaid work, this chapter turns to disadvantages people face when paid work is sought after but unavailable. Specifically it discusses the importance of guaranteeing a job for all citizens as a permanent policy and elaborates on the benefits of en-'gendering' such an active labor market policy. Making use of South Africa as a case study, it argues that should a framework be adopted that makes the importance of unpaid work visible, gender-aware project design can produce synergies that promote many policy goals simultaneously. It traces the macro- and micro-impacts of employment creation for unskilled, poor households in the areas of early childhood development and home-based care. The results obtained indeed warrant public policy consideration. Substituting paid for unpaid work delivers human development outcomes that are accompanied by pro-poor development and reduction in unpaid work.

The remaining chapters shift our attention to data collection and methodological issues. Chapters 8 and 9 discuss challenges and achievements in the context of data collection for African countries and Latin America, with a specific focus on Buenos Aires. Chapter 10 adds a new and unique voice to the book in that it expresses outrage and disappointment at the fact that unpaid work, after decades of mobilization and commitments, remains marginalized, misunderstood and misused, thus blinding policy to substantive issues relevant for the majority of the world's population and women in particular. It then presents selected findings on the Philippines. The final chapter, Chapter 11, offers a comprehensive presentation and unique assessment of TUS conducted to date in the Global South. To provide a bit more background, we summarize each one separately.

In Chapter 8, Valeria Esquivel presents 'Lessons from the Buenos Aires TUS: A Methodological Assessment.' The Buenos Aires TUS was a collaborative effort between a statistical agency and academia, and the author of the chapter offers unique and in depth insights, as she played a key role in all stages of the survey. The primary purpose of survey was to quantify unpaid care work performed mostly by women in the household and the findings of this survey are to be used to promote policies focused on enhancing the living conditions of women, as well as on the equitable integration of women and men into society. This chapter describes the methodological features of the survey and derives useful lessons to replicate the Buenos Aires TUS in similar contexts and/or on a nationwide scale. There are many useful lessons to be derived from the Buenos Aires TUS in terms of fieldwork organization, activity classification and the way simultaneous activities are captured. Above all, it is argued that even under circumstances where abandoning the idealized stand-alone time-use data collection approach is necessary, designing a TUS module within an ongoing household survey can yield valuable information. For, when it comes to policy making, recurrent surveys (and hence, timely data) are terribly important.

Chapter 9, 'issues in Time-use Measurement and Valuation: Lessons from African Experience on Technical and Analytical Issues,' by Jacques Charmes, presents technical and analytical issues in time-use measurement and valuation from the standpoint of African experiences. Since the middle of the 1990s, several TUS have been carried out in developing countries and especially in Africa; several are presently on-going. These various surveys have made evident several challenging methodological issues; largely these discrepancies arise from using surveys designed for developed countries in the context of the developing world. Based on field experience in Benin and Madagascar, as well as on various studies at the local level, this chapter addresses some technical issues arising from the implementation of TUS in rural traditional societies, such as the notion of time, seasonality, simultaneous activities and sampling procedures, among others. Also, in the present period when time poverty reveals itself more and more as a crucial dimension of poverty, especially for women, the paper stresses the weak use that is made of TUS results, both from an analytical point of view, as well as from a political point of view.

The penultimate chapter, Chapter 10, 'Removing the Cloak of Invisibility: Integrating Unpaid Household Services in National Economic Accounts: The Philippines Experience,' is written by Solita Collas-Monsod. The chapter is essentially concerned with the pervasive and enduring invisibility of unpaid household services in national income accounts and discusses this at some length before turning to the Philippines experience. The chapter begins with a key policy question: What can be done to increase the demand for time-use data so that women's contributions become visible? Having highlighted the processes and fora that raised consciousness in regards to women's contributions to the economy through their unpaid work, fault is found in the fact that unpaid work has not been integrated sufficiently into national income accounts. This is due to insufficient pressure to collect appropriate data, but also due to lack of awareness of the importance of linking the paid and unpaid economies. Turning to the Philippine experience, it presents data that highlight severe gender inequalities and the chapter ends by recommending mobilization strategies to place unpaid work center stage.

'Time Use Surveys in Developing Countries: An Assessment' is the final contribution by Indira Hirway. This comprehensive review of the available literature and data sets is informed by the first-hand practical experience of the author – who has been involved in conducting TUS and analyzing time-use data of different countries. As such, it offers a rich discussion of the multiple issues related to time-use methodologies and data analysis. Out of the 56 reviewed countries, less than half (27) have conducted a national survey, with the remaining being confined to pilot studies. Of these 27 countries, only four countries, namely Morocco, Mexico, Nicaragua and Ecuador, have conducted more than one national TUS. In short, TUS in developing countries are still in the exploratory stage and far from mainstreamed in their respective national statistical systems. The chapter concludes with an assessment of what is needed urgently at present. Two key recommendations emerge. First, harmonization of concepts and methods is important, not only to enhance cross-country comparability of the data, but also to ensure the quality of the data collected. Second, and equally important, is the need to analyze the available data and establish the utility of TUS in addressing some of the critical concerns on these economies. In this regard, much can emerge from existing studies. The hope is that the contributed chapters of this volume will provoke further research and produce valuable insights in this direction.

1
Unpaid Work and the Economy

Rania Antonopoulos and Indira Hirway

Introduction

This chapter is written at an introductory level and serves to contextualize issues that emerge later on in the contributed chapters. We have four tasks facing us. We begin with a purview of the concept of unpaid work so as to clarify terms used in this book, such as paid and unpaid work, system of national accounts (SNA) and non-SNA work and so on. We move then to establish some important linkages between unpaid work and the economy. Beyond an explication of intrahousehold inequalities, we point out some of the interconnections between unpaid work taking place within the institutional setting of the household and the institutions of the market and the state. Next, we turn to TUS data, as they are the primary tool for acknowledging and measuring unpaid work. Finally, we put forward some dimensions of unpaid work that are of specific importance in the context of development strategies for countries of the Global South.

Analytically speaking, people allocate their time to activities that can be classified as no work, paid work and unpaid work.[1] Leaving aside sleep time, the concept of 'no work' is commonly understood as consisting of free time spent on personal care and leisure activities.[2] No work is important because: (1) rest and leisure are necessary for physical and mental health of human beings; and (2) a part of it (namely, reading, studying, skill training, self-development activities and so on) contributes to improving human capabilities.

Paid work refers to time contracted out that receives remuneration. Work arrangements and the extent to which paid work is performed under decent conditions show extreme variations, with notable adverse effects on workers that have received considerable attention by academic

1

researchers, government and non-government organizations and trade unions. Labor market segmentation, wage differentials, unemployment and labor force participation rates are also relatively well-investigated subjects and national labor statistics departments routinely collect data on these issues.

Unpaid work has received less attention. Generally speaking, it includes all nonremunerated work activities. The allocation of unpaid work depends upon many factors; these include age, social class, presence of children and type of household structure, to name a few. Accordingly, the amount of time devoted to unpaid tasks is overall smaller for the very young, those that can purchase substitutes in the market, those with few or no children and non-single heads of households.

Equally important is the level of development of the economy, which affects not only the number of persons performing these tasks and the distribution of time between paid/unpaid work, but also the duration and allocation of unpaid time among different types of unpaid activities. In developing countries people tend to spend relatively more time on unpaid subsistence work, for example, production for self-consumption, unpaid work in family enterprises and on care related work; in wealthier countries, larger segments of the population have access to paid jobs. Furthermore, among those that work part-time or not at all, as one would expect, less time is devoted to activities such as subsistence cultivation or fetching water. Finally, and connected to the latter issue, public sector infrastructure and state provisioning regimes determine service delivery and hence play a role in the specific allocation of time among a variety of unpaid tasks. Universal free access to child and elder care, health services and water delivery to one's living quarters would reduce the amount of time needed in taking care of family/household members at home and in gathering and transporting water.

Nonetheless, and despite the above-mentioned differentiating elements, a most striking and well-known feature revealed by data collected through TUS is that women, as compared to men, perform unpaid work disproportionately in both developing and developed countries. In Figure 1.1, a simple tabulation of time-use data from UNDP (2006) and ECLAC (2007) shows, for example, that this gap ranges from two to five hours per day for countries as diverse as South Africa, Japan and the Netherlands, to France, Mauritius and the United States, and to India, Guatemala, Italy and Mexico.

We now turn to terminology. As unpaid work is unwittingly conflated with *nonproduction* work and, at other times, with performing production work (not destined for the market) some conceptual clarifications are in

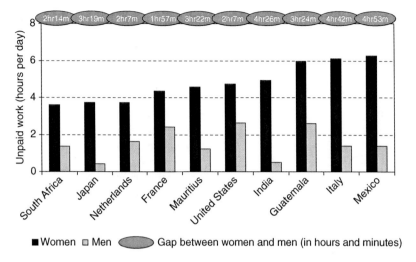

■ Women □ Men ◯ Gap between women and men (in hours and minutes)

Source: Antonopoulos, 2008, p. 9.
Figure 1.1 Time spent on unpaid work: selected developing and OECD countries

order. To complicate matters, unpaid work, unpaid *care* work, household production and household reproduction are used interchangeably. It is useful therefore, to devote a bit of time to clarify these terms.

We begin with the question of whether unpaid work is *economic* work or *non-economic* work. The United Nations System of National Accounts of 1993 (UN-SNA), provides the conceptual framework that sets the international statistical standard for the measurement and classification of economic activities;[3] it consists of an integrated set of macroeconomic accounts, balance sheets and tables based on internationally agreed upon concepts, definitions, classifications and accounting rules that delineate the market economy. In addition, it provides guidelines for constructing parallel (commonly referred to as satellite) accounts of unpaid work. Some types of unpaid work activities are deemed 'economic work' and, much like paid work, are considered to belong within the 'SNA production boundary.' Other unpaid work activities are classified as 'non-economic.'

The SNA 1993 convention indicates that the former (unpaid *economic* work) activities be measured and included in annual estimates of gross domestic product (GDP). These pertain to: (a) production of fixed assets for household use, such as building a house; (b) subsistence production work, such as crop cultivation, animal husbandry, forestry and fishery for own use; (c) collection of basic necessities, like water and fuel wood, from common lands or private lands; (d) collection of raw materials for *income* generating activities like crafts and other manufacturing; and (e) activities like unpaid family work for crop production that *reaches the market,* as well as animal grazing, agroprocessing and food processing *for sale.* Accordingly, unpaid economic work consists of activities in procuring inputs and producing for own use, as well as for the market. Unpaid agricultural family work for the market is also included here. In practice, data collection gaps make measurement and inclusion of many of the above-mentioned activities in national income and product accounts very difficult.

Other types of unpaid work are deemed by the SNA 1993 to be 'non-economic' and are relegated outside the SNA production boundary. Non-SNA unpaid work, often referred to as work that falls 'outside the SNA production boundary,' consists of household maintenance, cleaning, washing, cooking and shopping. It also consists of providing care to infants, children (active and passive care), the permanently ill or temporarily sick, older relatives and the disabled, as well as all volunteer work for community services. Recognizing these as contributing to society, but not to the 'economy,' the SNA recommendation is that parallel (satellite) accounts to the national income and product accounts (GDP) are constructed. Table 1.1 shows a schematic representation of the relationship between paid/unpaid work and SNA/non-SNA work. To reiterate, unpaid work is at times performed with a view to produce for the *market*, as in cell (B); it is considered to be *production* work, as in cells (B+C), whether it is destined for the market, as in cell (B), or for own use within the household, cell (C).

Regarding gender differences, it is not only the length of time devoted to unpaid work that puts women at a disadvantage. As mentioned earlier, it is also the types of activities and nature of the tasks that create (and reveal) further inequalities among women and between households. For instance, the exact duration and distribution among tasks of 'household reproduction time' – that is, time spent to ensure the physical and emotional well-being of household members – is determined, to a large degree, by income levels and availability of household appliances. The first allows for purchase of intermediate goods and services and the second for use of technologies, both of which reduce unpaid work time needed for food processing and preparation, cleaning up and performing daily maintenance work. Previous research and findings presented in this volume reveal that the distribution of time allocated to unpaid work across non-poor and poor households shows a lot of variation (Hirway, 2005; Blackden and Wodon, 2006).

Table 1.1 The overlap of paid/unpaid work and SNA/non-SNA work

SNA work (within the production boundary)	(A) Paid work (for the market)	(B) Unpaid work (ultimate purpose and destination of output is the market)	(C) Unpaid work for the household (ultimate destination is the household itself, namely, nonmarket)	
Non-SNA work (outside the production boundary)				(D) Unpaid work (nonmarket; household maintenance, care work and volunteer work)

Source: Antonopoulos (2008), p. 11.

Equally important is the existence of social and physical public infrastructure and/or ability to pay user fees that provide access to critical inputs such as water, sanitation, adequate health care services and energy resources. Existing time-use information reveals that the pattern of time distribution to access such vital inputs matters a lot from a gender perspective, as more unpaid work is needed to fill in infrastructural gaps. This implies that longer household overhead (unpaid work) production hours are necessary for poor households, which further exacerbates the burden of poor women.

Unpaid work and the macroeconomy

Among the contributions of gender-aware economic analysis is the reexamination of the function households play at the macroeconomic level of investigation. For our purposes it is worth noting that households have traditionally been presumed to supply labor to the business sector in return for income; they either consume or save this income. This, as feminist economists have pointed out, is a rather limited view, as it conceals the fact that households are also linked to the rest of the economy through their *production* capacity[4] in so far as they produce much of the basic needs and conveniences of life through unpaid work. Excluding the nonmonetized part of the economy is even more problematic for developing countries, where fully marketized activities comprise a small fraction of the economy. We wish to highlight three aspects here: (a) the fact that GDP should be expanded to include the value of economic unpaid work by including the SNA 1993 guidelines, as well as the portion deemed 'non-economic contribution'; (b) the link of unpaid work to the marketized part of the economy; and (c) the link of unpaid work to state provisioning of public goods and service delivery.

Expanding the measurement of GDP

Our starting point is that household production expands the available pool of necessities human beings rely upon for their physical and social reproduction. At one level then, household unpaid (care) work supplements the goods and services bought with income from the market and those made available through public sector provisioning. TUS data and the construction of parallel satellite accounts have made the contribution of household production transparent.[5] We will discuss briefly what TUS are in the section immediately following this one, but it suffices to say that for countries with available time-use data, satellite accounts estimates range from an additional 20 per cent to 60 per cent of GDP,[6] highlighting the contribution of this hidden sector of the economy and, in particular, women's contributions to economic well-being.

Even more important than assigning monetary value to the contributions of household production, awareness of unpaid labor's value leads to the recognition that the three sectors – households, markets and government (and for some developing countries the NGO sector) – are structurally interlinked at the economic level. Accepting such a vision implies that when investigating questions related to growth and policy (fiscal, monetary, international trade and financial sector), the household *production* sector should not be viewed as an afterthought, but rather as one of the fundamental building blocks.[7] From a policy point of view, how people divide their time between paid and unpaid work ought to be used to understand the impact of macropolicies on those performing unpaid work, as well as those that operate mostly within formal markets.

A gender-aware vision proposes that studying the economy entails specifying the processes that take place not only within and between the marketized parts of the economy and the government sector, but also those related to the nonmonetized household sector. Figure 1.2 shows a revised view of labor flows in the economy.

Unpaid work as a subsidy to the marketized part of the economy

Unpaid work activities entail everyday routine household maintenance work, such as cooking, cleaning, shopping, doing the laundry, caring for children and so on. Viewed from the point of view of classical economics,

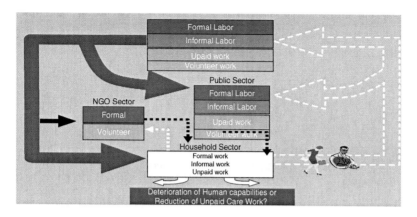

Source: Original graphic design is from E. Gomez Luna, *Unpaid Work and the System of National Accounts*, Conference on 'Unpaid Work: Gender, Poverty and the MDGs,' The Levy Economics Institute, 3–4 October 2005.

Figure 1.2 Unpaid work and the macroeconomy

this work lowers the cost of labor; at the macro-level, this allows for a smaller wage fund and thus a larger pool of profits, which facilitates the process of accumulation at any given time. Unpaid time spent on these activities, then, can be thought of as a 'subsidy' to the business sector, as a transfer, a 'gift' if you may, from one institution (the household/family) to the institution of the market.[8] That unpaid work may be important at a personal level, both to the giver and to the receiver, does not alter the fact that in its absence a higher real wage would be necessary to maintain the same standard of living for employees and their families, with consequences for cost structures and wage–profit rates. At the same time, the 'subsidies' unpaid work provides result in lower overall levels of labor force participation, income that could have been generated and lower levels of effective demand for goods and services that could be providing employment and generating further economic activity, especially in employment-intensive sectors.

A recent study on selected Latin American countries shows that over half of the women aged 20 to 24 stated their responsibilities at home as *the main reason* for not seeking a job in the labor market (ECLAC, 2007). This group is larger than those unable to find jobs due to lack of education. The study also reports that having someone in the household engaged exclusively in housework (for example, another relative or domestic worker) does not have much impact on the amount of time that men spend on unpaid domestic work, but it has a major impact on women who report a positive affect on time spent on other activities (including work in the labor market). The study validates the fact that women's domestic unpaid work forms a barrier in seeking or keeping a paid job. Women's inferior status, as well as their poor performance in the labor market, is closely linked with the division of labor between men and women in the household, as well as the social and cultural norms emanating from and reinforcing this division. Women's burden of unpaid domestic work, their poor access to education and skill development, restricted horizontal and vertical mobility and restricted choice of work – all of which are the consequences of unequal division of unpaid domestic work and the sociocultural norms – result in women's inferior status in the labor market (Hirway, 2008).

Unpaid work as a subsidy to state provisioning

A different linkage of unpaid work and the rest of the economy exists through its connection to public sector goods provisioning. For example, unpaid work provides care to the homebound and chronically ill or those in need of protracted treatment. Care is provided in hospitals due to lack of nurse-aides, sanitation personnel, cooks and so on or at home due to shortened hospital stays dictated by the structural adjustment policies of the late 1980s and 1990s. Time-use data and satellite accounts allow for estimations of the volume of unpaid work directed to the provisioning of goods and services that the public sector should be making available – health, education, transportation, water, sanitation and childcare. It is time spent performing unpaid work in these areas that we will refer to as *'subsidies'* to *public sector provisioning*. Included in these activities are the delivery of raw foodstuff, cooking, serving and cleaning up for (school) children's nutrition enhancement programs; fetching and carrying water and fossil fuels for sanitation and energy use in households; and childcare and eldercare provisioning for one's own family and for the community.

This work places an enormous time-tax on some people asymmetrically, particularly on women (especially on poor women) and children in developing countries, which limits other aspects of social engagement.[9] In some cases, it reduces the time spent in self-employment or market participation; a case in point is taking care of HIV/AIDS patients in sub-Saharan Africa (Akintola, 2004). In other cases it limits involvement in political processes, in attending school and medical appointments and skill upgrading or artistic expression. Yet at other times it reduces leisure and time available for self-care and sleep. At times of financial crisis, as in Argentina in 2001, as women increased their time for pay, the extra unpaid work was picked up by elder women (Esquivel, 2006). This can lead to social exclusion, time-poverty and depletion of human capabilities.[10] Internalized as one's 'destiny', the inviolable obligations of unpaid work deprives some of their 'rights' and citizenship by *de facto* segregation.

Unpaid work is interlinked with the location individuals occupy in paid work through many channels: it (a) shapes the ability, duration and types of paid work that can be undertaken and therefore limits access to existing and potential collective-action processes and social security; (b) does not offer monetary remuneration, which reduces the exercise of 'voice' over decision-making and ability to accumulate savings and assets; (c) is regarded a woman's 'natural' work, performed in the 'private' sphere of the family, and essentializes this work and strips it of its socioeconomic dimensions and contributions; and (d) assigns paid social reproduction (care) workers to jobs that are presumed to be unskilled, with low pay, slender options for promotion and scant social protection.

Taking care of one's own household and family members' needs may be labor of love, but it is also labor of sorrow and drudgery. In particular, unpaid care work, though embedded in feelings of obligation and commitment to others' well-being, is also rooted in patriarchal structures that interact with the rest of the economy in ways that need to gain more visibility. The male-breadwinner/female-caregiver polar representation perpetuates a 'gendering' ideology that distorts and limits human potential and narrows the range of experiences of 'being' and 'doing' for men and women. If we are to make further progress towards gender equality, we have to address the fact that it is neither 'normal' nor 'natural' for women to be performing most of the unpaid labor.

Most importantly, unpaid care work entails a systemic transfer of hidden subsidies to the rest of the economy that go unrecognized, imposing a systematic time-tax on women throughout their life cycle. These hidden subsidies signal the existence of power relations between men and women, but they also connect the 'private' worlds of households and families with the 'public' spheres of markets and the state.

Existing methodologies on data collection, production and analysis on unpaid work

The main tool for collecting information on unpaid work is the TUS. Historically, time-use statistics were first produced in the early years of the twentieth century in social surveys reporting on the living conditions of working class families. Later on, in the 1920s, TUS were carried out in some centrally planned economies, as well as in some industrialized countries (the United Kingdom and the United States). The first comprehensive multinational comparative time-use research project occurred in the 1960s. It consisted of data collected in twelve European countries, with the main objective being to understand the use of free time by people on hobbies, recreation, mass media and child care.

It was only in the 1970s that unpaid domestic work came to center stage as a particular interest emerged from within feminist groups in industrialized countries in the North to measure the 'invisible' unpaid care work of women to assess both the emerging 'double day' and to estimate women's contribution to human welfare. Subsequently TUS emerged as a tool of projecting the uneven distribution of total (paid and unpaid) work between men and women in an economy and a large number of industrialized countries, such as the United Kingdom, Germany, the Netherlands, Finland, Japan, Australia, Canada and others, started conducting periodical TUS. Over the years, the objectives behind conducting TUS have expanded to cover many socioeconomic objectives, including satisfaction with public services and overall happiness, with the objective of estimating the contribution of unpaid domestic work still remaining important.

The developing countries, however, saw that TUS could be very useful in measuring another dimension of unpaid work, namely, SNA work covered under the production boundary of the UN-SNA. This work is frequently not well-recorded in these countries through labor force surveys and mixed surveys (household cum enterprise surveys), as: (1) it is not always easy to distinguish between informal work and household work at the practical level (for example, cooking for hired farm workers and cooking for the family are not easy to separate from each other; another example may be the activity of cooking for unpaid family workers in a family business); (2) there are sociocultural biases on the part of respondents, particularly women, who fail to report themselves as workers; (3) there are also sociocultural biases on the part of interviewers or investigators who frequently fail to report women's economic work correctly; and (4) the nature of informal work is frequently temporary, seasonal or of short duration, scattered and sporadic, and is irregular and mobile, all of which makes it difficult to net this work through these surveys. TUS, which collect comprehensive data on how people spend their total time on different activities, are likely to help in overcoming these problems if the surveys are designed well and the data are analyzed systematically using a good classification of activities (Hirway and Charmes, 2006).[11] In addition, TUS: (1) provide information on subsistence work, which is uncounted or undercounted; and (2) highlight some of the characteristics of workforce, such as, multiple activities of workers (mainly women), the scattered nature of work and the time spent on different activities of men and women.

This new use of TUS for estimating and understanding the characteristics of a workforce engaged in economic work is now seen as relevant to industrialized countries also. This is because the labor markets in these countries, under increasing flexibilization, have a variety of production organizations with a wide range of work-time arrangements that cannot be captured through conventional surveys. Since women predominate as flexible labor (namely as part-time, home-based, casual and temporary workers), TUS are extremely relevant to understand gender differences in the labor market status of workers.

Recently, TUS have been recognized as a tool that provides comprehensive information on human life. Human activities can be broadly divided into three categories, namely, economic activities, or those activities falling within the production boundary of the UN-SNA, as discussed earlier; unpaid activities falling outside the production boundary, mainly domestic services, voluntary services and so on; and personal care and leisure activities like sleeping, watching TV, and so on, which cannot be delegated to others. Though all the three categories of activities contribute to human well-being and though national policies impact on all the categories of activities, many national statistical offices still collect data only on marketized and fully reported activities, so national policies are formulated and monitored using this partial picture. This approach of using a partial picture for formulating policies that affect the entire economy or society does not seem to be appropriate. Since unpaid activities are performed predominantly by women, it especially undermines women's interests.

Time-use studies improve estimates of macrovariables

Information on how people spend their time on the different paid and unpaid activities can be used in getting improved estimates of some macrovariables, which, in turn, can also be useful in macroeconomic modeling. These macrovariables are: (1) workforce estimates; (2) national income estimates; (3) valuation of 'unpaid' work; and (4) national time accounts. These areas are still a 'work in progress' in the sense that the methodologies in these areas are not yet firmed up. However, several countries have made considerable progress in compiling improved measurements.

A major difficulty in using time-use data for macroeconomic analysis is also related to the lack of timely produced data for unpaid work activities and the absence of regularly collected time-use statistics, as most developing countries have conducted only a single TUS. This prohibits analysts from having access to time series information regarding the allocation of time between the paid and unpaid sectors of the economy, which, in turn, limits the ability of modeling. The estimation of a variety of useful reaction coefficients, such as elasticities of the interaction of the paid and unpaid sectors to growth, balance of payments, reduced fiscal space and so on, is quite difficult to achieve unless one imposes very stringent assumptions. Although time allocation changes slowly, lack of comprehensive and consistent data when the economy undergoes changes (induced by either external shocks or policy decisions) makes it virtually impossible to engage in meaningful and scientifically robust analysis. Why such information is of paramount importance is discussed below.

Improving workforce estimates

As seen above, the workforce, particularly in developing economies, is underestimated in 'difficult to measure sectors' like the subsistence sector, home-based work, home work and other informal sector activities. TUS are likely to help in getting over these difficulties to a considerable extent if the right concepts and right methodologies (namely, the right survey design including sampling of households and time sampling, data collection methods, classification of activities, context variables and data analysis) are used. TUS should not replace labor force surveys, but they can definitely supplement the findings of labor force surveys and thereby can give improved estimates of the workforce, as well as throw light on some of its important characteristics. In India, for example, workforce estimates based on TUS data have given improved estimates of the workforce (Saha, 2003). One can therefore suggest that a labor force survey should have a time-use module or an independent TUS should be conducted when a labor force survey is conducted, say after every five years.

Improving national income estimates

There are three major sectors/subsectors that are underestimated or not estimated in national income estimates: (1) the informal economy; (2) production for self-consumption, as in a subsistence economy; and (3) the underground or illegal economy (OECD, 2002). The main reason for this non-/under-estimation is the lack of adequate statistics. The contribution of informal sector activities is frequently compiled by multiplying the number of workers in each of the activities with its average production (which is calculated by conducting special surveys). The total contribution of each of the activities is then added up to arrive at the total contribution of the informal sector to the national GDP. TUS are useful in improving these data, as they can provide better estimates of workers for the different informal sector activities. The contribution of the subsistence sector to national income also can be improved by using time-use data. The production boundary for the purpose of estimating national accounts (UN-SNA) was expanded in 1993 to cover nonmarketed production for own consumption. It is difficult to estimate the production for self-consumption through conventional surveys, as these activities frequently get mixed with unpaid domestic services and conventional surveys find it difficult to collect data on how many persons spend time on subsistence activities, how much do they produce for self-consumption and so on. A TUS is a suitable survey for collection of these data, as they collect comprehensive information on how people spend their time on difficult activities and how much they produce (collected through the suitable context variables).

Valuation of unpaid work/satellite accounts

Unpaid domestic services are outside the purview of national income according to the 1993 UN-SNA. However, these services contribute to human well-being in several ways. Since women are predominant in these services, it is important to estimate their contribution to the total welfare of the economy. That is, the valuation of unpaid domestic services is essential for making visible women's contribution to total welfare. However, there are several conceptual and methodological problems in this valuation, such as: (1) many domestic services do not have market prices available for valuation, as these activities are never marketed; (2) domestic services are performed in a noncompetitive, nonmarket environment, therefore it is not valid to use market prices to value these activities; and (3) the concept of time in the unpaid domestic sector is elastic, as the same work can be done in different time periods. In spite of these problems, attempts have been made to value these activities using the following approaches:

Input method   According to this method the time input in unpaid work is valued by multiplying it with an appropriate wage rate. The kinds of wages used are the specialized wage rate, the generalized wage rate and opportunity cost. This approach has several limitations, as it ignores the role of capital in the production.

Output method   According to this method, unpaid work is presented in output terms (for example, so many meals prepared, so many clothes washed and so on) so as to compute its value by multiplying the output produced by market prices. This approach also has several limitations, as not all domestic services can be converted into output. Also, the value of output needs to be expressed in terms of value-added.

Households input/output tables or national accounts of household economy   These are essentially an extension of SNA. They include unpaid household productive activities of men and women in a system of 'household' accounts, which is separate from, but consistent with, the main accounts. These are commonly referred to as Satellite national time accounts and we discuss them in the next section.

Satellite national time accounts   Satellite national time accounts are income and expenditure accounts of time, similar to the estimates of national income and expenditure that account for market transactions in monetary terms. The accounts present how households allocate time between paid work, unpaid work and leisure according to the standard categories of industrial activities (for paid work) and standard categories of household production and leisure. A system of national time accounts would provide a basis for international comparisons and for greatly improved modeling of economic and social systems. Regular national time accounts present a more complete perspective and understanding of the role of the household in the total economy, productive activities and leisure activities, and the interaction between the household and the market. So far, countries like the Netherlands, Canada, Australia and others have compiled national time accounts.

Unpaid work in the context of development

As we pointed out at the beginning of the chapter, in accordance to the SNA 1993, both paid and unpaid work are accepted as 'work,' namely, these are recognized as activities involving physical and mental effort that contribute to well-being of people and are to be included as constituent parts of total income. The recommendation of the Platform for Action (PFA) of the Beijing World Conference on Women 'to estimate all forms of work by men and women' and 'to value them in satellite accounts,' as well as the suggestion by the UN-SNA to all nations to compile household satellite accounts, emerges from this understanding of the total economy. The concepts of 'total work' and 'extended incomes,' developed by Statistics Canada, are very relevant here (Stone and Chicha, 1996).

Similarly, the contribution of unpaid work to human development is well-recognized in the literature. As mentioned earlier, unpaid work is related to social reproduction that rejuvenates the working population on the one hand and produces human capital by raising children and providing them with education, health and values to be good citizens on the other. In short, there is now a good understanding of how unpaid work is a part of the total economy, as well as how it contributes to human capabilities and to the total well-being in an economy.

In spite of this understanding, however, the implications of the organic relationship between paid and unpaid work are still not well understood and the policy inferences for integrating unpaid work into the total economic system are still not very clear. It is not yet realized, for example, that when we put unpaid work within the boundary of macroeconomics, it loses its female and familial connotation and becomes an important central question of the efficiency and sustainability of the whole economic system.

Two sets of questions become important here: (1) How does unpaid work affect the outcomes of the economy and how does the paid economy impact the unpaid economy?; and (2) How does one address unpaid work to integrate it with the development strategy of an economic system? This book deals with these questions.

Unpaid work and functioning of the total economy

The functioning of the total economy cannot be understood well without understanding the role of unpaid work in it.

The unpaid economy is the lagging economy that pulls back the overall economy, particularly in developing countries, as it poses several constraints to the development of the economy. To begin with, unpaid workers are constrained in multiple ways and are not able to reach their potential. Since unpaid work is repetitive, boring and offers limited scope for upward mobility, unpaid workers are not able to reach their potential in terms of productivity and earnings. This also does not allow the economy to reach its potential.

The workers (mainly women) who carry the burden of unpaid work enter the labor market with a highly disadvantageous position, with the result that they are denied a level playing field in the labor market. The low work participation rates, low human capital, low productivity and low wages, as well as poor diversification of work, higher incidence of unemployment and lower employment status of unpaid workers in the labor market are some of the consequences of their work burden.

Second, the size of the unpaid workforce is flexible, as they have the capacity to absorb shocks in the family and unpaid workers are pressured to bear a large burden of work in the event of crisis. This results in severe depletion of their capabilities and functioning. In the event of crisis, unpaid work increases, resulting in severe loss of unpaid workers' well-being.

Third, since no data are available on unpaid work and workers, there is no way of incorporating the disadvantages of unpaid workers in policy-making or of monitoring and understanding the impact of a crisis on their well-being. Hence it is difficult, for policy-making purposes, to establish the need for remediation.

Addressing unpaid work to integrate it in development strategy

Recognition of unpaid work as part of the total economy implies that: (1) this part of the economy is lagging behind, particularly in developing countries, as it operates with low technology and low productivity; and (2) unpaid workers are in a disadvantageous position in terms of accessing developmental opportunities in the economy. There is, therefore, a need to improve the productivity of this work on the one hand and create equal developmental opportunities for workers engaged in unpaid work on the other. Though 'recognition,' 'reduction' and 'redistribution' of unpaid work are valid and desirable in this context, for developing economies there are concerns over and above those of promoting gender equality. The point we wish to highlight is that the processes and targets that aim to address the unpaid economy need to be integrated within the framework of development strategies of these economies.

Though important in its own right, recognition of unpaid work should not merely mean giving visibility to this work by 'counting' it. Rather, what is needed is: (a) comprehensive information on the different categories of unpaid work as they relate to production processes and the daily fulfillment of basic needs; and (b) a clear understanding of how the conditions under which this work is performed hinders the integration of people's laboring capabilities within the development strategies of the economy. This necessitates a comprehensive and disaggregated view of the unpaid work in the economy. For developing economies the domains of unpaid work can be broadly categorized as follows:

Unpaid work of family workers in family enterprises

These workers, usually women and frequently children, are engaged in productive activities of family enterprises, while men perform the core production tasks, as well as sale- and purchase-related tasks. These workers are frequently underreported in workforce statistics and also suffer from low productivity and poor working conditions.

Subsistence work

Subsistence workers are usually engaged in nonmarket SNA work, including collection of free basic necessities like fuel wood, water and so on, as well as raw materials for family enterprises (fodder for animal husbandry, bamboo or wood for craft, leaves for manufacturing household products and so on). Primarily because of the poor public provisioning of these goods, these workers spend long hours collecting and transporting these goods, tasks that become all the more time consuming due to the depletion and degradation of environmental resources.

Unpaid household (non-SNA) work

Household maintenance, such as cleaning, washing and general household up-keep and grueling sanitation is another category of work. This work, particularly in the case of marginalized sectors of the population, is low technology/low productivity work, which is frequently drudgery for housewives. There is a need to improve the technology and productivity of this work.

Care of children, the sick, the old and others within the household

This work is highly time consuming in developing countries, as there are few public services available for child care or for taking care of the sick, the old and the disabled. Also, the care taken within families is not satisfactory, as families are not always equipped to give quality services to children and others. Apart from this, the time spent on these services restricts the access of the service providers (mainly women) to productive employment in the labor market.

Reduction and redistribution of these four categories of unpaid work is to be brought about in a manner that ensures the efficiency and improved productivity of this work, as well as making certain that unpaid work is integrated with the overall development process of the economy. That is, gender inequalities are intertwined with the need to reduce and reshape unpaid work so as to promote the overall development of the economy.

Reduction in unpaid family work in household enterprises requires improving technology, and hence labor productivity, to promote the livelihoods of people. This type of (low productivity) unpaid work needs to be transformed into productive work by improving the access of household enterprises to better technology and finance.

Reduction in some forms of subsistence work implies a transfer of this work to public provisioning. Pubic infrastructure facilities, such as the availability of drinking water at the doorstep, energy security through the cultivation of bio-fuels, provision of fuel efficient stoves, ensuring supplies of alternative energy sources and so on, will reduce the drudgery of the unpaid work time on acquiring basic necessities of life on the one hand and improve the quality of services on the other.

The issue of reduction in unpaid care needs to be addressed carefully. Transferring, for instance, the care of children from the realm of the household to pubic provisioning should be done with a view of ensuring satisfactory early childhood development. This includes physical and psychological security, as well as mental stimulation and social development of children. In turn, this calls for improved food intake by children, facilities for play and games, as well as a clean and healthy environment in child care centers. The public care facilities for the care of the old, sick and disabled also call for professional services with efficiency. The provision of these services can be organized not only through the state, but also through partnerships with civil society organizations and the market.

In concluding this chapter we wish to simply reiterate that the reduction and redistribution of unpaid work is as much a gender issue as it is an institutional and developmental one. The load carried by the (institution of the) household, which assumes most of the basic needs provisioning responsibilities in many developing counties, must be reduced by shifting parts of it to the institution of the state. Beyond reducing women's burdens, this will allow for a very different interconnection between households, markets and the state.

Instead of hidden subsidies, improved efficiency and productivity in household production will ensure that family enterprises are better integrated with the mainstream economy, receive higher income and, at the same time, release unpaid workers for undertaking productive work in the labor market. We wish to put forward also the idea that 'professionalization' and 'socialization' of tasks presently carried out under unpaid conditions must receive due policy consideration. Professionalization will result in remunerating and fully recognizing unpaid work for what it is – productive work that delivers goods and services to the economy. Socialization, namely provisioning under a shared responsibility framework with corresponding state budgetary allocations, will reduce unpaid work burdens for women and will redistribute them from the household sector to the state sector under more efficient conditions. Both processes essentially lead to the upgrading of the overall economy to a higher level while contributing to a key developmental goal – that of promoting gender equality.

Notes

1. This section is based Antonopoulos (2008).
2. We should note here the often-neglected distinction between 'no work' as voluntarily chosen free time and 'no work' as the outcome of enforced inactivity due to chronic lack of employment opportunities. Traditional economics presumed that within the span of a day what is not accounted for by work-time is leisure (Pigou, 1920; Becker, 1965; Linder, 1970). Keynesian theory and heterodox economic traditions warn that 'no work' can also be the outcome of social exclusion from paid work, in which case a person is rendered forcefully inactive for short or long periods of time (Vickery, 1977; Minsky, 1986).
3. It consists of an integrated set of macroeconomic accounts, balance sheets and tables based on internationally agreed upon concepts, definitions, classifications and accounting rules that delineate the market economy, but, in addition, for constructing satellite accounts of unpaid work. For details see http://unstats.un.org/unsd/sna1993/introduction.asp
4. *New Household Economics* (Becker, 1981) introduced in neoclassical microeconomics the idea that households also engage in production of goods and services. This field of study is predicated on unrealistic and gender-blind assumptions about preferences, behavior and choices; the further presupposition of similitude in regards to regulating principles of the institution of the market and the institution of the family renders its findings quite problematic. For a discussion see Ferber and Nelson (2000).
5. The measurement of unpaid work was one of the major challenges to governments that came out of the UN Third World Conference on Women in Nairobi in 1985, as well as the UN Fourth World Conference on Women in Beijing in 1995. The Platform for Action that developed out of Beijing called for national and international statistical organizations to measure unpaid work and reflect its value in satellite accounts to the GDP. Few counties have developed full accounts though.
6. For Canada it is estimated as more than 45 per cent (Harvey and Mukhopadhyay, 2007); for the United States 42 per cent of GDP. Japan ranges from 15 to 23 per cent and for the Philippines 38 per cent for the year 1997 (APEC, 1999); for Mexico and Nicaragua, the figures for the years 2002 and 1998, respectively, are 21.6 per cent and 30 per cent of GDP (ECLAC, 2007).
7. See *World Development*, special issue on Gender, Adjustment and Development, December 1995 and *World Development*, special issue on Growth, Trade, Finance and Gender Inequalities, July 2000.
8. Antonella Picchio (2003, pp.11–26), and the 1970s discussion on the productive/unproductive nature of reproductive labor.
9. Harvey and Mukhopadhyay (2007), estimating time-adjusted poverty thresholds taking into account the amount of time spent on unpaid housework in Canada, finds high incidence of time deficit among employed single parents with children.

10. For documentation, see various reports at http://www.levy.org/undp-levy-conference
11. The paper points out that TUS can provide estimates of informal employment only when the right context variables are selected, suitable classifications are used and the survey design is sound.

References

Akintola, O. (2004) 'Gendered Analysis of the Burden of Care on Family and Volunteer Caregivers in Uganda and South Africa', Research Report, Health Economics and HIV/AIDS Research Division (Durban: University of KwaZulu-Natal).

Antonopoulos, R. (2008) 'The Unpaid Care Work Paid Work Connection,' Working Paper 541 (Annandale-on-Hudson, NY: The Levy Economics Institute of Bard College).

APEC (1999) 'Time for Work: Linkages between Paid and Unpaid Work in Human Resource Policy,' Report of the APEC Human Resource Development Working Group. http://www.nsi-ins.ca/english/pdf/time.pdf

Becker, G.S. (1965) 'A Theory of the Allocation of Time,' *The Economic Journal*, 75(299), 493–517.

Becker, G.S. (1981) *Treatise on the Family* (Cambridge, MA: Harvard University Press).

Blackden, C.M. and Q. Wodon (eds) (2006) 'Gender, Time-Use and Poverty in Sub-Saharan Africa,' Working Paper 73. (Washington, DC: The World Bank).

Cagatay, N., D. Elson and C. Grown (eds) (1995) 'Special Issues on Gender, Adjustment and Macroeconomics,' *World Development* 23(11), 1825–2017.

ECLAC (2007) 'Women's Contribution to Equality in Latin America and the Caribbean,' Paper prepared by Women and Development Unit of the Economic Commission for Latin America and the Caribbean (ECLAC) for the Regional Conference on Women in Latin America and the Caribbean on 6–9, August Ecuador.

Esquivel, V. (2006) 'What Else Do We Have to Cope With? Gender, Paid and Unpaid Work during Argentina's Last Crisis', The International Working Group on Gender, Macroeconomics, and International Economics (GEM–IWG) Working Paper Series, No. 06-06 (Salt Lake City, UT: Department Of Economics, University Of Utah).

Ferber, M. and J.A. Nelson (eds) (2000) *Beyond Economic Man: Feminist Theory and Economics* (Chicago: University of Chicago Press).

Harvey, A.S., and A. Mukhopadhyay (2007) 'When Twenty-Four Hours is not Enough: Time Poverty of Working Parents,' *Social Indicators Research*, 82(1), 57–77.

Hirway, I. (2005) 'Understanding Poverty: Insights Emerging from Time Use of the Poor,' Paper presentation at UNDP–Levy Institute Conference, Unpaid Work and Economy: Gender, Poverty, and the Millennium Development Goals. The Levy Economics Institute of Bard College, 3–5 October.

Hirway, I. (2008) 'Equal Sharing of Responsibilities between Men and Women Some Issues with Reference to Labour and Employment,' Paper prepared for Expert Group Meeting on Equal Sharing of Responsibilities between Men and

Women, Including Caregiving in the Context of HIV/AIDS United Nations Office, Geneva, 6–9 October.

Hirway, I. and J. Charmes (2006) 'Estimating and Understanding Informal Employment through Time-Use Studies,' Paper presented at Delhi Group Meeting, New Delhi.

Linder, S.B. (1970) *The Harried Leisure Class* (New York: Columbia University Press).

Luna, E.G. (2005) 'Unpaid Work and the System of National Accounts,' Paper presentation at UNDP-Levy Institute Conference, Unpaid Work and Economy: Gender, Poverty, and the Millennium Development Goals. The Levy Economics Institute of Bard College, 3–5 October.

Minsky, H. (1986) *Stabilizing an Unstable Economy* (New Haven, CT: Yale University Press).

OECD (2002) *Measuring the Non-Observed Economy* (Paris: Organization for Economic Cooperation and Development).

Picchio, A. (ed.) (2003) *Unpaid Work and the Economy. A Gender Analysis of the Standards of Living* (London: Routledge).

Pigou, A. (1920) *The Economics of Welfare* (London: Macmillan).

UNDP (2006) *Human Development Report* (New York: UNDP).

Vickery, C. (1977) 'The Time Poor: A New Look at Poverty,' *The Journal of Human Resources*, 12(1), 27–48.

2
Understanding Poverty: Insights Emerging from Time Use of the Poor

*Indira Hirway**

Introduction

It is now widely recognized that to view poverty only as income poverty is far from adequate, because low income/consumption is only one dimension of the multiple dimensions of poverty. The other dimensions of poverty include low human capabilities (human poverty), vulnerability, exclusion and marginalization, chronic nature of poverty and so on, on which there is extensive literature. It is usually argued that a major reason why the poor are poor is that they possess no or low capital, where capital consists of: (1) physical capital; (2) financial capital; (3) human capital; and (4) social capital. Because of their low capital base the poor are restricted in terms of their access to better opportunities in the economy. That is, their access to productive employment and income declines considerably, as they do not have an adequate base of capital.

One missing asset or capital here however is time. The poor have as much time as the non-poor. Since time is a major asset of the poor, who have no/low assets otherwise, it is important to understand how they spend their time. Information on how the poor use their time, or rather how they are forced to use their time to fight their multiple deprivations, can provide useful insights into their poverty. Their time use can reveal their constraints and problems on the one hand and can throw light on the potential areas of interventions for poverty reduction on the other hand. Though some attention has been paid to time poverty in some recent literature (Charmes, 2006; Kes and Swaminathan, 2006; Blakden and Woden, 2006), this has been limited to time stress and time burden, particularly of women. There is a need to go beyond time stress to understand the nature of poverty as reflected in the time use of the poor.

Time-use data provide comprehensive information on how people allocate their time between different activities such as productive work in the labor market, subsistence work (for example, production for self consumption), unpaid domestic and community work, personal care, rest, relaxation, reading, writing, education and so on. It is possible that the allocation of time by the poor creates constraints for them for getting out of poverty. It will therefore be useful to study their time use systematically.

This chapter intends to do this. It discusses the conceptual issues related to time use and poverty and analyzes the Indian time use data to understand the time use of the poor in India. The chapter ends with drawing policy implications of the time use for poverty reduction.

Understanding poverty through time use

The time dimension of poverty seems to have two major components: (1) the unfavorable allocation of time of the poor; and (2) time stress of the poor. The former seems to constrain the participation of the poor in productive work and leaves less time for capacity building and for social networking (namely, social capital), while the latter tends to result in the depletion of human capital, particularly for women, and in reduction in their well-being. The time use of the poor thus tends to reinforce poverty of the poor.

Unfavorable allocation of time of the poor

Time is a major asset for the poor and the poor are likely to use it to fight their multiple deprivations and vulnerability. The time use of the poor is likely to be determined by their constraints and problems on the one hand and their priorities and preferences on the other hand. The different constraints of the poor are likely to reduce their freedom or choices available concerning their time use and this, in turn, is likely to create distortions and further constraints to limit their opportunities in life.

Struggle to acquire basic necessities in life and livelihood

The first major constraint of the ultra-poor households is that they are forced to spend long hours on unpaid subsistence activities like collection of free goods, mostly from common lands and forests, to acquire basic needs of life and to manage their livelihoods.

The first claim on the time of the poor is of the basic necessities in life. As observed in many developing countries, the poor spend a lot of time on collection of water for drinking and domestic use, as well as on fuel wood collection and making dung cakes (by mixing cow dung with charcoal waste) for cooking and heating. Water supply is frequently a scarce item in these countries and the poor have to travel long distances to fetch it from a well or a pond. Energy also is scarce in these countries and people frequently have to collect fuel wood for cooking and heating. The TUS in South Africa, for example, shows that in some regions women spend about 70 minutes per day on collecting water and 30 minutes on collecting fuel wood and making dung cakes for their household use. The corresponding figures for men are 18 minutes and 7 minutes, respectively (South Africa, 2000). Jacques Charmes also has noted that women in Benin spend 46 minutes per day on collecting water and 31 minutes on collecting fire wood, as against 19 and 16 minutes for men, respectively (Charmes, 2000). The situation in Madagascar and Ghana also is similar (Charmes, 2000). In addition, the poor also collect wood pieces/bamboo for construction of shelter, as well as vegetables, fruits, fish and so on for food from common resources. Usually the non-durable shelters of the poor need a lot of repair and maintenance, and fishing and hunting help the poor to survive. In many countries the poor are observed to be spending up to 20–25 per cent of their productive time on collecting the basic needs of the household. This leaves limited time for them for undertaking productive work in the labor market (Hirway and Jose, 2008). To put it differently, poor provisioning of basic infrastructure like water supply, energy and housing forces the poor to spend long hours on acquiring basic facilities.

Many economic activities of the poor on which their livelihood depends have low productivity, but are time consuming. The poor are forced to spend long hours on these activities in spite of their low returns. The poor in developing countries are frequently observed to be spending considerable time on: (1) collection of fodder for animals from common lands; (2) open grazing of animals including sheep, goat, camels and so on; (3) fishing from common water bodies; (4) hunting animals from common lands and forests; (5) collection of leaves, bamboo and grass as raw materials for traditional crafts; and (6) collection of fruits, vegetables and so on for family business. These materials are collected from common lands, common water bodies, common forests (outside the reserved forests) and wastelands (Charmes, 2006; Hirway, 2003b). The poor are observed to be spending increasingly long hours on these activities with the increasing depletion and degradation of natural resources. Degradation of natural resources and low returns are also observed in crop cultivation, which is frequently a subsistence activity of a large number of small farmers. In short, the poor and their management of natural resources and degradation observed in the recent years have forced the poor households at the bottom to spend long hours in collecting materials for managing their livelihoods in developing countries where the majority of people still depend on primary sectors for their livelihoods.

Time spent on household management and care of household members

Another set of activities on which the poor (particularly poor women) seem to be spending relatively more time is management of households and taking care of household members. These activities include broadly: (1) household up-keep related activities, namely cooking, cleaning, washing clothes, shopping for the household and so on; and (2) taking care of children, the old, the sick and the disabled in the household. The time spent on these activities is significant in both developed and developing countries. However, the time spent on these activities by the poor in developing activities is likely to be much longer, as: (1) there is no adequate public infrastructure/public provisioning of the basic needs in developing countries; (2) the cash-poor households try to access these facilities through free collection or within the home and do not buy in the market; and (3) the technology used by the poor is likely to be of a lower standard, demanding more time and more efforts.

Harvey and Taylor (2002) have developed a concept of 'household time overhead,' which is defined as 'the minimum number of hours that a household must spent on basic chores vital to the survival of the family.' These basic chores will include preparing meals, washing clothes, cleaning, fetching water and so on. We can also include care of children, the old, the sick and the disabled in this. It can generally be argued that a household with 'low household time overhead' will be better off than a household with 'high household time overhead.' This is because there will be more free time or more time with freedom of choice in the former households than in the latter households. Generally poor households are likely to have a high 'household time overhead' because: (1) the poor households tend to use a low level of technology in household chores (for example, traditional wood-based stove rather than an electric or a gas stove); (2) the poor household will perform most of the basic chores within the home, as they cannot usually afford to hire servants or buy the products from the market; and (3) as far as possible they will substitute family labor for hired labor (for example, taking care of children, the old and the sick at home with family labor). In other words, the poor households are likely to spend more time in household management as compared to the rich.

In short, the pattern of allocation of time that is forced on the poor in most developing countries restricts their participation in the market economy.

Time stress and time poverty

In the recent literature one finds the concept of time poverty or time stress, which refers to the burden of work on the poor (and mainly women) that restricts the choice that is available to them in selecting activities. That is, time poverty is defined in the context of the time burden of competing claims on individuals' time that reduce their ability to make unconstrained choices on how they allocate their time. This leads to work intensity on the one hand and trade-offs among various tasks on the other hand.

It is argued that the well-being of individuals and households is a function not only of income and consumption or health and educational capabilities, but also of time. One important indicator of well-being is leisure, the time spent on rest and relaxation. A person who gets good time to relax is considered to be enjoying good well-being. The concept of time poverty has been developed in this context. There is a need to include the time dimension of poverty or 'time poverty' for a broader and more inclusive definition of poverty (Blackden and Wodon, 2006; Kes and Swaminathan, 2006; Charmes, 2006). Time poverty is understood in the context of the burden of competing claims for individuals' time that reduce their ability to make unconstrained choices on how they allocate their time, leading frequently to work intensity and to trade-offs among various tasks. Time poverty is seen as a time burden on the poor, particularly women. It is also seen as time stress, due to the predominance of the poor in drudgery and in low productivity activities and limited time availability of the poor to productive work.

Understanding poverty from a time-use perspective

The two dimensions of the time use of the poor, namely, the unfavorable allocation of time and time stress, explain the constraints of the poor that trap them into poverty.

To start with, there is a trade-off between the unpaid work performed in acquiring basic services in life (like water, energy and housing), as well as for care and productive work in the labor market. The longer the time spent on the former work, the less will be the time available for the latter work. In other words, the poor, including poor women, are likely to have less time for undertaking productive work in the mainstream economy. Studies have shown that the poor spend up to 25 per cent of their productive time in collecting fuel wood, fodder, water, free goods and so on, leaving only 75 per cent of their productive time for market work. This is a severe constraint of the poor, as it limits their participation in the mainstream labor market. The burden of unpaid work also restricts their performance and prospects in the labor market, as they will be able to devote less time and less energy on market work compared to the non-poor.

Secondly, the longer time spent on unpaid work also means less time available for developing capabilities in terms of education, skills and so on. This, in turn, will imply low productivity of labor for the poor in the labor market.

Thirdly, the more time spent on unpaid work in poor households, the more likely it is that children will also be engaged in such work. In fact, there is ample evidence in developing countries that indicates that young boys graze animals, young girls take care of younger siblings and young children are engaged in collecting fuel wood, fodder, water and so on. This implies that the burden of unpaid work on poor households will tend to reduce the development of human capabilities in the next generation. The poverty is likely to be carried forward to the next generation.

Fourthly, the time stress or time poverty will have multiple impacts on people: It will reduce the level of well-being of time-stressed persons and it will result in the depletion of human capital, for example, reduction in health and nutrition status of the poor. This is likely to result in the reduction of labor productivity for poor households. Fifthly, the time shortage/stress felt by the poor is likely to reduce their social networking, as it will leave less time for social interaction. This will result in a lower level of formation of social capital among the poor. This is indeed a serious matter, as social mobilization, social networking and collective action are important for improving the bargaining power of the poor and enabling their poverty reduction.

Gender dimension of time use: intrahousehold division of work

An important advantage of analyzing time-use data for understanding the constraints of the poor is that it allows one to view the intrahousehold dimension of poverty. That is, it throws light on the poverty of women as separate from poverty of men. It helps in understanding the feminization of poverty, which is talked about a lot, but not well understood. As Charmes has put it, the time poverty approach can open up new horizons for policy-making for poverty reduction (Charmes, 2006).

The overall higher burden of unpaid work on households in developing countries has a clear gender dimension, as this work is observed to be distributed highly unevenly across the sexes. Women are considered to be primarily responsible for performing/managing household chores and care-related activities, with the result that they end up taking the lion's share in the total work. In addition, women also take on a higher share of subsistence work, like the collection of fuel wood, water and so on – all work that involves drudgery, has low productivity/low technology and is repetitive, boring and monotonous. Even among the poor, women are much worse off than men. Women tend to shoulder a disproportionately higher burden of drudgery. In addition, women also participate in paid work in the labor market as much as they can. Women from poor households are particularly keen on participating in the labor market, with the result that women carry a higher burden of total work.

In other words, when time-use data are included in analysis of poverty, intrahousehold inequalities emerge as a major issue, and women's poverty emerges as different from men's poverty; women are predominant in unpaid work, and they carry higher burden of total work. The former restricts their access to the labor market and, when they enter the labor market it limits their performance and prospects in the labor market. The latter limits their access to human capital formation (in fact, it tends to deplete their human capital) and their upward mobility in the labor market (Hirway and Jose, 2008).

In short, income poverty and the time use of the poor (including the time stress) are likely to reinforce each other, forming a vicious circle of poverty. The poor, with their adverse time use and time stress, are likely to acquire low capabilities and low productivity, which, in turn, is likely to trap them into poverty.

Developing indicators of poverty based on time use

Indicators of poverty can be developed to reflect the time-related constraints of the poor. These can be divided into two major categories: indicators referring to time stress of the poor and indicators referring to the allocation of time of the poor.

Indicators for measuring time poverty

Though it is difficult to say how much leisure or free time a person needs, one can say that a person who does not get enough leisure is under time stress. Another way of looking at it is to view time stress as the 'feeling of getting rushed' or 'not having enough time to do what one wants to do.' As is well known, time poverty can be experienced at all income levels, as people with high incomes also are frequently over-burdened with work, losing their freedom of choice in time use. However, this chapter develops indicators for households living in poverty so as to gain additional insights into poverty in developing countries.

In order to use the concept of time poverty, it is necessary to define a time-poverty line. Using the International Labour Organization (ILO) norms of weekly working hours, one can say that anybody working more than 40 hours can be considered as 'time poor.' This has been calculated on the assumption that a person needs (1): eight hours of sleep; (2) eight hours of work (for five days a week); and (3) eight hours of personal time. However, if we consider the fact that people in developing countries work for six days, the time poverty line can be put at forty-eight hours. This line should, of course, include SNA and non-SNA work together.

Based on the time poverty concept, the indicators of poverty can be listed as follows:

- Percentage of persons – men and women – working for more than forty-eight hours a week (SNA + non-SNA work)
- Percentage of persons – men and women – working for forty-eight hours on SNA work

Measuring poverty based on allocation of time

Indicators based on allocation of time refer to the freedom of choice that the poor have with respect to participating in productive work and particularly participating in diversified economic activities in the non-primary sectors (including manufacturing activities). These indicators can be listed as follows:

- time spent on subsistence/unpaid SNA activities (drudgery) as a percentage of total SNA time;
- time spent on non-SNA activities as a percentage of total work time (SNA + non-SNA time);
- time spent on total work (SNA + non-SNA) as a percentage of total time;
- time spent on education, skills and so on as a percentage of the total weekly time; and
- time spent on social networking as a percentage of the total time.

An economy gets diversified into non-primary sectors it grows and, in the process, creates new opportunities for productive employment. Diversified economic activities of households imply their participation in nonprimary activities, which are generally more remunerative. The diversification also implies access to upward mobility and to higher incomes. The indicators based on diversification of SNA activities of households can be listed as follows:

Workforce-participation-rate- (WPR) based indicators
- WPR in nonprimary sector activities; and
- WPR in subsistence activities (unpaid SNA).

Time-use based indicator
- Percentage of SNA time spent on nonprimary sector activities

Indicators of gender and poverty
The gender dimension of time poverty (time stress), as well as time-use (time allocation), can be measured with the help of the following indicators:

- female/male (F/M) ratio of time spent on total work;
- F/M ratio of time spent on unpaid work;
- F/M ratio of time spent on collection of free goods (subsistence work);
- F/M ratio of time spent on education and skill formation;
- F/M ratio of time spent on reading, using library, computers and so on; and
- F/M ratio of time spent on sleep, rest and personal hygiene.

Time-use statistics in India

The incidence of poverty has declined significantly in India during the past few decades, from 44.93 per cent in 1983, to 36.02 per cent in 1993–94 and to 28.27 per cent in 2004–05 (Planning Commission, 2008). There are interstate variations in the incidence with eight out of the eighteen major states having a less than 15 per cent incidence of poverty. However, a major concern relating to poverty is that in spite of a more than 8 per cent rate of growth of the economy during the past decade and a half, and in spite of the efforts made to reduce poverty through a large number of special programs and schemes, the level of poverty is still quite significant.

A major challenge identified by scholars in this context is the severity of poverty at the bottom. It is argued that the poor at the bottom suffer from chronic poverty, which is usually severe poverty, which is usually of long duration (frequently intergenerational) and is multidimensional. These poor are frequently socially marginalized, vulnerable and suffer from multiple deprivations. The growing literature on chronic poverty has analyzed this poverty systematically in India (CPRC, 2002, 2006). Scholars have observed that chronic poverty poses a serious obstacle to income poverty reduction, as well as to human poverty reduction (Thorat and Mahamallik, 2006). It is necessary to study the poverty at the bottom systematically. In this section we study this poverty at the bottom using time-use data.

TUS in India

The first (and the last so far) official TUS was conducted by the Government of India in 1998–99. It covered six major states in India, namely Gujarat (West India), Tamil Nadu (South India), Madhya Pradesh (Central India), Haryana (North India), Orissa (East India) and Meghalaya (North East India). It was an independent, stand-alone survey that covered 18,628 households and 77,593 people (members of the selected households who were 6 years old or older). The survey was conducted in four rounds of the year to capture seasonal variations in the time use of the population (Government of India, 2001).

Three schedules were designed to collect the relevant data: Schedule 1 was for collecting data on household characteristics and it collected some basic information on the household; Schedule 2 collected detailed information on the selected households and household members; and Scheduled 3 collected information on time use of the selected population. Information on time use was collected for the preceding 24 hours in a time diary and was collected by well-trained investigators using one-day recall method. Two context variables were used to collect contextual information; they were about the location of the activity (whether outside or inside home) and about the paid/unpaid nature of the activity. Special efforts, such as the preparation of a detailed instruction manual, intensive training and strong follow-up, were made to ensure good quality data (Hirway, 2003b).[1] The TUS had an elaborate classification of time-use activities in the SNA framework to distinguish between SNA, non-SNA and personal services.

The major groups of the classification are as follows:

1. Primary production activities
2. Secondary sector activities
3. Tertiary sector activities (trade, business and services)
4. Household maintenance, management and shopping for own household
5. Care of children, elderly and disabled for own household
6. Community services

7. Learning
8. Social and cultural activities
9. Personal care and self-maintenance

It is clear that the first three activities refer to SNA activities falling under the production boundary; the next three activities are non-SNA activities falling in the general production boundary; while the last three activities are personal activities that are nondelegable activities. These activities are further divided into two-digit classifications that cover the major dimensions of the first-digit activities. The first three major groups covering SNA activities are divided into two-digit groups. For example, the first major group of primary production activities is divided into six two-digit groups, namely: (1) crop farming; (2) animal husbandry; (3) fishing, forestry, horticulture and gardening; (4) fetching fuel, fodder, water, fruits and so on; (5) processing and storage; and (6) mining, quarrying, digging, cutting and so on. The second major group, secondary sector activities, is divided into: (1) construction activities; and (2) manufacturing activities, while the tertiary sector activities are subdivided into: (1) trade and business; and (2) services. Similarly, non-SNA activities and personal services are divided in to further subcategories and into three-digit activities (see Appendix). The subgroups are divided into three-digit activities that describe specific activities falling in the two-digit subgroups.

Using the state-level poverty lines determined by the planning commission for the year 1998–99, the incidence of poverty for the selected states was calculated as follows:

Table 2.1   Incidence of poverty in the selected states (1999–2000)

State	Rural		Urban	
	Poverty line (Rs)	% of poor population	Poverty line (Rs)	% of poor population
Haryana	363	11.67	420	10.98
M. Pradesh	311	38.80	482	38.92
Gujarat	319	15.19	474	24.05
Orissa	324	53.73	473	40.06
Tamil Nadu	308	25.46	476	24.48
Meghalaya	365	17.71	344	13.19

Source: Planning Commission, Government of India (2001).

Table 2.1 shows that Haryana is the least-poor state, followed by Meghalaya, Gujarat and Tamil Nadu. Orissa and Madhya Pradesh are the poorest states, Orissa being at the bottom with 53.73 per cent of the rural and 40.06 per cent of the urban population living in poverty.

Haryana is one of the most developed states in India with its second rank in per capita income among the twenty major states in India. With Punjab state (which ranks first in per capita income) and the union territory of Chandigarh, Haryana constitutes a prosperous northern region in India. Gujarat, which follows Haryana in the incidence of poverty, is one of the most industrialized states in India. It is a part of the western region that constitutes Maharashtra (another industrialized state), Goa and Rajasthan states. This region is known for its enterprising population, as well as for wide intrastate disparities. Tamil Nadu is a state in the south, which represents the southern region (consisting of Andhra Pradesh, Karnataka and Kerala), known for its progressive welfare policies. Madhya Pradesh, which represents central India, is a region lagging in terms of growth as well as poverty reduction. Orissa, an eastern state, is a part of the poverty-stricken eastern states of Bihar, Jharkhand, Chhatisgarh and also West Bengal. Meghalaya represents the northeast region of India (consisting of seven states), which is unique in terms of its physiographical, as well as sociocultural, characteristics. The six states thus differ widely, but represent the six main regions in the country.

Analysis of poverty using time-use data

This chapter uses time-use data for all of the six states put together, namely, data of combined states. This is because the sample of the combined states is observed to be fairly representative of the country, as it was drawn systematically from all the six major regions of the country. It was observed that the combined states sample was representative of India in depicting poverty, demographic characteristics, pattern of consumption expenditure and so on (Pandey, 2000).

In order to understand the time use of the ultra-poor, the total households have been divided into four categories based on the monthly per capita consumption expenditure (MPCE) of the households. This has been done with reference to the income poverty line determined by the planning commission for that year (Government of India, 2001), which is based on the minimum consumption expenditure required: (1) the nutrition intake in calories and (2) other essential expenditure. All the households are divided into four categories: ultra-poor (the poor below the mid-point of the poverty line); poor (the poor above the ultra-poverty line and below the poverty line); non-poor (non-poor above the poverty line but survival below the mid-point of the average consumption expenditure of the non-poor); and rich (the rest of the non-poor). The ultra-poor at the bottom, who pose a serious challenge to policy-makers at present, have been the main focus of the study.

Time use of ultra-poor and non-poor

Overall time use of ultra-poor and non-poor

Table 2.2 presents data on the overall time allocation by ultra-poor and non-poor on SNA activities,[2] non-SNA activities[3] and personal services.[4] SNA activities refer to activities included under national income accounts as per the UN-SNA; non-SNA activities refer to domestic services, including care-related activities and community services; and personal services refer to nondelegable personal activities, which include sleep, rest, study and education, personal hygiene, care and so on.

Table 2.2 refers to the average weekly time spent by people living in rural and urban areas combined for all the three categories of activities. It provides useful insights on the allocation of time by ultra-poor and non-poor.

A quick view at Table 2.2 reveals that men in general spend more time on SNA work while women spend more time on non-SNA work. For example, ultra-poor and non-poor men spend 42.13 hours and 44.71 hours per week, respectively, on SNA work, while the corresponding figures for women are 22.07 and 17.75. Compared to this, ultra-poor and non-poor women spend 31.25 hours and 35.43 hours, respectively, on non-SNA work, while the corresponding figures for men are 3.23 and 3.13. With regards to total work (SNA + non-SNA work), the time spent by ultra-poor women is 53.42 hours. Both these figures are much higher than the figures for men.

Table 2.2   Overall time use of ultra-poor and non-poor (R + U) (weekly average time)

Activity	Ultra-poor		Poor		Non-poor		Rich	
	Male	*Female*	*Male*	*Female*	*Male*	*Female*	*Male*	*Female*
Total SNA	42.13	22.07	43.66	22.66	43.11	18.79	44.71	17.75
activities (%)	*25.08*	*13.14*	*25.99*	*13.49*	*25.66*	*11.18*	*26.61*	*10.57*
Non- SNA	3.23	31.25	3.04	32.8	2.85	34.44	3.13	35.43
activities (%)	*1.92*	*18.60*	*1.81*	*19.52*	*1.70*	*20.50*	*1.86*	*21.09*
Personal	122.08	113.98	120.59	111.92	121.29	114.43	119.68	114.41
services (%)	*72.67*	*67.85*	*71.78*	*66.62*	*72.20*	*68.11*	*71.24*	*68.10*
Total time	168	168	168	168	168	168	168	168

Source: Calculated from the Indian TUS, 1998–99.

This pattern of time use has the following important implications:

• Ultra-poor women rank at the bottom in terms of burden of total work. They spend 32.74 per cent of their total time (53.42 hours) on work. They are followed by non-poor women (and not by ultra-poor men) who spend 31.66 per cent of their time (53.18 hours) on work. That is, rich women work much harder than ultra-poor men in terms of the time put into work.

• Men put in longer hours on SNA work, while women put in longer hours on non-SNA work. However, the SNA time of women is between 40–50 per cent of the SNA time of men, while men's contribution to non-SNA work is less than 10 per cent of women's contribution. This indicates a clear gender divide in non-SNA work compared to SNA work.

• Ultra-poor men spend less time on SNA activities than what the non-poor do. This reflects less availability of work for ultra-poor men. This is a severe limitation of ultra-poor men, as it indicates their much lower access to work.

• Table 2.2 also shows that there is a difference between the personal time enjoyed by men and women. Ultra-poor women have 10 hours less then ultra-poor men, while non-poor women have 5.5 hours less than non-poor men.

The broad picture emerging from Table 2.2 indicates that the gender differences in overall time use are much wider than the differences based on poverty.

Participation and time spent by ultra-poor and non-poor on SNA activities

The nature of workforce participation, as well as the time use of the ultra-poor and non-poor in SNA activities, throws useful light on the differences in their participation in SNA activities.

Workforce participation rate (WPR) of ultra-poor and non-poor

Table 2.3 presents the WPR of the ultra-poor and non-poor in the different categories of SNA activities. A striking feature of the table is that the ultra-poor men have a *higher* WPR than the non-poor men, the two rates being 79.4 and 74.6, respectively. However, they spend less time on SNA work (as seen above), as they do not get enough work. The WPR of ultra-poor women also is much higher (68.5) than that of non-poor women (58.5). In other words, the poor at the bottom participate in a significant way in SNA activities to make two ends meet.

There are, however, significant differences in the composition of respective SNA activities of the ultra-poor and non-poor. The most important activities for the ultra-poor are primary sector activities, where their WPR is 48.2 and 58.4 for men and women, respectively. For the non-poor the primary sector is also important, but the rates are much lower, 38.1 and 50.2 for men and women, respectively. The non-poor enjoy a much higher diversification of activities in the higher-productivity activities like manufacturing, trade and services. Again, within the primary sector, the WPR of the ultra-poor is higher in subsistence activities, such as the collection of water, fuel wood and other free goods, as well as fishing, forestry and so on. Also, a careful activity-wise analysis shows that the ultra-poor have a much higher WPR in the activities that are strenuous (for example, plowing, mining and quarrying) and have low productivity (for example, weeding).

Table 2.3   Workforce participation by ultra-poor and non-poor (R + U)

Activity	Ultra-poor		Non-poor	
	Male	*Female*	*Male*	*Female*
Crop farming	39.0	26.7	33.2	20.7
Animal husbandry	20.6	18.8	20.4	23.5
Fishing, forestry, horticulture, etc.	5.5	4.7	2.3	2.3
Collecting, water, fuel wood, fodder, etc.	6.7	31.0	5.3	22.9
Processing and storage	0.7	3.5	0.8	3.3
Mining, quarrying, digging, etc.	2.3	1.2	1.2	0.3
Total Primary	*48.2*	*58.4*	*38.1*	*50.2*
Construction activities	5.3	1.8	3.8	0.9
Manufacturing activities	5.5	4.2	8.6	5.7
Total Secondary	*10.8*	*6.5*	*15.5*	*7.7*
Trade and business	7.4	1.3	8.9	1.5
Services	10.5	6.2	20.0	7.6
Total Tertiary	*14.9*	*7.5*	*28.8*	*12.7*
Total SNA	*79.4*	*68.5*	*74.6*	*58.5*

Source: Calculated from the Indian TUS, 1998–99.

Both ultra-poor and non-poor women are particularly predominant in the collection of free goods (subsistence work), though the WPR of ultra-poor women in these activities is much higher (31.00) than that of non-poor women (22.9).

Weekly time spent by ultra-poor and non-poor on SNA work

It is important to note that though the WPR of the ultra-poor is much higher than that of the non-poor, the average time spent by the ultra-poor is much less than that of the non-poor. This is largely because of the low availability of work to the ultra-poor.

Table 2.4 Weekly average time (hours) spent on primary, secondary and tertiary activities by the ultra-poor and non-poor (R + U)

Activity	Ultra-poor		Non-poor	
	Male	Female	Male	Female
Crop farming	19.64	10.54	16.23	7.59
Collecting, water, fuel wood, fodder, etc.	1.09	3.78	0.76	2.05
Other primary activities	7.20	4.25	4.90	3.87
Total Primary	*27.93*	*18.57*	*21.89*	*13.47*
Construction activities	2.58	0.69	1.88	0.33
Manufacturing activities	2.76	1.21	5.01	1.38
Total Secondary Activities	*5.34*	*1.91*	*6.88*	*1.71*
Trade and business	4.31	0.33	5.34	0.39
Services	4.55	1.26	10.59	2.18
Total Tertiary	*8.85*	*1.59*	*15.94*	*2.56*
Total SNA	*42.13*	*22.07*	*44.71*	*17.75*

Source: Calculated from the Indian TUS, 1998–99.

Some of the striking differences in the composition of SNA time of the ultra-poor and non-poor men are worth noting. Ultra-poor men spend the bulk (two-thirds) of their SNA time on crop farming and animal husbandry, while the non-poor spend less than half of their SNA time on these activities. Ultra-poor men spend 14.19 hours per week on secondary and tertiary activities, as against 23 hours by the non-poor. Again, compared to non-poor men, ultra-poor men spend more time on construction work and less on manufacturing activities; they spend less time on government services and more time on *petty* services; and they spend more time on *petty* trade. In short, the ultra-poor men perform more subsistence work and are predominant in low productivity activities, which involve hard labor and/or low returns.

In the case of women, the WPR, as well as the time spent on SNA work, is much less for non-poor women compared to ultra-poor women. However, the SNA work of non-poor women is much more diversified into secondary- and tertiary-sector activities. The predominant activities of both the categories of women are crop farming and animal husbandry.

Within crop farming, they participate mainly in weeding and application of manure and fertilizer, preparation of land and transplanting. However, on average, non-poor women spend much less time on these activities. Again, ultra-poor women work for longer hours on relatively strenuous work, namely preparation of the land, sowing and transplanting, than the non-poor women.

An important activity of both the categories of women, however, is collection of necessities like fuel wood and water, fetching fruits, vegetables and minor forest produce, as well as collecting building materials or other raw materials for family enterprises, such as fodder for animals, raw materials for crafts and so on. These activities are particularly important for rural women.

Collection of water and collection of fuel wood/making dung cakes meets two major needs of life in India. These are time-consuming activities, as there is no provision for their supply locally. Both ultra-poor and non-poor women spend long hours on these activities, as these are 'women's activities.' The weekly time spent on these activities comes to 3.11 hours for ultra-poor women and 1.23 hours for non-poor women. In rural areas these figures are 3.52 hours and 2 26 hours, respectively. That is, in rural areas, ultra-poor women spend 14.75 per cent (one-seventh) of their total SNA time and non-poor women spend 10.50 per cent of their SNA time only on collection of water and fuel!

In addition to the above, considerable time is spent on other subsistence work like the collection of fruits, vegetables, edible goods, minor forest produce, leaves and bamboo, as well as collection of raw materials for crafts and collection of building materials for consumption or for family enterprises. The total time spent on all subsistence work in rural and urban areas combined comes to 5.22 hours for ultra-poor women and 2.16 hours for non-poor women. That is, ultra-poor women spend 23.6 per cent or almost one-fourth of their SNA time on this low-productivity subsistence work! The corresponding figure for non-poor women is 12.16 per cent, and for ultra-poor and non-poor men it is 2.82 per cent and 1.40 per cent, respectively.

This reflects poor public provisioning and poor basic infrastructure in the economy, where the households at the bottom are left to fend for themselves for their basic necessities. It also reflects blatant neglect of natural resources, on which the livelihoods of majority of people still depend. Some of the adverse impacts of the predominance of these activities for women are: (1) women spend up to 20–25 per cent of their SNA time on these activities, with the result that they get only 75 per cent of their productive time for market work in the mainstream economy;

(2) these activities have an adverse impact on their health, as this work is strenuous; and (3) it also adversely affects women's safety and security. Ultra-poor women are the worst victims of this adverse impact.

Table 2.5 Weekly average time (hours) spent on selected SNA activities by ultra-poor and non-poor (R + U)

Activity	Ultra-poor		Non-poor	
	Male	Female	Male	Female
Plowing, preparing land, cleaning of land	6.02	1.14	3.22	0.63
Supervision of farm work	0.43	0.13	1.45	0.26
Time spent on collection of water and fuel wood	0.05	3.11	0.05	1.23
Time spent on collection of other goods	1.14	2.11	0.58	1.13
Construction activities	2.58	0.69	1.88	0.33
Manufacturing activities	2.76	1.21	5.01	1.38
Trade and business	4.31	0.33	5.34	0.39
Services	4.55	1.26	10.59	2.18

Source: Calculated from the Indian TUS, 1998–99.

With regards to the secondary and territory activities, ultra-poor women spend more time on construction activities, as workers on public and private works, as compared to non-poor women. In the case of manufacturing activities, however, non-poor women spend more time, while in the case of services, non-poor women are more diversified into government and private services as compared to ultra-poor women.

To sum up, women lag far behind men in terms of diversification of their SNA activities. Women are also trapped in subsistence work, with the result that they get less time for productive work in the market. On the whole, however, non-poor men and women are more diversified in their SNA time use than the ultra-poor men and women.

Participation and time spent by ultra-poor and non-poor on non-SNA activities

Women participate in non-SNA activities at a much higher rate than men. While women's participation rate is more than 80 per cent in household management and 35–40 per cent in the case of childcare, men's participation rates are 21–24 for household management and 10–12 for care-related activities. These are clearly women's activities.

A striking feature, however, is that the participation of the non-poor is much higher in household management and upkeep than that of the ultra-poor, perhaps because the non-poor have bigger houses and a larger number of consumer goods to take care of; and it is much less in care-related activities than that of ultra-poor, perhaps because the non-poor have servants to take care of children.

Community services are not very important for either the ultra-poor or the non-poor, with the result that the WPR in these activities is 1.0 for the ultra-poor and less than one-half for the ultra-poor. We believe that these low rates are also because of the perception of community services in India. Indians seem to believe that these services have to be very formal and explicit.

Table 2.6 Participation of ultra-poor and non-poor in non-SNA activities

Activity	Ultra-poor		Non-poor	
	Male	*Female*	*Male*	*Female*
HH management	22.2	80.4	24.4	85.1
Care of children, old, disabled and so on	12.5	39.1	10.7	33.0
Community services	0.3	0.5	1.3	1.3
Non-SNA	30.4	89.16	27.3	88.6

Source: Calculated from the Indian TUS, 1998–99.

The time spent by them more or less confirms the above observation: As compared to the ultra-poor, non-poor spend more time on household upkeep and less time on care-related activities. Non-poor women spend 31.08 hours on upkeep of the household compared to 25.70 hours by ultra-poor women. The corresponding figures for men are 2.13 and 1.96, respectively. It appears that non-poor women spend much more time on cooking, serving and so on may be because they cook elaborate meals; they spend more time on care of textiles possibly for the same reasons. They also spend more time on shopping for the household.

In the case of care-related work, however, ultra-poor men and women spend more time on these activities than the non-poor, though women are the main caregivers in both the categories. However, ultra-poor women spend more time on physical care of children, as well as physical care of the sick, the elderly and the disabled, while non-poor women spend more time on the teaching and training of household children. Ultra-poor women hardly spend any time on the teaching and training of children.

Participation and time spent on personal services

Personal services can be broadly divided into three groups: (1) education, skill training and related activities; (2) sociocultural activities and use of mass media; and (3) personal care and related activities.

Table 2.7 Weekly average time (hours) spent on household upkeep by ultra-poor and non-poor (R + U)

Activity	Ultra-poor		Rich	
	Male	Female	Male	Female
Cooking food items, beverages and serving	0.49	13.77	0.12	15.10
Cleaning and upkeep of dwelling and surroundings	0.25	4.18	0.19	4.75
Household maintenance, management, etc.	0.32	1.90	0.22	1.84
Total household upkeep	*1.06*	*25.70*	*1.13*	*31.08*
Physical care of children	0.65	4.25	0.24	2.74
Teaching, training, etc.	0.12	0.14	0.18	0.22
Accompanying children to places	0.06	0.10	0.10	0.10
Total childcare	*1.18*	*4.98*	*0.76*	*3.90*
Other care	0.05	0.52	0.10	0.31
Care of children, the sick and elderly	*1.23*	*5.50*	*0.86*	*4.21*
Total non-SNA activities	*2.29*	*31.40*	*1.99*	*35.29*

Source: Calculated from the Indian TUS, 1998–99.

Table 2.8 Participation by ultra-poor and non-poor in personal services

Activity	Ultra-poor		Non-poor	
	Male	Female	Male	Female
Education-related activities	20.9	14.4	25.8	16.9
Sociocultural activities and use of mass media	49.6	37.9	66.3	58.7
Personal care	100	100	100	100
Total personal services	100	100	100	100

Source: Calculated from the Indian TUS, 1998–99.

Table 2.8 shows large variations in the participation rates of ultra-poor and non-poor households in these activities. The participation in the last category, personal services, is 100, as all need sleep, rest and personal hygiene. In education, the participation of men is much larger, with more than one-fourth of them participating in this activity, though the participation of ultra-poor men is much less at 20.9. Women's participation in education is even less at 14.4 and 16.9 for ultra-poor and non-poor women, respectively. It is worth noting that rich women's participation in education is much less than that of ultra-poor men. Women's education is badly neglected in rich as well as poor families.

In the case of social networking, however, non-poor men as well as women are far ahead of their counterparts in ultra-poor families.

*Weekly average time spent on education and related activities by the
ultra-poor and non-poor*

A careful look at the time spent by the ultra-poor and non-poor sheds
useful light on their involvement with education and related activities.
Ultra-poor women spend the least time (7.55 hours per week) on education, training and related activities, while non-poor men spend the most
time (14.53 hours) on these activities. Non-poor men are followed by
ultra-poor men and then by non-poor women, which again indicates the
neglect of women's education. As the data indicate, nonformal education
is not important for any group, but skill training is important for non-
poor men, who, on average, spend about half an hour per week on this.

On the whole, ultra-poor men and women get less time for developing
their capabilities through education, skill training and so on. Clearly,
the ultra-poor men and women get less time and fewer opportunities
to enhance their educational and skill-based capabilities. The poverty is
thus likely to be transferred to the next generation.

Social capital formation by ultra-poor and non-poor

Though participation rates of men and women in social activities are
relatively high, the time spent is very short.

The most important source of entertainment for poor people in India
appears to be watching the TV and listening to music, or games and
other pastime activities. The non-poor men spend almost ten hours on
these activities while the ultra-poor spend almost seven hours. Non-poor
women also spend more than seven hours on these activities. Ultra-poor
women get the least time, 4.50 hours per week, for these activities. This
is clearly due to their burden of other work.

As far as participating in social events is concerned, the ultra-poor men
and women are placed in a very unfavorable position. Except for religious
activities, they hardly get any time for social intervention. Table 2.9
shows that the non-poor men and women spend, on average, 0.07 and
0.05 hours on social networking compared to 1.60 hours by non-poor
men and 0.48 hours by non-poor women. The non-poor also spend
relatively more time in visiting the library, reading newspapers or magazines and computing. The non-poor are thus more aware and get more
opportunities to meet people and to build/strengthen social networks.

Women from the non-poor households also get more time for social
networking, largely due to their lower burden of work and their incomes
that allow them to participate in community and social activities.

Finally, one finds large differences in the personal time available across
the MPCE levels and across sex. In general, women get much less time

Table 2.9 Weekly average time (hours) spent on selected personal services by the ultra-poor and non-poor (R + U)

Activity	Ultra-poor		Non-poor	
	Male	Female	Male	Female
Education				
General education: school/university	6.96	4.58	9.30	5.36
Work-related training, training under government programs and other training	0.06	0.05	0.23	0.10
Learning total	*10.38*	*7.55*	*14.53*	*8.60*
Participating in social events: weddings, funerals, etc.	0.02	0.02	0.61	0.31
Participating in religious activities: church services, etc.	0.36	0.28	0.63	0.38
Participating in community functions: music, dance, etc.	0.01	0.01	0.81	0.01
Social and cultural activities, mass media, etc.	*8.94*	*6.07*	*13.34*	*10.41*
Sleep and related activities	63.59	62.62	60.40	60.30
Personal hygiene and health	8.20	7.47	9.36	8.57
Personal care and self-maintenance	*102.07*	*99.36*	*96.81*	*95.39*

Source: Calculated from the Indian TUS, 1998–99.

for sleep and rest than men in ultra-poor, as well as non-poor, categories. Women get 95.39 hours and 99 hours for personal work in non-poor and ultra-poor households, respectively, compared to 104 hours and 103 hours of men in the non-poor and ultra-poor categories. A careful look at Table 2.9 shows that women get: (1) less time to sleep than men; (2) less time to eat and drink; (3) less time for personal hygiene and care; and (4) less time for exercise and games.

To sum up, the time-use analysis of the ultra-poor, namely, the poor at the bottom, indicates that they are constrained by several factors: first, their participation in SNA activities is much higher than that of the non-poor, but the average time of SNA work available to them is much less. Secondly, on average, they spend more time on subsistence work (namely, unpaid SNA work) and their nonsubsistence work is less diversified in the sense that the ultra-poor participate predominantly in low-productivity and primary-sector activities. Thirdly, the ultra-poor get less time for capacity building and for social networking than what the non-poor get.

The gender dimension of poverty, however, is highly significant. In many time dimensions non-poor women are worse off than ultra-poor men! This clearly indicates that any analysis of poverty without looking into gender poverty is far from adequate.

Indicators and inferences

Poverty indicators based on allocation of time

The first set of indicators in Table 2.10 refers to allocation of time by the ultra-poor and non-poor.

Table 2.10   Poverty indicators based on allocation of time

Serial No	Indicator	Ultra-poor		Non-poor	
		Male	Female	Male	Female
1	Time spent on collection of water and fuel wood and making dung cakes as % of SNA time	1.80	14.07	0.55	6.92
2	Time spent on subsistence work as % of SNA time*	2.82	23.60	1.40	12.16
3	Time spent on non-SNA work as % of total work time (SNA + non-SNA)	7.13	63.61	6.53	66.63
4	Time spent on total work as % of total time	27.00	32.73	28.47	31.65
5	Average weekly time spent on education and skill training	10.38	7.55	14.53	8.60
6	Time spent on social networking as a % of total time	0.07	0.05	1.60	0.48

Note: *Subsistence work here includes free collection of goods, largely from common lands, forests, water bodies, etc.
Source: Calculated from the Indian TUS, 1998–99.

Table 2.11 shows that ultra-poor women and men spend a larger part of their SNA time on collection of water and fuel wood or in making dung cakes than their non-poor counterparts. Ultra-poor women spend the highest percentage of their SNA time (more than 14 per cent) on these activities. Public provisioning of water and energy would save this time to enable them to participate in productive activities in the labor market.

In addition, the ultra-poor spend almost one-fourth of their time on collection of free goods from common resources on which their livelihoods depend. This indicates that good management of natural resources can reduce this time drastically, and this can promote their livelihoods in primary-sector activities like crop cultivation, animal husbandry, forestry, fishing and so on.

The ultra-poor get much less time for education and skill-building than the non-poor get, and hardly any time for social networking and social capital formation.

What is important to note is that the deprivation of women is much more than men as far as their time allocation is concerned: Both ultra-poor and non-poor women spend more of their time on collection of water, fuel and free goods for their livelihoods than what men do.

Indicators of time poverty

The gender dimension of poverty is also reflected in the time poverty of women, as shown in Table 2.11.

Table 2.11 Indicators of time poverty

Sr. No	Indicator	Ultra-poor		Non-poor	
		Male	Female	Male	Female
1	Average weekly time spent on total work (SNA + non-SNA)	45.32	53.27	46.70	53.03
2	Time spent on SNA + non-SNA work as % of total time	26.97	31.70	27.79	31.56
3	Average weekly time spent on SNA work	42.13	22.07	44.71	17.75
4	% working for more than 48 hours	20.15	89.12	5.32	85.34

Source: Calculated from the Indian TUS, 1998–99.

On the whole, women are time stressed as, on average, they work for more than 48 hours a week. Men, on the other hand, work for less than 48 hours a week. However, when the distribution of men is considered, Table 2.11 indicates that about one-fifth of the ultra-poor work for more than 48 hours a week. The incidence of time stress is much higher on ultra-poor men as compared to non-poor men. This also indicates that the work time of ultra-poor men is relatively more unevenly distributed as compared to the non-poor men.

In the case of women, the incidence of time stress is much higher, with more than 85 per cent of women suffering from overwork. As expected, ultra-poor women have a higher incidence of time-stress.

Indicators based on diversification of SNA work

Poor diversification of SNA time is another important indicator of poverty. Clearly, the WPR, as well as the time use, of the ultra-poor is much less diversified than that of the non-poor.

Table 2.12   Indicators based on diversification of SNA work

Serial Indicator	Ultra-Poor		Non-Poor	
	Male	Female	Male	Female
WPR in nonprimary sector activities	25.69	14.10	44.31	20.42
WPR in subsistence activities (unpaid SNA)	6.71	31.21	5.32	22.93
% Of SNA time spent on nonprimary sector activities	33.71	14.86	51.05	24.11

Source: Calculated from the Indian TUS, 1998–99.

It is interesting to note that the SNA time of ultra-poor men is much more diversified than their WPR. As compared to their 25.69 WPR in non-primary sector activities, they spend 33.71 per cent of their SNA time on nonprimary activities. The same is true with non-poor men who also spend larger part of their SNA time on nonprimary activities than their WPR in these activities. This indicates that those involved in nonprimary activities are able to spend more time on their work than those working on primary activities. This also seems to be true for non-poor women. In the case of ultra-poor women, however, there is not much difference between their WPR and their time spent on nonprimary activities. This indicates that they get more or less the same time of work in the primary and nonprimary sectors.

Table 2.12 indicates a larger diversification of SNA work for the non-poor as well as for men. Non-poor men enjoy the highest diversification of work, followed by ultra-poor men and then by non-poor women. Women workers of ultra-poor households are, once again, in the worst position.

Indicators of gender and poverty

The gender dimension of time poverty (time stress) as well as time use (time allocation) is measured with the help of the following indicators, as shown in Table 2.13.

A striking feature of Table 2.13 is that gender inequalities in the time-use are higher in the case of non-poor than in the case of ultra-poor as far as work (SNA + non-SNA) is concerned. This is because ultra-poor women work for longer time than non-poor women on this work. For example, ultra-poor women spend 52 per cent of the male SNA time on SNA work, while the corresponding figure for non-poor women is 39 per cent. Similarly, ultra-poor women spend 17 per cent more time on

Table 2.13 Indicators of gender and poverty

Indicator	Ultra-poor	Non-poor
F/M ratio of time spent on SNA work	0.52	0.39
F/M ratio of time spent on total work	1.17	1.14
F/M ratio of time spent on collection of free goods (subsistence work)	4.39	3.42
F/M ratio of time spent on unpaid work	9.78	17.73
F/M ratio of time spent on education and skill formation	0.73	0.60
F/M ratio on time spent on reading, using the library, computers and so on	0.70	0.91
F/M ratio on time spent on sleep rest and personal hygiene	0.91	0.99

Source: Calculated from the Indian TUS, 1998–99.

work than what men spend, while the corresponding figure for non-poor women is 14 per cent.

However gender inequalities are less in the case of non-poor women when it comes to time spent on reading newspapers and other media, as well as on sleep and rest.

While concluding this chapter, one can observe that the poor at the bottom, the chronically poor, are constrained by the way they are forced to use their time to access some of their basic needs and to manage their livelihoods. They seem to be trapped in the vicious circle of unpaid work and poverty, and unless they are helped in getting out of this unpaid SNA and non-SNA work (which is usually drudgery) it will be difficult to bring them out of poverty. The following are important in this context:

- providing basic services/infrastructure at the door step, for example, water, energy, transport;
- ensuring public provisioning of care through organizing universal childcare (childcare centers for infants and children, midday meals and so on) and health services;
- bringing unpaid domestic work under the realm of technological upgradation to reduce drudgery of household work, for example, fuel-efficient cooking stoves, durable housing (that requires less maintenance); and
- the neoliberal policies that focus mainly on economic growth have neglected natural resources, resulting in their severe depletion and degradation in most developing countries, including India. This seems to have increased instability in the livelihoods of people, as the

majority of them still depend on primary sector activities for their livelihoods. It is clear that macropolicies will have to pay attention to natural-resource management. In other words, regeneration of natural resources is essential to enable the poor at the bottom to get out of the subsistence mode of production and to produce goods for the market at a higher and stable level of productivity.

Women in non-poor households are not necessarily out of poverty, as they are under tremendous time stress on the one hand and constrained by a highly unfavorable pattern of time use on the other hand. The former tends to deplete their well-being, as well as their human capital, while the latter restricts their access to developmental opportunities (including productive employment).

Reduction in the unpaid work of women calls for efforts in three major areas: (1) public provisioning of basic needs like drinking water, energy, housing, childcare and so on; (2) technological improvements for reducing the drudgery of unpaid work (for example, smokeless stoves that require only a fraction of fuel wood and do not release dangerous gases); and (3) environmental regeneration so as to reduce the strain of women in collecting inputs/raw materials for their income-generating activities (such as fodder for animal husbandry). Improving women's access to developmental opportunities, including opportunities for to their human development, is not feasible without addressing their unpaid work.

Notes

* The author is thankful to Professor Diane Elson for her comments on the earlier version of this chapter.
1. Since this was the first survey of this kind, care was taken to see that investigators were trained well and the instruction manual was clear and comprehensive. For details, refer to Hirway (2003a).
2. SNA activities are the activities falling within its production boundary. The production boundary, as per the 1993 SNA, includes production of all goods and the production of all services except personal and domestic services produced for own final consumption within households [other than the services of owner-occupiers of housing and of those produced by employing paid domestic staff (UN, 1993)].
3. Non-SNA activities are the activities falling outside the SNA production boundary, but within the general production boundary. An activity is included in general production boundary when: (1) it is carried out under the control and responsibility of an institutional unit exercising ownership rights on what is produced (natural processes without any human involvement are excluded);

and (2) there is marketability of being exchanged, though actual exchange is not necessary (UN, 1993).
4. 'Personal services' refer to activities that cannot be delegated to others, such as learning, studying, personal-hygiene-related activities, sleeping, eating and so on.

References

Charmes, J. (2000) *African Women in Food Processing: A Major, But Still Underestimated Sector of Their Contribution to the National Economy* (Ottawa: IDRC).
Charmes, J. (2004) 'Data Collection on the Informal Sector: a Review of Concepts and Methods Use Since the Adoption of an International Definition Towards a Better Comparability of Available Statistics' in Delhi Group on Informal Sector Statistics ILO-Bangkok, February.
Charmes, J. (2006) 'A Review of Empirical Evidence on Time Use in Africa from UN-Sponsored Survey,' in M. Blackden and Q. Wodon (eds), *Gender, Time Use and Poverty in Sub-Saharan Africa* (Washington, DC: The World Bank).
Chronic Poverty Research Center (CPRC) (2002) 'Chronic Poverty in India: Overview Study,' Working Paper No. 57 (Manchester: CPRC).
Chronic Poverty Research Center (CPRC) (2006) *Chronic Poverty Report* (Manchester: CPRC). Available at: www.chronicpoverty.org.
Bardasi, E. and Q. Wodon (2006) 'Measuring Time Poverty and Analyzing its Determinants: Concepts and Applications to Guinea' in M. Blackden and Q. Wodon (eds), *Gender, Time Use and Poverty in Sub-Saharan Africa* (Washington, DC: The World Bank).
Blakden, M. and Q. Woden (2006) 'Gender, Time Use and Poverty: Introduction' in M. Blackden and Q. Wodon (eds), *Gender, Time Use and Poverty in Sub-Saharan Africa* (Washington, DC: The World Bank).
Harvey, A.S. and M.T. Taylor (2002) 'Time Use' in M. Grosh and P. Glewwe (eds), *Designing Household Survey Questionnaires for Developing Countries* (Washington, DC: The World Bank).
Hirway, I. (2000) 'Estimating Workforce Using Time Use Data: Preliminary Analysis' in *Proceedings of the International Seminar on Time Use Studies* (New Delhi: CSO, Government of India).
Hirway, I. (2003a) *Indian Experience in Time Use Survey, in Application of Time Use Statistics* (New Delhi: Central Statistical Organization, Ministry of Statistics and Programme Implementation).
Hirway, I. (2003b) 'Using Time Use Data for Estimating Informal Sector in Developing Countries: Conceptual and Methodological Issues with Reference to South Asia,' Paper presented at the IATUR conference, Brussels 17–19 September.
Hirway, Indira (2006) 'Implications of Time Use Patterns for Public Employment Guarantee Programs in Global South,' Working Paper No. 42, Centre for Development Alternatives, Ahmedabad, India.
Hirway, I. and J. Charmes (2006) 'Estimating and Understanding Informal Employment through Time Use Studies,' Paper presented at the meeting of the Delhi Group on Informal Economy, Central Statistical Organization, Ministry of Statistics and Programme Implementation, New Delhi.

Hirway, I. and S. Jose (2008) *Understanding Women's SNA Work Using Time-Use Statistics: The Case of India* (Ahmedabad: CFDA).

Government of India (2000) *Report of the Time Use Survey* (New Delhi; Central Statistical Organization, Ministry of Statistics and Programme Implementation).

Government of India (2001) *Estimates of Poverty in India* (New Delhi: Planning Commission).

Government of India (2008) *Eleventh Five Year Plan Document (2007–12)* (New Delhi: Planning Commission).

Kes, A. and Hema Swaminathan (2006) 'Gender and Time Poverty in Sub-Saharan Africa' in C. Mark Blackden and Quentin Wodon (eds), *Gender, Time Use and Poverty is Sub-Saharan Africa*, World Bank Working Paper No. 73, The World Bank, Washington, DC, USA.

Pandey, R.N. (2000) 'Operational Issues in Conducting Pilot Time Use Survey in India, in *Proceedings of the International Seminar on Time Use Studies* (New Delhi: Central Statistical Organization, Government of India).

Planning Commission (2008) *Eleventh Five-Year Plan Document (2007–12)* (New Delhi: Government of India).

Shah, A. and Aasha Kapur Mehta (2006) 'Chronic Poverty in India: Evidences and Policy Imperatives,' *MARGIN*, 38–9, 63–81.

Statistics South Africa (2000) *A Survey of Time Use* (Pretoria: Government of South Africa).

Thorat, S. and M. Mahamallik (2006) 'Chronic Poverty and Socially Disadvantaged Groups: Causes and Remedies,' *MARGIN*, 38–9, 41–63.

United Nations (UN) (1993) *System of National Accounts.* (Washington, DC: IMF, OECD and the World Bank).

UNDP (2005) *Three Case Studies of Time Use Survey Application in Lower and Middle-Income Countries* (New York: UNDP).

Appendix: TUS – classification used in the Indian TUS

I Primary production activities

  11 Crop farming, kitchen gardening, etc.

    111 Ploughing, preparing land, cleaning of land
    112 Sowing, planting, transplanting
    113 Application of manure, fertilizer, pesticides and watering, preparing organic manure, harvesting, threshing, picking, winnowing
    114 Weeding
    115 Supervision of work
    116 Kitchen gardening – backyard cultivation
    117 Stocking, transporting to home, guarding or protection of crops
    118 Sale- and purchase-related activities
    119 Travel to the work

  12 Animal husbandry

    121 Grazing animal outside
    122 Tending animals – cleaning, washing shed, feeding, watering, preparation of feed
    123 Caring for animal – breading, shearing, medical treatment, grooming, shoeing and so on
    124 Milking and processing of milk collecting, storing of poultry products
    125 Making dung cakes
    126 Poultry rearing – feeding, cleaning
    127 Other related activities
    128 Sale- and purchase-related activities
    129 Travel to the work

  13 Fishing, forestry, horticulture, gardening

    131 Nursery – seedings
    132 Planting, tending, processing of trees
    133 Collecting, storing and stocking of fruits and so on
    134 Wood cutting, chopping and stocking firewood
    135 Fish farming, cleaning sea-bed, feeding fish, catching fish, gathering other aquatic life
    136 Care of house plants, indoor and outdoor garden work
    137 Flower gardening – landscaping, maintenance, cutting, collecting, storing
    138 Sale- and purchase-related activities
    139 Travel to the work

14 Fetching of fruits, water, plants, etc. storing and hunting
   141 Fetching of water
   142 Fetching of fruits, vegetables, berries, mushrooms, edible goods, etc.
   143 Fetching of minor forest produce, leaves, bamboo and so on
   144 Fetching of fuel/fuel, wood/twigs
   145 Fetching of raw material for crafts
   146 Fetching of building materials
   147 Fetching of fodder
   148 Sale- and purchase-related activities
   149 Collection of other items
15 Processing and storage
   152 Milling, husking, pounding
   153 Parboiling
   154 Sorting, grading
   155 Grinding, crushing
   156 Any other related activities
   157 Sale- and purchase-related activities
   158 Travel to the work
16 Mining, quarrying, digging, cutting, etc.
   161 Mining/extraction of salt
   162 Mining/digging/quarrying of stone, slabs, breaking of stones for construction of building road, bridges, etc.
   163 Digging out clay, gravel and sand
   164 Digging out minerals – major and minor
   165 Transporting in vehicles
   166 Storing and stocking
   167 Any other related activities
   168 Sale- and purchase-related activities
   169 Travel to the work

II Secondary activities

21 Construction activities
   211 Building and construction of dwelling (laying bricks, plastering, thatching, bamboo work, roofing), maintenance and repairing of dwelling
   212 Construction and repair of animal shed, shelter for poultry
   213 Construction of well, storage facilities, fencing, etc. for farms, irrigation work
   214 Construction of public works/common infrastructure – roads, buildings, bridges and so on

217 Any other related activities
218 Sale- and purchase-related activities
219 Travel to the work
22 Manufacturing activities
    221 Food processing and cooking for sale – making pickles, spices and other products; canning fruits, jams and jellies; banking; beverage preparation; selling ready-made food, etc.
    222 Butchering, curing, processing, drying, storing and so on of meat, fish, etc.
    223 Manufacturing of textiles – spinning, weaving, processing of textiles; knitting, sewing, garment making of cotton, wool and other materials
    224 Making handicrafts, pottery, printing and other crafts made primarily with hands (wood-based, leather-based crafts, embroidery work and so on)
    225 Fitting, installing, tool setting, tool and machinery – molding, welding, tool making
    226 Assembling machines, equipment and other products
    227 Production-related work in large and small factories in different industries – as production workers, maintenance workers, paid trainees and apprentices, sales administration and management activities
    228 Sale- and purchase-activity
    229 Travel for the work

III **Trade, business and services**
31 Trade and business
    311 Buying and selling goods – such as capital goods, intermediate goods, consumer durable and consumer goods – in the organized and formal sectors
    312 Petty trading, street and door-to-door vending, hawking, shoe cleaning, etc.
    313 Transporting goods in trucks, tempos and motor vehicles
    314 Transporting in hand carts, animal carts, cycle rickshaws, etc. or manually
    315 Transport of passengers by motorized and nonmotorized vehicles
32 Services
    321 Services in government and semi-government organizations (salaried)
    322 Services in private organizations (salaried)

323 Petty services – domestic servants, sweepers, washers, priest, cobbler, gardener, massaging, prostitution, (wages) watching and guarding

324 Professional services – medical and educational services (nonformal teaching, etc.) financial services, management and technical consultancy services

325 Professional services – computer services, xerox/photocopying services, beauty parlors, hair cutting salons, etc.

326 Technical services – plumbing, electrical and electronic repair and maintenance and other related services

327 Others

328 Travel to work

IV   Household maintenance, management and shopping for own household

411 Cooking food items, beverages and serving

421 Cleaning and upkeep of dwelling and surroundings

422 Cleaning of utensils

431 Care of textiles – sorting, mending, washing, ironing and ordering clothes and linen

441 Shopping for goods and nonpersonal services; capital goods, household appliances, equipment, food and various household supplies

451 Household management – planning, supervising, paying bills, etc.

461 Do-it-yourself home improvements and maintenance, installation, servicing and repair of personal and household goods

471 Pet care

481 Travel related to household maintenance, management and shopping

491 Household maintenance, management and shopping not elsewhere classified

V   Care for children, the sick, elderly and disabled for own household

511 Physical care of children – washing, dressing, feeding

521 Teaching, training and instruction of own children

531 Accompanying children to places – school, sports, lessons, Primary Health Centre (PHC) doctor, etc.

541 Physical care of sick, disabled, elderly household members; washing, dressing, feeding, helping

551 Accompanying, adults to receive personal care services – hairdresser, therapy sessions, temple, religious places, etc.

561 Supervising children, needing care with or without other activity

562 Supervising adults, needing care with or without other activity

571 Travel related to care of children

572 Travel related to care of adults and others

581 Taking care of guests/visitors

591 Any other activity not mentioned above

VI Community services and help to other households

611 Community organized constructions and repairs; buildings, roads, dams, wells, ponds and other community assets

621 Community organized work – cooking for collective celebration, etc.

631 Volunteering with/for an organization (that does not involve working directly for individuals)

641 Volunteering work through organizations extended directly individuals and groups

651 Participation in meetings of local and informal groups/caste, tribes, professional associations, union, fraternal and political organizations

661 Involvement in civic and related responsibilities; voting, rallies, attending meetings, panchayat

671 Informal help to other households

681 Community services not elsewhere classified

691 Travel related to community services

VII Learning

711 General education – school/university/other educational institutions attendance

721 Studies, homework and course review related to general education

731   Additional study, nonformal education under adult education programs
741   Nonformal education for children
751   Work-related training
761   Training under government program such as Training for Rural Youth in Self Employment (TRYSEM), Development of Women and Children in Rural Areas (DWCRA) and others
771   Other training/education
781   Learning not elsewhere classified
791   Travel related to learning

VIII   Social and cultural activities, mass media, etc.

811   Participating in social events – wedding, funerals, births and other celebrations
812   Participating in religious activities – church services, religious ceremonies, practices, kirtans, singing, etc.
813   Participating in community functions in music, dance, etc.
814   Socializing at home and outside the home
821   Arts, making music hobbies and related courses
822   Indoor and outdoor sports participation and related courses
831   Games and other pastime activities
832   Spectator to sports, exhibitions/museums, cinemas/theater/ concerts and other performances and events
841   Other related activities
851   Reading other than newspaper and magazines
852   Watching televisions and video
853   Listening to music/radio
861   Accessing information by computing
862   Visiting library
863   Reading newspaper and magazine
871   Mass media use and entertainment not classified elsewhere
891   Travel related to social, cultural and recreational activities, social cultural and recreational activities not elsewhere classified, mass media use and entertainment
892   Travel related to job search

IX   Personal care and self-maintenance

911   Sleep and related activities
921   Eating and drinking
922   Smoking, drinking, alcohol and other intoxicants

931 Personal hygiene and health
932 Walking, exercise, running, jogging, yoga, etc.
941 Receiving medical and personal care from professional
942 Receiving medical and personal care from household members
951 Talking, gossiping and quarreling
961 Doing nothing, rest and relaxation
962 Forced leisure of forced rest and relaxation – willing and available for work
971 Individual religious practices and meditation
981 Other activities
982 Resting/convalescing due to physical illness and physical unwell persons
991 Travel related to personal care and self-maintenance

3

Gender Inequalities in Allocating Time to Paid and Unpaid Work: Evidence from Bolivia*

Marcelo Medeiros,[1] Rafael Guerreiro Osório[2] and Joana Costa[3]

Introduction

In this chapter we are interested in how gender influences the allocation of time among adults and results in inequalities among individuals. The case we will analyze is that of urban Bolivia, an example of an urban population of a developing country in which the incidence of paid work is higher for men than for women, but where, nonetheless, more than two-thirds of the adult urban female population has a paid job and an even higher proportion of men report doing domestic work.

The available data about time use in developing countries are increasing in quantity, but are still limited. Bolivia was one of the few South American countries that collected time-use information in the early 2000s. The data we use were collected in a general-purpose household survey, using questions similar to those recommended by the ILO for collecting information on time spent in paid labor; as a consequence we were able to have data with national coverage, but with much less detail than would usually be collected by specialized TUS. To examine this data we deploy conventional tools used in income inequality studies and apply them to analyze inequalities in time allocation. It is not our intent to fully explain those inequalities, but to describe them and to understand, to a certain extent, how gender roles influence them.

In this chapter we show that the sexual division of labor in Bolivia is characterized mainly by differences in the duration of paid and unpaid work shifts of women and men. This division of labor is associated with a partial trade-off between paid and unpaid labor so that the longer the paid work shift, the shorter the unpaid work shift tends to be, and vice versa. However, this trade off, as we mentioned above, is only partial

58

and there is no complete substitution of activities; thus, females tend to accumulate a double work shift. The result of this accumulation is that women, overall, work longer hours than men in urban Bolivia. We also show that despite the clear gender-based division of labor, women and men do not form homogeneous groups. There is much within-group inequality in time allocation as a consequence of factors other than gender.

The chapter is divided into five sections including this introduction. The next section briefly points out the relevance of time allocation analysis for development policies and the third section deals with data issues, the definitions of the analytical concepts deployed and the methodology of our decompositions. In the fourth section we present the results of the study, using decompositions to show how the incidence and the duration of paid and unpaid work affect gender inequalities in work-time allocation. We also look more closely at within-group inequalities. The fifth section features our concluding remarks.

Time-use inequalities matter

In recent decades women in many countries have experienced increased freedom in defining what to do with their own lives, including participation in the labor market. However, this has not been accompanied by a reduction of their obligations in the domestic[4] realm. Many women who have overcome the barriers that prevented previous generations from full access to the labor market have shouldered a double work shift. This has meant less time for studying, resting, engaging in social relations and so on.

Such 'time deprivation' is indeed a problem, but the consequences of a differentiation in the patterns of time allocation extend far beyond it, affecting also women's economic autonomy. Time is a scarce resource and thus its allocation implies trade-offs. One of these trade-offs is between domestic and market work. Many women still have their autonomy restricted because much of their time is committed to caring for their households, reducing time that could be used for paid work. In addition, domestic work also restricts time available for socialization, which is a way to receive information and accumulate social capital that can influence their positioning in the labor market.

Policies seeking increases in employability and productivity of paid workers usually neglect the dimension of unpaid work. Time inequalities matter and by studying time allocation we will be able to have a better understanding of what can be done to reduce several other inequalities in society, particularly gender related inequalities. Notwithstanding, we argue that the reduction of domestic workloads or the increase in the productivity of household work contributes to removing barriers that prevent women from entering the labor market and, although it is not the subject matter of this chapter, it has been shown to have impacts on income inequality, poverty and growth.

Methodology

Data and definitions

This study was based on the unit-level datasets of the Bolivian general household survey, the Encuesta de Mejoramiento de Condiciones de Vida (MECOVI), fielded in 2001 by the Instituto Nacional de Estadística (INE). The MECOVI is not a TUS, but its 2001 round does have sections on market labor and domestic activities. The survey is representative of the urban areas of the entire country and has a sample size of over 25,000 interviews (the population of Bolivia at the time of the survey was 8.2 million people). The urban adults we are studying compose 29 per cent of the total population (a sample size of 5,723 observations). Case attrition due to missing or inconsistent data were irrelevant.

Information was collected by personal interviews in a period of less than a month. For household members over the age of seven, the survey recorded the time – hours and minutes per day and days per week – spent in 'activities for the household' and if any time was spent in any of a roll of seven activities – care for children and the elderly, cooking and cleaning the house, shopping, laundry, keeping animals and crops, fetching wood and water and household repairs – but did not differentiate between the time spent in each of them.

The survey also collected information on time spent in 'work,' this being understood as the production of goods and services against payment in cash on in kind, that is, paid work. The questionnaire for this collection followed international standards and covered time spent in primary and secondary jobs – hours and minutes per day and days per week. In this study we use this information and measure time spent in paid and unpaid activities in hours per week (h/w).

In view of the fact that we are dealing only with the urban population, domestic work is to be understood as mostly unpaid work oriented towards the family's own consumption – ranging from cooking to house repairs – while 'production of goods and services' tends to mean market-oriented work, which is paid. This last category includes work that receives nonmonetary payment, work that is paid indirectly (when one member of the family receives payment for all of the family's work) and the paid domestic work of servants.

To deal with the reporting of extreme work shifts that we consider unrealistic, we assumed that even in extreme conditions, individuals have to regularly spare at least eight hours a day for resting, personal hygiene and nourishment. Actually, this limit is very low and already bellow the necessary to maintain a person's biological functioning: on average a typical adult is recommended to sleep for eight hours a day (Ting and Malhotra, 2005; Heslopa *et al.*, 2002) and to this we should add time for other self-care activities – which, in Thailand and the US are, on average, around 2.3 hours a day (NSOT, 2001; USBLS, 2004). As a result, we imposed a ceiling of 112 hours per week for both paid and unpaid labor time, which corresponds to working for 16 hours a day, seven days a week.

It is obvious that the data we use here are limited, particularly for tackling issues such as child labor, farm labor and community work, just to name a few. To avoid those limitations, and in view of the fact that our main focus is on gender inequalities in time use, we restricted the study to the subsample of Bolivian urban adults. We considered adults as those aged 20 to 59 years.

Decomposition of total time

The averages of total time spent at work in the population can be decomposed in terms of the incidence of each activity and the duration of each type of work shift. By incidence we mean the proportion of the adult population engaged in one or another type of work, that is, the equivalent of an occupation rate in paid work. By duration we mean the average hours dedicated to the activity by those who do it:

$$\frac{T}{N} = \sum_{l=1}^{2} \frac{W_l}{N} \cdot \frac{T_l}{W_l} \tag{1}$$

Where T is the total time devoted to work; N the total population size; W the number of workers; and l the type of work (unpaid = 1 or paid = 2).

Letting T-bar represent the average of total time spent at work, p the incidence of labor types, and μ the duration of work shifts, we can rewrite (1) as:

$$\overline{T} = \sum_{l=1}^{2} p_l \mu_l \tag{2}$$

Equation (2) allows us to determine the weight of each factor component in the average of total time spent at work.

Results

Duration and incidence of work

Bolivian adults spend about one-third of their time working, be it market-oriented paid labor or unpaid domestic labor. In 2001, as shown in Table 3.1, adults allocated an average of slightly over 56 hours per week (h/w) to work, which represents 34 per cent of the 168 hours available in a week. This is the equivalent of working seven days a week for slightly more than eight hours a day.

Proportionally, paid work has a higher importance than unpaid work in the total (averages of 33.6 hours versus 22.7 hours). This result occurs despite the fact that there are more people doing unpaid labor. The reason is that the longer duration of paid work shifts is more than sufficient to compensate its significantly lower incidence in the population.

Table 3.1   Decomposition of the average total work hours per week for urban adults, Bolivia 2001

Total work average	Unpaid			+ Paid		
	Incidence (p_1)	*	Duration (μ_1) +	Incidence (p_2)	*	Duration (μ_2)
56.3412 =	0.9179	*	24.7822 +	0.7215	*	46.5604
		22.7472	+		33.5940	

Note: p_1 and p_2 are the proportions of the total population doing, respectively, unpaid and paid work; μ_1 and μ_2 the mean durations of work shifts of paid and unpaid labor in hours per week.
Source: Bolivia, Instituto Nacional de Estadística, Encuesta de Mejoramiento de Condiciones de Vida, 2001.

As Table 3.1 shows, about three-fifths of the total time is employed in paid work whereas the remaining two-fifths go to unpaid work. Decomposing the average by equation (2), we find that the proportion of people doing unpaid labor (92 per cent) is much higher than that of paid labor (72 per cent). Conversely, the average duration of paid work shifts (47 h/w) is higher than that of unpaid labor (25 h/w). In other words, on average there are more Bolivians doing unpaid work, but for less time; fewer of them are doing paid work, but for more time.

Between-groups gender inequalities in the total workload

Every individual is endowed with the same 24 hours per day, but the way people use their time for different activities is varied and determined by their social roles. In the case of Bolivian urban adults, the influence of gender roles on the allocation of time to work is clear. First, on average, women work longer hours than men. The data presented in Table 3.2 show that the average number of hours per week allocated to work by Bolivian women is ten hours higher than men's. Discounting a minimum of ten daily hours for resting and personal care, men allocate 46 per cent of their maximum net time to work, while women allocate 55 per cent. This heavier workload is basically due to the accumulation of paid and unpaid activities, that is, to the fact that women are submitted to a double shift of work.

This higher average is not the mere statistical result of a small but more heavily burdened group of women on the total. Looking at the entire distribution, we can see that women systematically work more than men. If we rank the male and female populations according to the amount of time people work, we always find that no matter the share of the population chosen, the cumulative workload of women is always higher than that of men.

To show this, we will use a graphical representation of inequality that gathers information about the shape and the level of men's and women's workload distributions, namely the generalized Lorenz curve, as depicted in Figure 3.1. The curves in the figure illustrate the distribution of the average workloads of men and women. The generalized Lorenz curve is a device that shows the cumulative average workload up to a given share of the population ordered by total time at work.

For instance, Figure 3.1 allows us to state that the half of the Bolivian urban adult women that commit less time to work spend on average 19 h/w working, while the equivalent half of the male population devote an average 15 h/w to work – a four-hour gap. This difference tends to increase as we move to higher shares of the population. Since the generalized Lorenz curve of women clearly dominates that of men, because the former always lies above the latter, we can state with certainty that the cumulative workload of Bolivian urban adult women is higher than that of men, regardless of the point of the distribution that we assess.

What is behind this difference in averages? One average can be higher than another due to more people working, people working for longer, or a combination of the two. By breaking down the averages using equation (2), we are able to determine the role of each of these factor components in determining the mean. Table 3.2 shows the results of this decomposition.

The incidence and, more importantly, the duration of the paid and unpaid activities show a clear sexual division of labor in Bolivia. The

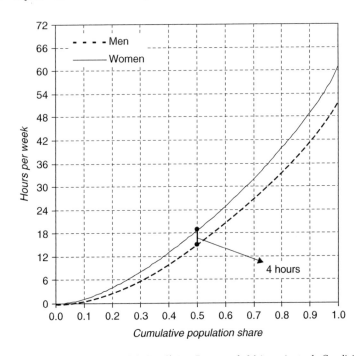

Source: Bolivia, Instituto Nacional de Estadística, Encuesta de Mejoramiento de Condiciones de Vida, 2001.
Figure 3.1   Generalized Lorenz curves for total work time, by gender, for urban adults, Bolivia 2001

incidences tell us that almost all, 98 per cent, urban adult women do unpaid labor. Among males we also find a high incidence of unpaid labor, even higher than that of their own paid labor, but still lower than the unpaid labor of females. Yet, it is the duration of unpaid labor that characterizes it as a predominantly feminine activity: it is more than three times higher among women.

With regard to paid labor, a different picture emerges: this activity is more masculine since both the incidence and the duration of the work shift are higher among men. It is clear that most of the gender differences in average work time have their origins in the duration of the shifts of unpaid labor and in the incidence of paid labor. Be it because of barriers to participating in the job market or because of labor supply factors, the average Bolivian woman commits 26 h/w to paid labor and 35 h/w to unpaid labor, whereas the average man dedicates 42 h/w to paid labor and 9 h/w to unpaid labor.

Table 3.2 Decomposition of the average work time according to type of work, by gender, for urban adults, Bolivia 2001

Sex	Total work (average)		Unpaid			+	Paid		
			Incidence (p_1)	*	Duration (μ_1)		Incidence (p_2)	*	Duration (μ_2)
Male	51.0538	=	0.8442	*	10.7184	+	0.8246	*	50.9429
				9.0487		+		42.0051	
Female	61.0585	=	0.9836	*	35.5516	+	0.6296	*	41.4397
				34.9687		+		26.0898	

Note: p_1 and p_2 are the incidences of, respectively, unpaid and paid work, as a proportion of the group population; μ_1 and μ_2 the mean durations of work shifts of paid and unpaid labor in hours per week.

Source: Bolivia, Instituto Nacional de Estadística, Encuesta de Mejoramiento de Condiciones de Vida, 2001.

To illustrate how the differences in incidences and duration influence the workload, Table 3.3 presents some simple counterfactual simulations using the factors shown in Table 3.2. The simulation consists of switching factors, one at a time, to estimate what would happen to the work time averages if the patterns of work of men were like those of women and vice versa.

Table 3.3   Simulated mean workload for urban adults, Bolivia 2001

Labor	Switched factor (males/females)	Simulated workload		Deviance from observed averages	
		Male	Female	Male	Female
Unpaid	Incidence (p_1)	52.5478	56.1030	1.4940	−4.9554
	Duration (μ_1)	72.0184	36.6325	20.9646	−24.4260
Paid	Incidence (p_2)	41.1215	69.1379	−9.9323	8.0794
	Duration (μ_2)	43.2179	67.0416	−7.8359	5.9831

Note: p_1 and p_2 are the incidences of, respectively, unpaid and paid work, as a proportion of the group population; μ_1 and μ_2 the mean durations of work shifts of paid and unpaid labor in hours per week.
Source: Bolivia, Instituto Nacional de Estadística, Encuesta de Mejoramiento de Condiciones de Vida, 2001.

Large differences in the existing working patterns would occur if men and women were to switch the duration of the unpaid work that they do. If men were to perform as many hours of unpaid work as women, the average male unpaid work time would increase by 21 h/w, thereby augmenting their total work time from 51 h/w to 72 h/w. Conversely, if women started doing unpaid labor for the same number of hours as men, their average unpaid work time would be reduced by 24 h/w. That is, their total work time would fall from 61 h/w to only 37 h/w. Switching paid work shifts would bring much less impressive, but still important, results. Men would have their average paid work shift reduced by about 8 h/w whereas women would experience an increase of about 6 h/w.

What really differentiates men and women in terms of unpaid work is the time that persons of each gender spend on it. Since almost everyone declares doing some sort of domestic work during the week, switching men's and women's incidences of unpaid work would not significantly change their workloads. The unpaid work time of men would rise by 1.5 h/w and women's would fall by about 5 h/w. Nevertheless, differences in the participation in the labor market are evident when we proceed with the simulations. If males were withdrawn from the labor market to the degree that women are, they would see a decrease of 10 h/w. For women, the equivalent change in the opposite direction would increase their paid work effort by about 8 h/w.

Examining the deviations from the observed averages shows that the duration of the shifts of unpaid work are the principal factor that influences the gender inequality in workloads, followed by the incidence of paid work. The duration of paid work is only slightly less important than the incidence of paid work. Since the incidence of unpaid work is high for both males and females, it is less important for gender differentiation than the other factors, although it does have a non-negligible effect.

Within-group inequalities

In the previous section we looked at differences between gender groups. Although we can use averages to be assertive about the existence of a clear gender-based division of labor in Bolivia, these averages mask high levels of inequality in time allocation within each gender group. In this section we turn to the analysis of the within-group inequalities by comparing women to other women and men to other men. To represent these inequalities we produced Lorenz curves for the distribution of the time spent in each activity, separately for males and females, as depicted in Figure 3.2. The Lorenz curve is the appropriate tool for the comparisons in this section because it is not affected by the absolute levels of the distributions (for example, the number of hours worked).

Figure 3.2 shows quite high levels of inequality in the distribution of time allocated to paid and unpaid labor both among males and among females. The patterns of the distributions of each activity are different, but are not the outcome of the interaction between paid and unpaid labor in terms of total work time. A quick comparison of the two panels shows that the most unequal distribution among women is that of time in paid labor, whilst for males it is that of unpaid labor. But with regard to the distribution of total time at work, the shapes of the curves are approximately the same. What is behind this result?

Almost 40 per cent of the urban adult women do not take part in the labor market and many have only part-time jobs, which results in extremely high levels of within-group inequality in the distribution of time spent in paid work. About half of all time allocated by females to paid work is spent by only one-fifth of the women. This suggests that participation and employment rates are insufficient indicators for the analysis of female labor market participation. The distribution of unpaid work time is less – but still very – unequal; although almost every woman does some domestic work, half of all unpaid work time is accounted for by one-quarter of women. The Lorenz curve for female total work shows much less inequality. This occurs because many women cannot have long paid work shifts (if any) due to their role as providers of unpaid work. Substitution for within-group paid/unpaid work is relatively high.

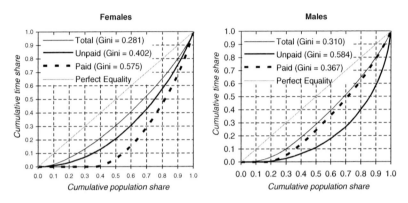

Source: Bolivia, Instituto Nacional de Estadística, Encuesta de Mejoramiento de Condiciones de Vida, 2001.

Figure 3.2   Total paid and unpaid work Lorenz curves by gender for urban adults, Bolivia 2001

Among males, time spent in unpaid work is much more unequally distributed than it is among females. About one-fifth of men do not do any type of unpaid work and half of all male unpaid work time is accounted for by little more than one-seventh of men. Conversely, most men have a full-time, paid job and therefore they end up working shifts of similar durations. However, these shifts are not completely uniform. Participation and employment rates tend to better reflect what happens among males than what happens among females. The much less unequal Lorenz curve for male total work time also indicates a gender specialization, that is, males reduce their unpaid work shifts due to their paid work efforts.

The Lorenz curves for the distributions of total time at work of Bolivian urban men and women have a similar shape because of a partial trade-off between paid and unpaid work. That is, adults who have long work shifts of paid labor tend to have short shifts of unpaid labor, and vice versa. This can be seen in Figure 3.3, which shows the joint distribution of paid and unpaid work for men and women.

The trade-off between paid and unpaid labor expresses a division of labor in which both men and women do both paid and unpaid work, but the duration of the work shifts in each of the activities tends to be

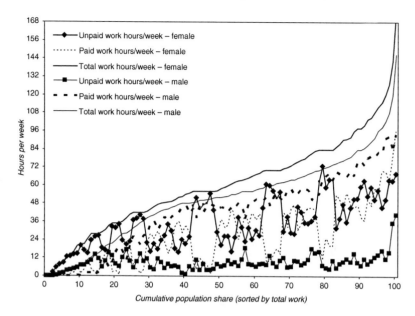

Source: Bolivia, Instituto Nacional de Estadística, Encuesta de Mejoramiento de Condiciones de Vida, 2001.
Figure 3.3 Total paid and unpaid work joint distributions by gender for urban adults, Bolivia 2001

differentiated by gender. In other words, the gender division of labor is not characterized by a polarization between the clear roles of the male breadwinner and the female housekeeper but by a partial specialization in either paid or unpaid work.

The substitution of activities is not complete and the result is a gender gap in the total workload, as we have seen above. As in other countries (Gershuny, *et al.*, 2005), for Bolivian women, the increase in the workload due to paid work is associated with a less than proportional decrease in unpaid work time. Conversely, for males, a decrease in paid work – unemployment, for instance – is not followed by an equivalent rise in time spent in domestic activities.

The high levels of inequality in the distributions of paid and unpaid work time among both men and women restrict the possibility of strong generalizations based only on the gender division of labor. Most likely there are other dimensions of social stratification – such as those based on having children, having certain family attributes or belonging to a social class – that influence most of the way that time is allocated. To evaluate the weight of these dimensions *vis-à-vis* gender, we will decompose total inequality into within-group and between-group shares in the next section.

Decomposing inequality within and between groups

There is a clear pattern of time allocation distinguishing gender groups. Still, time is also allocated differently by persons of the same sex. For example, some women do much more paid work than others. Therefore, we may speak of inequality between groups – all men compared to all women – and also of inequality within groups – men compared to men and women compared to women. By decomposing total inequality into between-group and within-group inequalities, we are able to better gauge the importance of gender in determining how time is allocated.

The Gini coefficient cannot be perfectly decomposable into groups, but the set of the generalized entropy inequality measures can be. The most well-known measure of this family is the Theil-T index. In its decomposition the contribution of within-group inequalities to total inequality is weighted by the share of the unequally distributed attribute – in our case, the weights represent differences in time allocated to paid/unpaid work among women themselves (Theil, 1967, p. 93). We present the measures for each distribution along with the decompositions in Table 3.4.

Table 3.4 is divided into three groups of four rows, one group for each distribution. The first row, 'Theil-T,' presents the inequality measure calculated just for men, just for women, and then for both genders together. The next row, 'share of total time,' presents the share of the total time held by each group. The row 'decomposition of Theil-T' presents the decomposition of the total Theil-T for each type of work, in absolute values. Those are obtained by multiplying the gender group Theil-T by the share of total time held by the group. The between-group inequality measure is obtained by subtracting the absolute contributions of the inequality within each gender group from the inequality measure in each type of work. The next row, '% contribution to inequality,' is just the previous row expressed as a percentage of the total Theil-T: it gives the relative contribution of each component.

When we decompose this index by gender, we find that 34 per cent of the total inequality in time spent in unpaid work is due to net differences between women's and men's allocations of time. The same decomposition, applied to the inequality in time spent in paid work, indicates that between-group inequality is responsible for only 6 per cent of the total inequality. The results of these decompositions highlight the fact

Table 3.4 Theil-T measure of inequality and its gender decomposition for the distributions of total work time, time spent on paid labor and time spent on unpaid labor, for urban population 20–59 years old, Bolivia 2001

	Distribution	Between men and women	Within men	Within women	Total inequality
Total work time	*Within group Theil-T*		0.1843	0.1385	**0.1620**
	Group share of total time		42.73%	57.27%	100.00%
	Decomposition of Theil-T	0.0039	0.0787	0.0793	0.1620
	% Contribution to inequality	2.43%	48.61%	48.96%	100.00%
	Within group Theil-T		0.6246	0.2694	**0.5125**
	Group share of total time		18.76%	81.24%	100.00%
Unpaid work time	*Decomposition of Theil-T*	0.1765	0.1171	0.2189	0.5125
	% Contribution to inequality	34.43%	22.86%	42.71%	100.00%
	Within group Theil-T		0.2879	0.6345	**0.4581**
	Group share of total time		58.96%	41.04%	100.00%
Paid work time	*Decomposition of total Theil-T*	0.0280	0.1697	0.2604	0.4581
	% Contribution to inequality	6.11%	37.05%	56.85%	100.00%

Source: Bolivia, Instituto Nacional de Estadística, Encuesta de Mejoramiento de Condiciones de Vida, 2001.

that the gender division of labor in Bolivia is marked particularly by a differentiation of how much unpaid labor is done by each person.

However, because of the trade-off between paid and unpaid labor and the very high levels of heterogeneity among men and women, the disparities between genders are not as important as within-group differences in explaining overall inequality in the allocation of total time to work. In fact, gender accounts for a small share of total work-time inequality, to be precise, only 2.4 per cent. The inequality within each gender group contributes a similar percentage, namely, about 49 per cent, to total work time inequality. For unpaid work time, inequality among women accounts for about 43 per cent of total inequality; for paid work, inequality among women accounts for about 57 per cent.

Although it is important to explain differences in the patterns of allocation of paid and unpaid work, gender is, comparatively, a less important variable for explaining why the total workload is unequally distributed in society. Much of the total inequality in paid, unpaid and total work time is located within – not between – gender groups. It is not the goal of our study to identify the determinants of these inequalities, but we speculate that they are likely to be related to the demographic composition of families and their position in the class structure.

Three remarks are warranted about the results of these decompositions. First, it should be stressed that the 34 per cent of total inequality in unpaid work time accounted for by gender is a very high share for a binary division of the population by a single variable. For the sake of comparison, such a value is almost six times higher than the one calculated for paid work using the same partition by sex. Usually, the smaller the number of partitions, the smaller the share of between-group inequality, but the high share observed is not common even when the population is partitioned in several groups. For instance, switching the focus to the position of individuals in the life cycle produces even more modest results: only 2 per cent of unpaid work inequality is due to differences between age groups despite the fact that, in this case, we are partitioning the society into forty groups.

Second, although gender accounts for a small share of total inequality, the consequences of gender differences for total time allocation are not negligible. As we saw before, they result in a total work effort of women that is, on average, 10 h/w higher than men's. The gender share is proportionally small because inequalities within groups are very high. If men and women formed more homogeneous groups, the gender (between-group) share of total inequality would probably increase substantially above the observed 2 per cent.

Finally, although the gender differences in the patterns of work-time allocations confirm that there is a clear gender division of labor in the Bolivian society, we must introduce a word of caution about the difference between the decompositions above and any inferences about causality. Stating that inequality between men and women accounts for 34 per cent of total inequality in unpaid work time does not mean, in net terms, that gender inequalities determine 34 per cent of the total inequality in time allocation between people. This decomposition does not take into account several other variables that could affect time allocation by increasing or reducing the net effect that gender has on total time use.

Conclusions

The way that people allocate time affects inequalities in various dimensions. Allocation of work time is particularly important, as work is one of the main activities of adults. This allocation is bounded by several constraints, among them social roles, particularly the ones related to gender.

Also, since certain activities bring more advantages than others, gender roles in work time allocation end up influencing the well-being of men and women in many spheres of life.

There is little doubt about the importance of work for the understanding of time-use patterns. In our study we found that, on average, Bolivian urban adults spend about one-third of their time working in either market-oriented paid labor or unpaid domestic labor. Discounting the time needed for rest and caring for oneself, the total rises to more than half of the maximum time a person has available to use in all of his/her social activities.

Moreover, paid work and unpaid work have approximately the same importance in time allocation. Although there are more people doing unpaid labor, the longer duration of paid work shifts is enough to compensate for its lower incidence in the population. As a result, paid work has a higher weight in total time allocation in Bolivia. Paid work is responsible for three-fifths of total time employed in work.

The proportion of people doing unpaid work among urban adults is high, even higher than the proportion of people doing paid work. In spite of a gap of 15 percentage points in these rates, the gender differentiation in unpaid work occurs more in the duration of the shifts: women tend, on average, to have unpaid work shifts that are more than three times higher than those of men. Regarding paid work, the gender differences are more pronounced in terms of incidence. The gap approaches 20 percentage points, but the duration of the shifts, although shorter for women, are not as substantially different as they are in the case of unpaid work.

When comparing men to men and women to women, we find much intragroup inequality in the distributions of paid and unpaid work time. About half of all unpaid work time is accounted for by one-quarter of women and half of all time allocated by females to paid work is accounted for by only one-fifth of them. Among males, time spent in unpaid work is much more unequally distributed than it is among females: one-fifth of men do not do any type of domestic work and half of all male unpaid work time is accounted for by little more than one-seventh of them.

However, when the distribution of total time at work is considered, the levels of inequality are much lower for both males and females. Behind this result is a partial trade-off between paid and unpaid work. The longer the paid work shift of adults, the shorter tends to be their unpaid work shifts, and vice versa. This trade-off is accompanied by a specialization that expresses the gender division of labor prevailing in Bolivia. As in other countries, men tend to specialize in paid work while women do so in unpaid work. Nevertheless – and, again, as in other countries – this trade-off is not a mere reproduction of the classic role models of 'male breadwinner' and 'female housekeeper.'

What characterizes gender differences is not only who does one particular type of work, but mainly how much work that person does. By a partial trade-off we mean there is no complete substitution between paid and unpaid work. Women are in the labor market and men have responsibilities for domestic work, but women have a higher workload. On average, women work more than men, basically due to a double shift of work, that is, an accumulation of both paid and unpaid work responsibilities.

The high levels of within-group inequality in the distributions of paid and unpaid work time for both men and women limit the explanatory power, at the individual level, of the gender division of labor. Gender is an important variable for explaining how much paid and unpaid work is done by individuals, but is proportionally less important for explaining why some people work more than others. In fact, due to the extremely high levels of within-group inequality among women and among men, only a small share of total work-time inequality is explained by the inequality between men and women. Evidently, there are other dimensions of social stratification determining how much work individuals undertake. We believe that further research might provide better explanations by examining, for example, the demographic composition of families and their position in the class structure.

Notes

* Many ideas in this chapter were presented at 'The Global Conference on Unpaid Work and the Economy: Gender, Poverty and the Millennium Development Goals,' which was held in 2005 at the Levy Economics Institute in Annandale-on-Hudson, NY and later discussed at the International Poverty Centre. The authors would like to thank Rania Antonopoulos, Indira Hirway and an anonymous reader for valuable feedback as well as Diane Elson, Sanjay Reddy, Eduardo Zepeda, Terry McKinley, Dag Ehrenpreis and Imraan Valodia and Karla Correa for their comments and suggestions.
1. International Poverty Centre and CSC/Cambridge University.
2. International Poverty Centre.
3. International Poverty Centre.
4. 'Domestic' refers to unpaid household production.

References

Gershuny, J., M. Bittman and J. Brice (2005) 'Exit, voice and suffering: do couples adapt to changing employment patterns?,' *Journal of Marriage and the Family* 67(August), 656–65.

Heslopa, P., G.D. Smith, C. Metcalf, J. MacLeod and C. Hart (2002) 'Sleep duration and mortality: the effect of short or long sleep duration on cardiovascular and all-cause mortality in working men and women,' *Sleep Medicine* 3, 305–14.

National Statistics Office Thailand (NSOT) (2001) *Time-use Survey* (Bangkok: NSOT).

Theil, H. (1967) *Economics and Information Theory*, Ch. 4 (Amsterdam: North Holland).

Ting, L. and A. Malhotra (2005) 'Disorders of Sleep: An Overview,' *Primary Care: Clinics in Office Practice* 32, 305–18.

United States Bureau of Labor Statistics (USBLS) (2004) *American Time-use Survey* (ATUS) (Washington, DC: USBLS).

4
Unpaid Work, Poverty and Unemployment: A Gender Perspective from South Africa

Emel Memis* and Rania Antonopoulos

Introduction

It has long been recognized that income poverty, joblessness and lack of access to public goods and services reduce people's ability to lead productive and healthy lives. The effects of such inequalities are, at times, devastating. Among them, malnutrition, bad health, social exclusion, violence and political instability, have led governments and international development organizations to take notice and introduce policies that redress such inequities. To date, and despite mixed results, commitments to bring about much needed change remain prevalent on the international agenda and the Millennium Development Goals (MDGs) speak to that effect.[1]

Another form of inequality that shapes life experience and circumscribes present capabilities and future options pertains to unpaid work.[2] Spending long hours performing unpaid family work, fetching wood, collecting and carrying water, preparing and cooking meals and devoting much of the day to cleaning up and performing sanitation work instead of attending school as a young person and working for pay later in life delineate very different life trajectories. Inequalities in this area need to be recognized and redressed as well.

Data collection on how individuals use their time is highly irregular. Yet one stylized fact shows up persistently across time and space. In terms of 'who' engages in unpaid work, including unpaid care work, it is women and girl children who perform most of it. This is the case in developing, as well as developed, countries.[3]

Figure 4.1 illustrates that despite variations between countries this is indeed the case: at the low end, women in South Africa and France spend, on average, about two more hours per day than men do, in Mauritius

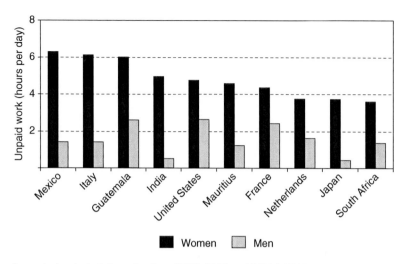

Source: Authors' tabulations; data from UNDP (2006) and ECLAC (2007).
Figure 4.1 Time spent on unpaid work: selected developing and OECD countries

and Japan about three and a half hours, four and a half extra hours in India, and Italy and close to five extra hours per day in Mexico.

Stark as this picture may be, averages and median values only partially reveal the differences between men and women. Looked at through the lens of other socioeconomic identifiers, women of some subgroups end up performing out of necessity even more unpaid work, leading to aggravated time-tax burdens for them. This is the topic of investigation of this chapter. Specifically, we are interested in the influence that: (a) poverty; (b) employment status; and (c) area of residence exert on unpaid work.

It is reasonable to expect that location affects the amount of required contributions of unpaid work. Households located in relatively remote areas may, for example, have more difficulty accessing publicly provided goods and social services, such as water and electricity, and may be required to travel longer distances to reach markets, clinics, schools and so on; equally probable is that poverty and unemployment increase unpaid work burdens as lack of income reduces the ability of households to purchase basic necessities and services from the market. Whether caring for the very young and the old, collecting and transporting water, gathering free goods and processing them into usable raw food ingredients, searching for fuel wood and cooking or spending long hours in performing sanitation tasks, unpaid work burdens are potentially exacerbated in all above stated cases.

Making use of the 2000 South African TUS data (TUS SA, 2000) we address two questions: first, we investigate whether indeed these three socioeconomic identifiers (namely poverty, employment status and geographic location of residence) affect unpaid work in general; and second, for households that face higher unpaid work requirements, we investigate whether men and women share unpaid work burden more equitably.

The section below briefly introduces the South African TUS and describes the time-use activity classification we employ in our investigation. Finally, it describes briefly the meanings of the categorical variables we use within the context of South Africa, namely of geographic location, poverty and unemployment. The subsequent section presents our findings in terms of patterns of gender distribution of unpaid work across groups with regard to poverty, employment status and geographic location, while the penultimate section reports multivariate analysis results by Tobit estimation of the patterns we observe.

Data, time-use activity classification and contextualization of our variables of choice

Data

The data we use is provided by the first TUS conducted in South Africa in the year 2000 (TUS SA, 2000). The overall objective of this survey is to provide information on how individual South Africans spend their time. Gender equity is a major emphasis of the survey; it delivers greater insight into the division of both paid and unpaid labor between men and women. The survey covers all nine provinces of South Africa. Within each province, four different settlement types were visited: formal urban, informal urban, commercial farms and other rural settlements. The sample size includes 8,564 households and data was collected for 14,553 respondents. The survey was conducted in three rounds (tranches) in order to capture potential seasonal variations in time use. These rounds were carried out in February, June and October 2000 (SSA, 2001).

The South African TUS 2000 consists of two sections, the first of which involves a household questionnaire with many standard questions used in Statistics South Africa (Stats SA) household surveys. This first section allows for comparison with the other surveys. One member per household was required to provide basic information about the household characteristics as a whole. In the second section, two people (aged ten years or above) from each household were systematically selected and questioned about the activities they had performed the previous day. Each respondent was also required to provide basic demographic information about themselves, for example their age, gender, race, education level and work status. The activities performed by each respondent were recorded in a 24-hour diary, which had been divided into half-hour slots. In each time slot, at most three activities could be recorded.

Activity classification

The South African TUS 2000 followed the activity classification system developed by the 1993 UN Statistics Division, which provided a much more detailed classification of economic activities to allow 'visibility' of informal and unpaid work activities.[4] As discussed in a previous chapter in this volume, the UN classification system of 1993 consists of ten broad categories: (1) work in establishments, such as in a factory, mine or for the government; (2) primary production, for example, growing fruits or vegetables on a household plot for sale or for own use; (3) work in nonestablishments, which includes street vendors, hair salon services run from home and so on; (4) household maintenance, for example, cleaning and cooking; (5) caring for the ill and the elderly and looking after children; (6) community service; (7) learning, for example, being in training or attending school; (8) time spent attending social and cultural events, for example, participating in religious activities or socializing with friends and family; (9) mass media use; and finally category 0, which stands for personal care and self-maintenance activities. Categories 7–9 and 0 are nonproductive activities and, though important in their own right, they are of no concern to this study.

For this study, in regards to paid work and in accordance to the conceptual framework of the SNA (1993), we group activities in categories 1–3 as 'paid work.' The remaining categories comprise 'total unpaid work.' For the purpose of our investigation, we have regrouped unpaid activities in three broad categories: water and firewood collection; social care; and home and community maintenance. Table 4A.1 in the Appendix provides the list of all activities included in each group, disaggregated at the three-digit level. Our aim in constructing a three-pronged unpaid work classification is to make evident how each one of these unpaid work groupings interacts with poverty, unemployment and location.

Contextualizing location of residence, poverty and unemployment

Unemployment and income poverty have remained serious challenges in post-apartheid South Africa, but some population groups have been disproportionately affected. Before we answer the questions we pose above, we must regroup the sample population of TUS SA 2000 according to the three individual and household characteristics mentioned above, namely unemployment, poverty and location of residence. Luckily the background schedule used in the TUS provides sufficient information, which allows us to also use and make comparisons with the Labour Force Survey (LFS) 2000 and Household Survey (HS) data 2000 of South Africa. Prior to presenting and discussing our results, we proceed to contextualize these socioeconomic identifiers and begin with a description of location of residence.

Location

The first important split Stats SA uses in many of the surveys it conducts, including the HS and LFS, is between urban and rural areas. As can be seen in Table 4.1, urban households are further subdivided into: (a) formal; and (b) informal ones. Here, the formal/informal classification refers to the type of housing in which the household lives in, and not to conditions of labor market employment. Formal urban residential areas refer to traditional residential suburban areas and city or town centers, with those residing within these areas being typically middle-income or wealthy households. Informal areas, on the other hand, are comprised of shantytowns and slums. Households living in shacks or huts often lack access to basic services and are generally classified as poor or very poor. Linkages to formal employment are also weaker than in formal areas. As can be seen in Table 4.1, 94.5 per cent of the population living in these informal areas are Africans. Rural commercial households

Table 4.1   Distribution of population by household types (%)

	African	Coloured	Asian	White	Total
Urban formal	63.2	12.1	4.4	20.2	100
Urban informal	94.5	4.7	0.6	0.1	100
Rural commercial	85.6	9.1	0.4	4.9	100
Rural ex-homeland	99.6	0.2	0.0	0.1	100

Source: Authors' calculations based on TUS South Africa (2000).

reside in geographic areas where economic activity is either commercial farming or other commercial activity (such as mining).

The remainder of the category 'rural areas' in South Africa consists of what was formerly known as 'homelands.' As part of the racist regime's apartheid policy, they were set aside as 'reservations' for Africans, dividing the population according to ethnic/tribal origin. Homelands were either partially self-governed or, in some cases, independent from the Republic. The ex-homeland areas constitute less than 13 per cent of the total land of the country; one in three Africans still live in ex-homeland territories and 99.6 per cent of the homeland population are Africans (as Table 4.1 indicates). Among these households, 54 per cent are female-headed households. Outward migration, rampant unemployment, inactivity and the worst poverty rates in the country are the result of decades of underfunding, as well as economic and geographical isolation.

Poverty status

Poverty estimates place 50–60 per cent of the population below the poverty line.[5] Overall, the incidence of poverty among women is quite high in South Africa; in a population of about 44 million, among the poor, 11.9 million (54.4 per cent) are female as compared to 10 million poor males (Sadan, 2006). Stats SA (2007) also concurs with this finding.

In our work here, we grouped households using the per capita household income as a criterion using data we pulled from the TUS 2000, which contains a categorical variable on the usual monthly income of the household. Respondents were asked to indicate their monthly income based on a range of ten values and, for the purposes of our study, the midpoint value for each category was allocated as the actual monthly income per household.

We created a total of three income groups, namely ultra-poor (<1,333 Rand), poor (<3,210 Rand) and non-poor (>3,210 Rand), by splitting households around the 25th and 50th percentiles of per capita income.[6] Table 4.2 provides some statistics on income distribution across a variety of population groups. As can be seen from the zero entries, there are no white people in the ultra-poor or poor category. More than 40 per cent of the African people living in ex-homeland areas are ultra-poor, while all of the white people living in urban formal areas are non-poor. Among those who are ultra-poor and poor, 94 per cent and 88 per cent, respectively, are Africans and, overall, they constitute the vast majority of the bottom 50th percentile. By any measurement, poverty in South Africa is extremely concentrated among a single population group.

Table 4.2   Distribution of population across income groups, location and race (%)

	Ultra-poor	Poor	Non-poor	Total
Row shares				
Urban formal African	21.7	28.5	49.8	100.0
Urban informal African	31.7	31.1	37.1	100.0
Rural commercial African	38.8	27.7	33.6	100.0
Ex-homeland African	43.8	33.2	23.0	100.0
Urban formal colored/Asian	10.2	17.8	72.0	100.0
Rural commercial colored/Asian	16.2	37.9	45.9	100.0
Urban Formal White	0.0	0.0	100.0	100.0
Rural commercial white	0.0	0.0	100.0	100.0
Column shares				
Urban formal African	20.2	26.6	25.9	24.6
Urban informal African	27.3	26.9	17.8	22.7
Rural commercial African	17.2	12.4	8.3	11.8
Ex-homeland African	29.3	22.2	8.6	17.6
Urban formal colored/Asian	3.7	6.4	14.4	9.5
Rural commercial colored/Asian	2.3	5.5	3.7	3.8
Urban formal white	0.0	0.0	15.7	7.4
Rural commercial white	0.0	0.0	5.6	2.6
Total	100.0	100.0	100.0	100.0

Source: Authors' calculations based on TUS South Africa (2000).

In order to understand the dynamics of poverty better, we looked at the distribution of population according to their employment and poverty status. We categorized individuals according to their employment status as employed, unemployed, economically inactive and not working age (age <16 and >65). We observed that the incidence of poverty is not only high among the unemployed individuals, but also quite high among the employed. Accordingly, around 68 per cent of the unemployed individuals live under poverty. This figure is 67 per cent for the economically inactive South Africans and 44 per cent among the employed individuals (Table 4.3).

The high rate of poverty among the employed raises the issue of inadequate income source. Exploration on the primary source of income here might give significant insights in understanding poverty and also in designing effective anti-poverty policies through effective targeting.

Among the poor and employed, 56 per cent report that their primary source of income is wages/salaries (Table 4.4). This figure is 39 per cent among the ultra-poor and employed people. Around 18 per cent of the ultra-poor people specify state grants (old pension, child support,

Table 4.3 Employment status and poverty (%)

	Ultra-poor	Poor	Non-poor	Total
Row shares				
Employed	24.1	20.3	55.6	100.0
Unemployed	37.0	31.4	31.7	100.0
Econ. inactive	38.0	28.1	33.9	100.0
Not working age	40.9	26.9	32.2	100.0
Column shares				
Employed	28.4	32.0	52.2	39.2
Unemployed	8.0	9.1	5.5	7.2
Econ. inactive	30.2	29.7	21.4	26.4
Not working age	33.4	29.3	20.9	27.2
Total	100.0	100.0	100.0	100.0

Source: Authors' calculations based on TUS South Africa (2000).

Table 4.4 Poverty and primary source of household income of the employed (%)

Primary source of household income	Ultra-poor	Poor	Non-poor	Total
Row shares				
Wages/salaries	13.9	16.6	69.5	100.0
Earnings from business or farm	37.0	19.1	43.9	100.0
State grants*	44.8	47.6	7.6	100.0
Private pension	30.6	26.1	43.3	100.0
Unemployment insurance fund	17.2	36.6	46.2	100.0
Investments	41.4	16.1	42.5	100.0
Remittances**	67.2	19.5	13.3	100.0
Private maintenance***	47.0	34.4	18.6	100.0
Other	71.5	16.0	12.5	100.0
Column shares				
Wages/salaries	39.3	55.6	85.3	68.2
Earnings from business or farm	19.7	12.1	10.2	12.9
State grants*	18.4	23.1	1.4	9.9
Private pension	1.5	1.6	0.9	1.2
Unemployment insurance fund	0.2	0.6	0.3	0.3
Investments	0.4	0.2	0.2	0.2
Remittances**	13.9	4.8	1.2	5.0
Private maintenance***	0.8	0.7	0.1	0.4
Other	5.0	1.3	0.4	1.7
Total	100.0	100.0	100.0	100.0

Source: Authors' calculations based on TUS South Africa (2000).
Note: *old pension, child support, disability, foster care grant; ** from people outside the household; ***from ex-spouse or father of the children.

Table 4.5   Unemployment rates (%)

	Men	Women
Urban formal African poor	60.8	58.7
Urban formal African ultra-poor	81.1	74.2
Urban formal colored/Asian poor	54.2	58.7
Urban formal colored/Asian ultra-poor	62.3	71.5
Urban informal African poor	48.0	55.4
Urban informal African ultra-poor	69.0	75.1
Rural commercial African poor	32.9	44.7
Rural commercial African ultra-poor	56.2	60.7
Rural commercial colored/Asian poor	14.9	30.1
Rural commercial colored/Asian ultra-poor	24.8	58.9
Ex-homeland African poor	42.3	41.0
Ex-homeland African ultra-poor	59.5	54.3

Source: LFS South Africa (2000).

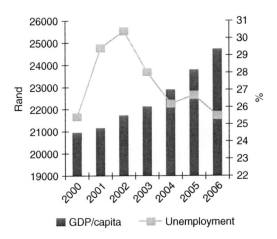

Source: LABORSTA, ILO (2008).
Figure 4.2   Persistent high unemployment

disability, foster care grant) and 14 per cent report remittances from people outside the household as the primary source.

Unemployment status

Despite the moderate economic growth of GDP per capita over the last decade, the official unemployment rate has been over 25 per cent, with

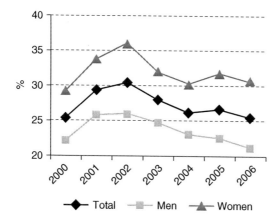

Source: LFS South Africa, 2008
Figure 4.3 Higher unemployment for women

about 31 per cent at the peak in 2002 (Figure 4.2). The expanded rate of unemployment, including discouraged job seekers, was as high as 42.5 per cent in 2001. Currently, the official and expanded unemployment rates are at 25 per cent and 37.1 per cent, affecting predominantly unskilled and low-skilled workers. Moreover, much like poverty, unemployment in South Africa continues to have racial, gender and spatial characteristics. In March 2007 the official unemployment rate (a measure that excludes discouraged workers) among the African population was 36.4 per cent for women and 25 per cent for men, while for white women it was 4.6 per cent and 4.1 per cent for white men.[7]

While unemployment among affluent white segments remains below 5 per cent, the case is quite clear that unemployment increases with poverty, reaching 81 per cent among African ultra-poor males in urban areas. The correlation between poverty and unemployment is consistently evident across geographic location and race/population group (Table 4.5).

But gender is also important here. As can be seen in Table 4.5, for eight out of twelve poor and ultra-poor household types, female unemployment is higher than male, with the trend reversing for African poor and ultra-poor households in urban areas and in ex-homelands.

This last finding of an overall higher unemployment rate among women when compared to their male counterparts is corroborated in Figure 4.3 which shows this to be the case for the entire post-2000 period.

Gender analysis of average time spent on unpaid work

Women are income-poor, but also taxed in terms of the time they allocate to caring for the sick, fetching the wood, collecting the water, preparing meals and so on. Using the TU activity classification groups we developed above (water and fuel collection, social care and household maintenance), we turn now to report our findings on how men and women spend their time, first according to their geographical location, then by income poverty level and finally by employment status. In all figures, the vertical axis measures time and the unit of measurement is hours and minutes.

Gender

In South Africa, women account for 74 per cent of unpaid work contributions. We begin by checking whether the differences between men and women are statistically significant in regards to the three groups of unpaid work activities we identified above. T-test analysis is a widely used statistical method to compare subpopulation means.[8]

Table 4.6 tabulates the average number of minutes and mean standard errors (SE) for water and fuel collection, social care and home maintenance. Our results show that the t-statistic is significant for all three groups of activities at the 0.05 level (the null hypothesis of no difference between means is rejected in all three cases) and, as expected, the difference between mean (men)-mean (women) is negative in all cases, thus the t-test values are negative.

Table 4.6   Time spent on different activities by gender

Weighted means, standard errors and comparison of means

Activity	Women		Men		t-stat
	Mean	SE	Mean	SE	
Water and fuel collection*	12.83	0.97	3.93	0.62	−7.67
Social care*	45.09	1.65	10.77	1.32	−16.24
Home maintenance*	205.25	3.50	79.88	2.41	−29.48

Note: Observation numbers for working age women and men are 6,028 and 5,246, respectively. Means are calculated in minutes. SE stands for standard errors.
* The t-statistic shows that the null hypothesis of no difference between means is rejected at the 0.05 level. The difference between men and women the mean (men)-mean (women) is negative.
Source: Authors' calculations from TUS South Africa (2000).

Location

Figure 4.4 provides supporting evidence for the fact that the gap between women and men expands as they move from urban areas to rural areas;[9] people living in ex-homeland areas spend even more time as compared to those in rural areas. Differences in time spent on water and fuel collection partly explain the difference in total unpaid work time. Similar evidence is also found in Charmes (2006), who points out that a big part of the gap between women and men in unpaid work in Africa is due to water and fuel collection, which depends on the rural and urban divide.

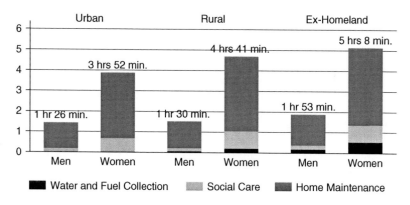

Source: Authors' calculations from TUS South Africa (2000).
Figure 4.4 Average time spent on unpaid work activities by location

Between respondents living in urban versus rural areas, we identified statistically significant differences for water and fuel collection, as well as for home maintenance, but not on time spent on social care (Table 4.7).

With respect to all three groups of activities, mean differences among the respondents living in urban settlements and ex-homeland areas are statistically significant (Table 4A.2). A similar pattern is observed between ex-homeland and rural areas on water and fuel collection, as well as on home maintenance; mean differences among the respondents living in ex-homeland areas and rural settlements are statistically significant, but not on social care. Tables 4A.2 and 4A.3 present the full report of our findings.

Income-poverty level

Figure 4.5 summarizes the average time spent by income level. Both female and male individuals who are poor spend more time on unpaid

Table 4.7   Time spent on different activities by location

Weighted means, standard errors and comparison of means

Activity	Urban		Rural		t-stat
	Mean	SE	Mean	SE	
Water and fuel collection*	0.88	0.11	8.93	0.85	−9.41
Social care	26.32	1.26	29.63	2.15	−1.33
Home maintenance*	134.64	3.31	151.12	3.94	−3.20

Note: Observation number for working age South Africans living in urban and rural are 6,520 and 2,936, respectively. Means are calculated in minutes.
* The t-statistic shows that the null hypothesis of no difference between means is rejected at the 0.05 level. The difference between respondents living in urban and rural areas the mean (urban)-mean (rural) is negative.
Source: Authors' calculations from TUS South Africa (2000).

work compared to those living in non-poor households. We also observe that as the household income level deteriorates the gap between women and men in terms of total unpaid work time increases. While female individuals living in non-poor households spend double of the amount of time spent by male, in ultra-poor households, women's total unpaid work time corresponds to around three and a half times of that spent by males. Our hypothesis is that lower levels of earned income would be correlated with a need to perform longer hours of unpaid work in order to provide for goods and services they are not able to buy in the market due to lack of income. The subsequent question is whether we can find any patterns that show redistribution (for example, more equitable sharing of unpaid work) among men and women who find themselves unemployed and/or in poverty.

Statistical test results comparing the average time spent on unpaid work activities by poverty status support the illustrations presented above. In Table 4.8 we present the tests results obtained comparing the averages corresponding to the poor respondents and non-poor respondents. The t-statistic is significant and indicates clearly that poor people spend a higher amount of time on water and fuel collection and home maintenance. The mean difference for time spent on social care is not statistically significant. The results for the other two cross-pair comparisons (ultra-poor respondents with non-poor, as well as poor, respondents) present significant mean differences on all activities among ultra-poor and non-poor South Africans. Except for the mean time spent on home

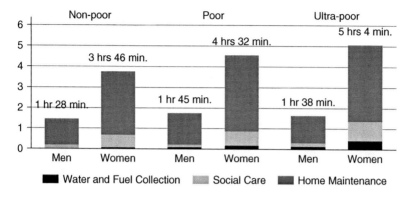

Source: Authors' calculations from TUS South Africa (2000).

Source: Authors' calculations from TUS South Africa (2000).

Figure 4.5 Average time spent on unpaid work activities by poverty status

maintenance, differences among the poor and ultra-poor respondents are also statistically significant. These can be found in the Appendix, Tables 4A.4 and 4A.5.

Table 4.8 Time spent on different activities by poverty status

Weighted means, standard errors and comparison of means

Activity	Poor		Non-poor		t-stat
	Mean	SE	Mean	SE	
Water and fuel collection**	8.83	0.97	2.39	0.36	6.21
Social care	26.14	1.67	25.27	1.54	0.38
Home maintenance**	161.87	4.18	129.61	3.97	5.59

Note: Observation numbers for working age South Africans who are poor and non-poor is 5,587 and 2,870, respectively. Means are calculated in minutes.
** The t-statistic shows that the null hypothesis of no difference between means is rejected at the 0.05 level. The difference between respondents living in urban and rural areas the mean (poor)-mean (non-poor) is positive.
Source: Authors' calculations from TUS South Africa (2000).

Unemployed and economic inactivity

Unemployed and economically inactive[10] South Africans do more unpaid work than employed people. As can be seen in Figure 4.6, this is true both for female and male South Africans; yet, female individuals who are unemployed end up performing, on average, the highest amount of time on unpaid work across all categories, totaling more than six hours of unpaid work a day. As compared to unemployed men, they spend almost three times more doing unpaid work.

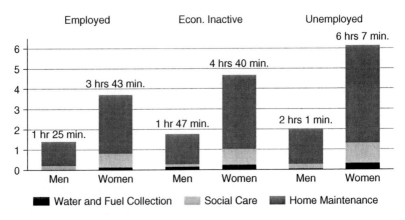

Source: Authors' calculations from TUS South Africa (2000).

Figure 4.6   Average time spent on unpaid work activities by employment status

Table 4.9 tabulates the test results comparing the means by employment status. We observe that employed respondents spend a lower amount of time on unpaid activities (such as water and fuel collection and social care) compared to the unemployed correspondents, which might be pointing to forced idleness rather than 'choice' to remain outside the labor market. Again, t-statistic results indicate that the null

Table 4.9   Time spent on different activities among employed and unemployed individuals

Weighted means, standard errors and comparison of means

Activity	Employed		Unemployed		t-stat
	Mean	*SE*	*Mean*	*SE*	
Water and fuel collection*	5.08	0.56	12.13	2.44	−2.81
Social care*	24.73	1.41	39.90	3.73	−3.81
Home maintenance*	119.06	2.57	207.25	12.68	−6.81

Note: Observation number of employed respondents is 6,534, where unemployed respondents' number is 1,116.

* The t-statistic shows that the null hypothesis of no difference between means is rejected at the 0.05 level. The difference between employed and unemployed the mean (employed)-mean (unemployed) is negative.

Source: Authors' calculations from TUS South Africa (2000).

hypothesis of no difference between means is rejected for all three groups of activities at the 0.05 level and that the difference between employed and unemployed respondents – as the mean (employed)-mean (unemployed) – is negative. Tables 4A.6 and 4A.7 in the Appendix provide test results of the comparison between economically inactive respondents with the employed and unemployed, respectively.

Tobit estimation of the determinants of time spent on unpaid work

In analyzing the time spent on unpaid work, the previous section has shown that gender, employment status, poverty status and area of residence are important categorical variables to consider. In addition to these variables, the decision to participate in doing unpaid work and the duration of unpaid work time contributions might depend on a variety of social, demographic and economic factors. These include household characteristics (household composition, such as number of preschool children, number of young children, number of adults who are at working age and resources available to a household including income and public resources), and individual characteristics (marital status of a person, educational status, person's age representing the phase of the household member's life-cycle). In this part, we discuss the influence of such determinants of unpaid work. Our methodology entails asking how do the four factors we have already identified (gender, employment status, poverty status and area of residence) influence the time spent on unpaid work, controlling for other possible factors that are likely to affect unpaid work time.

One common problem in the data provided by TUS is the large number of zero responses, which is also the case in our data set. A significant portion of the respondents in the TUS South Africa appear to spend zero time on unpaid work activities. It's a well-known fact that data sets of this sort with truncation require specific methods to deal with omissions (Wooldridge, 2009). As discussed in the literature, apart from the usual technical problems in data collection, there are two sources for zero observations in TUS (Flood and Grasjö, 1998; Ruuskanen, 2004). One is that there are individuals who never participate in doing the work. The other is that although individuals perform the work activities in general, for some reason, they spend zero time on the day selected for the interviews.

Three different estimation methods are suggested in the literature in order to solve the problem of the large number of individuals reporting zero hours of work, these being the double-hurdle model, Heckman's model and Tobit model. Unlike the Tobit model, the former two models consider the decision to participate in doing work as an independent process from the decision on the duration of work, thus they require a specific equation for participation decision separate from the equation designed for the amount of work. Flood and Grasjö (1998) provides a comparison of the suitability of these three estimation methods within the context of labor supply estimation. In labor supply models, since hours of work are only observed for the individuals with market wage, the zero observations are taken as an outcome of a well-defined participation decision process that creates selection bias, where Heckman's or the double-hurdle method is used to remedy this problem. We believe modeling the participation decision process of doing unpaid work is not as straightforward as in the case of market work and, as Flood and Grasjö (1998) points out, using a misspecified participation equation in the double-hurdle and Heckman's model can produce worse results than a Tobit model. Therefore, we select the Tobit model for our estimations and assume the decision to participate in doing unpaid work and the decision on duration of unpaid work are simultaneously determined, that is, we treat zero observations as individuals' desired amount of unpaid work.

More concretely, we specify the following reduced form equation:

$$\text{unpaid}_i^* = \beta' x_i + \varepsilon_i \tag{1}$$

where unpaid_i^* is the latent (noncensored) variable representing time allocated to unpaid work activity by individual I; x_i is a vector of explanatory variables including household, as well as individual characteristics; β is a vector of parameters; and ε_i is the error term. The observed time spent on unpaid work (unpaid_i) is related to the corresponding latent time-use variable by:

$$\text{unpaid}_i = \text{unpaid}_i^* \text{ if } \text{unpaid}_i^* > 0, \qquad \text{unpaid}_i = 0 \text{ otherwise} \tag{2}$$

Our sample includes 11,274 observations (working age population: ages between 16 and 65 years old) where 53 per cent are women. We estimate four different Tobit models, each differing in terms of the independent variables included. First we estimate a basic model (model 1) to examine the effects of gender, area of residence, poverty status and employment status[11] on time spent doing unpaid work then we add other possibly relevant explanatory variables to check for robustness of the results.

In model 1, the explanatory variables involve a dummy variable indicating gender (women); dummy variables for the area of residence (rural and ex-homeland); dummy variables indicating the individual's poverty status (ultra-poor, poor); and dummy variables representing the employment status of the individual (unemployed and inactive).

Based on the findings presented in section 3, we expect to see a statistically meaningful discrepancy between women's and men's time spent on unpaid work that is unfavorable for women. This would mean a significant and positive coefficient for the gender dummy (for example, conditional on all the other factors included, being a woman should imply higher amount of time spent on doing unpaid work).

Our expectations with regards to the coefficients of the residential location dummies is that they will be significant and positive which would suggest that compared to South Africans living in urban areas, people living in rural and ex-homeland areas spend longer hours doing unpaid work. Existing differences among residential locations in terms of time spent on water and fuel collection, as well as on home maintenance, mentioned above, shape these expectations. In a similar manner, we expect to obtain statistically significant and positive coefficients for the employment status dummies if we compare unemployed and economically inactive respondents with the employed South Africans.

Models 2 to 4 are extended versions of the basic model with new variables added sequentially to control for the possible effects of each additional variable. Adding new variables at the same time enables us to test the robustness of our estimation results. In model 2, in addition to the variables included in the first model, we also consider the effects of the variables that represent the household composition. First, we added dummies for the number of adults living in the household (two adults, three adults, four or more adults). Compared to single-adult households, we expect to get negative and significant coefficients for these dummies, namely, the existence of other adults is highly likely to have a decreasing impact on the share of the burden of unpaid work within a household. However, a higher number of adults might also indicate existence of elderly members of the household who are in need of health and social care. In order to accurately account for the third-adult effect on unpaid work, we considered the adults who are of working age (age >16 and <65) for whom the possibility of doing unpaid work is high without their being in no need of help from others.

Secondly, we added dummies representing the number of preschool children under 7 years old (one child7 and two or more children7) to control for their impacts and we expect to see significant positive coefficients for these dummies, which would suggest that in comparison to the individuals living in the households with no dependent children, those with children do more unpaid work. We also included the number of young children (7–17 years old) (one child18 and two or more children18).

Based on the evidence presented in Ilahi (2000) that indicates young children also spend a considerable amount of time helping their parents in unpaid work activities. There is a strong possibility that the two dummies will have negative coefficients.

In the third model we added variables that represent individual characteristics indicating if the person is married or cohabiting with a partner (married*women and married*men), considering also sexual difference and age, as well as the square of age, of the person (age and age_2), we added the square of age of the person in order to check for any non-linearities with respect to age, for instance, relatively young and elderly people might do more unpaid work than the middle-aged individuals; and educational status dummies (educ*women and educ*men).

With respect to the marital status, earlier findings point to its asymmetric impact on women's and men's time spent on unpaid work. Studies have shown that while married women do more housework than single women, men do less housework after they get married (Gupta, 1999; Couprie, 2007). As we expect to see opposite impact of marital status (positive coefficient for married women and negative coefficient for married men) on the unpaid work time spent by women and men, we added two separate dummies representing the marital status (married*women and married*men).

Regarding the age of the person, our results might reflect that as people get older they do more unpaid work until they reach an age after which they start doing less. These expectations imply a positive coefficient for the age and a negative coefficient for the age-square variable.

Similar to marital status, educational status might also exert an asymmetric influence on women's and men's time use. If the educational attainment of women is higher, the probability for her participation in the paid labor market is higher, while the time she spends on unpaid work gets lower. On the other hand, with regards to men, one might expect to get a positive impact on unpaid work time in the case of better educated men. There tends to be a more egalitarian division of labor at home, as better-educated men do more housework (Huber and Spitze, 1983). Thus, we added two dummies – one for educated women and the other for educated men – in order to capture these possible impacts.

For the variable that represents educational attainment, TUS 2000 provides answers varying from no education to grade 12. We selected two educational categories as 'none through GET (grade 1 to 10)' and 'matriculation to tertiary' in order to split higher educational attainment from primary school and lower secondary school, which results in obtaining the General Education and Training Certificate (GET).[12] Our distinction is meaningful given the findings by Oosthuizen (2005) and Van der Westhuizen *et al.* (2007) which show clearly that the decision to participate in the labor market only increases significantly once a person has a grade 12 qualification. Using this categorization for educational attainment, we introduced two dummies representing women and men with matriculation to tertiary education, educ*women and educ*men, respectively, expecting to see a negative coefficient for the former and a positive one for the latter.

Lastly, in model 4, including all the variables of third model, we also added a dummy variable (homeapp) that represents home appliances in order to identify the households that make use of any of appliances (specifically, a washing machine, a vacuum cleaner and a refrigerator) (homeapp=1 if any of these are present in the home, whereas homeapp=0 represents a household with none of the three appliances). There are contradictory findings in the literature on the impacts of home appliances on unpaid work. While some argued that there has been a decline in homemaking with these machines (Greenwood *et al.*, 2005), others have shown no sign of decline in housework despite the diffusion of appliances. This is called the 'Cowan paradox,' arguing that while technological innovations may have greatly reduced the drudgery of housework, they did not decrease the time devoted to it (Ramey, 2009). Our expectations on the coefficient of homeapp cannot be determined a priori.

In the fourth model, we also added a variable (tv) that shows whether the households have the use of a television in order to introduce a proxy variable for a possible negative impact of passive leisure time on unpaid work time. Unlike other time-saving home appliances, television is a typical time-using good. Here we suppose the amount of time spent on unpaid work might be negatively affected with the presence of a television at home.

The results are presented in Table 4.10. The specification of the model is jointly highly significant for all four estimations: The χ^2 statistics of 206.81, 118.78, 93.67 and 85.11, respectively, indicate rejection of the null hypothesis that all slope coefficients are zero. The results are robust to different specifications that aim to control for household composition,

Table 4.10 Tobit estimation results for time spent on unpaid work

	Model 1	Model 2	Model 3	Model 4
constant	15.522**	36.857***	−125.380***	−114.797***
	(4.93)	(6.81)	(27.14)	(27.43)
women	188.010***	180.437***	146.634***	146.781***
	(5.70)	(5.75)	(8.14)	(8.14)
ex-homeland	47.802***	44.836***	46.430***	42.299***
	(6.61)	(6.45)	(6.37)	(6.57)
rural	25.738***	20.186**	17.552**	13.601*
	(6.43)	(6.31)	(6.38)	(6.44)
ultra-poor	24.132***	30.470***	34.779***	29.102***
	(7.28)	(8.23)	(7.69)	(8.03)
poor	17.077*	20.424**	22.816**	19.451**
	(6.89)	(7.63)	(7.09)	(7.28)
unemployed	99.644***	99.970***	98.962***	98.916***
	(14.08)	(14.49)	(13.50)	(13.45)
inactive	36.875***	43.462***	58.376***	58.141***
	(6.05)	(6.09)	(7.01)	(7.03)
No. of adults in the household				
two adults		−20.596**	−20.453**	−18.947*
		(7.36)	(7.63)	(7.65)
three adults		−31.264***	−25.287**	−22.580**
		(8.32)	(8.19)	(8.29)
four or more adults		−47.634***	−34.725***	−30.235***
		(8.08)	(7.90)	(8.20)
No. of children under 7 years old				
one child7		40.563***	42.793***	42.925***
		(6.94)	(7.10)	(7.10)
two or more children7		58.236***	53.192***	53.390***
		(11.16)	(11.28)	(11.30)
No. of children older than 6 and under 18 years old				
one child18		6.483	−2.671	−1.433
		(9.62)	(8.70)	(8.77)
two or more children18		−12.987	−26.519***	−24.767**
		(8.30)	(7.92)	(8.00)
Marital status				
married*women			55.012***	55.527***
			(8.90)	(8.89)
married*men			−40.163***	−39.537***
			(9.55)	(9.53)
Age				
age			9.030***	8.970***
			(1.39)	(1.39)
age_2			−0.105***	−0.104***
			(0.02)	(0.02)

(Continued)

Table 4.10   Continued

	Model 1	Model 2	Model 3	Model 4
Educational status				
educ*women			−13.747	−10.739
			(8.47)	(8.60)
educ*men			13.302	15.672
			(8.33)	(8.42)
Time-saving/-using home appliances				
homeapp				−12.948
				(6.90)
tv				−3.976
				(6.72)
sigma	175.346	173.239	169.836	169.748
Censored observations	1549	1549	1549	1549
Uncensored observations	9725	9725	9725	9714

Note: The dependent variable is amount of time spent on unpaid work activities (unpaid). Robust standard errors in parentheses. Marginal effects of the variables are not presented here as the marginal effect of a dummy variable is equal to its coefficient.
* significant at 10% level; ** significant at 5% level; *** significant at 1% per cent level.

individual characteristics. No evidence of multicollinearity is found (as the variance inflation factor [VIF] for each variable ranges from 1.11 to 2.07) except for age and age_2 (VIF equals to 22.76 and 21.13 for these variables).

The estimated coefficients confirm most of our a priori expectations. The positive and highly significant coefficients of rural and ex-homeland indicate that compared to South Africans living in urban areas, people living in rural and ex-homeland are more likely to spend longer time on unpaid work. This is consistent with our earlier observations where we find that the discrepancy between the average time spent in urban-living households and others is more due to the time spent on water and fuel collection.

Another reason behind the significance of rural and ex-homeland might be the effect of increasing participation in paid work and higher wages in urban areas. Studies have argued that employment and higher wages increase time pressure of people and result in a decline in time spent on unpaid work (Gronau, 1980). One might consider that higher employment in urban areas explains the urban/rural and urban/ex-homeland divide in terms of unpaid work time. However, when we look at the unemployment rates above, we observe that unemployment rates are higher in urban areas when compared to rural and ex-homeland areas. This points to the second-shift (Hochschild, 1989) of South Africans living in rural and ex-homeland areas, performing both paid work and higher unpaid work simultaneously.

In addition to these, the significance of rural and ex-homeland may also be explained by the fact that time buying strategies, for example, meals away from home, purchase of child care and so on (Nickols and Fox, 1983), are more viable in urban areas compared to rural and ex-homeland areas.

Confirming earlier studies (Antonopoulos, 2008), in all four estimations the gender variable strongly shows that women spend more time on unpaid work than their male counterparts. Despite the fact that at a global scale there has been a long-term trend increase in women's participation in paid work (ILO, 2007), the statistical significance of gender in our estimation reflects that when it comes to bargaining power, intrahousehold division of labor is still highly 'gendered' (Cook, 2005). Our results provide further support to this argument.

The coefficients of employment status (inactive and unemployed) strongly suggest that when a person is economically inactive or unemployed, she/he spends a longer time on unpaid work compared to a fully employed person. Effects of the variables are significant in all four estimations. This is also an expected result supported by observations on the average time spent by individuals across employment categories. Both the figures for time spent on home maintenance, as well as social care, suggest the same outcome.

It is not surprising that time spent on household maintenance and care shows large variations among employed and unemployed or inactive persons in general and women in particular (Walker, 1973). What is interesting to note is that when the employment status of men is reported as 'unemployed,' women still perform more unpaid work than men do. Yet some studies do report increases in the relative proportion of housework done by men after layoffs (Wilkinson, 1992; Strom, 2002). In this context, our results, confirm the statistical significance of inactivity and unemployment as well.

The positive coefficients of variables representing the poverty status of individuals (poor and ultra-poor) indicate that in comparison to nonpoor people, poor and ultra-poor individuals spend a higher amount of time performing unpaid work activities. Considering our analysis of average time spent on different unpaid work activities, the result here might reflect the differences among poor and non-poor people with respect to their time spent on water and fuel collection.

Coefficients for ultra-poor and poor are significant in four models. The coefficient of poor is significant at the 10 per cent level in the first model, while it is significant at the 5 per cent level in the other three models. Significance of the two coefficients indicate that the higher the burden of poverty (for example, the lower the household income), which might reflect the lower the access to market-purchased substitutes of social care and meals cooked at home, the higher the amount of unpaid work time controlling for the effects of all other variables included.

With respect to the composition of households, the coefficients for variables representing the number of adults living in the household (two adults, three adults, four or more adults) are all negative and significant in the last three models. Confirming our expectations, the existence of other adults living in the household decreases the amount of time spent on unpaid work activities.

The effect of the number of preschool children under 7 years old (one child7, two or more children7) on unpaid work is positive and significant. This reflects an increase, particularly in time spent caring for children with the number of children, which is expected. Despite this result, the number of children does not always have an increasing effect on the unpaid work burden of the adults. For instance, we do not observe a significant effect on unpaid work time in the case of the number of children between 7 and 18 (one child18, two or more children18) in model 2. Rather than an increasing effect of number of children, the reverse is pointed out by earlier research on children's time use. Evidence that shows that children also allocate significant amounts of time to household maintenance, as well as to the care of younger siblings (Ilahi, 2000), is supported by our findings in the third and fourth models. The negative coefficient for two or more children18, which is significant at the 1 per cent level in model 3 and significant at the 5 per cent level in model 4, suggests the fact that if there are young children (older than 6 and younger than 18) living in the household, then the amount of time spent on unpaid work by the adult members in that household is lower in comparison to other households.

The effect of marriage or cohabiting in case of women is positive and significant in models 3 and 4, suggesting that married/cohabiting women spend more time on unpaid work compared to single ones, which supports earlier evidence provided by Gupta (1999) and Couprie (2007). On the other hand, regarding men's marital status, our results depict a negative influence of marriage/cohabiting on unpaid work time that is highly significant at the 1 per cent level. These results provide supporting evidence for earlier findings as well.

Confirming our expectations, coefficients of the age and square of age variables (age and age_2) are positive and negative, respectively, and both significant at 1 per cent, which reflects the existence of a nonlinear relationship between the age of a person and the time spent on unpaid work activities (models 3 and 4).

Coefficients for the educational status variables (educ*women and educ*men), which are not significant (in models 3 and 4), do not confirm our expectations. Results show that educational status has no significant impact on time spent on unpaid work activities and this is true both for women and men.

Similarly, the coefficients for homeapp and tv are also not significant, implying that whether the households have the use of any the time-saving/-using home appliances or not, the amount of time they spend on unpaid work is not influenced by this factor.

Examination of the determining impacts of a variety of household and individual characteristics on unpaid work time showed the significant influence of gender, employment status of the individual, area of residence, poverty status of the household, marital status, household composition and the age of the individual. Educational status and presence of home appliances and television are not significant factors in determining time spent on unpaid work. Our results are found to be robust.

Conclusions

Chapter 2 of this book argued that from a structural point of view, unpaid work provides important inputs in transforming market goods and those collected from common lands into final consumable goods that are necessary for the daily reproduction of household members. Whether women are self-employed, home-based informal workers or members of the formal market, unpaid work patterns clearly show that the costs of daily reproduction of generation after generation falls onto their shoulders (Folbre, 1994). What we have shown in this chapter is that, in the context of poverty, unemployment and geographic location of households, if and when more unpaid inputs are observed (or required), apparently the supply of unpaid labor response is highly gendered.

According to new home economics, which is an extended version of neoclassical economic theory onto nonmarket work (Becker, 1965; Gronau, 1980), what lies beneath the gendered nature of unpaid work are women's and men's rational choices, namely, women choose to specialize in nonmarket production because it is the best option for them as they have a comparative advantage in caring for children and homemaking. Folbre (2004), in her article entitled 'A Theory of the Misallocation of Time,' criticizes this choice-determined approach for overstating the role of individual decisions where she calls attention to the role of social institutions, for example, cultural norms, legal rules and discriminatory rules against female participation in the labor force that govern allocation of time. Unlike how it is presented in Becker's theory of allocation of time, time allocation does not conform to the idealized processes of competitive markets (Folbre, 2004). Having the view on the determinants of allocation of time, which agrees with Folbre (2004), we do not discuss the individual choice versus social institutions issue in this study, as it would be a topic for another paper.

For socioeconomic groups that face higher unemployment and poverty, or reside in rural or underserved areas, we hypothesized that it is reasonable to expect that what cannot be bought in the market (due to lack of income) and what is not delivered by the state (due to infrastructural and public sector service delivery gaps) may be made up by unpaid work. Based on South African time-use data, we explored how poverty, unemployment and location act as stratifiers that impact the overall amount of unpaid work burdens on households. We then turned to examine whether these exert some influence in the distribution of unpaid work between men and women. The answer is no. Under strained conditions that require households to spend more time on unpaid work, women spend significantly more of their time to fulfill these obligations. Whether it is a labor of love or drudgery, there is nothing natural nor romantic about women performing most of it. It presents us with a challenge of an inequality that needs to be recognized and redressed.

Notes

* While taking full responsibility for all the views and analyses in the chapter, the authors gratefully acknowledge the suggestions made by Indira Hirway on an earlier version of the paper, and our colleagues at The Levy Economics Institute of Bard College, Kijong Kim, Thomas Masterson and Ajit Zacharias.
1. Declared government commitments to achieving the Millennium Development Goals are but a manifestation of this. Policy responses have ranged from market-based solutions at the household micro-level, such as better access to credit and promotion of self-employment, to structural macroeconomic measures including land reform, trade agreements, efforts to transform the development agenda path across pro-poor growth dynamics and expanding direct government poverty alleviation programs. See Duncan and Pollard (2002) and Cagatay (1998).

2. For an excellent review on why we should care about the division of one's time between paid and unpaid activities, see the seminal work of Budlender (2004). For an extensive discussion on the linkages between paid and unpaid work, see Antonopoulos (2008).

3. Another stylized fact is that in most developing countries, when we combine paid and unpaid work, on average, women spend more of their time working than men do (Antonopoulos, 2008). Burda, Hamermesh and Weil (2007) have argued that in most European countries, total work time (paid and unpaid combined) is higher for men than women with the exception of Italy, France and Spain. Measured in annual days, a simple tabulation using the same data sources as in Figure III-2 in Antonopoulos (2008: 21) shows considerable differences among advanced countries, with Austria, for example, witnessing women working an average 22.5 extra days per year and 30 extra days in Korea, while in Denmark, where men work an extra 9 minutes per day, males work longer by an average of 4.5 days per year.

4. The SNA is used to calculate various macroeconomic indicators such as GDP. Certain productive activities are taken into account by SNA, yet it does not account for activities that occur outside of the paid economy. Activities referred as 'reproductive' activities correspond to the ones such as cooking and cleaning, as well as caring for children and other household members. These activities are most likely to be performed by women, whilst men are more likely to produce goods and services for the market economy. Even though many reproductive services have an equivalent in the market economy, the majority of these activities are provided on an unpaid basis. The TUS provides data on activities produced outside the paid economy and, therefore, establishes a foundation for the elaboration of GDP through parallel (satellite) national accounts.

5. At the time this work was undertaken, there was no official poverty line in South Africa, although the Treasury was in the process of finalizing documentation that will establish such a threshold. Some researchers adopt R5,057 per annum, according to which the headcount ratio (defined as the proportion of the population living below the poverty line) for South Africa is 49.8%. The 20th percentile cut-off of adult equivalent income (R2,717 per annum) is sometimes used as the 'ultra-poverty line.' About 28.2% of the South African population lives below this poverty line. For this study we have adopted comparable measures using 2000 prices and poverty levels.

6. Annual per capita income was calculated by dividing monthly household income by the household size and then multiplying by 12. Income data was recorded as missing for 458 observations. In order not to lose these observations and, thereby, further reduce the sample, it was decided to impute income values for these observations. Income values were imputed based on the following demographic indicators, which, in previous studies, have been shown to be reliable predictors of income: the household's main source of income, the household's main source of lighting energy and the household's main source of water.

7. Banerjee *et al.* (2007) provide excellent review of the South African labor market.

8. If two independent subpopulations have equal variances then the t-test uses the pooled variance (otherwise individual variances are used in the

denominator). If the population size is large, as in our case, correction for unequal variances is not required. Thus we do our analysis under equal variance assumption. The null hypothesis in comparing the means of two independent subpopulations hypothesizes whether the mean difference between the two groups' means is zero. For detailed information on how to do a t-test using a survey data, see Bruin (2006).

9. Here we use three categories for settlement types as: (1) urban, covering formal urban and informal urban settlements; (2) rural (commercial farming); and (3) ex-homeland, which refers to other rural areas.

10. We restrict our analysis to the working-age population, aged between 16 and 66, and proceed to group individuals into three groups according to their employment status.

11. Details on these selected characteristics have been presented in the section on gender analysis, pp. 86–90.

12. The current education policy in South Africa determines that school attendance is compulsory until the completion of grade 9, with most students acquiring at least a grade 10 GET.

13. The following activity groups are created with a corresponding list of activities included in each group. A complete list of the activity codes, based on the activity classification system used in TUS 2000, is accessible in SSA (2001): http://www.statssa.gov.za/publications/TimeUse/TimeUse2000.pdf.

References

Antonopoulos, R. (2008) 'Unpaid Care Work-Paid Work Connection,' Working Paper No. 541 (Annandale-on-Hudson, NY: The Levy Economics Institute of Bard College).

Banerjee, A., S. Galiani, J.A. Levinsohn, Z. McLaren and I. Woolard (2007) 'Why Has Unemployment Risen in the New South Africa,' Working Paper No. W13167 (Cambridge, MA: National Bureau of Economic Research).

Becker, G.S. (1965) 'A Theory of the Allocation of Time,' *The Economic Journal* 75, 493–517.

Berk, S.F. (1985) *The Gender Factory: The Apportionment of Work in American Households* (New York, NY: Plenum Pres).

Breen R. and L.P. Cooke (2005) 'The Persistence of Gender Division of Domestic Labor,' *European Sociological Review* 21(1), 43–57.

Budlender, D. (2004) *Why Should We Care About Unpaid Care Work?* (New York: UNIFEM).

Bruin, J. (2006) 'Newtest: command to compute new test,' UCLA: Academic Technology Services, Statistical Consulting Group. http://www.ats.ucla.edu/stat/stata/ado/analysis/.

Burda, M., S. Hamermesh and P. Weil (2007) 'Total work, Gender and Social Norms,' Working Papers No. 13000 (Cambridge, MA: National Bureau of Economic Research).

Cagatay, N. (1998) 'Gender and Poverty,' Working Paper Series No. 5 (New York: Bureau for Development Policy SEPED, UNDP).

Charmes, J. (2006) 'A Review of Empirical Evidence on Time Use in Africa from UN-sponsored Surveys, ch. 3.' Working Paper No. 73. (Washington DC: The World Bank).

Couprie, H. (2007) 'Time Allocation within the Family: Welfare Implications of Life in a Couple,' *Economic Journal* 117(516), 287–305.

Duncan, R. and S. Pollard (2002) 'A Framework for Establishing Priorities in a Country Poverty Reduction Strategy,' Working Paper No. 15 (Manila, Philippines: ERD, Asian Development Bank).

ECLAC (2007) 'Women's Contribution to Equality in Latin America and the Caribbean,' Paper prepared by Women and Development Unit of the Economic Commission for Latin America and the Caribbean (ECLAC) for the Regional Conference on Women in Latin America and the Caribbean on 6–9 August, Ecuador.

Flood, L. and U. Grasjö (1998) 'Regression Analysis and Time Use Data A Comparison of Microeconometric Approaches with Data from the Swedish Time Use Survey (HUS),' Working Papers in Economics No. 5 (Göteborg, Sweden: Department of Economics, School of Economics and Commercial Law, Göteborg University).

Folbre, N. (2004) 'A Theory of the Misallocation of Time,' in N. Folbre and M. Bittman (eds), *Family Time: The Social Organization of Care* (New York, NY: Routledge).

Greenwood, J., A. Seshadri and M. Yorukoglu (2005) 'Engines of Liberation,' *Review of Economic Studies* 72(1), 109–33.

Gronau, R. (1980) 'Home Production – A Forgotten Industry,' *Review of Economics and Statistics* 62(3), 408–16.

Gupta, S. (1999) 'The Effects of Transitions in Marital Status on Men's Performance of Housework,' *Journal of Marriage and the Family* 61(3), 700–11.

Heckman, J.J. (1979) 'Sample selection bias as a specification error,' *Econometrica* 47, 153–61.

Hochschild, A. (1989) *The Second Shift: Working Parents and the Revolution at Home.* (London: Piatkus Ltd).

Huber, J. and G.D. Spitze (1983) *Sex Stratification: Children, Housework, and Jobs* (New York, Academic Press).

Ilahi, N. (2000) 'The Intra-household Allocation of Time and Tasks: What Have We Learnt from the Empirical Literature?,' Policy Research Report on Gender and Development, Working Paper Series No. 13 (Washington, DC: The World Bank).

ILO (2007) 'Global Employment Trends for Women,' March 2007, http://www.ilo. org/public/english/employment/strat/download/getw07.pdf

Nickols, S.Y. and K.D. Fox (1983) 'Buying Time and Saving Time: Strategies for Managing Household Production,' *Journal of Consumer Research* 10(September), 197–208.

Oosthuizen, M. (2005) 'The Post-Apartheid Labour Market: 1995–2004,' Development Policy Research Unit, University of Cape Town, Working Paper 06/103 (Cape Town: University of Cape Town, Development Policy Research Unit).

Ramey, V.A. (2009) 'Time Spent in Home Production in the Twentieth-Century United States: New Estimates from Old Data,' *The Journal of Economic History* 69(1), 1–47.

Ruuskanen, O.P. (2004) *An Econometric Analysis of Time Use in Finnish Households*, Doctoral Thesis, Helsinki School of Economics. Available at: http://hsepubl.lib.hse.fi/pdf/diss/a246.pdf

Sadan, M. (2006) 'Gendered Analysis of the Working for Water Program,' Occasional Paper. (Pretoria: Southern African Regional Poverty Network).

Statistics South Africa (SSA) (2001) 'A Survey of Time Use: How South African Women and Men Spend Their Time' Available at: http://www.statssa.gov.za/publications/TimeUse/TimeUse2000.pdf, date accessed 10 November 2008.

―― (2002) *Labour Force Survey*, September 2000 (Pretoria: Statistics South Africa).

―― (2007) *Labour Force Survey*, March 2007 (Pretoria: Statistics South Africa).

Strom, S. (2002) 'Unemployment and Gendered Divisions of Domestic Labor,' *Acta Sociologica* 45(2): 89–106

UNDP (2006) *Human Development Report* (New York: UNDP).

Van der Westhuizen, C., S. Goga, L. Ncube and M. Oosthuizen (2007) 'Women in the South African Labour Market, 1995–2005,' Working Paper No. 9610 (Cape Town: University of Cape Town, Development Policy Research Unit).

Walker, K. (1973) 'Household Work Time: Its Implications for Family Decisions,' *Journal of Home Economics*, 7–11 October.

Wilkinson, D. (1992) 'Change in Household Division of Labour Following Unemployment in Elliot Lake,' ELTAS Analysis Series #2A3, Elliot Lake Tracking Study, Paper presented to the 27th Annual Meeting of the Canadian Sociology and Anthropology Association on 31 May, in Charlottetown, Prince Edward Island.

Wooldridge, J. (2009) *Introductory Econometrics: A Modern Approach*, fourth edition (Florence, KY: South Western Cengage Learning).

106

Appendix

Table 4A.1   Activity list by codes[13]

Total unpaid work activities

1. *Water and fuel collection*
236   Collecting fuel, firewood or dung
250   Collecting water

2. *Social care*
511   Physical care of children: washing, dressing, feeding mentioned
        spontaneously
512   Physical care of children: washing, dressing, feeding not mentioned
        spontaneously
521   Teaching, training and instruction of household's children mentioned
        spontaneously
522   Teaching, training and instruction of household's children not mentioned
        spontaneously
531   Accompanying children to places: school, sports, lessons, and so on
        mentioned spontaneously
532   Accompanying children to places: school, sports, lessons, and so on
        not mentioned spontaneously
540   Physical care of the sick, disabled, elderly household members: washing,
        dressing, feeding, helping
550   Accompanying adults to receive personal care services: such as
        hairdressers, therapy sessions and so on
561   Supervising children and adults needing care mentioned spontaneously
562   Supervising children and adults needing care not mentioned
        spontaneously
580   Travel related to care of children, the sick, elderly and disabled in
        the household
590   Care of children, the sick, elderly and disabled in the household not
        elsewhere classified
610   Community organized construction and repairs: buildings, roads, dams,
        wells, and so on
615   Cleaning of classrooms
620   Community organized work: cooking for collective celebrations
        and so on
630   Volunteering with or for an organization
650   Participation in meetings of local and informal groups/caste, tribes,
        professional associations, union, political and similar organizations
660   Involvement in civic and related responsibilities: voting, rallies
        and so on
671   Caring for non-household children mentioned spontaneously

(Continued)

Table 4A.1 Continued

Total unpaid work activities

672	Caring for non-household children not mentioned spontaneously
673	Caring for non-household adults
674	Other informal help to other households
680	Travel related to community services
690	Community services not elsewhere classified

3. Home maintenance

410	Cooking, making drinks, setting and serving tables, washing up
420	Cleaning and upkeep of dwelling and surroundings
430	Care of textiles: sorting, mending, washing, ironing and ordering clothes and linen
440	Shopping for personal and household goods
441	Accessing government services, such as collecting pension, going to post office
448	Waiting to access government service
450	Household management: planning, supervising, paying bills, and so on.
460	Do-it-yourself home improvements and maintenance, installation, servicing and repair of personal and household goods
470	Pet care
480	Travel related to household maintenance, management and shopping
490	Household maintenance, management and shopping not elsewhere classified
491	Chopping wood, lighting fire and heating water not for immediate cooking purposes paid work activities
111	Wage and salary employment other than domestic work
112	Outworkers/home-based work for an establishment
113	Domestic and personal services produced by domestic work
114	Unpaid employment in establishment
115	Work as employer/self-employed for an establishment
130	Working in apprenticeship, internship and related positions
140	Short breaks and interruptions from work
150	Seeking employment and related activities
180	Travel to/from work and seeking employment in establishments
190	Employment in establishments not elsewhere classified
210	Crop farming and market/kitchen gardening: planting, weeding, harvesting, picking and so on
220	Tending animals and fish farming
230	Hunting, fishing, gathering of wild products and forestry
240	Digging, stone cutting, splitting and carving
260	Purchase of goods for and sale of outputs arising from these activities
280	Travel related to primary production activities (not for establishments)

(Continued)

Table 4A.1 Continued

Total unpaid work activities

290	Primary production activities (not for establishments) not elsewhere classified
310	Food processing and preservation activities: grain processing, butchering, preserving, curing
320	Preparing and selling food and beverage preparation, baking confectionery and related activities
330	Making and selling textile, leather and related craft: weaving, knitting, sewing, shoemaking, tanning, products of wood
340	Building and extensions of dwelling: laying bricks, plastering, thatch, roofing, maintaining and repairing buildings: cutting glass, plumbing, painting, carpentering, electric wiring
350	Petty trading, street/door-to-door vending, shoe-cleaning and other services performed in non-fixed or mobile locations
360	Fitting, installing, tool setting, maintaining and repairing tools and machinery
370	Provision of services for income such as computer services, transport, hairdressing, cosmetic treatment, baby-sitting, massages, prostitution
380	Travel related to services for income and other production of goods (not for establishments)
390	Services for income and other production of goods (not for establishments) not elsewhere classified

Table 4A.2 Time spent on different activities by location (urban *vs* ex-homeland)

Weighted means, standard errors and comparison of means

Activity	Urban		Ex-homeland		t-stat
	Mean	SE	Mean	SE	
Water and fuel collection*	0.88	0.11	22.71	1.80	−12.12
Social care*	26.32	1.26	34.28	2.49	−2.85
Home maintenance*	134.64	3.31	168.60	4.65	−5.95

Note: Observation number for working age South Africans living in urban and ex-homeland is 6,520 and 1,818, respectively. Means are calculated in minutes.
* The t-statistic shows that the null hypothesis of no difference between means is rejected at the 0.05 level. The difference between respondents living in urban and rural areas the mean (urban)-mean (ex-homeland) is negative.
Source: Authors' calculations from TUS South Africa (2000).

Table 4A.3 Time spent on different activities by location (rural *vs* ex-homeland)

Weighted means, standard errors and comparison of means

Activity	Rural		Ex-homeland		t-stat
	Mean	*SE*	*Mean*	*SE*	
Water and fuel collection*	8.93	0.85	22.71	1.80	−6.93
Social care	29.63	2.15	34.28	2.49	−1.41
Home maintenance*	151.12	3.94	168.60	4.65	−2.87

Note: Observation number for working age South Africans living in rural and ex-homeland is 2,936 and 1,818, respectively. Means are calculated in minutes.
* The t-statistic shows that the null hypothesis of no difference between means is rejected at the 0.05 level. The difference between respondents living in rural and ex-homeland areas the mean (rural)-mean (ex-homeland) is negative.
Source: Authors' calculations from TUS South Africa (2000).

Table 4A.4 Time spent on different activities among ultra-poor and non-poor households

Weighted means, standard errors and comparison of means

Activity	Ultra-poor		Non-poor		t-stat
	Mean	*SE*	*Mean*	*SE*	
Water and fuel collection**	18.06	1.71	2.39	0.36	8.93
Social care**	37.54	2.48	25.27	1.54	4.21
Home maintenance**	161.82	4.45	129.61	3.97	5.40

Note: Observation number of ultra-poor respondents is 2817, where non-poor respondents' number is 5591.
** The t-statistic shows that the null hypothesis of no difference between means is rejected at the 0.05 level; the difference as mean (ultra-poor)-mean (non-poor) is positive.
Source: Authors' calculations from TUS South Africa (2000).

110

Table 4A.5 Time spent on different activities among ultra-poor and poor households

Weighted means, standard errors and comparison of means

Activity	Ultra-poor		Poor		t-stat
	Mean	SE	Mean	SE	
Water and fuel collection**	18.06	1.71	8.83	0.97	4.67
Social care**	37.54	2.48	26.14	1.67	3.81
Home maintenance	161.82	4.45	161.87	4.18	−0.01

Note: Observation number of ultra-poor respondents is 2,817, where poor respondents' number is 2,870.
** The t-statistic shows that the null hypothesis of no difference between means is rejected at the 0.05 level; the difference as mean (ultra-poor)-mean(poor) is positive.
Source: Authors' calculations from TUS South Africa (2000).

Table 4A.6 Time spent on different activities among employed and economically inactive

Weighted means, standard errors and comparison of means

Activity	Employed		Econ. inactive		t-stat
	Mean	SE	Mean	SE	
Water and fuel collection*	5.08	0.56	13.17	1.27	−5.79
Social care*	24.73	1.41	32.95	1.95	−3.41
Home maintenance*	119.06	2.57	172.62	3.87	−11.52

Note: Observation number of employed respondents is 6,534, where unemployed respondents' number is 3,628.
* The t-statistic shows that the null hypothesis of no difference between means is rejected at the 0.05 level. The difference between employed and unemployed respondents as the mean(employed)-mean(econ. inactive) is negative.
Source: Authors' calculations from TUS South Africa (2000).

Table 4A.7   Time spent on different activities among unemployed and economically inactive

Weighted means, standard errors and comparison of means

Activity	Unemployed		Econ. inactive		t-stat
	Mean	SE	Mean	SE	
Water and fuel collection	12.13	2.44	13.17	1.27	−0.38
Social care***	39.90	3.73	32.95	1.95	1.65
Home maintenance**	207.25	12.68	172.62	3.87	2.61

Note: Observation number of employed respondents is 1,116, where unemployed respondents' number is 3,628.
** The t-statistic shows that the null hypothesis of no difference between means is rejected at the 0.05 level; the difference as mean (unemployed)-mean (econ. inactive) is positive:
*** The t-statistic shows that the null hypothesis of no difference between means is rejected at the 0.10 level; the difference as mean (unemployed)-mean (econ. inactive) is positive.
Source: Authors' calculations from TUS South Africa (2000).

5
Unpaid HIV/AIDS Care, Gender and Poverty: Exploring the Links

*Olagoke Akintola**

Introduction

Traditionally, women are known worldwide to be the main care providers in families and households, devoting much of their time to carrying out domestic work, which includes household maintenance, shopping and care of children and the sick, without being remunerated. Much of the value of these activities has gone unrecognized. However, the domestic work carried out by women in sub-Saharan African countries has recently received greater attention due to the consequences of the AIDS epidemic, which has necessitated the introduction of home-based care on a wide scale. The impact of the HIV/AIDS epidemic on southern African countries, which have consistently recorded the highest global HIV/AIDS-prevalence rates in the past five years (UNAIDS, 2004), has been particularly severe. As matters stand, the southern African region is currently home to three of the countries with the highest prevalence of HIV/AIDS in the world. Swaziland, with an HIV/AIDS prevalence rate of over 26 per cent, is currently the country with the highest prevalence rate in the world, followed by Botswana with 24 per cent and Lesotho with 23 per cent (UNAIDS, 2008). Although South Africa has the fifth highest prevalence in the region, it has the highest number of people living with HIV/AIDS in the whole world, with about 5.5 million people infected in the region.

Although recent studies have focused on women's role in the care of people living with AIDS, showing evidence of an increase in magnitude of care work carried out by women, little is to be found in the way of comprehensive information on the extent and forms of care provided and how these contribute to women's time burdens or impact on poverty in HIV/AIDS-affected households and communities. In this paper I explore the links between unpaid HIV/AIDS care and poverty from a gender perspective.[1] I argue that the home-based care results in a dramatic increase in women's care work and is contributing to the feminization of poverty.

The rise of unpaid care

Unpaid AIDS care did not begin with the introduction of home-based care policies. Families were already providing some degree of care to ill members at home before the advent of home-based care. This care covered a whole range of activities described for home care later, but was less demanding since family members only needed to provide supportive care to patients. This is because most bedridden patients would either be hospitalized for extended periods of time, while those who were asymptomatic or showing severe symptoms would visit hospitals frequently.

A number of factors have contributed to bringing the AIDS care agenda in sub-Saharan Africa to the fore in recent times. In the past few years, health systems have been under enormous strain due to a myriad of factors. The introduction of structural adjustment policies (SAP) in the region has led to health-sector reforms in many countries in Africa which require massive cut backs in spending on public healthcare and development programs. At the same time, the numbers of infected people who need medical care is growing rapidly. The cost of medical care for people living with HIV/AIDS (PLWHA) is exorbitant, sometimes costing twice as much as that of other illnesses (Hansen *et al.*, 2000). This has increased government spending on hospitals dramatically, imposing untold pressure on the health sectors of these countries. In addition, due to poor remuneration and poor working conditions, there is a massive brain drain as a result of large scale emigration among healthcare professionals, especially nurses and doctors (Aitken and Kemp, 2003). For instance, an estimated 18,000 Zimbabwean nurses work overseas and in South Africa about a third to half of medical graduates emigrate to the developed world (Pang *et al.*, 2002). In Malawi, between 1999 and 2001, over 60 per cent of all registered nurses in a single tertiary hospital emigrated abroad (Buchan and Schalski, 2004). All these have caused a significant reduction in human capacity in hospitals across the continent. In the absence of finances to expand existing facilities to cater to the large number of patients who require care, many governments in seeking ways to reduce the costs[2] to public health facilities, have enacted home-based care policies. Home-based care policies require that the home becomes the primary place of care for people living with HIV/AIDS, with family members serving as the main providers of care (South African Department of Health, 2001; WHO, 2002). As a result of the introduction of these policies, there has been an increasing shift in the primary place of patient care from formal health facilities to patients' homes, as hospitals discharge AIDS patients in an attempt to maximize patient turnover (Fox *et al.*, 2002). This has led to more AIDS patients dying at home (Nsutebu *et al.*, 2001; Steinitz, 2003; Uys, 2003). These patients are typically cared for by family members with little support in the provision of home-based care from the formal health care facilities in the public health care sector (Robson, 2000; Akintola, 2004a). This is all despite the scale of the epidemic and the pressing need to provide care and support for those dying at home, as well as for their care providers across the subregion. Accordingly, many community-based organizations, faith-based organizations and other nongovernmental organizations have developed, spontaneously and somewhat chaotically, in various communities across the subregion. These organizations typically recruit and train community members who volunteer their services to assist AIDS-affected households in caring for PLWHAs. As volunteer caregivers, these community members are not typically remunerated for their work. The crucial need for active involvement of community volunteers and family members in providing care to the ill has led to a renewed focus on women's unpaid care work. While there are clear benefits of home-based care, including a reduction of the burden on public health facilities and, thus, cost savings to the formal health care sector, information on the relationship between this form of care and poverty is scant.

Unpaid HIV/AIDS care is gendered

Feminist economists have written extensively about the gendered dimensions of different forms of unpaid caring labor, but little about unpaid AIDS care. Unpaid HIV/AIDS care refers to a wide range of care activities performed for people who are infected with HIV/AIDS. It has variously been referred to as home-based care or community home-based care. This form of care is informal because it is carried out by people who have received little or no training, mostly outside of formal hospital structures (Akintola, 2006). It is unpaid care because most, but not all, of those who provide home care do so without receiving any pecuniary reward. The focus of this chapter is on caregivers who carry out informal AIDS care without remuneration. Like other forms of unpaid care work documented in the feminist economics literature, the care of people living with HIV/AIDS is gendered, with women predominating among AIDS caregivers. This is consistent with women's traditional roles as nurturers in the home. Although available evidence on the proportion of men and women providing unpaid care for AIDS patients across the region and the amount of time spent on care are drawn from a nonrepresentative sample (Akintola, 2008), there is enough qualitative evidence to suggest that unpaid AIDS care is overwhelmingly gendered. Research across the southern African subregion shows that the typical care provider is a woman (Nnko *et al.*, 2000; Robson 2000; Akintola, 2004a; Chimwaza and Watkins, 2004; Orner, 2006); caregivers are commonly mothers, grandmothers, sisters, female friends, wives or girlfriends and rarely brothers, husbands or boyfriends of the patients (Nnko *et al.*, 2000; Chimwaza and Watkins, 2004; HelpAge International, 2004; Akintola, 2006; Orner, 2006). Although most of the available evidence is drawn from nonrepresentative samples (see Akintola 2008), women predominate among primary, as well as secondary, caregivers in the different kinds of family structures prevailing in Africa for various reasons.

Because AIDS is mainly transmitted through heterosexual intercourse and from mothers (during pregnancy, at birth and breastfeeding) in Africa, HIV usually infects both spouses in a marriage or sexual relationship and often one or more of their children. This creates a situation whereby AIDS clusters in households. Women are likely to be the caregivers in relationships where the male partner or both partners are ill. In the latter circumstance, women who are ill provide care for themselves as well as their male spouses. They also take on the responsibility of caring for the ill children. Further, separation and divorce are consequences of AIDS on households. This is often a result of gendered patterns of blame where men accuse women of being responsible for AIDS in the family and so some chase them out of the home or leave them at home without providing any form of support (Akintola, 2006; Rajaraman *et al.*, 2006). Women who are separated or divorced have to provide care alone without help from their male partner or his family (Lindsey *et al.*, 2003; Akintola, 2006; Rajaraman *et al.*, 2006). On the contrary, women still provide care to men responsible for infecting them with HIV (Akintola, 2005).

Across Africa, high rates of AIDS deaths have left numerous widows in their wake. The widows (who are most likely infected) are left to provide care for themselves and their children, some of whom may be infected as well. In circumstances where the female spouse dies leaving a widower, the care of the male survivor and the children usually rests with female members of the family (Akintola, 2004b). Additionally, men tend to remarry earlier than women (Wiegers *et al.*, 2006), increasing the probability that women will be the ones providing care for orphaned children and the surviving widower who may be living with HIV/AIDS. The southern Africa region has the highest average proportion of female-headed households in sub-Saharan Africa. Females head 30 per cent of households with children. The proportion of female-headed households is highest in Botswana (52 per cent); Namibia (47 per cent) and South Africa (46 per cent) (UNAIDS, 2004). These figures are even higher in AIDS-affected households. For instance, in these households, women who are the caregivers are usually also the only people who provide financial support in addition to performing other caring activities (Akintola, 2004b; Wiegers *et al.*, 2006). Although there are few quantitative estimates, many of the female heads of households combine the roles of breadwinner or main income earner and caregiver in HIV/AIDS-affected households (Akintola, 2004b). In a study conducted in the Bergville district of the KwaZuluNatal Province, South Africa, primary caregivers were also the head of the household in 42 per cent of the cases (Gow and Desmond, 2002).

Nonmarriage is a common feature in southern Africa and, together with labor migration and desertion of women by male spouses, has contributed considerably to the high proportion of female-headed households in the region (Denis and Ntsimane, 2006; Montgomery *et al.*, 2006; Wiegers *et al.*, 2006). Women who are not married, or are separated or divorced, usually live alone as single parents and heads of households/breadwinners, cohabiting with their male partners or living with their parents in multigenerational households (Akintola, 2004a). There is a high proportion of unmarried women who are heads of households or living in single-parent households among HIV/AIDS caregivers (Robson, 2000; Lindsey *et al.*, 2003; Chimwaza and Watkins, 2004; Akintola, 2006). The fact that there is no contractual agreement in cohabiting relationships makes it easier for men to leave without any obligation to their partners and children from such relationships. These women typically have children with men who may not take full responsibility for their children (Denis and Ntsimane, 2006; Rajaraman *et al.*, 2006). In these households many of the care providers are usually unable to readily access support from men or the man's family. (Steinberg *et al.*, 2002; Akintola, 2006; Wiegers *et al.*, 2006). Similar behaviors have also been documented among men in legal marriages. Denis and Ntsimane's (2006) study of a small sample of AIDS-affected families in KwaZuluNatal, South Africa found that men were absent in 72 per cent of AIDS-affected households; 10 per cent of these men had left because of divorce or separation, while the remaining 62 per cent were absent and were, at the time of the interview, not in regular contact with their children. Only 34 per cent of fathers provided any emotional or material support to their children.

A major consequence of the lack of support from men and the breakdown in traditional family structures as a result of the AIDS epidemic is the increasing number of children who become caregivers of PLWHAs. The burden of caregiving has fallen to children in many parts of the southern African subregion. In some households where there are adult relatives who could be potential caregivers, they may be working or in school (Akintola, 2004a; Robson, 2000, 2004). About 7 per cent of caregivers in a study in South Africa were less than 18 years old (Steinberg *et al.*, 2002). It is worthy to note that there is also a greater likelihood of girls serving as caregivers than boys among children who become caregivers. Only one of the nine young care providers in a Zimbabwean study was a boy (Robson, 2000). Similarly, in Botswana, a substantial proportion of young girls were serving a secondary caregivers, playing supportive roles or providing respite to the primary caregivers, although a few of them were also primary caregivers in homes where adults were not available (Lindsey *et al.*, 2003). Elderly people also participate in caring for the ill and especially for children orphaned by AIDS. In a Botswana study, 54 per cent of caregivers were 54 years or older (Lindsey *et al.*, 2003). In Tanzania, a large proportion of elderly women are involved as primary caregivers (HelpAge International, 2004).

In addition to family members, there are other people in the community who contribute their time in providing care for the ill. While some volunteer individually to assist their neighbors or friends, the majority of volunteers are those who enroll with voluntary organizations as volunteer caregivers. Referred to as 'volunteer caregivers,' this later group is usually recruited from the communities by community-based, faith-based or nongovernmental organizations and local hospitals. They are trained to support and train primary caregivers. Yet, in many cases, volunteers end up serving as the primary care providers in many households where there is no one else available or willing to provide care to the ill (Akintola, 2006). Again, most of those who volunteer their services as caregivers are women (Blinkhoff *et al.*, 2001; Steinitz, 2003; Akintola, 2006; Montgomery *et al.*, 2006). Studies of various community care programs providing home-based care services show an overwhelmingly higher proportion of women enrolled as volunteers than men (see Akintola, 2008).

Across the world, TUS reveal strong asymmetries of unpaid work between men and women and southern Africa is not an exception. In South Africa, for instance, women perform over 76 per cent of unpaid work (Stats SA, 2000) and research has shown that alongside gender, poverty and unemployment are correlated with higher levels of unpaid work contributions (Kizilirmak and Memis, 2009). Women do not only predominate among HIV/AIDS caregivers, but there is also a gendered dimension to the nature and level of care provided. The various forms of care provided for people living with HIV/AIDS necessitate time allocation over and above the normal unpaid household work performed by women. In addition to the need for supplemental income generation, collecting water and fuel, bathing the sick, cleaning and washing, child care and socialization, growing, harvesting, storing, preparing, cooking and serving/distributing food, ministering to the sick comprises part of the daily activities when caring for PLWHA (Robson, 2000; HelpAge International, 2004; Ogden *et al.*, 2004). Yet, overall levels of time spent in the above-mentioned care activities do not shed light on the specific forms caring assume (Akintola, 2008). Caring for the ill can be classified into activities of daily living (ADL), instrumental activities of daily living (IADL), management of instrumental activities for daily living, provision of moral and spiritual support, provision of basic nursing care, assistance with finances and care for children and orphans. The type and division of task allocation between men and women has implications that extend beyond the requisite amount of time and this is what I turn to next.

Assistance with daily and other activities

HIV/AIDS care often involves helping the ill to carry out ADL. These include feeding, bathing, dressing, going to the toilet and ambulating among others (Akintola, 2006). In addition, caregivers typically assist with IADL. These include tasks such as housework, shopping, cooking, moving within the home, transportation to health facilities and making telephone calls (Lindsey *et al.*, 2003; Orner, 2006). Caregivers also assist with activities that relate to the management of the affairs of the sick person, such as the management of the PLWHA's financial and legal affairs, dealing with doctors or other medical personnel and taking care of other activities left undone by the patient, such as taking care of the children of the patient.

Moral, spiritual and other forms of support

Moral and spiritual care forms the thrust of the care that is provided by caregivers, particularly volunteers. For volunteers, emotional support entails showing love, understanding, compassion and tolerance. It also involves 'being there' for the patients, having contact and spending time with them as well as engaging them in conversation and listening to them (Akintola, 2004a; Orner, 2005). In addition, volunteer caregivers link patients and their families with clergy and sources of spiritual support, such as churches or mosques. Volunteers also provide counseling to patients and family members and refer them to sources of support.

Provision of basic nursing care

Volunteer caregivers are trained to provide basic nursing care to patients. They, in turn, pass on the skills to primary caregivers who provide such care on a daily basis to patients. Basic nursing care includes help in cleaning of wounds, skin care, mouth care, monitoring treatment compliance, massaging patients' body, providing guidance, offering support necessary for adequate nutrition, turning bedridden patients and helping to manage incontinence among those with frequent diarrhea (Akintola, 2004a, 2005). In addition, family and volunteer caregivers monitor the diets of the patients to ensure that they adhere to the diet recommended by health workers. This sometimes requires the preparation or purchase of special foods for the patients. They also assist with fetching medication from health facilities and monitoring adherence to prescribed medication.

Assisting with finances, material resources and social resources

Caregivers frequently assist in sourcing and distributing material support, as well as linking patients with support systems (Akintola, 2004a; Boswky, 2004). Given the extreme poverty or illness that may occur in their patients' homesteads, volunteer caregiving also involves out-of-pocket expenses on the part of the caregivers who often have to borrow money from neighbors and friends to take care of their patients' financial needs (Chimwaza and Watkins, 2004; Akintola, 2004a).

Other activities

In order to deal with the poverty in HIV/AIDS-affected homes in South Africa, volunteers assist family members with the preparation of documents necessary for accessing social grants. Volunteers also assist with funeral policies and arrangements for their patients, spending a considerable amount of time in community mobilization, monitoring and supervision, as well as attendance of community home-based care and other related meetings. After the death of patients, caregivers are usually left to care for the patient's children, some of whom may also be HIV positive.

It is the case that women perform more of the ADL, as well as IADL (Akintola, 2004a). Although men sometimes assist with IADL such as transport to health facilities and finances, they are usually more involved in carrying out management activities of daily living than any other activity. However, they do not provide support or care in certain instances, in which case women and children (usually female) have to shoulder these responsibilities (Akintola, 2006). In female-headed households and households where women are the breadwinners, the provision of financial support for various activities in the home usually falls to women alone. While men are not completely absent in the AIDS-caring arena, their participation in caregiving is usually low, gendered and also poorly researched (Akintola, 2006; Montgomery *et al.*, 2006). Montgomery and colleagues' study in South Africa showed that although some men participate in caring for family members in HIV/AIDS-affected families, these experiences usually are underreported or not reported at all. The authors also argue that prevailing social norms about appropriate men's behavior remains a barrier to men's involvement in caring. The fact that men who are involved in caring usually take on secondary roles in physical care activities, as discussed earlier, mean that their work is invisible to families and researchers.

Unpaid HIV/AIDS care and poverty

In Africa, poverty is common and had been a feature of many households long before the HIV/AIDS epidemic (UNAIDS, 2004; Bachmann and Booysen, 2003). This is linked to a high rate of unemployment among urban and rural dwellers. In South Africa, for instance, the lack of employment opportunities has been linked to structural reasons, for example, an overall inability of economic growth to absorb surplus labor and the low level of education and skills among this population, largely a legacy of apartheid policies. At the same time, AIDS has aggravated preexisting poverty levels in many affected households across the continent and has made income generation and recovery from poverty more difficult for HIV/AIDS-affected households (Bollinger and Stover, 1999; Barnett and Whiteside, 2002; Shaibu, 2006; Yamano and Jayne, 2004). Although comprehensive data and surveys are lacking (Akintola, 2008), findings from studies to date on HIV/AIDS care show that care is being provided within this context of poverty and deprivation (Bollinger and Stover, 1999; Booysen, 2002; Oni *et al.*, 2002; Samson, 2002; Steinberg *et al.*, 2002; Lindsey *et al.*, 2003; Akintola, 2004a). Studies in Botswana, Malawi, Lesotho and South Africa provide information on the context of poverty prevalent in HIV/AIDS-affected households and communities

(Lindsey *et al.*, 2003; Chimwaza and Watkins 2004). A longitudinal study conducted in the Free State province of South Africa compared 202 households with an HIV-infected member and 202 unaffected neighboring households. The study found that affected households tended to be larger, poorer and have lower employment rates than unaffected households. Incomes in affected households were about half of that of affected households (Bachmann and Booysen, 2003). The level of unemployment in affected households implies that most of the unpaid caregivers live in very poor homes where no one is employed or, at best, have temporary employment. Unfortunately there is very little data on the socioeconomic profile of unpaid caregivers living in these households since questions on socioeconomic status in surveys are asked on the households as a whole (Akintola, 2008).

Nonetheless qualitative studies provide insight into the socioeconomic characteristics of unpaid caregivers. A study in Botswana found that 57 per cent of the caregivers that made up the sample had low socioeconomic status. Only four of the thirty-five caregivers interviewed were employed and two of these had only temporary employment. Many of HIV/AIDS-affected households were wholly dependent on pensions, amounting to approximately US$26 per month, but available only to households where there was an elderly person (Lindsey *et al.*, 2003). In a more recent study in South Africa, only a few of the primary caregivers had any employment. Those who did were employed as temporary domestic workers with an average income of R15 per day, and most were working only about two days in a week (Akintola, 2004a). The study also showed that seven of the twenty-one HIV/AIDS-affected families were very poor using relative measures of wealth. Another seven were classified as poor, while six were classified as having moderate socioeconomic status. Only 5 per cent of HIV/AIDS-affected households were classified as well-off by local standards.[3] While data on the socioeconomic profile of caregivers reveal that most live in poverty, little is known about their socioeconomic profile prior to assumption of caregiving duties, therefore it is difficult to quantify the impact of AIDS care. There is also a limited understanding of the processes through which home care contributes to poverty. How then is home-based care related to poverty? Unpaid AIDS care is inextricably linked to poverty in a variety of ways. To begin with, home-based care policies mainly target and impact poorer families for a variety of reasons. Poor households constitute the majority of AIDS-affected households and most of the people who use public hospitals across the region come from the poorer segment of society and are therefore more likely to be those without access to medical insurance.[4]

Given that home-based care policies are aimed at addressing capacity problems in public hospitals, the very same poor families who can not afford to pay for care in private hospitals are often the ones who are being asked to provide home care for their sick family members. Poorer families are therefore the ones most affected by the home-based care policies. On the contrary, the well-off are likely to be able to afford to pay for health care in private hospitals, semiprivate hospitals, hospices or employ a paid home caregiver. Indeed, some well-off or middle class families with white-collar jobs have medical insurance that covers treatment of AIDS.[5] Families that are well-off are thus less likely to be affected in any significant way by home-based care policies since they are more likely to be able to afford to pay for care.

The fact that poor families spend more time providing unpaid AIDS care means that the provision of care aggravates poverty in previously poor households. I discuss two major pathways and the processes through which home-based care exacerbates poverty, namely, the opportunity costs, as well as the financial and material costs, of caregiving.

Opportunity costs of caregiving

Time spent providing unpaid care to people living with AIDS has serious implications for the household economy. The opportunity costs sustained by those caring for people living with HIV/AIDS refer to the costs of the alternative activities they could have engaged in, alternatives they must forgo in order to provide care for the ill. These activities may include, but are not limited to, paid employment, subsistence production, social activities (like visiting friends, attending community meetings or religious programs) and time devoted to reading or self-care. The opportunity cost of caring for PLWHAs is one of the most neglected and least researched areas relating to caregiving. Currently, there is little information about such costs incurred by the caregivers, as time-use data is too sporadic and small scale to provide a comprehensive picture. Furthermore, existing studies do not disaggregate time-use data sufficiently to provide an appreciation of the time taken for the performance of AIDS-related care. As a consequence there is dearth of quantitative information about the specific activities that caregivers forego (see Akintola, 2008).

Prior to the wide-scale introduction of home-based care policies, family members only needed to provide supportive care to patients and make occasional visits to public clinics and/or hospitals since most patients would be in their care for varying lengths of time depending on the severity of their illness. But with the introduction of home-based care policies, public hospitals, in a bid to reduce length of stay, began to discharge

HIV/AIDS patients early to be cared for at home, leading to a marked increase in the burden of caring for family members (Van Dyk, 2001; Fox *et al.*, 2002; Makoae and Jubber, 2008). While hospitals are able to achieve a shorter length of stay for HIV/AIDS patients, this increases the responsibility of caregivers at home who become the primary caregivers of patients. A shorter hospital stay therefore means greater opportunity costs for families.[6]

Because time spent on care depends on the kind and level of care provided, caregiving is often shared and not the responsibility of just one person. The amount of time spent on caring will therefore depend on whether or not one is the primary, secondary or tertiary caregiver. Accordingly, the opportunity costs incurred by household members vary with the amount of time and kind of care provided. Research has pointed out that indeed, primary caregivers who have to be on standby 24-hours usually have the least time to carry out other economic and social activities, while caregivers providing respite care spend less time. Steinberg *et al.* (2002) found that caregivers in HIV/AIDS-affected households in South Africa had to take time off from work and other income-generating activities or school in 40 per cent of households. In almost 12 per cent of households, time was taken from formal employment.

Research has shown that the majority of the unpaid caregivers are self-employed or working in temporary and casual jobs where they are often unable to take extended paid leave, sick leave or even unpaid leave (Rajaraman *et al.*, 2006, 2008). The opportunity costs to them are therefore usually enormous. A recent Botswana study comparing HIV caregivers and non-HIV caregivers found that HIV caregivers were more likely to take leave from work for caregiving (53 per cent versus 39 per cent), and for longer periods of time (13 versus 7.6 days) (Rajaraman *et al.*, 2008). Staying away from work even for a short period could lead to loss of income since casual workers are not paid for those days they are absent. The caregivers could also lose their jobs when they absent themselves from work for extended periods. Subsistence farming, which provides a substantial proportion for the food needs of most of the population of most countries in southern Africa, is often severely affected by caregiving. Because small-scale farming relies heavily on family labor, particularly that of women (Wiegers *et al.*, 2006), the inability of caregivers to participate in farming results in reduction in household food production. The impact of caregiving on both formal and subsistence work is profound, resulting in severe food shortages and severe threats to household food security (Rajaraman *et al.*, 2006; Wiegers *et al.*, 2006). Rajaraman and colleague's (2006) study in Botswana showed that one in five caregivers lost substantial income due to caregiving. Caregivers took leave and, as their patients' health deteriorated, had to extend leave repeatedly in order to continue to provide care. This often resulted in loss of jobs, as some of them were not able to return to their work due to caregiving commitments. This led to severe food shortages, as was the case with one caregiver (Ramjaran *et al.*, 2006, p.660):

> We would go for days without food until perhaps neighbours noticed we didn't have any food. Then they'd come and help us.

In a South African study (Akintola, 2004a), caregivers' normal daily lives were affected considerably by the performance of caregiving activities, with some having to restructure their normal daily program to suit their new role as a caregiver. Many had to give up certain commitments in order to provide care to the recipients. Although none of the caregivers in this study had a permanent/regular job, the few who had temporary jobs reported having to cut down on the time spent on work, and some others indicated that they lost opportunities to increase income by spending more time doing temporary jobs. One of the family caregivers who had been employed as a domestic worker said she worked twice a week, but could not use an opportunity to improve her earnings by increasing the number of days because there was nobody to care for her mother when she was away at work. Yet, this family was living in abject poverty and desperately needed money to feed and take care of the sick person. In many households the only source of income has to be foregone because of caregiving activities (Akintola, 2004a). Volunteers providing care also incur opportunity costs. In a South African case study (Akintola, 2004a), a 40-year old volunteer caregiver who took temporary jobs as a domestic worker was denied an opportunity for a more regular contract job because of her daily caregiving routine:

> Sometimes if I wake up in the morning, I do my house chores and instead of going to town (to look for work) I have to go and help the terminally ill people. There was a time when I lost my temporary job. There was a neighbour who came to call me for a temporary job but when she came I was already gone to help the sick people. So I lost the opportunity for that job.

It is often difficult for these caregivers to estimate the amount of money they lose in the process, as these jobs are sometimes irregular and dependent on client flow, which is also often unpredictable and, therefore, difficult to estimate. Furthermore, volunteer caregivers who give money or other material resources to patients often have to sacrifice to do it. It often means that these caregivers forego things related to personal comfort or material resources that would otherwise have benefited them. For example, a volunteer caregiver in KwaZuluNatal province of South Africa indicated that she used money meant for electricity to transport her patient to the hospital and had to live in darkness for a few days (Akintola, 2004a). Despite wide acknowledgment in the literature and among advocacy groups that caregivers, particularly women, sacrifice a lot of their time, money and other resources to provide care, only a few studies have attempted to quantify the cost of time that caregivers forego when providing care (see Hansen *et al.*, 1998; Akintola, 2008). One exception is a Zimbabwean study that found that volunteers provided between 2.5 to 3.5 hours of care per day and the opportunity cost was estimated at US$22 per month[7] (Hansen *et al.*, 1998).

The time spent in caring for the ill and, therefore, the opportunity costs of care are mediated by a number of factors including the household size/composition/structure, severity of illness, quality of care provided and number of patients in the household. Primary caregivers living in households with many able-bodied adults are more likely to have less time burdens than those with fewer members since other household members usually provide support and respite to the primary caregivers. In reality, however, AIDS kills adults in the reproductive and productive ages leaving, in many cases, female-headed households which mainly contain older people and children, elderly-headed households containing children and child-headed households also containing children. These households usually do not have adult members who can carry out productive labor. Wiegers *et al.* (2006), in a study in Zambia, found that female-headed and elderly-headed households had less total labor compared with male-headed households affected with AIDS and unaffected households. Since agricultural activities are gendered, with men carrying out slash-and-burn cultivation, fishing, poaching and charcoal burning, women who need these activities to be done for them can only access male labor through exchange of local beers, which are usually brewed by women (Wiegers *et al.*, 2006). Women caregivers in female-headed households carry a double burden because they are not only unable to participate in agricultural production (because of the caregiving duties), but also do not usually have male adult productive labor that could help them on the farm and provide for their subsistence agricultural needs. Furthermore, while male-headed households are able to draw on women's labor from other households, female-headed households are usually unable to solicit and receive help from males from other house-holds (Wiegers *et al.*, 2006). This has implications for household food security and livelihoods. The impact on caregivers' ability to participate in agricultural production is even more severe in elderly- and female-headed households where there are few secondary caregivers to relieve the primary caregiver. Not only will these households be unable to access the labor necessary for the activities largely carried out by men, the care-giver will also have to combine provision of care with income generation for sustenance of livelihood (see Wiegers *et al.*, 2006).

Caregivers of patients with full-blown AIDS spend more time providing care because they are more likely to require more attention for physical support and changing of soiled clothes and bed linen than those in the early stages of the disease (such as those with symptomatic illnesses). The former are also likely to have more frequent diarrhea and require fre-quent bathing. Given that there is often limited access to water among poor households, the time required for fetching water from rivers, wells or public standpipes is usually longer than from pipes connected to the home or yard and could result in heavy time burdens for caregivers. Ngwenya and Kgathi's (2006) study in Botswana showed that time spent in fetching water increased considerably when there were disruptions in water supply and people had to travel to neighboring villages, a distance of about 10 km (6 hours), to fetch water, leading to huge opportunity costs for the caregivers. Carers of patients receiving high quality care, such as those that have access to well-resourced home-based care orga-nizations, are likely to spend less time caring than those receiving poor quality care, since the latter will have more recurring illness episodes than the former. Unfortunately, most patients fall in the later group because home-based care coverage is very low in Africa, with only a few of the affected households able to access support from home-based care organizations (Blinkhoff *et al.*, 2001; Nsutebu *et al.*, 2001; Steinberg *et al.*, 2002; Steinitz, 2003; Akintola, 2004b). A South African study showed that less than 50 per cent of AIDS-affected households received care and support from any home-based care organization. The situation is similar in Lesotho, Malawi, Zimbabwe and Zambia (Woelk *et al.*, 1995; Blinkhoff *et al.*, 2001; Nsutebu *et al.*, 2001; Bowsky, 2004; Chimwaza and Watkins, 2004). Access to antiretroviral (ARV) therapy can also mitigate the time burdens of caregivers, as patients who are on ARVs will require less time to be cared for than those who are not. However, ARV coverage is also low and many infected people still don't have access to ARVs or only access them when it is too late (Mutombo, 2007). Home-based care orga-nizations also provide varying degrees of financial and material support depending on the resources available to the care organization. Given that AIDS clusters in households, caregivers in households with more than one HIV/AIDS patient will spend more time providing AIDS care and, thus, incur greater time costs than those with just one patient. Caregiving for patients with AIDS also affects other housework. Caregivers are often not able to devote enough time to do their other chores while providing AIDS care and other people, particularly children who were previously receiving care from the caregiver, suffer neglect as a consequence. In Steinberg's study, almost 60 per cent took time from other housework or vegetable gardening activities to provide care. This has implications for the health and future economic well-being of those affected.

However, those who provide secondary care, particularly men and male children, often have more time to engage in productive, as well as social, activities. This could potentially help with food production and income generation activities as they have time to work to earn an income to maintain the family, but, as noted earlier, many affected households do not have male productive labor to carry out certain activities necessary for subsistence farming. Child caregivers also incur opportunity costs because they spend school time at home providing care or on the farm assisting in carrying out home production work that caregivers are unable to do because of their caring work. Steinberg and colleagues indicated that 20 per cent of research participants spent school/study time caring for the sick person. Girl children were more likely than boys to be withdrawn from school for any of these reasons (Steinberg *et al.*, 2002). This has serious implications for the educational development of these individuals. Children who are not caregivers, but whose parents are providing care to HIV patients, are also more likely than those whose parents are noncaregivers to have academic problems since their parents do not have enough time to provide academic support at home (Rajaraman *et al.*, 2008). Another study by Samson (2002), also in South Africa, corroborates the impact of caregiving on children's schooling. Samson (2002) indicated that HIV/AIDS reduces the opportunities and support for education by debilitating the caregiver and reversing roles, thereby turning the child to a caregiver. Although Samson's study did not find a strong direct link between household health status and educational outcomes, he found that children who dropped out of school form a small proportion of households with members reporting HIV/AIDS symptoms. This suggests that some might have dropped out as a consequence of lack of finances arising from the impact of HIV/AIDS. However, we do not have sufficient data on children whose primary reason for dropping out of school is because of the need to provide AIDS care. It is common for children to drop out of school for a variety of other reasons or a combination of several other reasons which include lack of finances for school fees, books or uniforms, participation in subsistence agricultural/home production or caring for other ill relatives (Samson, 2002; Steinberg *et al.*, 2002; Bennell, 2005; Wiegers *et al.*, 2006). While any or a combination of these factors may be the primary reasons for withdrawing children from school, they may also be the secondary reasons. For example, children may be withdrawn from school to provide other forms of care for younger siblings while the primary caregiver provides AIDS care. They may also be withdrawn from school or miss school occasionally to work on the farm (Wiegers *et al.*, 2006) or to participate in other kinds of subsistence productive activity. The opportunity and financial costs of providing unpaid care can also have knock-on effects on finances in the households, thereby making education unaffordable for HIV/AIDS-affected households. For example, in a South African study, 4 per cent of AIDS-affected households reported not paying school fees as result of having an AIDS-sick person to care for.

Financial and material costs

It is ironic that poor households who provide care at home are also the ones that have the least ability to bear the financial and material cost of home-based care. In discussing the financial and material costs associated with AIDS care, one should pose two critical questions. What are the costs associated with unpaid AIDS care and who bears these costs? With respect to the former, the financial costs documented in household impact studies are not strictly those incurred in the care of AIDS patients, but include all costs incurred as a result of AIDS in the household. However, few studies distinguish costs associated with AIDS care from other costs (see Hansen *et al.*, 1998). Although it may seem reasonable to suppose that most of the financial costs of AIDS will be associated with the provision of care for the ill person, there is evidence to suggest that this is not always the case. Some of the costs are associated with income loss from the death of adult breadwinners in HIV/AIDS-affected households (Bollinger and Stover, 1999; Booysen, 2002; Yamano and Jayne, 2004). There is therefore a need to disentangle costs related to the care of AIDS patients from other costs in the household.

Following Akintola (2008), two broad kinds of costs associated with unpaid AIDS care can be distinguished. First is the cost incurred in providing care in cases where the ill person is receiving public institutional care. In such cases the costs incurred by the families will be those extra costs that are not covered by public hospitals. Since the cost of medical care will be covered by the hospital, one would expect the cost to the family to be minimal and may include, but not limited to, cost of transport to hospitals and out-of-pocket medical related expenses, such as extra medication. The cost of diapers and other medical-related material inputs would ideally be covered by hospitals in economies that are fairly well-resourced, such as that of Botswana and South Africa.[8] The second kind of cost relates to incremental costs associated with providing home-based care.[9] Incremental costs refer to costs incurred as a consequence of home-based care policies. They are incremental because these costs would not have been incurred by households had the patient been in public institutional care where they would have been covered by government hospitals.[10]

With the introduction of home-based care across the region, the incremental costs of home-based care have increased remarkably. Since patients are now cared for at home, costs previously covered by hospitals are inevitably transferred to families. These include cost of diapers, bed linen, gloves, mackintosh, soaps and detergent, water and special or extra food.

These costs are mediated by support received from individuals, family members, community members, home-based care organizations and governmental structures and/or organizations. As mentioned earlier, there is a wide variation in the type and quality of care provided across countries and within public hospitals in each country, as well as the kind of financial and material support provided by these organizations. The degree to which unpaid care contributes to poverty in these households will therefore vary with the level of support received not only from the care organizations, but also from informal sources like individuals or families outside the household. In addition to the provision of care, many home-based care organizations provide varying degrees of material support to affected households. Therefore, households that do not have access to home-based care organizations will spend more time, as well as financial and material resources, on home care-related expenses than those who have support from care organizations. However, many of the home-based care organizations do not even receive any kind of support from governments and are financially constrained and operating on shoestring budgets (Russel and Schneider, 2000; Nsutebu *et al.*, 2001; Akintola, 2004a); this makes it impossible for them to reach many HIV/AIDS-affected households (Russel and Schneider, 2000; UNAIDS, 2000; Nsutebu *et al.*, 2001; Steinberg *et al.*, 2002).[11] In Lesotho, for instance, most HIV/AIDS-funded activities are located in urban and periurban areas where only 20 per cent of the population resides (Bowsky, 2004). In South Africa, only a few households have access to support from home-based care organizations (Steinberg *et al.*, 2002). In households that have access to care organizations, they do not receive the necessary medical and material support to mitigate their financial and material burdens. This implies that there are many households that are vulnerable to being impoverished by unpaid AIDS care.

Policies on public health care vary across countries, with countries providing varying degrees of subsidies. In countries where public health care is free because of government subsidies, hospital care affords poor families the opportunity to save on some of the costs that would have been incurred in home care, for example, the cost of medicine, diapers, gloves and so on. However, in countries where subsidies on public health care are low and user fees are charged, hospital care may be unaffordable for poor families. Home-based care could therefore provide some savings on the cost of hospital care, at least in the short run (Akintola, 2008). While home-based care will relieve them of the need to pay hospital fees, it nonetheless introduces other costs that family members have to bear and may have profound negative consequences in the long run. This may include the costs of materials necessary for home-based care such as diapers, gloves, bed linen, disinfectants and so on.

In Africa, many of the public health facilities are located quite a distance from the communities they serve. Although there may be dispensaries or health posts located close to rural communities, these do not always have the necessary infrastructure and personnel to care for diseases such as AIDS and its sequalae. These health facilities are usually the first port of call for ill people, from where they are then referred to other district or specialist hospitals far away from their communities, necessitating that caregivers and their patients incur transport costs. This has consequences for patients' health-seeking behavior. Patients may miss appointments in hospitals when they cannot afford transport fare (Mtika, 2001; Akintola, 2004a); They may also resort to buying medication at exorbitant prices from private dispensaries in the vicinity instead traveling to government hospitals that are far away to consult with medical personnel (see Mtika, 2001). In a Botswana study (Rajaraman *et al.*, 2006), a round trip has been shown to cost as much as the total monthly income of a poor family. As a consequence, patients may choose not to go to the hospital. This could lead to deterioration in their health, which may lead to more spending. Transporting bedridden patients is even more expensive because families have to hire cars to take the caregiver and the patient to the hospital. This is usually far more expensive than public transport. Even in circumstances where patients are in institutional care, the cost of visiting them can be enormous for the caregiver. In countries like Malawi, where lack of capacity in public hospitals implies that there are not enough nurses or nursing assistants to bath patients, family members have to travel to some public institutions to bathe patients (Mtika, 2001). This creates additional expenses for transport to hospitals and for feeding when they have to sleep in or around the hospital.

The cost of water can be enormous for families. In Tanzania, for example, where there is poor access to water in rural areas, already-poor caregivers have to purchase water. Women who can not afford to pay for water are compelled to exchange sex with young men selling water (Help Age International, 2004, p. 9), exposing themselves to the risk of HIV infection. In Botswana, where water is provided 'free of charge' through public standpipes, problems with service delivery leading to unreliable water supply compels caregivers to purchase 'expensive' water from donkey-cart owners (Ngwenya and Kgathi, 2006). Given that patients with diarrhea require between 20–80 litres of water per day (Ngwenya and Kgathi, 2006), the cost of water may further impoverish poor families. Those who are unable to afford the cost resort to using river water or reducing the number of times they bathe patients, all of which may predispose people to diarrhea and other infections or aggravate existing infections among patients.

Who bears these financial and material costs of unpaid AIDS care? Just as caring tasks are disproportionately shared among family members, so are costs also shared disproportionately among family members providing care to the ill. But while there are qualitative and quantitative studies that provide some indication of how caregiving tasks are shared in AIDS-affected households,[12] we do not have a clear sense of who bears the financial costs of home care. This is largely because most studies that estimate costs only provide aggregate costs that households as a whole incur as a result of having an HIV/AIDS patient and not for any particular household member (Booysen, 2002; Bachmann and Booysen, 2003) making it difficult to ascertain who bears which of the various costs associated with HIV/AIDS. Yet this information is critical in order to determine what proportion of the costs of AIDS care unpaid caregivers incur.

Notwithstanding the paucity of information on the demographics of those who bear costs associated with caregiving, some insight could be obtained from anecdotal evidence and a few available studies. Various members of households contribute to the financing of care-related activities, as well as other AIDS-related costs, therefore each will incur varying amounts of costs. The financial costs are shouldered not only by the people within the household, but also by neighbors, community members and nonresident relatives who contribute through financial and material gifts, loans and remittances. Mike Mtika (2001), in a study in rural Malawi, found that 91 per cent of AIDS-affected households received help from relatives with food and taking care of the ill during a ten-week research period. Affected families reported receiving financial support for medical expenses and transport assistance, as well as others, from family and community members. Intrahousehold contributions of financial and material resources could help reduce the impoverishing impact of home-based care on AIDS-affected households. However, this may not be sustainable in the medium to long run with many rural and semirural communities in southern Africa experiencing generalized AIDS epidemics.[13] The impact of AIDS in communities with high HIV/AIDS prevalence can be so huge that it undermines social immunity.[14] Mtika's study in three rural villages in Malawi showed that support for AIDS-affected households declined with time. This was due to the fact that illness and death had reached a threshold in the villages that made it difficult for households to help each other. First, the long, drawn-out nature of AIDS illnesses requires long-term financial outlays that are difficult to sustain by poor and middle-income households. Second, the number of people who required help, as well as the total amount of financial help they required, has increased beyond a threshold that 'helping households' could sustain. Third, the households that initially provided help eventually had someone infected with HIV in their own households. In those instances it was observed that the 'helping households' now had to direct all resources to care for their own members, making it practically impossible to continue assisting others. All these led to a weakening of social immunity – a situation where people who previously provided help that mitigated the burden of financial expenses associated with caregiving for the ill could no longer do so.

The fact that sick individuals eventually die and have virtually little or no opportunity to reciprocate for the help they received contributes to the weakening of social capital (Mtika, 2001; Wiegers *et al.*, 2006). Thus, as seen above, the weakening of social immunity could lead to food insecurity in affected households, as well as in helping households, which could increase aggregate poverty levels of affected communities.

Conclusions and recommendations

In this paper, I have discussed how home-based care increases caregivers' time burdens and reduces participation in paid labor, subsistence production and the care of other members of the households, thereby undermining health and socioeconomic well-being among previously poor unpaid caregivers of people living with HIV/AIDS. Most of the impact of HIV/AIDS on households disproportionately affects caregivers who are predominantly women and who do not receive remuneration for their labor, but nevertheless have to give of their time and financial and material resources to provide care. The impact on women is made worse because they are more likely to be the primary and secondary caregivers. While many men restrict their physical, financial and emotional involvement in the provision of care, others are hindered by sociocultural norms. The training of men from a young age within families and institutional settings could capacitate men to better negotiate greater involvement and more effective roles in caregiving.

The impact of AIDS is so severe that it is eroding social immunity, which could mitigate the effects on caregivers and their patients and this highlights the need for urgent policy interventions at the household and community level to prevent the total erosion of social cohesion and social capital. Additionally there is a gendered dimension to the impact on households in rural agrarian economies where AIDS-affected female-headed households and AIDS-affected elderly-headed households have less access to the male labor necessary for subsistence production than AIDS-affected male-headed households and unaffected households. Children are particularly vulnerable as caregivers and child laborers, but they also face neglect from parents who are caregivers with consequences for their health and educational development. Since the girl child is the one most likely to provide respite to the primary caregiver, this could lead to a cycle of poverty where previously poor women are prevented from accessing the healthcare and education that has the potential to liberate them from the shackles of poverty. This will in turn exacerbate gender inequality by widening the gap between men and women in terms of educational achievement and future livelihoods.

Little data exists on the impoverishing impact of home-based care on caregivers. This study highlights the need for studies that aim to better understand the processes through which various models of home-based care contribute to nonparticipation in paid and subsistence production, which, in turn, lead to poverty in various kinds of economies. For instance, longitudinal cohort data on the socioeconomic conditions and time use among unpaid caregivers versus noncaregivers can help shed more light on the role that home-based care plays in the feminization of poverty.

The study also reveals the need for policies that aim to protect children from experiencing the adverse effects of providing care, as well as to keep them protected from being removed from school to provide care. Such policies should include interventions that target poor families and guarantee education for all children, particularly those in poor and HIV/AIDS-affected families who can not afford education. The fact that caring work increases caregivers' time burdens underscores the importance of respite care so that caregivers have more time to participate in the labor force. Respite care will need to be carried out within the framework of well-funded and resourced community-based care programs.

As has been shown in this study, proximity to quality health care facilities and access to quality health care services, as well as other public services (such as water supply) can help reduce women's time burdens. It can also help patients to improve health-seeking behavior and ensure patients receive quality care, thereby reducing recurrent episodes of illness, waiting time in hospitals and the out-of-pocket costs. In this regard, provision of anti-retrovirals (ARVs) to poor, infected people remains one major way of reducing the impact of home-based care on women's time. Measures should be taken to ensure food security, particularly in AIDS-affected communities, through the provision of social safety nets and the provision of institutional support for caregivers of PLWHAs. Poor, as well as HIV-affected, households should be given access to sustainable technology that can reduce their dependence on labor and help them improve agricultural production. Training is needed in economies that are not predominantly agrarian to provide women with skills they can use for home or subsistence production and reduce their dependence on menial jobs that have less security and little opportunities to take leave. All these will require substantial investments from governments and structural changes in the allocation of funds. More equitable distribution of government resources is needed to combat the devastating effects of home-based care on households.

Notes

* I would like to thank the reviewers and editors for their valuable comments and suggestions. In particular, I thank Rania Antonopoulos for her support throughout the time of writing this article. I owe a debt of thanks

to Olubunmi Akintola for assistance with literature searches, reading and suggestions. The writing of this article was made possible by funds from the 'Mellon Merit Awards for Young Scholars' from the Mellon Foundation through the Faculty Office of Human Development and Social Sciences, University of KwaZuluNatal, Durban, South Africa, as well as a Competitive Research Grant from the Research Office of the University of KwaZuluNatal, Durban South Africa.

1. This study builds on a previous study (Akintola, 2008) which explored issues relating to the cost-effectiveness of home-based care versus hospital care.
2. Here 'cost' is used very broadly to imply financial costs as well as the human capacity necessary for caring for people living with HIV/AIDS.
3. For a detailed description of the living conditions of caregivers see Lindsey *et al.* (2003), Akintola (2004a), Chimwaza and Watkins (2004).
4. In countries such as Botswana, which provide comprehensive care to citizens in public hospitals that are accessed by poor people as well as middle income groups, poorer segments of the society are still more likely to use public hospitals and will likely revert to home-based care while richer people who use public hospitals will likely revert to paid care as a result of the home-care policies.
5. Some medical insurance covers the cost of antiretroviral therapy which significantly improves health and reduces dependence on caregivers. I discuss this in the section on opportunity costs.
6. Nonetheless, we must keep in mind that big variations do exist across and within countries in regards to what is provided by public health facilities. Even in circumstances where patients are in hospital care, shortcomings in health service delivery can lead to major time burdens for caregivers, as they become responsible for activities such as cleaning, cooking, feeding and bathing patients. This is a problem facing many sub-Saharan African countries, including Uganda, Kenya and Malawi (Mtika, 2001).
7. The study used the minimum wage in the country to estimate opportunity cost of time spent in caring.
8. Although these countries provide heavy subsidies to public health service users, shortcomings in service delivery, as well as cut-backs in spending, imply that there are variations in the provision of material resources across public health institutions.
9. In countries where public health care is free and home-based care is not being promoted or a where a government policy is not in place, the costs associated with care will be less, since most of the costs associated with medical care will be borne by the hospitals.
10. In practice, not all costs are borne by the government hospitals. The cost covered by public hospitals depends on the degree of subsidies provided by government. This point is discussed later.
11. A slight exception is Botswana, which provides a wide range of support services to home-based care programs across the country. Even so, there are still a large number of people who are not reached by these programs (Lindsey *et al.*, 2003; Shaibu, 2006).
12. This point is discussed in the section that follows under the theme opportunity costs of care.
13. These are epidemics where more than 5% of the population is infected with HIV/AIDS.

14. Social immunity refers to 'coping mechanisms' adopted by communities to deal with the impact of an affliction in this case HIV/AIDS. This entails the sharing of resources among households belonging to the same extended family network.

References

Aitken, J. and J. Kemp (2003) 'HIV/AIDS, Equity and Health Sector Personnel in Southern Africa,' Discussion Paper 12. [Harare, Zimbabwe: Regional Network for Equity in Health in Southern Africa (EQUINET)].

Akintola, O. (2004a) 'Home-Based Care: A Gendered Analysis of Informal Care Giving for People with HIV/AIDS in a Semi-rural South African Setting,' Unpublished PhD Thesis (Durban, South Africa: University of KwaZulu-Natal).

Akintola, O. (2004b) 'A Gendered Analysis of the Burden of Care on Family and Volunteer Caregivers in Uganda and South Africa,' A Research Report for Health Economics and HIV/AIDS Research Division. (Durban, South Africa:.University of KwaZulu-Natal). Available www.heard.org.za

Akintola, O. (2005) 'Community Responses to HIV/AIDS: The Role of Volunteers in Home-based Care for People Living with HIV/AIDS in South Africa,' Research Report for Centre for Civil Society (Durban, South Africa:.University of KwaZulu-Natal).

Akintola, O. (2006) 'Gendered Home-Based Care in South Africa: More Trouble for the Troubled,' *African Journal of AIDS Research*, 5(3), 537–47.

Akintola, O. (2008) 'Unpaid HIV/AIDS Care in Southern Africa: Forms, Context and Implications,' Paper presented at the International Association for Feminist Economics Conference, Torino, Italy.

Bachmann, M.O. and L.R. Booysen (2003) 'Health and Economic Impact of HIV/AIDS on South African Households: A Cohort Study,' *BMC Public Health*, 3(14), http://www.biomedcentral.com/1471-2458/3/14, date accessed 1 October 2003.

Bachmann, M.O. and L.R. Booysen (2004) 'Relationship between HIV/AIDS, Income and Expenditure Over Time in Deprived South African Households,' *AIDS Care*, 16(7), 817–26.

Barnett, T. and A. Whiteside (2002) *AIDS in the Twenty-First Century: Disease and Globalization*. (Basingstoke, UK: Palgrave/Macmillan).

Bennell, P. (2005) 'The Impact of the AIDS Epidemic on the Schooling of Orphans and Other Directly Affected Children in Sub-Saharan Africa,' *Journal of Development Studies*, 41(3), 467–88.

Blinkhoff, P., E. Bukanga, B. Syamalevwe, and G. Williams (2001) *Under the Mupundu Tree: Volunteers in Home Care for People with HIV/AIDS and TB in Zambia Copperbelt*, Strategies for Hope Series No 14. (London, UK: ActionAid).

Bollinger, J. and L. Stover (1999) *The Economic Impact of AIDS in Zambia* (Washington, DC: Futures Group International).

Booysen, F. (2002) 'Financial Responses of Households in the Free State Province to HIV/AIDS-related Morbidity and Mortality,' *The South African Journal of Economics*, 70(7), 1193–215.

Bowsky, S. (2004) 'Matla ea Lesotho ke Sexhaba: Hlahlobo ea Kokelo ea Bakuli ma Haeng – Lesotho's Strength is its People: A Rapid Appraisal of Home and

Community Based Care,' Summary Report. (Durham, NC: Care Lesotho/Family Health International).

Buchan, J. and J. Sochalski (2004) 'The Migration of Nurses: Trends and Policies,' *Bulletin of the World Health Organisation*, 82(8), 587–94.

Chimwaza, A.F. and S.C. Watkins (2004) 'Giving Care to People with Symptoms of AIDS in Rural Sub-Saharan Africa,' *AIDS Care*, 16(7), 795–807.

Denis, P. and R. Ntsimane (2006) 'The Absent Fathers: Why Do Men Not Feature in the Stories of Families Affected by HIV/AIDS in KwaZulu Natal?,' in Linda Richter and Robert Morrell (eds) *BABA: Men and Fatherhood in South Africa* (Cape Town: Human Sciences Research Council Press), pp. 237–48.

Fox, S., C. Fawcett, K. Kelly and P. Ntlabati (2002) *Integrated Community-based Home Care (ICHC): A Review of the Model Implemented by the Hospice Association of South Africa* (Pretoria: Centre for AIDS Development and Evaluation).

Gow, J. and C. Desmond (2002) 'Households,' in J. Gow and C. Desmond (eds) *Impacts and Interventions: The HIV/AIDS Epidemic and the Children of South Africa* (Scotsville: UNICEF).

Hansen, K., G. Woelk, H. Jackson, R. Kerkhoven, N. Manjonjori, P. Maramba, J. Mutambirwa, E. Ndimande and E. Vera (1998) 'The Cost of Home-based Care for HIV/AIDS Patients in Zimbabwe,' *AIDS Care*, 10(6), 751–9.

Hansen, K., G. Chapman, L. Chitsike, O. Kasilo and G. Mwaluko (2000) 'The Costs of HIV/AIDS Care at Government Hospitals in Zimbabwe,' *Health Policy and Planning*, 15(4), 432–440.

HelpAge International (2004) *The Cost of Love: Older People in the Fight Against AIDS in Tanzania* (Tanzania: HelpAge International).

Kizilirmak, B. and E. Memis (2009) 'The Unequal Burden of Poverty on Time Use,' Working Paper 572 (Annandale-on-Hudson, NY: The Levy Economics Institute of Bard College).

Lindsey, E., M. Hirschfeld and S. Tlou (2003) 'Home-based Care: Experiences of Older Women and Young Girls,' *Health Care for Women International*, 24(6), 486–501.

Machipsa, L. (2001) 'Confronting HIV/AIDS: Women and Girls Bear the Burden in Zimbabwe,' *CHOICES*, 10(4), 20–1.

Makoae, M.G. and K. Jubber (2008) 'Confidentiality or Contintuity? Family Caregivers' Experiences with Care for HIV/AIDS Patients in Home-based Care in Lesotho,' *Journal of the Social Aspect of HIV/AIDS*, 5(1), 36–46.

Montgomery, C.M., V. Hosegood, J. Busza and I.M. Timaeus (2006) 'Men's Involvement in the South African Family: Engendering Change in the AIDS Era,' *Social Science and Medicine*, 62, 2411–19.

Mtika, M. (2001) 'The AIDS Epidemic in Malawi and its Threat to Household Food Security,' *Human Organisation*, 60(2), 178–88.

Mutombo, N. (2007) 'Care and Support Services for People Living with HIV/AIDS in Zambia,' *Population Review*, 46(1), 59–74.

Ngwenya, B.N. and D.L. Kgathi (2006) 'HIV/AIDS and Access to Water: A Case Study of Home-based Care in Ngamiland, Botswana,' *Physics and Chemistry of the Earth*, 31, 669–80.

Nnko, S., B. Chiduo, F. Wilson, W. Msuya and G. Mwaluko (2000) 'Tanzania: AIDS Care-Learning from Experience,' *Review of African Political Economy*, 27(86), 547–57.

Nsutebu, E.F., J.D. Walley, E. Mataka and C.F. Simon (2001) 'Scaling-up HIV/AIDS and TB Home-based Care Lesson from Zambia,' *Health Policy and Planning*, 16(3), 240–7.

Ogden, J., S. Esim and C. Grown (2004) *Expanding the Care Continuum for HIV/AIDS: Bringing Carers into Focus*. Horizons Report. (Washington, DC: Population Council and International Center for Research on Women).

Oni, S.A., C.L. Obi, A. Okorie, D. Thabede and A. Jordan (2002) 'The Economic Impact of HIV/AIDS on Rural Households in Limpopo Province,' *The South African Journal of Economics*, 70(7), 1173–91.

Orner, P. (2005) 'The Psychosocial Impact on Caregivers of People Living with AIDS: A Qualitative Study to Determine Gender, Program, and Policy Implications,' Research Report for the Medical Research Council, London.

Orner, P. (2006) 'Psychosocial Impacts on Caregivers of People Living with AIDS,' *AIDS Care*, 18(3), 236–40.

Pang, T., A. Lansang and A. Hainers (2002) 'Brain Drain and Health Professionals,' *British Medical Journal*, 324; 499–500.

Rajaraman, D., S. Russel, and J.S. Heymann (2006) 'HIV/AIDS, Income Loss and Economic Survival in Botswana,' *AIDS Care*, 18(7), 656–62.

Rajaraman, D., A. Earle and J.S. Heymann (2008) 'Working HIV Caregivers in Botswana: Spill-over Effects on Work and Family Well-being,' *Community, Work and Family*, 11(1), 1–17.

Robson, E. (2000) 'Invisible Carers: Young People in Zimbabwe's Home-based Healthcare,' *Area*, 32(1), 59–69.

Robson, E. (2004) 'Hidden Child Workers: Young Carers in Zimbabwe,' *Antipode*, 36(2), 227–48.

Rugalema, G. (1998) 'It is Not Only the Loss of Labor: HIV/AIDS, Loss of Household Assets and Household Livelihood in Bukoba District, Tanzania,' Paper presented at the East and Southern Africa Regional Conference on Responding to HIV/AIDS: Development Needs of African Smallholder Agriculture, Harare, Zimbabwe.

Russel, M. and H. Schneider (2000) *A Rapid Appraisal of Community-based HIV/AIDS Care and Support Programmes in South Africa*. A report by the Centre for Health Policy, University of Witwatersrand.

Russell, S. (2004) 'The Economic Burden of Illness for Households in Developing Countries: A Review of Studies Focusing on Malaria, Tuberculosis, and Human Immunodeficicency Virus/Acquired Immunodeficiency Syndrome,' *American Journal of Tropical Medicine and Hygiene*, 71(supplement 2), 147–55.

Samson, M.J. (2002) 'HIV/AIDS and Poverty in Households with Children Suffering from Malnutrition: The Role of Social Security in Mount Frere,' *The South African Journal of Economics*, 70(7), 1148–72.

Shaibu, S. (2006) 'Community Home-Based Care in a Rural Village: Challenges and Strategies,' *Journal of Transcultural Nursing*, 17(1), 89–94.

South African Department of Health and Department of Social Development (2001) *Integrated Home/Community Based Care Model Options* (Pretoria: DOH South Africa).

Steinberg, M., S. Johnson, G. Schierhout and D. Ndegwa (2002) *Hitting Home: How Households Cope with the Impact of the HIV/AIDS Epidemic: A Survey of Households Affected by HIV/AIDS in South Africa* (Washington, DC: Henry J. Kaiser Family Foundation and Health Systems Trust).

Steinitz, L. (2003) 'When Spider Webs Unite: The Work of Volunteers in Providing Home-based Care in Namibia,' *Journal of HIV/AIDS & Social Services*, 2(1), 45–65.

Stover, L. and J. Bollinger (1999) *The Economic Impact of AIDS in Zambia. Report for the Futures Group International.*

Tlou, S. (2000) 'The Girl Child and AIDS: The Impact of Secondary Care Giving in Rural Girls in Botswana,' Paper presented at the XIIIth International AIDS Conference, Durban.

UNAIDS (2000) *Caring for Carers: Managing Stress in Those who Care for People with HIV and AIDS* (Geneva. Joint United Nations Programme on HIV/AIDS).

—— (2004) *Report on the Global AIDS Epidemic* (Geneva: Joint United Nations Programme on HIV/AIDS).

—— (2005) *AIDS Epidemic Update* (Geneva: Joint United Nations Programme on HIV/AIDS).

—— (2008) *AIDS Epidemic Update* (Geneva: Joint United Nations Programme on HIV/AIDS and World Health Organisation).

Uys, L. (2003) 'Aspects of the Care of People with HIV/AIDS in South Africa,' *Public Health Nursing*, 20(4), 271–80.

Van Dyk, A. (2001) *HIV/AIDS Care and Counselling: A Multidisciplinary Apporach*, 2nd edn. (Cape Town: Pearson Education South Africa).

Wiegers, E., J. Curry, A. Garbero and J. Hourihan (2006) 'Patterns of Vulnerability to AIDS Impacts in Zambian Households,' *Development and Change*, 37(5), 1073–92.

Woelk, G., H. Jackson, R. Kerkhoven, K. Hansen, N. Manjonjori, P. Maramba, J. Mutambirwa, E. Ndimande, and E. Vera (1995) 'The Cost and Quality of Community Home-based Care for HIV/AIDS Patients and Their Communities in Zimbabwe,' *SAfAIDS News*, 3(3), 2–5.

World Health Organization (WHO) (2002) *Community Home-based Care in Resource-limited Settings: A Framework for Action* (Geneva: WHO).

Yamano, T. and T.S. Jayne (2004) 'Measuring the Impacts of Working-Age Adult Mortality on Small-scale Farm Households in Kenya,' *World Development*, 32(1), 91–119.

6
Public Investment and Unpaid Work in India: Selective Evidence from Time-Use Data

Lekha S. Chakraborty*

Introduction

In recent years there has been an increased awareness of the need to lift the veil of statistical invisibility that covers unpaid work. The theory of allocation of time revealed that throughout history the amount of time spent on work in the market economy has never consistently been greater than that spent at nonmarket work and other activities (Becker, 1965). Becker therefore argued that allocation and efficiency of nonmarket working time may be more important to economic welfare than that of market working time, yet the attention paid by the economists to the market economy skews any paid to latter. Time-budget data, in this context, are increasingly becoming important as they capture the burden of unpaid work (in addition to the market economy), which, in turn, has significant macropolicy implications, in particular public investment.

The time-budget data challenged the existing theories on allocation of time where time was dichotomized into market time and nonmarket time and, moreover, nonmarket time aggregates leisure and work at home. The justification for aggregating leisure and unpaid work at home into a single category rests on two assumptions: (a) the two elements react similarly to changes in socioeconomic environment and therefore nothing is gained by studying them separately; and (b) the two elements satisfy the conditions of a composite input, that is, the relative price is constant and there is no interest in investigating the composition of the aggregate since it has no bearing on production and the price of the output (Gronau, 1977). The time-budget findings did reveal that these two assumptions are wrong, as unpaid work at home and leisure are not affected in the same way by changes in socioeconomic variables and the composition of the aggregate affects many facets of the intrahousehold behavior, such as labor supply, specialization in the household and demand for children.[1] These findings from time-budget data suggest that it is preferable to tricotomize the allocation of time into work in market, work at home and leisure. Doing so has serious policy implications in integrating the unpaid work into economic modeling and, in turn, in macropolicy making. This is particularly relevant in the context of developing countries where infrastructure deficit induces locking of time in unpaid work, eroding leisure or resulting in a trade off with the time otherwise spent in the market economy activities.

The public infrastructure deficit in rural areas may enhance rural poverty due to women's time being allocated excessively towards unpaid work, time which would otherwise be available for income-earning activities. Public investment in infrastructure like water and fuel can have positive social externalities in terms of educating the girl child and improving the health and nutritional aspects of the household. Studies note that easy accessibility to drinking water facilities might lead to an increase in school enrollment, particularly for girls; in Madagascar, 83 per cent of the girls who did not go to school spent their time collecting water, while only 58 per cent of the girls who attended school spent time collecting water (Bredie and Beehary, 1998). In the light of above issues, it is important to analyze time-use statistics and value unpaid work, as it can help in providing valuable insights in fiscal policy-making especially in terms of public investment in infrastructure.

This chapter looks into the extent of statistical invisibility of unpaid work and its valuation aspects and highlights the policy alternatives, especially in reducing the infrastructure deficit through the analysis of time-use statistics in India. The chapter is divided into following sections. The section below discusses the statistical invisibility of unpaid work, while the subsequent section interprets the time-use data of selected states in India and the valuation issues related to unpaid work. The penultimate section discusses the fiscal policy issues emanating from the analysis of time-use statistics, in particular related to public investment. The final section summarizes the findings and draws conclusions.

Statistical invisibility of unpaid work

Unpaid work remains significantly invisible in national accounts. The global estimates suggest that US$16 trillion of global output is invisible and US$11 trillion is the nonmonetized, invisible contribution of women (UNDP, 1995). Although a certain degree of statistical invisibility of unpaid work in the economy is a global phenomenon, it is particularly predominant in India and other South Asian nations due to the orthodox sociocultural milieu. The attempt of United Nations Statistical Division to extend the production boundary of the SNA 1993 has led to the inclusion of the activities of unpaid work into the national accounting system as satellite accounts. This extended production boundary of SNA 1993 provides a better understanding of women's contribution to the economy.[2]

TUS have been an effective tool in unfolding the statistical invisibility of unpaid work across countries. The most reliable way of obtaining time-use data has been by the use of the time-diary method, confined to a probability sample of all types of days (weekdays and weekends) and of different seasons of the year. Time diary is a retrospective method in which the respondents are asked to keep an account of a recent 24-hour chronology of the use of time and the researchers code the responses to a standard list of activities. Time-use diaries are preferred over the other methods as they tend to be more comprehensive, they enable respondents to report activities in their own terms and they have some form of built-in check that increases the reliability of the data (Juster and Stanford, 1985). However, unless one is careful about designing a space in the diary for reporting multitasking, a part of multitasking is likely to be missed out in data collection. The possibility of this arises from the imposition of a rigid time constraint, namely, the fact that no person has either more or less time available than 24 hours per day; therefore the duration of the entire set of activities described and analyzed must add up to a fixed number of hours (24) (Floro, 1995). Theoretically, it can be solved by defining the new activity as joint activity, but the codes for possible diary activities would explode in number. The practical way of solving this problem is to indicate one activity as primary and the other as 'secondary.' Yet another way to conceptualize secondary activities is to argue that there is really only one activity at any given time, but there are frequent switches between activities and if the time grid were fine enough, the issue of secondary activities would then effectively disappear. Finally, it seems plausible that the issue of multiple or joint activities is the key source of the major failure of alternative recall methods. Recall accuracy falls when the respondents make primitive attempts to respond to questions about hours of an activity in the last week or month by engaging in a kind of *temporal double counting* – adding in periods when the activity was secondary to periods when it was central (Juster, 1985).

Time-use data helps in public policy-making at two realms: at the macrolevel and at the microlevel. At the macrolevel, time-use data

Table 6.1 Time allocation by women and men: selected industrial countries (as % of total working time)

Countries	Year	Total work time		Female		Male	
		SNA	Non-SNA	SNA	Non-SNA	SNA	Non-SNA
Industrial		49	51	34	66	66	34
Australia	1992	44	56	28	72	61	39
Canada	1987	52	48	39	61	65	35
Norway	1990/91	50	50	38	62	64	36
Denmark	1987	68	32	58	42	79	21
Netherlands	1987	35	65	19	81	52	48
USA	1985	50	50	37	63	63	37
United Kingdom	1985	51	49	37	63	68	32

Source: Compiled from Human Development Report, 1995 and 2000.

have been used in the construction of augmented economic and social accounting systems (conventional economic accounting systems provide only the productive activity in market economy and ignore the productive use of nonmarket time and leisure). At the microlevel, intrahousehold behavioral models are built using the time-use data, which have implications in terms of fiscal policy. For instance, studies have focused on the use of nonmarket time in childcare and in the care of elderly, intrahousehold division of labor, analysis of leisure activities and time stress, a set of production activities and so on (Becker, 1965).

Table 6.1 provides data on time allocation across selected developed countries. The data are not fully comparable due to the differences in concepts and methodological issues in TUS conducted across countries, which is reflected in the microdata files of time-use allocation. In the TUS, time is subdivided into work time, which is further subdivided into market work and care (household) work, personal care (dominantly sleep and rest) and a number of leisure activities. The work in the market economy is termed as SNA and the rest as non-SNA. Non-SNA activity (predominantly the extended SNA activities including those in the care economy) is as large as recorded SNA activity, both in industrial and developing countries.

In industrial countries, a little less than half of the total work time is spent in paid SNA activities and little more than half in unpaid non-SNA activities. It is interesting to note that men spend about two-thirds of the total work time in SNA activities and earn income and recognition, with only one-third of their time devoted to unpaid non-SNA activities.

Table 6.2 Time allocation by women and men: selected developing countries (as % of total working time)

Countries	Year	Total work time		Female		Male	
		SNA	Non-SNA	SNA	Non-SNA	SNA	Non-SNA
Developing		54	46	34	66	76	24
National	1990	45	55	34	66	56	44
Rep. of Korea							
Rural		59.2	40.8	37.8	62.2	76.2	23.8
Bangladesh	1990	52	48	35	65	70	30
Guatemala	1977	59	41	37	63	84	16
Keyna	1988	56	44	42	58	76	24
Nepal	1978	56	44	46	54	67	33
Highlands	1978	59	41	52	48	66	34
Mountains	1978	56	44	48	52	65	35
Rural Hills	1978	52	48	37	63	70	30
Philippines	1975–77	73	27	29	71	84	16
Urban		54.4	45.6	31	69	79.2	20.8
Columbia	1983	49	51	24	76	77	23
Indonesia	1992	60	40	35	65	86	14
Keyna	1986	46	54	41	59	79	21
Nepal	1978	58	42	25	75	67	33
Venezuela	1983	59	41	30	70	87	13
India	1998–99	–	–	19	34.6	42	3.6

Source: Compiled from Human Development Report, 1995 and 2000 and TUS, India, 2000.

The shares are reversed for women. Among industrial countries, women's share in non-SNA activities ranges from 61 per cent of total work time in Canada to 81 per cent in the Netherlands; while male's share in non-SNA activity ranges from 21 per cent in Denmark to 48 per cent in the Netherlands (Table 6.1).

Time-use data of developing countries suggests that women work significantly more hours in the non-SNA activities than men. The proportion of total time spent on the non-SNA by women in the developing countries ranges from 76 per cent in urban Columbia to 52 per cent in the mountainous region of Nepal. The proportion of time spent by men in non-SNA activities is as little as 13 per cent in urban Venezuela and 14 per cent in urban Indonesia (Table 6.2).

The Indian data is not strictly comparable with that of other countries because of different categorization of activities and time band. Furthermore, the Indian figures are based on only six states of India (Table 6.3). In India, on an average, a male spends about 42 hours per week in SNA

Table 6.3 Time allocation by women and men, selected states of India (weekly average time in hours)

States	Female			Male			Total		
	SNA	Non-SNA	Residual	SNA	Non-SNA	Residual	SNA	Non-SNA	Residual
Haryana	21.26	31.06	115.67	37.72	1.99	128.23	30.19	15.24	122.52
Madhya Pradesh	19.85	35.79	112.38	42.07	4.43	121.47	31.54	19.22	117.19
Gujarat	17.6	39.08	111.36	43.63	3.19	121.12	31.24	20.27	116.44
Orissa	17.07	35.70	115.20	40.12	4.47	123.45	28.69	19.91	119.36
Tamil Nadu	18.97	30.46	118.61	42.54	3.19	122.27	30.68	16.87	120.45
Meghalaya	26.34	34.52	107.15	45.94	7.16	114.78	35.88	21.28	110.84
Combined States	18.72	34.63	114.58	41.96	3.65	122.42	30.75	18.69	118.62

Source: CSO, TUS, 2000.

activities as compared to 19 hours by a female. However, in non-SNA activities (extended SNA activities), an average male spends only about 3.6 hours as compared to 34.6 hours by an average female.

Interpreting time-use data in India

TUS are increasingly accepted for getting better statistics on the size of the labor force of a country, as well as the contribution of women to the economy.[3] The recent major macrolevel TUS conducted in six major states, namely, Gujarat, Haryana, Madhya Pradesh, Meghalaya, Orissa and Tamil Nadu, during July 1998 to June 1999 by the Central Statistical Organization of India is a pioneering attempt not only in South Asia, but also among developing countries. This large-scale survey of 18,591 households in India gives a better understanding of how time is allocated across gender in the economy and provides some insight into the extent of statistical invisibility of women's work in India. The TUS covered all members of the household aged six years and above.

The TUS in India categorized activities into three classes: SNA activities (which comprises GDP and also includes, as per the 1993 SNA recommendations, unpaid work for water and fuel collection),[4] unpaid non-SNA activities (that do not get included in GDP, but should be included in the satellite accounts) and residual time (non-SNA activities that meet the third-party criteria such as personal care, sleep time, relaxation and so on).[5] The non-SNA category of activities in Table 6.3 can be compared to the category of extended SNA activities of the TUS conducted in India.

Table 6.4   Time-use statistics for water collection (weekly average time in hours for persons participating in the activity)

States	Rural			Urban			Total		
	Male	Female	Total	Male	Female	Total	Male	Female	Total
Haryana	3.2	5.54	5.38	3.08	4.79	4.71	3.19	5.48	5.33
Madhya Pradesh	3.21	5.4	5.03	1.21	2.96	2.76	3.11	5.22	4.88
Gujarat	14.00	0.00	14.00	0.00	0.00	0.00	14.00	0.00	14.00
Orissa	5.96	8.02	7.83	0.00	5.21	5.21	5.96	7.94	7.76
Tamil Nadu	3.85	4.79	4.69	2.56	4.62	4.26	3.33	4.74	4.57
Meghalaya	4.69	5.21	5.04	9.54	7.08	8.31	5.34	5.34	5.34
Combined States	3.83	5.11	4.97	3.02	4.63	4.35	3.61	5.02	4.85

Source: CSO, TUS, 2000.

The survey found that in the production of own-account services that qualify for inclusion in the satellite accounts as per SNA 1993, on average, a female spent 34.6 hours per week compared to 3.6 hours by a male (Table 7.3). In these activities, females in Gujarat scored the highest time spent (39.08 hours per week) on such activities, followed by Madhya Pradesh (35.79 hours) and Orissa (35.70 hours).

Specific to water-sector statistics, there is a clear link between access to water and time allocation of women, who have the primary responsibility to ensure drinking water to their households, which suggest that that changes in the availability of water infrastructure can lessen their burden in fetching the water as well as release their time locked up in care economy for the income-earning market economy activities. Table 6.4 shows the gender disaggregated statistics of time use in fetching water across selected six states in India, which clearly revealed that women spent more time in fetching water than men, except in Gujarat. Therefore infrastructure investment in water can help women in reallocating their labor time and reduce the stress related to walking long distances to fetch water.

Apart from the time allocation in the activity, it is to be noted that the travel time for fetching water, fuel and so on, is also equally time consuming. Table 6.5 provides the travel time data across states of India related to fetching water, fodder, fuel and so on, which is as high as seven to eight hours per week in Madhya Pradesh and Meghalaya as compared to around four hours in Tamil Nadu. The data revealed the gender differentials in travel time, too.

Table 6.5 Time-use statistics of travel time for collecting water, fodder and fuel (weekly average time in hours for persons participating in the activity)

States	Rural			Urban			Total		
	Female	*Male*	*Total*	*Female*	*Male*	*Total*	*Female*	*Male*	*Total*
Meghalaya	5.95	6.67	6.28	0.00	4.00	4.00	8.30	6.60	6.30
Orissa	6.93	6.63	6.78	0.50	7.68	6.98	6.70	6.90	6.80
Haryana	6.20	4.00	5.67	7.00	5.72	6.72	6.20	4.00	5.70
Madhya Pradesh	7.73	6.79	7.28	2.60	5.42	4.45	7.50	6.70	7.10
Tamil Nadu	3.83	5.44	4.30	1.20	1.70	1.44	3.30	4.20	3.60
Gujarat	5.45	5.78	5.57	7.60	42.00	39.15	5.50	11.00	7.80

Source: CSO, TUS, 2000.

Table 6.6 Value of unpaid work as compared to state domestic product

States	Value of unpaid work (Rs. crores)			SDP (Rs. crores)	'Unpaid work' as a % of SDP		
	Male	*Female*	*Total*	*1997–98*	*Male*	*Female*	*Total*
Haryana	928.74	10,209.30	11,138.04	37,427	2.48	27.28	29.76
Madhya Pradesh	4,466.03	29,034.09	33,500.12	70,832	6.31	40.99	47.30
Gujarat	2,209.55	22,577.63	24,787.18	86,609	2.55	26.07	28.62
Orissa	1,463.78	11,343.88	12,807.65	32,669	4.48	34.72	39.20
Tamil Nadu	3,073.37	19,922.04	22,995.40	87,394	3.52	22.80	26.31
Meghalaya	260.45	862.97	1,123.42	2,250	11.58	38.35	49.93

Source: NIPFP (2000).

Before discussing the public investment issues, the valuation of unpaid work and its proportion to state domestic product (SDP) is given in Table 6.6.[6] In theoretical literature, there are two main approaches to the valuation of the unpaid work: (i) the input-related method, based on imputing value to labor time spent on unpaid work; and (ii) the output-related method, based on imputing market prices to goods and services produced (for example, imputing market price to the fuel wood collected, homemade utensils and so on).[7] From the perspective of accounting for unpaid work, input-related accounting is superior to output-related accounting. For example, if women have to walk longer to fetch water, input-related accounting will show an increase in the time input, though there is no increase in output. Thus, the intensified effort of women is valued in input-related accounting. The results from the input-related global substitute method (improvised) for valuing the unpaid work in India are given in Table 6.6.

District-wise data on wage rates for agricultural labor and wage rates for urban unskilled manual labor have been used for valuing unpaid work in rural and urban areas, respectively. With this methodology, projecting the TUS results by age-wise, district-wise population, valuation of time spent on unpaid activities by females in Gujarat and Haryana indicates that the value of unpaid activities could be as much as 26–28 per cent of the relevant SDP. For example, the total value of such activities by females was Rs22,578 crore and Rs10,209 crore in Gujarat and Haryana, respectively, relative to SDP of Rs86,609 crore and Rs37,427 crore in these two states (Table 6.6). Compared to females, the valuation of unpaid activities by males was limited to only about 2–3 per cent of SDP in these two states. The unpaid work, as a proportion of SDP, is as high as 49.93 per cent in Meghalaya and 47 per cent in Madhya Pradesh.

Implications of time-use statistics for public investment

Fiscal policy, in particular the capital expenditure in infrastructure, can redress the time burden of women in unpaid work and release their time for market economy activities, which can earn them a livelihood or otherwise increase their leisure and well-being. Fiscal policy interventions in terms of infrastructure can lead to substitution effects in time allocation of women from the care economy to the market economy, which has implications for reducing the poverty in the household and also for enhancing the education and health status of the household. Therefore the analysis of time-use statistics can help in formulating better fiscal policies in terms of infrastructure requirements. Infracture development deficits vary across regions and, again, time-use statistics can be revealing. There is a need to ensure *complementary fiscal services* for better gender-sensitive human development as gender related issues cut across sectors. Time-use statistics can reveal, for instance, the fact that investing in water supply infrastructure may improve the enrollment of girl children in school.

The time-use statistics can be useful in formulating macropolicies in terms of public investment in three realms: at *ex ante* expenditure interventions, *ex post* expenditure incidence analysis and in public service delivery.

Ex ante interventions in terms of public investment

In case of *ex ante* expenditure interventions, Sen's capability approach provides an advanced analytical framework over mainstream economic

welfare criteria and its overemphasis on GDP.[8] It has brought attention
to a much wider range of issues on people's well-being than in earlier
economic planning and budgeting. However, the scope of time-budget
statistics in identifying the capability deprivation and related functioning across gender has been an underresearched area. In terms of public
investment, Sen's capability approach points to three crucial layers that
need interpretation in the context of time use, unpaid work, and macro-
polices. These crucial layers are capabilities, functioning and commodi-
ties. The first step is to propose a list of basic capabilities. Basic capabilities
can be a set of capabilities that should have only a few elements and this
set is common for all individuals. These capabilities can be capability to
stay alive and live long, capability to lead a healthy life, capability to
have knowledge, capability to have social interaction and so on.

The second step would be to gather relevant information on those *functionings* that are observable (gender disaggregated to the largest possible
extent). In this step of listing the functionings, the data from time-use
budgets needs to be incorporated along with life expectancy, age-specific
mortality rates, literacy rate, nutritional disadvantage, enrollment ratio,
participation in governance process, and so on (Table 6.7). Time-use
statistics provide a gamut of functionings that are more revealing in
terms of capability deprivation.

The third step is to estimate the optimal *commodity space*, especially
the fiscal policy stance in terms of public investment, which is necessary
to be at an individual's command to match commodity characteristics
and capability requirements and then to analyze the actual commodity
space to identify the gaps. For instance, in terms of public investment in
water supply, time-use statistics revealed the extent of the requirement
of infrastructure across regions and, in turn, its impact on capabilities
across gender.

Ex post incidence analysis of public investment

Theoretically, there are two approaches to analyzing the distributional
impacts of public expenditure: benefit incidence studies and behavioral
approaches. The behavioral approach is based on the notion that a
rationed publicly provided good or service should be evaluated at the
individual's own valuation of the good, which Demery (2000) called a
'virtual price.' Such prices will vary from individual to individual. This
approach emphasizes the measurement of individual preferences for the
publicly provided goods. The methodical complications in the valuation of revealed preferences based on the microeconomic theory and the
paucity of unit record data related to the knowledge of the underlying

Table 6.7 Relating Sen's capability framework to time-use budgets, non-market work and investment

Capabilities	Functioning*	Commodity space (in terms of fiscal stance)
Capability to stay alive and live long	1. Life expectancy 2. Time use and percent access to water and sanitation 3. Time use and percent access to health infrastructure, including travel time 4. PEM malnutrition 5. IMR/CMR/sex ratio 6. Time-stress data (non-SNA activity)	1. Food security 2. Infrastructure policies in terms of water, fuel and sanitation 3. Environmental policies 4. Immunization/nutrition programs
Capability to have knowledge	1. Gross enrollment ratio 2. Time use of child on care economy and schooling 3. Time-use budgets of unpaid work of school-going children 4. Literacy rate/drop-out rate/completion rate	1. Education policy with complementary fiscal services, viz., water infrastructure projects
Capability for social/economic activity	1. Mobility: travel time in time-use statistics for economic activities, paid and unpaid 2. Security and safety 3. Time-use budgets in community activities (including participatory process of building local infrastructure)	1. Public transport system 2. Better road infrastructure 3. Public safety and security (law and order)
Capability to earn livelihood	1. Work participation rate, estimated from time-use statistics 2. Time use in care economy activities (dual burden) 3. Time-poverty data	1. Employment policies 2. Microfinance programs
Capability to communicate/ decision making/governance	1. Time use in participation in decision making 2. Time use statistics in governance of publicly provided services	1. Policies for decentralized provisioning of public services with client participatory approach

Note: *The list of capabilities, functionings and commodity space is open-ended.

demand functions of individuals or households led to less practicability of the behavioral approaches in estimating the distributional impact of public expenditure. However, time-use data can provide insights into the estimation of efficiency of public expenditure based on perceived measurement of individual preferences for publicly provided goods.

The second approach, benefit incidence analysis (BIA), is a relatively simple and practical method for estimating distributional impact of public expenditure across different demographic and socioeconomic groups. The genesis of this approach lies in the path-breaking work by Meerman (1979) on Malaysia and Selowsky (1979) on Colombia. BIA involves allocating *unit cost* according to individual utilization rates of public services. BIA can identify how well public services are targeted to certain groups in the population across gender, income quintiles and geographical units. The studies on BIA revealed that a disproportionate share of the health budget benefits the elite in urban areas, or that the major part of the education budgets benefit the schooling of boys rather than girls, which has important policy implications. However, BIA studies have been largely confined to education and health sectors due to the comparative richness of unit utilized data from the secondary sources. To analyze the distributional impact of public expenditure on water supply and energy is difficult to undertake at the macrolevel due to paucity of data on units utilized. The point to be noted here is that time-use statistics may provide these data on unit utilized of other social sector expenditure.

Following Demery (2000), there are four basic steps towards calculating benefit incidence.

Estimating unit cost

The unit cost of a publicly provided good is estimated by dividing the total expenditure on that particular publicly provided good by the total number of users of that good. This is synonymous to the notion of per capita expenditure, but the denominator is confined to the subset of population who are the users of the public good. For instance, the unit cost of the elementary education sector is total primary education spending per primary enrollment, while the unit cost of the health sector could be total outpatient hospital spending per outpatient visit.

The unit cost of the water sector is estimated through a two-fold procedure. Using the finance accounts data, we have estimated the revenue and capital expenditure of major rural and urban water supply schemes across selected states in India. The net expenditure on rural and urban water supply is derived by deducting the cost recoveries from the total expenditure.

Identifying the users

Usually the information on the users of publicly provided goods is obtained from household surveys with the standard dichotomy of data into poor and non-poor, male- and female-headed households, rural and urban and so on. We have attempted an illustrative calculation of gender disaggregated benefit incidence for water supply from unit utilization data using TUS, applying the time budget ratio of persons involved in fetching of water across gender to the rural and urban population separately. The derived unit utilized data revealed that more women engage in collection of water than men across states. Gujarat is exempted from the analysis of benefit incidence due to restrictions related to the sample engaged in the fetching of water as per time-use data under code 140 of economic activity. These ratios obtained from the TUS are applied to the mid-year estimates of decennial census figures of the rural and urban population of these states, adjusted for the age group to above five years.

Aggregating users into groups

It is important to aggregate individuals or households into groups to estimate how the benefits from public spending are distributed across the population. Empirical evidence has shown that the most frequent method of grouping is based on income quintiles or MPCE quintiles. The aggregation of users based on income or MPCE quintiles could reveal whether the distribution of public expenditure is progressive or regressive. As the TUS of India does not provide data on users by quintiles, we have only a broad grouping of users categorized into states. After categorizing the unit utilized based on geography, we created yet another set of significant groups based on gender units. Though spatial differentials in the public expenditure delivery cannot be fully captured through the rural–urban dichotomy, it can provide broad policy pointers with regard to the distributional impact of publicly provided goods across rural and urban India. We have attempted yet another significant grouping based on gender, after categorizing the unit utilized based on geographical units. The grouping of users based on gender is often ignored in studies on benefit incidence analysis. The derived unit utilized data based on rural–urban disaggregations and gender disaggregation are given in Table 6.8.

Calculating the benefit incidence

Benefit incidence is computed by combining information about the *unit costs* of providing the publicly provided good with information on the *use* of these goods (which is obtained from the TUS of households).

Table 6.8 Deriving unit utilized data on water supply from time-use budgets (%)

	Rural		Urban		Total	
	Male	Female	Male	Female	Male	Female
Meghalaya	31.08	68.92	40.00	60.00	33.08	66.92
Orissa	7.14	92.86	–	100.00	6.67	93.33
Haryana	6.58	93.42	7.69	92.31	6.71	93.29
Madhya Pradesh	16.17	83.83	14.63	85.37	15.99	84.01
Tamil Nadu	10.41	89.59	13.32	86.68	11.23	88.77
Gujarat	100.00	0.00	–	–	100.00	0.00
Combined	13.42	86.58	17.07	82.93	14.23	85.77

Source: Basic Data, TUS, India (2000).

Mathematically, benefit incidence is estimated by the following formula:

$$X_j \equiv \sum_i U_{ij}(S_i/U_i) \equiv \sum_i (U_{ij}/U_i)S_i \equiv \sum_i e_{ij}S_i$$

where X_j = sector specific subsidy enjoyed by group j;

U_{ij} = utilization of service i by group j;

U_i = utilization of service i by all groups combined;

S_i = government net expenditure on service i; and

e_{ij} = group j's share of utilization of service i.

The unit cost for rural and urban provisioning of water supply is obtained from the public expenditure on rural water supply schemes separately normalized to the derived global unit utilized.[9] The estimates of BIA for rural areas across states is given in Figure 6.1. The gender disaggregated benefit incidence results need to be interpreted with caution, as the higher per capita benefit incidence of water for women *per se* does not translate into women having higher distributional incidence in regards to water than men. It requires a judicious interpretation that as women are involved in fetching of water more than men, the incidence figures became higher for women than men. These results can give policy signaling in the sense that higher provisioning of water can benefit women, as ensuring clean water is the primary responsibility of women in the household across states in rural India.

The spatial differences in the distributional incidence of water ranges from Haryana and Meghalaya being the highest to Orissa being the lowest. This benefit incidence in per capita terms is closely correlated to

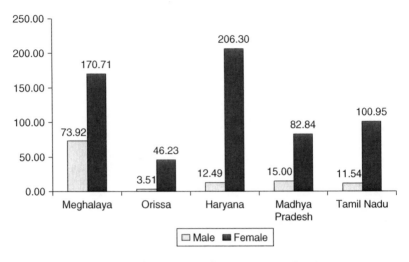

Figure 6.1   Per capita benefit incidence of rural water supply scheme

the time-use budgets. As discussed in the above section the time budgets of women in Haryana and Meghalaya are much higher than that
of other states, Orissa being the lowest. In terms of public investment,
there is an increasing recognition of direct policy interventions in reducing gender gaps to alleviate poverty, especially in terms of reducing their
unpaid work burden related to deficit in public infrastructure. This can
release their time for more market-oriented activities that help them in
earning income for the household. Fiscal policy redresses inequalities
in the intrahousehold division of labor by providing infrastructure that
can reduce the time allocation of women spent in unpaid care economy
work. Such policy interventions can be in terms of improved water supply and sanitation services, along with better transport infrastructure,
rural electrification and better access to fuel. The significance of infrastructure in redressing gender equities and promoting development needs
to be incorporated in framing water policies and energy policies.

This is particularly significant in the context of the fact that public
investment in water supply and sanitation across selected states is only
around 2–4 per cent of the total expenditure, except for Meghalaya,
where it is around 6 per cent, as is given in Table 6.9.

A caveat must be mentioned at this point. Our assumption is that
a higher expenditure on water supply results in better access of people/
women to water supply. This is not always true in India, as in many

Table 6.9 Share of public expenditure on water supply and sanitation in selected states in India (%)

States	1999–2000			2000–2001			2001–2002			2002–2003		
	Plan	Non-plan	Total	Plan	Non-plan	Total	Plan	Non-plan	Total	Plan	Non-plan	Total
Gujarat	10.23	0.49	3.12	14.15	0.83	4.06	7.75	0.40	1.76	8.49	0.44	2.27
Haryana	6.90	3.43	4.24	6.78	2.88	3.77	9.02	3.04	4.25	6.74	2.91	3.73
Madhya Pradesh	6.93	1.59	2.78	6.60	1.64	2.83	5.54	1.27	2.59	4.76	1.49	2.66
Meghalaya	10.76	3.93	6.15	10.21	4.02	6.41	11.80	3.87	7.00	12.57	4.21	7.58
Orissa	5.28	1.37	2.41	4.99	0.94	2.00	4.51	0.92	1.75	4.53	0.78	1.77
Tamil Nadu	1.41	0.04	0.29	9.97	0.07	2.08	10.50	0.04	2.04	7.42	0.03	1.81

Source: Finance Accounts (various issues).

developing countries. This is because: (1) different regions have different requirements depending on the specific geohydrological conditions and therefore different expenditure needs; (2) in many cases public expenditure on water supply provides temporary or nonsustainable solutions, with the result that the expenditure does not ensure sustainable water supply (Lodhia and Raval, 2008); and (3) there are leakage as well as inefficiencies in implementing water related programs. These data therefore need to be read keeping in mind this limitation.

Provisioning of public infrastructure

Provisioning of public goods is equally as important as investment in public goods. High budgetary allocation *per se* does not necessarily ensure quality in delivery of public goods. Provisioning of public goods can be better assessed through the client participatory approach. The time-use data disaggregated for the community level voluntary activities across gender can capture the time allocation in the participatory process of provisioning of public goods. For instance, the time-use statistics of participation in infrastructure building and maintenance can be collated from code 611 of the TUS, which is mainly the unpaid work related to public infrastructure. The link between the involvement of clients in the public provisioning of services and the quality of provisioning, *prima facie*, appears to be positively related. The time-use statistics may provide some valuable information regarding the hypothesis including spatial and gender differentials. This analysis is particularly important when the quality of infrastructure investment, apart from the quantity, also affects the time allocation of women. The positive externalities of infrastructure investment go beyond the efficiency in the production boundary to improvements in the standard of living and, therefore, the well-being of the household. The higher the public investment in infrastructure in water and sanitation, the higher the health and education status of children in the household. Increased access to public delivery of water can improve the health status of children, as the quality of water will be better than the other available sources of water in the rural areas. Given existing is evidence that girl children help their mothers in fetching water, public investment in water supply infrastructure can also release the time of girls to attend school or participate in income-generating activities.

Link between public infrastructure and time allocation: empirical evidence

It is often argued that mainstream expenditure, such as public infrastructure, is nonrival in nature and applying a gender lens to these public expenditures is not feasible. This argument is refuted by the time-budget statistics. The time-budget data revealed that this argument is often flawed, as there is an intrinsic gender dimension to the nonrival expenditure. The time allocation in activities like fetching of water and fuel involves more girls and women, so infrastructure investment with gender-sensitive water and energy policies can really benefit women.

Prima facie, increase in public investment in infrastructure is negatively related to the time-burden of women in fetching of water and fuel. There can be possibilities of substitutability between unpaid work and market work by women through increased investment in infrastructure by government. There can be a link between deterioration in infrastructure and rural poverty. In terms of fiscal policies to redress poverty, the aspect of *time poverty* is often forgotten. Time poverty affects income poverty. Fiscal policies designed to redress income poverty can be partial if they do not take into account the aspects of time poverty. This policy discussion has a gender dimension, as women are time poor and fiscal policies designed for poverty alleviation need to incorporate the time allocation aspects across gender.[10] In this section, we undertake an empirical investigation of these issues in the context of India using the data of the TUS and finance accounts. However, the time-use data across income quintiles is not available in India, so the poverty-related aspects of time allocation across gender and their implications for public investment cannot be analyzed.

The empirical investigation of the link between public infrastructure and time allocation related to water supply requires comprehensive time-use data either in terms of longitudinal surveys or across considerable cross-section units. An illustrative analysis is undertaken to examine the link between infrastructure and time allocation within the data constraints of 12 cross-section units of time-use data conducted for rural and urban regions of six states of India.[11] The direction of regression coefficients suggests that fiscal policy interventions in terms of public infrastructure investment affect market work, nonmarket work and leisure time in different ways. The gender-differentiated effects of public infrastructure are also evident in the results summarized in Table 6.10. The results, though tentative due to data constraints, give certain broad inferences in terms of policy suggestions. The results revealed that investment in public infrastructure has effects in terms of travel time related to collection of water rather than in terms of the time allocation in the activity, per se, or the number of persons involved in the activity; moreover, the effects are significant only in the case of women.

Table 6.10   Public infrastructure and time allocation link: sign of regression coefficients

	Female	Male	Total
Time allocation	−	−	−
Number of persons involved in activity	+	−	−
Travel time	−*	−	−
SNA	−*	−	+
Extended SNA	−	+	−
Non-SNA	+ *	−	−

Note: Denotes significant regression coefficients.
Source: Finance Accounts and TUS, 2000 (basic data).

The time allocation of women in SNA activities of women is found to be inversely related to the public infrastructure. This result indicates that better infrastructure can lessen the unpaid SNA work of women. But there is no evidence that the release of time locked up in the unpaid SNA work of collecting water has a substitution effect towards market work. This gets further reinforced by the positive link between infrastructure and time allocation in non-SNA activity. It is to be noted that a rise in the time allocation in non-SNA work for women is *forced leisure* due to the paucity of opportunities in terms of employment. The policy suggestion arising from this analysis is that infrastructure investment lessens the time stress of women in unpaid SNA activity, but complementary employment guarantee policies are required along with infrastructure investment to ensure the substitution effect of unpaid work with market work, which, in turn, can have impact on household poverty. Time poverty affects income poverty, but infrastructure in tandem with employment policies are required for redressing the capability deprivation of the household. The point to be noted here is that employment guarantee policies without sufficient public investment in infrastructure can be equally flawed, as women are time poor and better infrastructural facilities are required to release the time locked up in the unpaid activities to have a smooth transition towards market economy.

Summary and policy conclusions

This chapter examined the link between public infrastructure investment and time allocation across gender in the context of selected states in India. The direction of the regression coefficients suggests that public infrastructure investment affects market work, nonmarket work and leisure time in different ways, with evident gender differentials. The time allocation in the SNA activity of women is found to be significant and inversely related to the public infrastructure related to water supply. But there is no evidence that the release of time locked up in unpaid SNA work through better infrastructure can have a substitution effect towards market work. This gets further reinforced by the significant positive link between infrastructure and time allocation in non-SNA activity, which manifests *forced leisure* in the context of India. The policy suggestion arising from the analysis is that although infrastructure investment lessens the time stress in unpaid SNA activity, complementary employment policies are required along with infrastructure investment to ensure the substitution effect of unpaid work with market work, which, in turn, can have an impact on household poverty.

In particular, the time-use statistics of water revealed that they are significantly higher for girls in both rural and urban areas, which, in turn, points to the deficiency in adequate infrastructure in water and sanitation. It has significant fiscal policy implications, as easy accessibility to drinking water facilities might lead to an increase in school enrollment, particularly for girls, by reducing the time utilized for fetching water. In other words, time-budget statistics enable the identification of the *complementary fiscal services* required for better gender-sensitive human development.

This paper also suggests that there is a need to integrate time budgets in *ex ante* expenditure interventions (Sen's capability approach, Table 6.7) and also for *ex post* benefit incidence analysis using *unit utilized* data from time budgets.

The overall conclusion of this chapter is that fiscal policies designed to redress income poverty can be partial if they do not take in to account aspects of *time poverty*. This paper is confined only to the SNA sector in terms of paid and unpaid work and their implications for fiscal policy. The analysis of extended SNA activities in the *care economy* and their implications for public investment is an area for future research.

Notes

* The author is a Fellow at National Institute of Public Finance and Policy, India and a Research Associate at The Levy Economics Institute of Bard College. This is the revised version of the paper presented at UNDP Bureau for Development Policy-Levy Conference on 'Unpaid Work and the Economy: Gender, Poverty and the Millennium Development Goals' at The Levy Economics Institute of Bard College, New York, 1–3 October 2005. The author sincerely acknowledges the comments from Diane Elson, Rania Antonopoulos, Indira Hirway,

Rathin Roy, Mark Blackden and Pinaki Chakraborty. The usual disclaimer applies.

1. Gronau (1976), in the context of Israel, empirically analyzed the determinants of time allocation of market work, non-market work and leisure.

2. The 1993 SNA however limits economic production of households for their own consumption to the production of goods alone, and excludes the own-account production of personal and domestic services (except for the services produced by employing paid domestic staff and the own-account production of housing services produced by employing paid domestic staff and the own account production of housing services by owner occupants). This allows the SNA to avoid valuing activities such as eating, drinking and sleeping, which are difficult for a person to obtain from another person. But, in the process, activities such as fetching water from the river or the well, collecting fuel wood, washing clothes, house cleaning, preparation and serving of meals, care, training and instruction of children and care of sick, infirm or old people also get excluded from the definition of economic activity. These services are mostly performed by women, but can also be procured from other units. While these activities are excluded partly because of the inadequate price systems for valuing these services, this exclusion principle leads to the economic invisibility and a statistical underestimation of women's work.

3. A major finding of TUS across the globe is that women carry a disproportionately greater burden of work than men. Since women are responsible for a greater share of non-SNA work in the care economy, they enter the labor market already overburdened with work. This dual work burden or unequal sharing of work borne by women is neither recognized in the data nor considered adequately in socioeconomic policy-making.

4. For details on SNA and non-SNA production categories see chapter 1 in this volume.

5. In Tables 6.1 and 6.2, non-SNA and residual time have been aggregated as non-SNA; while for Indian data in Table 6.3.

6. SNA 1993 suggests development of estimates for the value of household production of services for own use in satellite accounts of an alternative concept of GDP. Estimation of the 'unpaid' work of women can suggest a quantification of the contribution of women to the economy. The quantification can also be useful for two more reasons. First, it would provide a fuller understanding of how resources and time are allocated in the economy. Second, it allows for a more accurate assessment in regards to increases in standard of living that are truly the result of market-oriented economic growth. It is quite misleading to interpret the marketization of goods purchased for home consumption as a new improvement in standard of living if, for example, the same items were previously the result of home production.

7. The major problem related to the input-related approach is to decide which value to impute to labor time. Three methods have been used for this purpose. The global substitute method uses the cost of a hired worker, paid to carry out the different tasks in the care economy. The specialized substitute method uses the costs of a specialized worker that would perform each specific task according to his/her specialization. The opportunity cost method is based on the wage that the person carrying out the domestic work would receive if she/he worked in the market. Each method suffers from its own

merits and demerits. The global substitute method tends to underestimate unpaid work, as it uses the wages at the lower end of the wage category. On the contrary, specialized substitute method tends to overestimate the unpaid work though they are more indicative of its market value. The opportunity cost method, on the other hand, tends to generate the widest range of estimates, depending on the skills and the opportunity wage of the individuals performing it (Beneria, 1992).

8. The capability approach has been central to the Human Development Reports series (HDR) launched by UNDP in the 1990s by Sen's close associate, the late Mahbub ul Haq, and has subsequently influenced policy at the World Bank during the Wolfensohn era (Gasper, 2002). It provided a channel for alternative economic development thinking, which goes beyond the undue emphasis on economic growth – as in the economic planning of 1970s and its trickling down effects. It revealed that GDP (economic growth) was never suited to be a measure of well-being, as it conceals extreme deprivation for large parts of the population.

9. The finance accounts data across states provide the expenditure disaggregated by urban and accelerated rural water supply schemes under revenue and capital accounts. However, some negligible schemes on water supply under 'others' category are not used in the analysis due to the problem in segregating into rural and urban. The per capita benefit incidence of urban water supply schemes has been calculated for Meghalaya, Haryana, Madhya Pradesh and Tamil Nadu, though not reported. The estimates showed similar patterns across gender to that of rural areas.

10. For instance, public policies on microfinance designed to address income poverty cannot have a full impact unless time-poverty issues are addresses simultaneously.

11. The chapter has depended on several assumptions while analyzing the links between the time spent on water collection and public investment in infrastructure, largely due to the paucity of data. However, such assumptions are inevitable given the availability of the data. The need for an updated TUS for not only six states, but for all states of India, is emphasized. From a macroeconomic policy perspective, it is important to integrate TUS into the statistical system of India.

References

Becker, G.S. (1965) 'A Theory of the Allocation of Time,' *Economic Journal*, 75(299), 493–517.

Beneria, L. (1992) 'Accounting for Women's Work: The Progress of Two Decades,' *World Development*, 20(11), 1547–60.

Bredie, J. and G. Beehary (1998) 'School Enrolment Decline in Sub-Saharan Africa,' Discussion Paper No. 395 (Washington, DC: World Bank).

Central Statistical Organisation (2000) *Report of the TUS* (New Delhi: Ministry of Statistics and Programme Implementation, Government of India).

Demery, L. (2000) 'Benefit Incidence: A Practitioner's Guide,' Poverty and Social Development. Group (mimeo). (Washington, DC: World Bank).

Floro, M.S. (1995) 'Economic Restructuring, Gender and the Allocation of Time,' *World Development*, 23(11), 1913–29.

Gasper, D. (2002) 'Is Sen's Capability Approach an Adequate Basis for Considering Human Development?,' *Review of Political Economy*, 14(4), 435–61.

Gronau, R. (1973) 'The Intrafamily Allocation of Time: The Value of the Housewives' Time,' *American Economic Review*, 63(4), 634–41.

Gronau, R. (1976) 'The Allocation of Time of Israeli Women,' *Journal of Political Economy*, 84(4), S201–20.

Gronau, R. (1977) 'Leisure, Home Production and the Theory of the Allocation of Time Revisited,' *Journal of Political Economy*, 85(6), 1099–1123.

Hirway, I. (2000) 'Tabulation and Analysis of the Indian TUS Data for Improving Measurement of Paid and Unpaid Work,' United Nations Statistical Division, http://unstats.un.org/unsd/methods/timeuse/xptgrpmeet/hirway.pdf

Juster, F.T. and F. Stanford (1985) *Time Goods and Well-Being* (Ann Arbor, MI: Institute for Social Research, University of Michigan).

Juster, F.T. and F. Stanford (1991) 'The Allocation of Time: Empirical Findings, Behavioral Models, and Problems of Measurement,' *Journal of Economic Literature*, 29(2), 471–522.

Lahiri, A., L. Chakraborty, and P.N. Bhattacharryya (2002) 'Gender Budgeting in India,' Discussion Paper. [New Delhi: National Institute of Public Finance and Policy (NIPFP)], http://www.nipfp.org.in/genderbudgetlink.asp.

Lodhia, S. and A. Rava (2008) *Slippage in Water Services in India* (Ahmedabad: CFDA and Netherlands: IRC).

Meerman, J. (1979) *Public Expenditures in Malaysia: Who Benefits and Why?* (New York: Oxford University Press).

NIPFP (2000) 'Women's Contribution to the Economy through Their Unpaid Household Work,' Discussion Paper Series (New Delhi: NIPFP).

Pollak, R.A. and M.L. Wachter (1975) 'The Relevance of the Household Production Function and its Implications for Allocation of Time,' *Journal of Political Economy*, 83(2), 255–77.

Selowsky, M. (1979) *Who Benefits from Government Expenditure?* (New York: Oxford University Press).

Sen, G. and C. Sen (1984) 'Women's Domestic Work and Economic Activity: Results from the National Sample Survey,' Working Paper No. 197. (Thiruvananthapuram, India: Centre for Development Studies).

United Nations Development Programme (UNDP) (1995) *Human Development Report* (New York: UNDP).

7
Unpaid Work and Unemployment: Engendering Public Job Creation

Rania Antonopoulos *

Introduction

A great paradox of too much unemployment and plenty of unpaid work confronts countries around the world. While large numbers of the population are condemned to forced idleness at the moment, TUS data reveals that women, and especially poor women and children in developing countries, spend long hours performing unpaid work to sustain their families and communities.

It is by now well documented that the distribution of unpaid work is characterized by gender asymmetries. When the differences are taken on an annual basis, the result is that women perform between twenty days and up to three and a half months of unpaid work, depending on the particular country. This is the case in developing and developed countries alike.[1] A further disturbing finding is that households subjected to high levels of poverty and joblessness devote substantially greater amounts of time to unpaid work. Yet, even in cases where all household members are unemployed, intrahousehold gender inequalities in unpaid work become even more accentuated to women's disadvantage (Antonopoulos, 2007, 2008).

In this context, it is worth noting that, historically, the above patterns are exacerbated during periods of economic turbulence. On the one hand, unemployment and declining personal income reduce the purchasing power of households, while on the other, with an overall decline in economic activity government revenues are squeezed, resulting in decreasing sources for financing public provisioning. In these circumstances decreased work is relied upon to, as best as it can, fill in newly created gaps. With the 2008 subprime mortgage crisis in the United States spreading to all parts of the world and transforming itself

163

into a severe worldwide recession and job crisis, there is good reason for renewed concern.

Chapter 1 of this book discussed, among other issues, the need to use a gender lens to make visible the disadvantages women face in allocating time disproportionately on unpaid work. Such a lens is also needed in en-'gendering' a specific government policy gaining currency amidst responses to the economic crisis as part of stimulus packages, namely, *direct public job creation*. It will be argued that a framework should be adopted that makes the importance of unpaid work *visible*.

This chapter is organized as follows: The next section introduces some key ideas that link unpaid work, poverty and the economy; the following section discusses direct job creation policy with the idea of the state acting as the employer of last resort (ELR); the subsequent section deals with gender dimensions of employment guarantee programs, highlighting the need for a gender-aware, unpaid-work focus of public job creation; the penultimate section presents empirical findings from a case study recently completed that documents the positive outcomes of *social sector* public works projects. The final section concludes.

Unpaid work, the economy and poverty

Unpaid work consists of a wide range of activities such as subsistence production, unpaid family work contributions in small businesses and agriculture and collection of free goods to be processed and transformed into consumable meals or to produce items for eventual sale in the market. It also encompasses the everyday routine household production and maintenance work, such as cooking, cleaning, shopping and caring for family and community. Unpaid work takes place not only at home, but also in public spaces. For example, the provisioning of home-based care due to shortened hospital stays and the caring of patients in hospitals due to lack of nurse-aides, sanitation personnel, cooks, and so on, are the domains of unpaid work. Women, primarily, must find the time to provide this unpaid care, often by reducing time previously allocated to types of activities involving, more specifically, paid employment and subsistence production, as is the case in sub-Saharan Africa and in the context of high infection rates of HIV/AIDS (Akintola, 2004).

Although some unpaid work is based on feelings of care, obligation and reciprocity, time spent performing unpaid work has also been conceptualized as systemically linked to the rest of the economy in complex ways. For instance, it can be thought of as a 'subsidy' to the *public sector,* providing services to those in need at no cost to the state (Picchio, 2003); it may also be considered as providing a 'gift,' transferred from some household members to the *market* because it contributes – at no charge – to the daily maintenance and rejuvenation of the labor force and the raising of the next cohort of workers (Folbre, 1994, 2001). The fact that some, though not all, unpaid activities may be embedded in feelings of love and care does not alter the structural function unpaid work performs within the economy. The point here is that there are *redistributional effects.* As unpaid work absorbs the costs other sectors of the economy would have to incur, the 'workers' performing these activities are unremunerated, unprotected, undervalued and unrecognized. They coutribute to the economy but invisible as they are, remain nonetheless intertwined with the rest of the economy.

This becomes clearer if one thinks of the counterfactual. In the absence of household production of goods and services, most activities currently performed via unpaid work would either have to become socialized or made available for purchase in the market. 'Socializing' means spreading the cost of activities for provisioning of goods and services over the entire economy. This entails an expanded welfare state function, which, in turn, would make necessary the collection of new tax revenue. In other words, the structure of taxation would have to be altered to expand physical infrastructure and delivery of services with clear distributional implications.

This would be possible only for countries with the capacity to expand their fiscal space. Many developing countries would be hard-pressed to accomplish that. With limited sources of earning foreign exchange, multiple obligations to international lending institutions and balance of payments concerns, this state of affairs dictates, more often than not, restrictions on fiscal expenditures and limitations in deficit spending. In either case, as it now stands, unpaid work subsidizes what the state is not providing for: that is, collecting water in the absence of water delivery systems; performing arduous and unpleasant sanitation work due to lack of proper waste and drainage infrastructure; and taking care of the permanently ill and those unable to care for themselves due to insufficient levels of dedicated budgetary allocations to health.

Alternatively, to make the purchase of market-based goods and services possible, wages would have to increase across the board. This would imply a different sharing arrangement of total national output, changing the functional distribution of income – a larger proportion being shifted to wages paid to employed persons and a lesser fraction going to profits for the entrepreneurial sector.

Consequently, labor costs of production would rise, with some complicated effects leading to structural changes in production. These changes would, for example, reduce profits for some sectors while enlarging them for others. With higher wages, many service industries would flourish and new ones would spring up. After-school programs, full-time eldercare, early childhood development, preparation of cooked meals, laundry and housecleaning services would have to be provided somehow.

It is in this sense that arguments portraying unpaid work as a 'subsidy' and 'gift' merit full consideration. The corollary to the above argument is that during periods of economic turbulence, retrenchment in the public sector (due to reduced revenues) and reduced household incomes (due to unemployment, underemployment and wage stagnation) are certain to increase unpaid work requirements.

In the context of development, we must also pay attention to the disproportional vulnerability[2] of some segments of the population to poverty, which is linked to the gendered division of labor in paid and unpaid work through another channel. Although not the case in every single country, the majority of the world's poor (1.4 billion people) are women. This is an important, yet complicated, issue, but it is beyond the scope of this chapter; it suffices to say that this is linked to the fact that women are overrepresented in unpaid family work. In 2006, in South Asia, 62.6 per cent of women were working as unpaid family members while the corresponding figure for men was 16.2 per cent; in East Asia, it is 20.9 versus 12.8; in the Middle East and North Africa the rates are 28.4 per cent and 11.9 per cent, respectively and in sub-Saharan Africa it was 40 per cent for women *vis-à-vis* 23.3 per cent for men.[3] Being an unpaid family worker comes with no protection whatsoever when there is loss of ability to work – whether this is due to an economic crisis, personal injury or old age.

Beyond being unpaid workers, an intuitive way of grasping poor women's predicament in terms of time use dedicated to either unpaid or paid work can be determined by estimating: (a) the number of paid hours they would need to work to reach the poverty line given the wages they can command; and (b) adding to that, the number of hours of unpaid work they perform.[4] In South Africa for the year 2000 (leaving aside the fact that employment opportunities may not even exist for women), unskilled women would have had to work four extra hours[5] per day to earn the poverty-level income as compared to unskilled men.[6] Meanwhile, the South African TUS data (Statistics SA, 2001) reveal that women spend, on average, an extra 2 hours and 15 minutes on unpaid work each day.[7] Poor women – under the best of circumstances in terms of availability of jobs, are certain to experience both income and time poverty.

To reiterate, there are two points that need emphasis. First, that although unpaid work contributes to the well-being of family members and community, at the same time, it is linked to the rest of the economy. Second, during periods of economic upheavals, as incomes and public services decline, women's standard of living declines while unpaid work burdens increase. Consequently, women are not only income-poor, but time-poor as well.[8]

The state as employer of last resort (ELR): historical foundations of ELR and employment guarantee programs (EGP) in the North and Global South

The government acting as the ELR has a very long history and was introduced as a policy centuries ago to avert famine by enlightened rulers in India[9] – as far back as the fourth and fourteenth century (Drèze and Sen, 1989). Over the years, many countries have undertaken similar initiatives for a variety or reasons; these initiatives have been variably known as 'employment guarantee schemes' (EGS), 'public employment programs,' 'food for work' and 'public works programs.' India, South Africa, Argentina, Ethiopia, Korea, Peru, Bangladesh, Ghana, Cambodia, France, Australia, Sweden, the United States and Chile, among many others, have intermittently adopted policies that effectively rendered the state as ELR. In most cases, these were temporary emergency programs that were phased out as conditions improved.[10] However, the case has also been made for using such measures on a permanent basis, not only as automatic stabilizers to guard against the many undesirable effects of underemployment but also to promote the right to a job as a guaranteed entitlement (Papadimitriou, 1998; Mitchell, 2001; Wray, 2007).

The necessity of such a policy is rooted in the development of capitalism itself. In the period following the Industrial Revolution, countries with relatively well-developed markets in the North experienced production and financial problems with surprising regularity. Despite colonial rule that provided them with cheap raw materials, ample product markets and other privileges, stock-market crises kept reoccurring and unemployment swings followed suit. J.M. Keynes understood early on that underemployment of labor and other resources was part and parcel of the *normal* functioning of the market-oriented economic system and the Great Depression validated his views quite powerfully. The New Deal program, introduced by President Franklin Roosevelt in the United States in 1933, was an intervention beyond countercyclical fiscal and monetary policy, as it aimed at reviving the economy but not by waiting for market activity to pick up, which would entail the rehiring of workers. Instead, it sought to directly provide publicly funded jobs to the unemployed in a host of different project areas such in electrification projects or construction of new roads, bridges and schools, but also in environmental and cultural areas. Some economists – prominently among them Sir William Beveridge,[11] John Pierson and John Philip Wernette – called for the government to guarantee full employment through direct job creation at fair wages as needed (Kaboub, 2007). Although other Keynesian policies of a countercyclical nature were adopted widely in many countries, beyond the aftermath of the crisis, the institutionalization of employment guarantee as a policy instrument was short lived and overall it did not take a stronghold.

At the same time, around the middle of the last century, economists concerned with developmental issues began to view public employment creation programs as a means to address the endemic problem of low levels of employment and the underutilization of labor resources. Hirway (2006) traces this view to Nurkse and Hirchman, and more recently to Tinbergen, who viewed public works programs as transitional ones that moved an economy closer to full employment through 'strategic use of surplus labor' that the private sector could not provide.[12] Finally, Hyman Minsky (1986), an economist mostly known for his work on financial fragility, cited the need for governments to serve as an ELR.

Concerned with poverty in the United States, Minsky advocated that the 'war on poverty' ought to be fought through a permanent public job creation program. Much like the liquidity role that the U.S. Federal Reserve facilitates in financial markets, in labor markets, he argued, only the government could create 'an infinitely elastic demand for labor at a floor or minimum wage that does not depend upon long- and short-run profit expectations of business. Since only government can divorce the offering of employment from the profitability of hiring workers, the infinitely elastic demand for labor must be created by government'[13] (Minsky, 1986).

These ideas were forgotten in the 1980s and 1990s. The role of the government as provider of social entitlements and guarantor of employment literally disappeared from the policy dialogue all together. Deregulation and the safeguarding of laissez faire principles became the rather limited scope of government activity. This has brought questionable results. Income distribution between and within countries has deteriorated;

poverty is still a huge challenge and recurring financial crises have not been prevented or dealt with effectively (for instance, in Brazil, Mexico, Argentina and Russia or during the Asian crisis and the worldwide crisis of 2008–2009). As a result, the old orthodoxy, which claimed that markets left alone deliver efficient outcomes, has lost credibility. Instead, an expanded role of government is being contemplated and the hope is that spaces will emerge to redress inequalities between and within countries, as well those across race, ethnic and gender lines.

Gender-awareness of EGP

Gender dimensions of EGP, and ELR in general, are pertinent along two interrelated axes.[14] The first relates to equitable access for women to newly created public jobs. Much like women's participation in labor markets, this requires that the female supply of labor is carefully thought about and facilitated (Krishnaraj *et al.*, 2004a, b). The second entails project design that is responsive to asset creation and service delivery that will benefit people in poverty, especially women (King-Dejardin, 1996).

Equitable female participation

Female participation rates in public job creation programs vary. In cases when they are low, quotas can and have been put in place in many instances. But overall, participation rates have been very high. In the state of Maharashtra, India, where an EGP was in effect for many years starting in the late 1970s, women comprised 53 per cent of the program participants (Engkvist, 1995). Chile's Minimum Employment Program (PEM), originally set up in 1975, had reached a 73 per cent female participation rate by 1987 (Buvinic, 1996). Finally, the *Jefes y Jefas de Hogar* program was introduced in Argentina in the post-2001 crisis period. Originally, the program anticipated that 400,000 heads of households would register. In a year's time, 75 per cent of registered participants were women and, to the surprise of officials, close to two million people declared interest and became beneficiaries, amounting to 5 per cent of the population (Tcherneva, 2005).

The above cases confirm the existence of much higher unrecorded unemployment rates among women in addition to the erroneous category of 'inactive persons' used by statistical agencies for persons not interested in gainful employment. In addition to providing what turns out to be much desired work opportunities for women, high female response to EGP has the added benefit of introducing gender equality standards in remuneration, at least for minimum-wage workers. As these programs offer a uniform wage for men and women alike, public works programs set in effect a nondiscriminatory wage floor for their hourly compensation.

Despite the high participation rates of women in these programs, there has not been adequate cross-country evaluation from a gender perspective.[15] For many women, taking up paid work will result in much longer hours dedicated to total work. This can be partly addressed by establishing conditions that facilitate women's participation. India's National Rural Employment Guarantee Act (NREGA) program, for instance, has incorporated the following stipulations in this regard: works provided must be within 4 km from the place of residence of (all) participants; shade and water must be provided; and crèche facilities for supervision of children must be provided as a part of the public works. These are very important issues and we now turn to the second dimension, which is of paramount importance from a gender perspective – the choice of public works projects.

The right to a job, the right types of projects: a gender perspective

High levels of female participation are an indication that women with low prospects of finding paid work are willing to work if offered a job opportunity. This being said, the gendered nature of paid and unpaid work makes matters somewhat more complicated. To make sensible use of public funds, a selection criterion for EGP projects requires that participants be provided with productive and socially useful jobs. A review of such programs across time and space reveals that the vast majority of projects are of a relatively large-scale, tangible *physical infrastructure nature,* such as intercity roads and bridges, upgrading and maintenance work on public structures and the like. As much as these are needed, more emphasis must also be placed on projects that provide *social services* or those that target *the efficiency and enhancement of public service delivery.*

While creating job opportunities in socially beneficial projects, the invisibility of unpaid work detracts from project selection by not identifying very useful but 'hidden' types of jobs that are ideally suited for public employment programs. Should it be required that half of the new employment must be generated with the goal of reducing unpaid work burdens, the 'hidden' vacancies would become immediately indentifiable.[16] Such employment opportunities can serve as a vehicle for transforming women's lives by reducing the unpaid work burden and thus altering the paid–unpaid gender division of labor. We will provide a concrete case study for South Africa in the next section that we hope will make the case clearer.

Prioritizing public investment in infrastructure that reduces unpaid work can take the form of rural irrigation projects, building of ecological latrines, aforestation and reforestation or establishing woodlots, all of which would reduce the time allocated to fetching water and fuel wood, sanitation and collection of free goods. By reducing the unpaid work component of these tasks, the reduction in drudgery will be accompanied by increases in productivity of unpaid work for household production and maintenance as well. In other instances, projects can directly target unpaid care work activities such as eldercare and care of the chronically ill.

Substituting paid employment for portions of currently performed unpaid work will have to be context specific and the best way to achieve this is by ensuring women's participation in the selection processes regarding such publicly funded projects. If designed with these concerns in mind, three distinct benefits should be expected: first, it will generate income for participants, both men and women, allowing for the possibility of gender bending in skill acquisition, as potentially some women may wish to be employed as construction workers, while young men could provide home-based care to the chronically ill; second, the social infrastructure and services delivered will become part of the basket of consumption for underserved communities and populations, in itself a contribution towards filling in existing gaps; third, and quite significant for promoting gender equality, this may turn out to be a very powerful redistributive policy of unpaid work burdens in both the short and medium run.

Finally, public works ought to create useful jobs. Project selection therefore is meant to identify existing gaps so that besides the income participants would be earning, the work they perform would benefit society. Much as large infrastructural projects yield benefits, so too will community-based projects enhance the productivity of unpaid work and substitute significant portions of it. As we mentioned above, we now turn to a specific case study that focuses on precisely this issue.

The case of a social sector public works program: evidence from South Africa

Background on South Africa and the Expanded Public Works Program (EPWP)

While many positive developments have taken place in post-apartheid South Africa, unemployment and poverty remain serious challenges; that is despite economic growth, which in the past seven years has ranged between 3–4.5 per cent. In the last decade the official unemployment rate in South Africa has hovered around 25 per cent. The expanded unemployment rate (a measure that includes discouraged workers) is about 37.1 per cent, affecting predominantly unskilled and low-skilled workers.[17] These rates correspond to about around 7.2 million persons out of work.

Both unemployment and poverty in South Africa continue to have racial, gender and spatial characteristics. In some parts of the country (ex-homelands, urban slums and deprived rural areas), joblessness among African women and youth is as high as 70 per cent and poverty estimates place 50 per cent of the population below the poverty line.[18] Overall, a larger number of women are in poverty; for example, in a population of about 44 million, among the poor, 11.9 million (54.4 per cent) are female, as compared to 10 million poor males (Sadan, 2006).

To redress the serious problem of chronic unemployment, among other measures, in 2004 the government of South Africa introduced the EPWP. This active labor market policy is a public job creation program that provides the unemployed with a paid work entitlement and has set a target to create one million job opportunities within five years. In retrospect, EPWP has set deeply transformative objectives. Besides job creation, it aimed at substantially reducing poverty while creating skills and providing exit strategies for participants in these programs. Within a short-term period of time and with small budgetary allocations, this proved hard to achieve. In the 2004–2005 period, the EPWP to GDP ratio was only 0.3 per cent; mid-term reviews by independent researchers revealed that budgetary allocations were incommensurable to the problem at hand.

A pleasant surprise: policy space for gender-aware design within the EPWP

As country-wide deliberations pointed to scaling-up EPWP, several efforts were undertaken to contribute to the policy dialogue, including the one we report below.[19]

We have noted earlier two findings: that women carry out unpaid work disproportionately and that lack of acknowledgment of such activities as 'work' precludes them from being given due consideration in policy discussions, including the realm of public job creation. Making use of the TUS data of 2000, we find that South Africa is not an exception to our first observation. Time spent on unpaid work is higher for women – in contrast to adult men, women perform 76 per cent of the total unpaid work. We also find evidence that time burdens increase with poverty and unemployment status of households and are particularly acute among African poor women in ex-homelands and urban slum areas.

Unique among similar government initiatives, EPWP provides policy space to consider issues pertinent to unpaid work. EPWP programmatically recognizes that it is unpaid work that provides home- and community-based care (HCBC) and early childhood development (ECD), both of which are performed primarily by women, mostly unemployed, who also join the ranks of poor 'volunteers.' Substituting paid for unpaid work by creating job opportunities that upgrade skills for men and women while extending service delivery to underserved communities in both areas is part of South Africa's mandate. This we consider a very important feature.

Case study and results of scaling-up the social sector EPWP

The EPWP jobs we propose below extend in substantive ways the scope of the social sector of the program.[20] Evaluation documents have noted that the social sector has been primarily focused on facilitating skill upgrading through learnerships.[21] Given its small budgetary allocations, it only provided for a very short duration of employment and has not expanded service delivery adequately.

In contrast, the jobs we propose are full-time, year-round jobs based on service delivery targets. They are meant to create jobs while providing services that reach infants, young children and the sick of vulnerable households. These services will also be available to households from within which newly hired EPWP workers will come, enabling women's participation in the program without adding to their already heavy burdens of unpaid work. Delivery of services will entail the hiring and development of an ECD and HCBC cadre that ranges from child-care workers, school nutrition workers, teacher aids, school caretakers and school clerical workers, to cooks, vegetable gardeners and administrators for local ECD sites, as well as community health workers, nutrition and food security workers, directly observed therapy, voluntary counseling and testing and TB and malaria health officers. These services, among other benefits yielded, will alleviate unpaid care burdens by providing support for the raising of children and the care of the ill.

Unpaid work performed by poor women in South Africa includes care for the sick and permanently ill, such as malaria and TB patients and people living with the HIV/AIDS virus. It also consists of care provisioning with meager means and under impoverished conditions for children during their early childhood development stages. This work extends beyond child minding. Proper early childhood development includes securing adequate nutrition and clean water, collecting fire wood to prepare meals, accessing health services, providing mental stimulation and creating a secure, clean, warm and nurturing environment, which is critically important for the physical and psychological development of children. In South Africa, the two care areas of ECD and HCBC are critically interconnected. As a result of the high HIV/AIDS prevalence rates among the mid-aged part of the population, older children and older women become the primary caretakers of orphans and children living in households with HIV patients and, hence, the jobs described above are meant to provide these services to all children in the bottom half of the income distribution (50 per cent) and to all vulnerable HIV/AIDS households (estimated to comprise 20 per cent of the population).

To assess the impact of scaling-up the EPWP social sector job creation, we developed a gender disaggregated social accounting matrix for South Africa (SAM-SA). The model shows the use of male and female labor (skilled and unskilled) in paid work from within several stratified household types. Parallel satellite time-use accounts were constructed to shed light on the distribution of unpaid work for the same stratified household types. We also made use of models that allowed us to determine the types and numbers of new jobs needed to expand service delivery. From these estimates we calculated the corresponding budgetary allocations that would allow for such scaling-up to take place. Lastly, it should be mentioned that during the month of October 2007, a total of seventeen interviews with government officials and EPWP beneficiaries were conducted and five project sites were visited in the provinces of KwaZulu Natal and Limpopo. These provided valuable insights and enhanced our understanding of both the importance of scaling-up and the challenges the EPWP faces.

The results of the policy experiment we report stem from a suggested budgetary allocation of approximately R9.2 billion. The annual cost of this policy covers all labor payments and all other costs associated with service delivery and human capital development, such as food, other agricultural inputs for meal preparation and supervisory costs, as well as training and certification expenses. The proposed full-time, year-round jobs primarily reach unskilled workers that are members of ultra-poor and poor households. Wages are stipulated at R500 per month, with some jobs requiring higher skill levels paying up to double that amount. The labor supply response is presumed to be the same for all households below the poverty line. The key findings are as follows:

- the injection of R9.2 billion corresponds to creation of 771,505 new full-time jobs, 571,505 of which are direct EPWP social sector jobs;

- almost 60 per cent of these jobs are estimated to be filled by women;
- in 2000 prices, the R9.2 billion corresponds to 3.5 per cent of government expenditures or 1.1 per cent of GDP, commensurable to other countries' initiatives;
- the total impact on GDP growth is in the order of 1.8 per cent;
- new direct and indirect taxes are generated equal to about R3 billion, which pays for one-third of the cost of the program;
- the resultant growth is pro-poor. The overall *incremental* change in income is 9.2 per cent for ultra-poor households, 5.6 per cent for poor households and 1.3 for non-poor households. These overall changes are instructive, but do not shed light on those households from whose ranks participants of the scaled-up social sector EPWP come from (we discuss this issue below);
- all EPWP-participating ultra-poor households cross the ultra-poor poverty line datum and depth of poverty is reduced by 60–80 per cent. Among them, poor households previously located above or around the poverty line are lifted above the poverty line; and
- overall, social sector job creation is more labor intensive than the infrastructure sectors of the EPWP. Budgetary allocations in the social sector result in higher levels of job creation and a larger depth of poverty reduction.

We must emphasize that this exercise serves as a hypothetical policy experiment and its aim is to identify *orders of magnitude* of economy-wide impacts should scaling-up be implemented. Many of the specific assumptions can be easily changed to reflect different initial conditions, as well as diverse objectives set by beneficiary communities, policy-makers and other stakeholders at the national, provincial and municipal levels.

Beyond job creation

We have argued that job creation through a government employment guarantee can be designed in ways that promote multiple policy objectives. The allocation of women's time in unpaid work activities sheds light and makes transparent a variety of types of jobs and projects that can be beneficial on many fronts. If project design is informed by these 'hidden' vacancies, in addition to jobs created, incomes received and pro-poor growth results, we also reach three important outcomes.

First, enhanced service delivery. Children of all households across the country would be able to enroll in early childhood development programs that should lead to better nutrition, health, education and overall well-being, especially those in vulnerable households. About 20 per cent of (the most vulnerable) households with people living with HIV/AIDS would be receiving home-based care, counseling and better nutrition. Such extended services would reduce demands placed on women's time for unpaid care work.

Second, participants would increasingly experience a renewed sense of dignity, fulfillment and self-worth. Our hypothetical policy scenario limits our capacity to directly conduct such an impact-assessment study emanating from the proposed intervention. Nonetheless, existing literature on this subject, as well as visits to various EPWP sites and other public works project evaluations, confirms this is indeed the case. Even critics of such programs have acknowledged the increase in self-esteem and fulfillment stemming from being able to work, save, afford better clothing, participate in community events and help family members financially.

Last, and most importantly from the stand point of this volume, creating job opportunities is a big step forward, while recognizing that it is neither eternal nor 'natural' for women to provide care under unremunerated conditions; that it is not the obligation nor the purview of households to be extracting unpaid work from their members in order to meet their minimum health, sanitation and other basic needs requirements.

Concluding remarks

There is a particular urgency, and immense opportunity, to place employment guarantee job creation in the public dialogue. International attention is gathering energy on the idea that where markets fail, governments must step in to regulate the economy and create jobs. This renewed emphasis on the importance of public investment and employment generation must be informed by real needs of real people.

Gender-informed, well-designed public job creation has the potential to steer the economy in a direction that is both efficient and equitable, as well as to improve women's status, helping promote the realization of their human rights. Access to a job is not a panacea. Healthy growth rates, environmental sustainability, decent work conditions and a government that safeguards public good provisioning on a permanent basis and strives for universal entitlements are key ingredients for a humane and caring society.

For the poor and ultra-poor willing to work and not having access to a job, public inaction constitutes social assignment of some to extreme hardship, poverty and social exclusion.

Notes

* Data used in this chapter originate in a research project undertaken by The Levy Economics Institute of Bard College in 2006–2007, titled 'Impact of Public Employment Guarantee Strategies on Gender Equality and Pro-poor Development.' The project received partial support from the UNDP Gender Team and a full report is available upon request. Many thanks to Kijong Kim, Dimitri Papadimitriou and Nilüfer Çağatay for useful comments and feedback.

1. With the exception of two countries, Denmark and the Netherlands, even when we measure total time contributions to both paid and unpaid activities, women work longer hours; see Antonopoulos (2008).

2. Vulnerable employment is a newly introduced concept by ILO, describing people who are employed under relatively precarious circumstances with lack of access to benefits or social protection and, thus, more 'at risk' to economic cycles. Unpaid family workers are part of this group, as vulnerable employment is calculated as the sum of own-account workers and unpaid family workers.

3. ILO (2007), Table 5.

4. This is a modified version of Vickery's (1977) seminal paper on time poverty, which was based on the idea that the working poor (versus the non-poor) need to spend longer hours performing paid work if they are to secure sufficient income just to reach the poverty line. She then proceeded to argue that they would have less time for household production, keeping free time as an inviolable constant at about ten hours per day, while in our view it is the 'free time' that is reduced, resulting in decreasing human capabilities and health effects.

5. Author's calculation: women received, on average, roughly R7–8 per hour and men around R11–12. Given existing wage differentials of unskilled females to males, to earn 2560 per month men needed to work fifty hours per week; women needed to devote 40% more hours to reach the level of income. The four extra hours estimate is based on a five day week at ten hours per day for men. Alternatively, for a six day per week work schedule, men would need to work around eight hours a day and women around thirteen hours.

6. Hourly wage calculations are based on LFS 2000 and TUS 2000. The year 2000 is chosen for consistency purposes, as the TUS was conducted in this year. Calculations are from the Levy research project on 'Impact of Employment Guarantee Policies on Pro-poor Growth and Gender Equality,' with particular contributions from Kalie Pauw and Rosemary Leaver.

7. For comparison, it is worth noting that the equivalent figure in the Netherlands and France is around two hours, while in Italy and Mexico it is over four and a half hours; see UNDP (2006) and ECLAC (2007). In Benin, for instance, collecting water and wood and carrying it home takes, on average, three and a half months of women's time per year (Charmes and Hirway, 2006). We must also note that for the majority of countries the combined paid/unpaid work time for women is higher (Antonopoulos, 2008).

8. For an interesting methodological and empirical discussion see Vickery (1977) and Harvey and Mukhopadhyay (2007).

9. India holds a very special place in this regard. See www.nrega.gov for National Rural Employment Guarantee Act (NREGA), 2005; Registered No. DL–(N)O4/000/72 003–5. New Delhi.

10. For a detailed country review, see Kaboub (2007) and Antonopoulos (2006), Hirway and Terhal (2004).

11. In his book, *Full Employment in a Free Society*, Beveridge advocated that the government ought to guarantee full employment, which for him was defined as always having more available vacancies than unemployed people, not slightly fewer jobs than those who need them.

12. See Hirway (2006), Hirway and Terhal (1994).

13. Minsky envisioned ELR as a permanent policy whereby the state assumes a buffer-stock employment role, absorbing the unemployed during contractionary periods and releasing them back into the market as needed. In addition to providing much needed jobs, ELR would have the added benefit of price stabilization, as it would reduce wage fluctuations over the medium term.

14. For a thorough introduction, see King-Dejardin (1996).

15. For research work that explicitly addresses differential impacts on men and women see Tcherneva and Wray (2005) and Krishnaraj *et al.* (2004a, b).

16. One exception is the *Jefes* program in Argentina; a large number of projects are designed specifically to cater to community needs by providing a wide range of goods and services (Tcherneva and Wray, 2005).

17. See Statistics South Africa (2007), Labour Force Survey.

18. There is no official poverty line in South Africa, although the Treasury is in the process of finalizing documentation that will establish such a threshold. Some researchers adopt R5,057 per annum, according to which the headcount ratio (defined as the proportion of the population living below the poverty line) for South Africa is 49.8 per cent. The 20th percentile cut-off of adult equivalent income (R2,717 per annum) is sometimes used as the 'ultra-poverty line.' About 28.2 per cent of the South African population lives below this poverty line. For this study we have adopted comparable measures using 2000 prices and poverty levels.

19. The design and results we report in the subsection 'case study and results of scaling-up the social sector,' are based on a proposal to scale-up social sector job creation undertaken at the Levy Economics Institute during 2006–2007, with valuable input received from the PROVIDE team (Department of Agriculture, University of Elsenburg, South Africa) Dr Irwin Friedman, Research Director of Health Systems Trust and multiple interviews and conversations with many government officials. The project received partial support from the United Nations Development Program (UNDP) Gender Team. A full report of the study is available upon request.

20. Other types of interventions have been modelled and are available upon request from the author.

21. A learnership combines work-based experience with structured learning and results in a qualification that is registered within the National Qualifications Framework (NQF) by the South African Qualification Authority (SAQA). A learner who completes a learnership will have a qualification that signals occupational competence and is recognized throughout the country.

References

Akintola, O. (2004) 'Gendered Analysis of the Burden of Care on Family and Volunteer Caregivers in Uganda and South Africa,' Research Report (Durban: Health Economics and HIV/AIDS Research Division, University of KwaZulu-Natal).

Antonopoulos, R. (2007) 'The Right to a Job, the Right Type of Projects: Employment Guarantee Policies from a Gender Perspective,' mimeo (Annandale-on-Hudson, NY: The Levy Economics Institute of Bard College).

Antonopoulos, R. (2008) 'The Unpaid Care Work-Paid Work Connection,' Working Paper 541 (Annandale-on-Hudson, NY: The Levy Economics Institute of Bard College).

Buvinic, M. (1996) 'Promoting Employment among Urban Poor in Latin America and the Caribbean: A Gender Analysis,' Discussion Paper 12 (Geneva: International Labour Organization).

Charmes, J. and I. Hirway (2006) 'Estimating and Understanding Informal Employment through Time-Use Studies,' Paper presented at the Expert Group Meeting on Informal Sector Statistics (Delhi Group), Centre for Development Alternatives, Ahmedabad, India, 11–12 May.

Drèze, J. and A. Sen (1989) *Hunger and Public Action* (Oxford: Oxford University Press).

ECLAC (2007) 'Women's Contribution to Equality in Latin America and the Caribbean,' Paper prepared by Women and Development Unit of the Economic Commission for Latin America and the Caribbean (ECLAC) for the Regional Conference on Women in Latin America and the Caribbean on 6–9 August, Ecuador. http://www.eclac.cl/mujer/noticias/paginas/8/29288/WomensContribution. pdf.

Engkvist, R. (1995) 'Poverty Alleviation and Rural Development through Public Works: The Case of the Employment Guarantee Scheme in Maharashtra,' Minor Field Study Series 57 (Sweden: University of Lund, Department of Economics).

Folbre, N. (1994) *Who Pays for the Kids?: Gender and the Structures of Constraint* (New York: Routledge).

Folbre, N. (2001) *The Invisible Heart: Economics and Family Values* (New York: The New Press).

Harvey, A.S. and A.K. Mukhopadhyay (2007) 'When Twenty-Four Hours Is Not Enough: Time Poverty of Working Parents,' *Social Indicators Research* 82(1): 57–77.

Hirway, I. (2006) 'Enhancing Livelihood Security through the National Employment Guarantee Act,' Working Paper 437 (Annandale-on-Hudson NY: The Levy Economics Institute of Bard College).

Hirway, I. and P. Terhal (1994) *Towards Employment Guarantee in India and International Experiences in Rural Public Works Programmes* (New Delhi: Sage Publications).

Hirway, I. (2009) 'Implications of Time Use Patterns for Public Employment Guarantee Programmes in Global South,' Background paper prepared for The Levy Economics Institute of Bard College Project: Impact of Employment Guarantee Programs on Gender Equality and Pro-Poor Economic Development, in collaboration with UNDP (forthcoming).

ILO (2007). *Global Employment Trends for Women.* http://www.ilo.org/public/
english/employment/strat/stratprod.htm

Kaboub, F. (2007) 'Employment Guarantee Programs: A Survey of Theories and
Policy Experiences,' Working Paper 498 (Annandale-on-Hudson, NY: The Levy
Economics Institute of Bard College).

King-Dejardin, A. (1996) 'Public Works Programmes, a Strategy for Poverty Alleviation: the Gender Dimension,' Issues in Development Discussion Paper 10
(Geneva: ILO, Development and Technical Cooperation Department).

Krishnaraj, M., D. Pandey and A. Kanchey (2004a) 'Does EGS Require Restructuring for Poverty Alleviation and Gender Equality? Part I – Concept, Design and
Delivery System,' *Economic and Political Weekly*, 17 April.

Krishnaraj, M., D. Pandey, and A. Kanchey (2004b) 'Does EGS Require Restructuring for Poverty Alleviation and Gender Equality? Part II – Gender Concerns and
Issues for Restructuring,' *Economic and Political Weekly*, 24 April.

McCord, A. (2004) 'Policy Expectations and Programme Reality: The Poverty
Reduction and Employment Performance of Two Public Works Programmes
in South Africa,' Working Paper 8 (London: Overseas Development Institute, Economics and Statistics Analysis Unit & Public Works Research Project,
SALDRU).

Minsky, H. (1986) *Stabilizing an Unstable Economy* (New Haven, CT: Yale University
Press).

Mitchell, W. (2001) 'Fiscal Policy and the Job Guarantee,' Working Paper 01/09
(Newcastle, Australia: Center for Full Employment and Equity).

NREGA (2005) http://nrega.nic.in/ (home page), date accessed 15 January 2009.

Papadimitriou, D. (1998) '(Full) Employment Policy: Theory and Practice,' Working Paper 258 (Annandale-on-Hudson, NY: The Levy Economics Institute of
Bard College).

Picchio, A. (ed.) (2003) *Unpaid Work and the Economy. A Gender Analysis of the
Standards of Living* (London: Routledge).

Sadan, M. (2006) 'Gendered Analysis of the Working for Water Program,' Occasional Paper (Pretoria: Southern African Regional Poverty Network).

Statistics South Africa (2001) *A Survey of Time Use: How South African Men and
Women Spend their Time – A Report on the 2000 Time Use Survey* (Pretoria: Statistics
South Africa).

Statistics South Africa (2007) *Labour Force*, September (Pretoria: Statistics South
Africa).

Tcherneva, P. (2005) 'The Art of Job Creation: Promises and Problems of the
Argentinean Experience,' Special Report (Kansas City, MO: Center for Full
Employment and Price Stability).

Tcherneva, P. and R. Wray (2005) 'Gender and the Job Guarantee: The Impact of
Argentina's *Jefes* Program on Female Heads of Poor Households,' Working Paper
50 (Kansas City, MO: Center for Full Employment and Price Stability).

UNDP (2006) *Human Development Report* (New York: UNDP).

Vickery, C. (1977) 'The Time Poor: A New Look at Poverty,' *The Journal of Human
Resources*, 12(1), 27–48.

Wray, R. (2007) 'The Employer of Last Resort Programme: Could It Work for Developing Countries?,' ILO, Employment Analysis and Research Unit, Economic
and Labour Market Analysis Department, Economic and Labour Market Papers,
#5 (Geneva: International Labour Organization).

8
Lessons from the Buenos Aires Time-Use Survey: A Methodological Assessment

*Valeria Esquivel**

Introduction

Supported by the women's movement and in the spirit of the Beijing Platform for Action, the Buenos Aires legislature passed a law at the end of 2003 (*Ley N° 1168*, 4 December 2003) that mandated the Directorate-General of Statistics and Census of the city government (*Dirección General de Estadística y Censos, DGEyC*) to collect information on the distribution of time use by women and men living in the city of Buenos Aires on a systematic and periodic basis (Consejo Nacional de la Mujer, 2006). The primary purpose of such a survey would be to quantify unpaid care work performed mostly by women in the household. According to the same law, the findings of this survey are to be used to promote policies focused on enhancing the living conditions of women, and on the equitable integration of women and men into society.

As a result of this mandate, in November–December 2005 the DGEyC decided to conduct a TUS in Buenos Aires as a module of its Annual Household Survey. TUS survey was the first to be conducted in the country following the publication of United Nations guidelines (UNSTAT, 2005).[1] Its methodological approach builds from the 2000 TUS SA – albeit in a smaller geographical scale (Budlender, 2007) – though a closer look reveals a number of methodological variations, particularly with respect to fieldwork organization, activity classification and the way simultaneous activities are captured. The Buenos Aires TUS is also a unique experience in the Latin American context since, in spite of being a module attached to an ongoing multipurpose household survey, it departed from the widely used short tasks list approach to collecting time-use data using the 24-hour recall activity diary (Esquivel, 2008a). The survey was collected under a cooperation agreement between DGEyC and Instituto de Ciencias, Universidad Nacional de General Sarmiento, Argentina.[2]

As a researcher from the university, I have been in charge of designing the Buenos Aires TUS methodological approach (DGEyC, 2007a:7). My role within this agreement involved designing survey instruments, coordinating the pilot test and training fieldworkers before fieldwork launching, supervising fieldwork, coordinating the edition, processing and analysis of time-use data and preparing press reports. This was an unusual and fruitful collaboration between statistical information producers and academia – who are typically only end users of it. This fact allowed for finding satisfactory solutions to the many tensions involved in designing and collecting a module attached to an ongoing household survey and shows up in many of its methodological features.

This chapter describes the methodological features of the survey and infers useful lessons to replicate the Buenos Aires TUS in similar contexts and/or on a nationwide scale.

The Buenos Aires TUS

Methodological approach

A module of the 2005 Buenos Aires Annual Household Survey

The Buenos Aires Annual Household Survey has been conducted every year since 2003 from October to December by the Directorate-General of Statistics and Census of the city government. This multipurpose household survey collects information on demographics, health, education, migration, labor market (labor force participation; employment, unemployment and underemployment) and earnings to describe the socioeconomic situation of the Buenos Aires city, which has approximately three million people[3] and which is the biggest Argentinian city, with its capital district accounting for 8 per cent of the country's population according to the last National Population Census (2001). The two features that distinguish this survey from other household surveys (notably *EPH*, the urban Continuous Household Survey conducted by INDEC,[4] which produces labor market and poverty indicators at the local and national levels) are its *larger sample size*, which makes it representative of the city's population as a whole *and* of smaller administrative units within the city (*Centros de Gestión y Participación*) as well as its *thematic flexibility*, which has made it possible to explore diverse issues of interest in the past as add-on modules (DGEyC, 2006:1) and has also allowed incorporation of the time-use module in the 2005 survey.

Typically, add-on modules are incorporated in the main questionnaire and share the same selection rules. The time-use module, however, was administered using a separate questionnaire. While the main survey collected information on the entire household, the dwelling and on all individual household members, the time-use module collected information from only *one randomly selected household* member between the ages of 15 and 74 (refer to discussion on sampling design).[5] However, as in all TUS, *no one else but the person who was selected to answer the time-use module is allowed to respond about their own time use*, hence, one extra household visit (over the two already planned for the survey) was allowed in order to find the designated member. Also, completing the interview on the phone as a last resort was allowed and clear replacement rules were designed in case the selected member could not be contacted (DGEyC, 2005b:3).[6]

The main survey contributed to the TUS as it provided good identification of household members and their ages, which was important to rapidly single out target population and correctly select at random one respondent for the time-use module. The Annual Household Survey had a well-designed questionnaire reception, which allowed for correcting errors and solving fieldwork problems related to the TUS as they arose. Extra resources were provided to complete the TUS and to undertake after fieldwork activities – edition, data entry, weights calculation and data processing.

Methodological features of the survey

Survey instrument   The TUS had three data collection instruments, the *cover*, which included a selection grid and a list of reasons for nonresponse in case it happened; the 24-hour recall *activity diary*, followed by three probing questions and a question asking whether the day reported was typical; and the *card* aimed at aiding the time-use interview. The *activity dairy* was a closed grid consisting of 48 30-minute long time slots with room for up to three consecutive and/or simultaneous activities. It started at 4 am of the day before the interview ('yesterday') and lasted until 4 am of the interview day (DGEyC, 2005c).[7]

This diary was filled in by fieldworkers (not by respondents) during the interview. Descriptive texts, simultaneity codes and location marks for each activity were filled while the respondent spoke about her/his previous day. Activity codes were added by fieldworkers *after* the interview. Activity diaries were checked for completion when received and eventually edited (refer to discussion on post-fieldwork). The interview was organized through a series of questions that prompted respondents' recall, read aloud by fieldworkers from a *card*, starting by '*What were you doing between ... [hour] and ... [half an hour later] yesterday?*' Respondents reported in their own words their previous day's activities, starting with their waking time and ending when the respondent went to sleep. Questions on waking up/going to bed times framed 'yesterday' and avoided both unnecessary repetitions of prompting questions. A question 'confirming' that the person slept between 4 am and the time she/he woke up and from the moment she/he went to sleep to 4 am of the day of the interview was added to check for sleeping time. A special set of questions was designed to ease the reporting of paid working hours. This again aimed at avoiding unnecessary repetition and identifying activities that were frequently missed because they were performed while doing paid work.

Probing questions   Wording of probing questions on child and adult care resulted from the pilot test and aimed at collecting underreported child and adult care time while avoiding affirmative answers from professional paid carers. An extra probing question was included to check whether any of the activities mentioned by respondents was done for pay – thus helping postcoding.

Simultaneous activities   Respondents were asked whether they did anything else in the same half hour (*'Did you do anything else between ... [hour] and ... [half an hour later]?'*) once or twice and reported on their activities. Simultaneity was captured by asking *'Did you do (the second activity) at the same time as (the first activity)?'* and, in the case of three activities, asking whether the third activity was performed at the same time as the first activity and at the same time as the second activity. Though complex, the answers to these questions were filled in a built-in grid in every time slot by introducing yes/no codes, which eased interview flow (DGEyC, 2005c). Simultaneous activities were not hierarchical: there was no 'main' and 'secondary' activity, as activity ordering was considered irrelevant. There were specific provisions while training fieldworkers on how to proceed where more than three activities were reported in a given time slot. Instructions were aimed at preserving events – the total duration of an activity – that comprised more than the conflictive time slot and prioritized care activities. However, there was very little need of these provisions because respondents very rarely reported more than three 'true' activities, as defined in the Activity Classification System used (see the point below).

As it was mentioned, the Buenos Aires TUS drew heavily on the 2000 South African TUS methodological approach.[8] In particular, the South African 24-hour recall activity diary included up to three nonhierarchical simultaneous activities, simultaneity and location codes, a probing question on childcare and a question on whether the day was typical[9] (Budlender *et al.*, 2001). However, the Buenos Aires survey introduced several methodological changes related to location marks (there was no provision to identify modes of transport) and simultaneity of activities. While in the case of South Africa, an activity could either be simultaneous or consecutive to all others in a given time slot, in the case of the Buenos Aires TUS, simultaneity was defined *pair-wise:* two activities were simultaneous if they were performed jointly at the same time. In other words, 'simultaneity is measured within a 30-minute time slot *between pairs of activities'* (DGEyC, 2007b: 7, in Spanish in the original). This allowed for a fairly complex, but exact, method to assign time (duration) to each activity.

The Buenos Aires Activity Classification System   The Activity Classification System was based on the first trial International Classification of Activities for Time-Use Statistics (10 major divisions ICATUS) and had up to three digits, although the third digit was used to differentiate certain activities (prompted/spontaneously reported, corrected while editing and so on), rather than to disaggregate them. This classification used only one SNA-work major division (100), while divisions within SNA-work distinguished between first and second jobs rather than employment status. The survey did not use the major divisions 200 and 300 of ICATUS. This is because very little (if any) primary production for self-consumption takes place in the Buenos Aires city and there was no need to differentiate between production for 'establishments' and 'nonestablishments.' The fact that specific questions on labor force participation were asked as part of the core survey (to the survey respondents and to all household members above ten years of age) made this omission relatively safe.[10]

Other major divisions are related to unpaid care work [400, household maintenance; 500, unpaid care for children and/or adults for own household; 600, unpaid community services and help to other households (relatives, friends, and neighbors)] and nonproductive activities (700, education; 800, social and cultural activities; 900, mass media use activities; 000, personal care activities).[11] A particular note should be added on the definition of childcare. Supervision and being on-call were regarded as caring activities, even if they were 'passively' performed (as opposed to the active content implied in the very concept of 'activity'). This feature was particularly emphasized in fieldworkers' training. The Activity Classification System therefore differentiated between active and passive childcare, as well as between spontaneously reported childcare and that reported as a result of the above mentioned probing question.

Children 17 years and below were considered as recipients of childcare – even though those between the ages of 15 and 17 were also potential respondents and, as such, also potential care givers.

The Buenos Aires Activity Classification System design was closely related to the length of time slots. First, by encompassing 30 minutes, prompting questions themselves signaled what a *significant* activity was; for example, respondents did not report on activities that were either too short or thought of as irrelevant (like blowing one's nose). Secondly, 30-minute time slots are associated with a high degree of activity aggregation (as opposed to 10-minute long time slots[12]). Shorter time slots would allow identifying very detailed/precise activities – feeding a baby, changing her/his diapers, cooking, setting the table and so on, would all have their own codes. They are, however, ill-suited to 24-hour recall activity diaries since it becomes extremely burdensome to conduct an interview that asks about the activities performed in 10 or 15 minute intervals for the entire 24-hour day. It is also practically impossible for the respondent to answer such questions.

Indeed, even simultaneity was 'filtered' by the degree of aggregation implied in the classification system. Given simultaneity was defined as *the performance of two (or up to three) different activities at the same time*, a crucial aspect in identifying simultaneous activities was indeed the way activities were defined. Since all actions that become aggregated in a single activity code (for example, cooking and setting the table, feeding a baby, changing her/his diapers) become *indistinct* behind that code (for example, 'preparing meals,' 'actively taking care of household children'), simultaneous activities can only take place between *different activities* (for example, between 'preparing meals' and 'actively taking care of household children'). A lower degree of aggregation would allow us to differentiate between simultaneous/consecutive activities within those that, by construction, become only one (cooking might have happened before setting the table; feeding a baby before changing her/his diapers and so on). Aside from the Activity Classification System, fieldworkers also had an 'activity dictionary' at their disposal, which listed activities in alphabetical order and their codes, to facilitate coding.

Data collection approach: how to fill in activity diaries through face-to-face interviews

Compared to self-administered activity diaries, the 24-hour recall activity diary minimizes respondent's burden by shifting responsibility to fieldwork and sampling design. The success of field work ultimately depends on fieldworkers' ability to transform respondents' answers into diary activities. This requires that fieldworkers know the Activity Classifica-tion System and can distinguish between activities that were aggregated under the same code (and therefore were written on the same activity line in a given time slot) from those that were not *in the course of the inter-view*. Following the South African example, it was therefore decided that fieldworkers would post-code activities, a feature that not only guaran-teed the gathering of complete diaries in a timely fashion, but also that time-use data was correctly collected in the first place.

Two difficulties were distinguished during the pilot test and empha-sized in fieldworkers' training: the avoidance of 'instantaneous' activities and the identification of activities behind respondents' reports. Some plausible answers to the prompting question (*'What were you doing...yes-terday?'*) were labeled 'instantaneous' activities ('I woke up', 'I arrived at...' and so on) because they are so short that they should not be recorded. Truly, they were not activities at all, but breaking points sig-naling the moment when an activity ended and a different one started (sleeping/being awake, traveling/being at the destination and so on). To emphasize that these actions should not enter the activity diary, field-workers were trained to mark them as breaking points in the diary's right margin. This helped them to be as accurate as they could in their report-ing of respondent's activities, but placed these answers *outside* the activity diary, where they would not take up room from 'true' activities and, therefore, would not be processed. Fieldworkers were trained to identify these activities using examples similar to the above mentioned. The cor-rection of wrongly coded activities during fieldwork showed fieldworkers their mistakes and enhanced the data collection process.[13]

In general, there was a strong emphasis on minimizing respondents' recall effort and reducing interview time, as a pilot test demonstrated that interview time was critical in reducing refusal rates – particularly bearing in mind there were high chances the time-use module would be collected immediately after the core survey.[14]

Sampling design

Reference population The 2005 Annual Household Survey used strati-fied multistage random sampling, based on the last National Popula-tion Census.[15] Three sampling frameworks were identified – residential dwellings, hotels/pensions and shanty towns. Sampling framework number one, comprising all residential dwellings, was organized around six independent tranches designed in two stages (first one with replace-ment, second one without replacement), each of them representative of the *total* Buenos Aires population living in residential dwellings (DGEyC, 2006).

The Buenos Aires TUS was collected in tranches one and two of sampling framework number one, between 20 November and 15 December 2005. The different working of sampling in hotels/pensions and shanty towns – that took place over the whole sampling period, from September to December 2005 – impeded the collection of time-use data in these subpopulations. As was already mentioned, only one randomly selected household member, either a woman or a man between 15 and 74 years of age, answered to the activity diary. This contrasts with other surveys that either target two randomly selected household members (the 2000 TUS SA) or all household members above a certain age (most of Latin American TUS). The relative small average size of the Buenos Aires city households (2.6 members) provides the rationale behind the choice of only one individual per household.

Also, only one activity diary per sampled individual was collected in order to minimize the fieldwork burden (because it would have required coming back to the household) and ultimately avoid confusion on the reference period (see below). In all, the sample comprised 1408 individuals (815 women and 593 men) who are representative of 1.18 million women and 0.96 million men between the ages of 15 and 74 living in residential dwellings. This excludes population out of age range (children below 15 and seniors over 74) and persons within the age range that live hotels/pensions and shanty towns.[16]

Reference period   The TUS produced estimates for an average day, an average week day and an average weekend day, based on random sampling respondents' 'yesterday'. Random-day sampling was decided on in order to give flexibility to fieldworkers to find the selected household member irrespective of when she/he could be contacted. Indeed, instruction to fieldworkers was 'always ask about yesterday,' even if the interview took place in a day of the week that differed from that of the initial household contact.

To guarantee the integrity of the process of receiving completed diaries, monitoring regarding the distribution of data per week day revealed the fact that fewer interviews were conducted on Sundays. Attempts to increase them were not very successful, since their relative under-representation was related both to fieldworkers' working schedules and household members' willingness to answer the interview on Sundays. The final was sample was comprised of 16 per cent Mondays, 16 per cent

Tuesdays, 15 per cent Wednesdays, 13 per cent Thursdays, 18 per cent Fridays, 7 per cent Saturdays and 14 per cent Sundays.

Clearly, Buenos Aires time-use estimates refer to a short period of the year, considered relatively 'normal'. This is, however, an assumption. The Buenos Aires TUS cannot provide information on seasonal variations.

Post-fieldwork

Editing, data entry and consistency checks   All activity diaries were edited during January–March 2006. Most of them were of good or very good quality – in only 6 per cent of cases was it necessary to make substantial changes to activity codes. A series of criteria were established to homogenize the use of certain codes to describe particular activities. Most notably, care was taken to differentiate between active and passive childcare or taking children to school as opposed to traveling associated with personal care including personal hygiene. These differences were checked for during editing. All changes made to activity codes initially assigned by fieldworkers were documented. Data compiled in electronic form included the descriptive text of all activities, something that might allow a closer analysis of respondents' reports and be used to improve future Activity Classification Systems.

Consistency checks were performed on simultaneous activities and location codes, traveling and location codes, random sampling and member selection, day of the week (since both the date of the interview and the day of the week it referred to were collected) and so on.

Assigning times to activities   Having detailed pair-wise information on simultaneous activities allowed for two different methods to assign minutes to activities. The '24-hour time' resulted from assigning average minutes to each of the activities performed in a given time slot (30 minutes where only one activity was reported, 15 minutes to each where two activities were reported and 10 minutes where three activities were reported), irrespective of their being performed either simultaneously or consecutively. The advantage of this time-assigning rule is that all respondent's activities add up to 24-hours a day. The obvious drawback is that the more simultaneous activities performed, the less time is allocated to each of them.

Having each and all possible combinations of simultaneous/consecutive activities (11 combinations of the number of activities recalled and yes/no answers to the simultaneity questions) allowed for assigning 'full-minute time' to all activities by accruing the full time length devoted to each activity, regardless of whether another activity was occurring at the same time. Thus, two simultaneous activities in the same time slot (for example, 'washing the clothes' at the same time as 'minding the children' or 'doing SNA work' at the same time as 'listening to the radio') each totaled 30 minutes.[17]

Quality indicators

The nonresponse rate (outright rejection, noncontacted respondents and so on) of the survey was 10.7 per cent among the households that responded to the Annual Household Survey and had at least one member between the ages of 15 and 74. This nonresponse rate was highly satisfactory, as it was significantly lower than nonresponse rates in the international context. As a result, checks for socioeconomic structure and labor force status indicate that the population surveyed by the Buenos Aires TUS did not significantly differ from that of the city, as surveyed by the Annual Household Survey.[18]

Random sampling of household members was equally satisfactory. Of the total number respondents to the TUS 32 per cent were not Annual Household Survey respondents. Though the probability of being chosen as a respondent in the TUS was higher in smaller the households, a crosstab between household type and selected members shows that the bigger and more complex the household, the higher was the chances of choosing nonheads/spouses. The final structure of the sample comprised 57 per cent household heads, 25 per cent were spouses, 12 per cent were daughters/sons and 6 per cent were other household members.

Over 80 per cent of time-use interviews were conducted in 20 minutes or less. This did not conspire against diary quality; the average number of episodes registered in each diary was 21 (23 among women and 19 among men), indicating fairly complex recall reports.

The probing question on childcare worked well: 24 per cent of all persons that reported childcare for either their household or other household's children did so partly because of this probing question and 8 per cent did so because they were prompted to do so – for example, they had not recalled having taken care of children altogether before being asked about it explicitly. However, the probing question aimed at identifying activities that were SNA work, even if the respondent would not consider them as such,[19] amounted to a marginal addition to the measurement of total SNA work (only 0.6 per cent affirmative answer from those who engaged in SNA work, 90 per cent of them women).

Considering simultaneous activities proved crucial for the measurement of activity times: if the 'full-minute time' assignation rule is used, the average day stretches to 28:15 hours. The highest simultaneity ratios were recorded in social and cultural activities (43 per cent), mass media use (37 per cent), unpaid community services (34 per cent) and unpaid care for children and/or adults for own household (32 per cent).

Lessons learned from the methodological approach

TUS as a module of an ongoing household survey

The Buenos Aires TUS shows that apart from cost considerations there are several advantages of the modular approach to TUS over stand-alone surveys. First and foremost, the very existence of an ongoing household survey made it possible to conduct the TUS. Deciding on survey frameworks, selecting households to be surveyed, training fieldworkers and conducting fieldwork for the time-use module became a marginal effort – as opposed to a new survey that might exceed both the budgets and the technical/operational capabilities of the Directorate General of Statistic and Census of the city government or those of any statistical office.

In methodological terms, the most obvious advantage of the modular approach is that the core survey provides information that usually exceeds in scope and detail the data that would be collected by stand-alone TUS, particularly on income and other socioeconomic stratification variables. In the case of the Buenos Aires TUS, the database comprises both time-use data *and* household and individual information for *all* members of the household to which the respondent belongs. The availability of this information improved both ex post analysis and data cleaning, as it allowed for editors to detect errors that could be eventually rectified.[20]

The other side of the coin is that a TUS collected as a module is a part of the household core survey it is attached to: it shares all its virtues *and* weaknesses in the form of operational definitions, global nonresponse rates, survey framework and fieldwork. In the case of this TUS, this meant missing the chance to collect information on hotels/pensions and shanty towns and having no chance of measuring seasonality in time use.

Ad hoc modules are not generally favored by household surveys designers, as they fear they might spoil core survey information by raising nonresponse rates and/or compromising the continuity of long-term series. They are usually collected after the core survey has finished and its information has been secured. In the case of the Buenos Aires TUS, there were also built-in restrictions in its design, precluding those features that could raise drop-out/rejection rates (for example, long interview times, fixed week days to collect information on and so on). However, some methodological features had to be guaranteed *in spite* of the core survey design, particularly the way respondents were selected: there was no possibility of giving up on randomly selecting the module respondent if huge biases and overrepresentation of population not in the labor market was to be avoided. The Directory General's experts advised on allowing replacements after the second visit, considering that the most difficult part – getting households to open their doors and accept responding to the survey – was in those cases already achieved. Fortunately, there were unexpected synergies between the module and the survey, particularly by allowing for an extra revisit. The possibility for revisits was instrumental in collecting better information and allowing fieldworkers to check on the data that the respondent had provided, and in decreasing nonresponse rates on particular questions (like those related to hours of paid work and income from paid work). Indeed, double-checking was two-sided and took place at many stages.

Use of a 24-hour recall activity diary

The TUS proves that in some circumstances, provided the core survey is flexible enough to cater for very specific requirements (for example, respondent selection; sufficient week day variability), it is possible to collect a time-use module that follows the 24-hour recall activity diary form. Indeed, there is no need to equate the modular approach to time-use data collection with tasks list surveys, as it has been frequently the case in Latin America (Esquivel, 2008a). Conversely, TUS based on activity diaries needn't be collected as stand-alone surveys. Even more, they needn't be self-administered to be activity diaries in the first place![21]

Activity diaries are less prone than task-list surveys to reflect designers' objectives and views, even if they are not 'value-free' data collection instruments. At the very least, they don't put words into the respondent's mouth, even if they shape answers by selecting time slots' length (which signal the respondent a minimum significant time for an activity to be so) and by filtering them through the Activity Classification System. In this respect, activity diaries allow for a more comprehensive measurement of the whole of the person's activities, since problems of 'missing activities', frequent in tasks lists survey, do not arise; rarely performed activities will simply come up less frequently and their total absence will never mean that the tasks list's designer forgot about it. Also, activity diaries provide information for the chronology of events, for example, not only the time devoted to a certain activity, but also when that activity takes place.

It cannot be sufficiently stressed that activity diaries are the only time-use collection instrument that satisfactorily caters to the collection and analysis of simultaneous activities. The Buenos Aires survey proves that simultaneity is an essential feature of time use, as simultaneity ratios and the length of the 'full-minute' average day show. Moreover, the satisfactory working of the probing question on childcare emphasizes the fact that unpaid care work is frequently performed in parallel with other activities and respondents tend to 'skip' their unpaid care work when socially more valued activities take place at the same time. Given this fact, instruments that cannot collect information on simultaneous activities have a built-in undue downward bias in their measurement.

Selected results from the Buenos Aires TUS and their relation to methodological features

Time-use estimates with nonhierarchical simultaneous activities

Time-use estimates result from the time length assigned to activities, for example, depending on whether '24-hour time' (the time assigned to activities so that all respondent's activities add up to 24 hour) or 'full-minute time' (the total number of hours per person may exceed a 24-hour period) is used to calculate them. None of these two ways of calculating time can be said to be better than the other. However, since not all activities are performed simultaneously with others with the same frequency and duration, using '24-hour time' results in a downward bias to activities more frequently performed simultaneously (unpaid care work, socializing).[22] In the same breath, it overrepresents those activities less affected by simultaneity, such as personal care activities – particularly sleeping – that cannot be performed simultaneously. In this survey, non-sleeping time amounts to 15:48 hours, on average, and simultaneity adds 4:15 hours to an average day, implying over one-quarter of average wakeful time is devoted to two or three simultaneous activities!

A comparison of population averages[23] further illustrates this point. As it is clear from Tables 8.1 and 8.2, the least simultaneously performed activities (SNA work, personal care activities and education) are the ones that lose the most in terms of the proportion of average time devoted to them when full-minute time is computed. Major gains in terms of population average time are recorded in those activities that are most extended in the population (for example, that record very high participation rates, as it will be explained further on) and present high simultaneity ratios, like social and cultural activities (including socializing) and mass media use. Among productive activities, unpaid care for children and/or adults

Table 8.1 Buenos Aires city, 2005: activities on an average day using 24-hour time, by sex

Activities on an average day (Monday through Sunday)	Total population			Women			Men		
	Hours	%	CV time	Hours	%	CV time	Hours	%	CV time
Total	*24:00*	*100.0*	*2.7*	*24:00*	*100.0*	*4.7*	*24:00*	*100.0*	*5.3*
100: SNA work	03:52	16.1	6.8	02:45	11.5	9.0	05:14	21.9	9.6
400: Household maintenance	02:11	9.1	5.9	03:03	12.8	7.4	01:06	4.6	11.5
500: Unpaid care for children and/or adults for own household	00:41	2.9	11.0	00:58	4.1	13.7	00:22	1.5	18.6
600: Unpaid community services and help to other households (relatives, friends, and neighbors)	00:11	0.8	18.9	00:16	1.1	22.1	00:05	0.4	34.4
700: Education	00:42	3.0	18.5	00:42	2.9	26.1	00:42	3.0	28.5
800: Social and cultural activities	03:01	12.6	5.1	02:56	12.3	6.4	03:07	13.0	8.7
900: Mass media use activities	02:32	10.6	5.4	02:28	10.3	7.3	02:37	10.9	8.2
000: Personal care activities	10:46	44.9	2.6	10:47	45.0	4.7	10:43	44.7	5.3

Source: Author's calculations based on the Buenos Aires TUS and DGEyC (2007a).

Table 8.2 Buenos Aires city, 2005: activities on an average day using full-minute time, by sex

Activities on an average day (Monday through Sunday)	Total population			Women			Men		
	Hours	*%*	*CV time*	*Hours*	*%*	*CV time*	*Hours*	*%*	*CV time*
Total	*28:15*	*100.0*	*2.9*	*28:28*	*100.0*	*4.8*	*28:00*	*100.0*	*8.2*
100: SNA work	04:07	14.6	6.9	02:54	10.2	9.1	05:37	20.1	9.6
400: Household maintenance	02:31	9.0	5.7	03:34	12.5	7.0	01:14	4.4	11.2
500: Unpaid care for children and/or adults for own household	00:55	3.3	10.6	01:16	4.5	13.1	00:29	1.8	18.8
600: Unpaid community services and help to other households (relatives, friends, and neighbors)	00:15	0.9	18.9	00:21	1.2	21.6	00:08	0.5	32.9
700: Education	00:45	2.7	19.1	00:47	2.8	27.1	00:44	2.7	28.8
800: Social and cultural activities	04:20	15.3	5.2	04:16	15.0	6.2	04:23	15.7	8.4
900: Mass media use activities	03:29	12.3	6.0	03:26	12.1	8.0	03:33	12.7	7.8
000: Personal care activities	11:50	41.9	2.6	11:51	41.6	4.6	11:48	42.2	5.2

Source: Author's calculations based on the Buenos Aires TUS and DGEyC (2007a).

for own household present the highest simultaneity ratios, though this feature is less evident from the comparison of Tables 8.1 and 8.2 due to its relatively low population incidence.

Not considering simultaneous activities presents obvious gender biases, even at this very aggregate level, women devote 7:03 hours (24-hour time) or 8:06 hours (full-minute time) to productive activities, for example, SNA work and unpaid care work (involving unpaid domestic work, unpaid care for children and/or adults for own household and unpaid community services[24]), while men devote 6:48 hours (24-hour time) or 7:30 hours (full-minute time). As women engage in simultaneous activities for a half an hour more than men, the gender gap between productive and nonproductive activities (all others) increases when simultaneous activities are fully taken into consideration.

Noticeably, gender-based differences emerge strongly *within* productive activities. Women and men distribute their work burdens in highly dissimilar ways. While the average time used for domestic work, care for children and adults for own household and community services by women was three times that used by men both in 24-hour and full-minute times, the time men devote to SNA work is roughly twice that used by women (Figure 8.1).

Unpaid care for children and/or adults for own household takes up 1:16 hours among women and 0:29 hours among men (full-minute time). Community services are the less frequently performed activities by the population (only 0:15 hours, on average, in full-minute time), which reflects the extremely low participation rate recorded in these activities (see below).

Time-use estimates and their statistical significance

Compared to the variations in the time spent on small individual activities, time spent on aggregate activities present relatively lower coefficients of variation (CV). CVs here are calculated both for time estimates and for the estimate of the number of persons engaging in a given activity. This is the 'bottom-up approach' in time-use data collection and analysis, in the sense that the degree of statistically significant activity disaggregation is determined ex post by activity frequency – as opposed to tasks lists, in which the degree of disaggregation is determined ex ante by the detail and length of the activity list. The highest CVs in Tables 8.1 and 8.2 correspond to unpaid community services, which are the least frequent activities and the ones in which participants engage in during the shortest average time. As Table 8.3 shows, 11 per cent of women, but only 5 per cent of men, engage in unpaid community services and

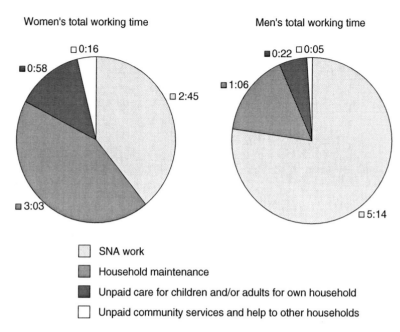

Women's total working time

Men's total working time

- SNA work
- Household maintenance
- Unpaid care for children and/or adults for own household
- Unpaid community services and help to other households

Source: DGEyC (2007a).

Figure 8.1 Buenos Aires city, 2005: total working time using 24-hour time, by sex

help to other households. As in all unpaid care working time activities, women participate more *and* the time female participants devote to these activities is higher than men's. This difference peaks in household maintenance (400), in which over 90 per cent of women participate (as opposed to 66 per cent men) and time devoted by women who participate is twice as much as the time devoted by men. Low CVs allow for the making of this comparison.[25]

As a general rule, CVs are lower for participation rates than for the time used in the activity, though patterns are similar. Table 8.3 shows particularly low CVs for participation rates in social and cultural activities, mass media use activities and household maintenance. Social and cultural activities present very high participation rates (and simultaneity) and quite high times by participant because this category includes socializing. This is the result of spontaneous accounts of activities by respondents, as well as of the instruction given to fieldworkers to record 'socializing with others' if respondents stated that they were 'with others' (like family or friends).[26] Given this approach, the difference between

Table 8.3 Buenos Aires city, 2005: participation rates and time by participant on an average day, by sex

Activities on an average day (Monday through Sunday)	Total population				Women				Men			
	Hours by participant		Part rate	CV pers.	Hours by participant		Part rate	CV pers.	Hours by participant		Part rate	CV pers.
	24-hour	Full-minute			24-hour	Full-minute			24-hour	Full-minute		
Total	*24:00*	*28:15*	*100*	*2.7*	*24:00*	*28:29*	*100*	*4.7*	*24:00*	*28:00*	*100*	*5.3*
100: SNA work	08:26	09:00	46	5.4	07:43	08:09	36	8.5	08:59	09:39	58	8.4
400: Household maintenance	02:42	03:08	81	3.8	03:18	03:51	93	5.5	01:40	01:53	66	6.7
500: Unpaid care for children and/or adults for own household	02:42	03:34	26	8.6	03:07	04:07	31	10.7	01:52	02:30	20	14.2
600: Unpaid community services and help to other households (relatives, friends, and neighbors)	02:16	03:02	8	14.8	02:29	03:13	11	16.0	01:43	02:33	5	29.8
700: Education	05:06	05:31	14	12.9	05:01	05:34	14	16.9	05:11	05:27	14	22.7
800: Social and cultural activities	03:20	04:47	90	2.9	03:13	04:41	91	5.2	03:30	04:55	89	5.9
900: Mass media use activities	02:51	03:54	89	3.1	02:45	03:49	90	5.1	02:58	04:02	88	5.8
000: Personal care activities	10:46	11:50	100	2.7	10:47	11:51	100	4.7	10:43	11:48	100	5.3

Source: Author's calculations based on the Buenos Aires TUS and DGEyC (2007b).

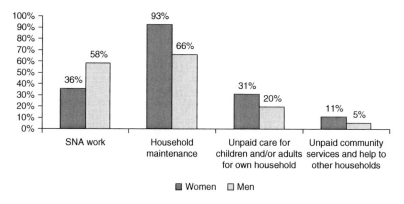

Source: DGEyC (2007a).

Figure 8.2 Buenos Aires city, 2005: participation rates in different types of work, by sex

participation rates for weekdays and weekend days' in these activities was not as strong as expected.[27] The same pattern is evident in mass media use activities, though in this case there is the possibility of recalling up to three nonhierarchical activities that 'made room' for reports on listening to the radio and watching TV *while* doing other things (1 hour out of the 3:54 hours devoted, on average, by participants).

Only 35 per cent of women between 15 and 74 years of age engage in SNA work, as opposed to 58 per cent of men. Coefficients of variation for these participation rates are similar (8.5). Differences in average hours between men and women who engage in paid work are not that important (1:30 hours in full-minute time).[28] Indeed, those who are working for pay do have very long working days, irrespective of their sex.[29]

Daily rhythms

The 24-hour recall activity diary allows for the analysis of daily rhythms in time use, a rich time-use dimension that adds to activity duration analysis.

Figures 8.3, 8.4, 8.5 and 8.6 show average full-minute time devoted to different activity types[30] for employed men, employed women, not-employed men (either unemployed or inactive) and not-employed women (either unemployed or inactive) in Buenos Aires city. These figures are built by adding up average full-minute time devoted to each one-digit activity, at every half hour. In doing so, they graphically show

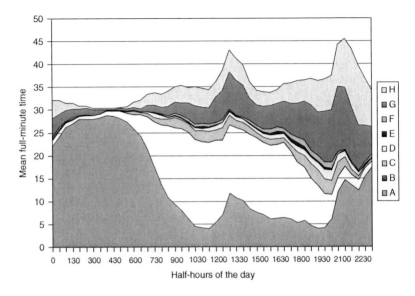

A – Personal care activities; B – SNA work; C – Household maintenance; D – Unpaid care for
children and/or adults for own household; E – Unpaid community services and help to other
households (relatives, friends and neighbors); F – Education; G – Social and cultural activities;
H – Mass media use activities.
The structure of total Buenos Aires TUS's population is as follows: 34% are employed men,
30% are employed women, 11% are not-employed men and 25% are not-employed women.
Source: Author's calculations based on the Buenos Aires TUS.
Figure 8.3 Employed men: full-minute time during the half hours of an aver-
age day

both daily rhythms *and* simultaneity patterns for selected population
groups.[31]

At every half hour, times exceeding 30 minutes reflect simultaneously
performed activities. The least simultaneous activities (personal care)
explain the 'shorter' half hours at the beginning of the days. For all
subgroups, peaks in simultaneity arise at lunch and dinner time, though
they are less marked among not-employed men.[32] Also, women engage
more regularly in simultaneous activities than men, so their total time
frontier is higher than 35 minutes for almost all half hours from 9 am
onwards.

Personal care daily rhythms coincide, on average, among employed
women and men, as does the productive frontier (paid plus unpaid care
work) for most of the daylight hours – though women's productive time

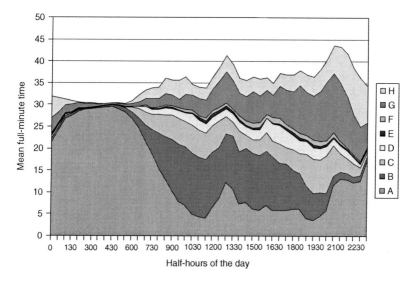

Notes:

A – Personal care activities; B – SNA work; C – Household maintenance; D – Unpaid care for children and/or adults for own household; E – Unpaid community services and help to other households (relatives, friends and neighbors); F – Education; G – Social and cultural activities; H – Mass media use activities.

The structure of total Buenos Aires TUS's population is as follows: 34% are employed men, 30% are employed women, 11% are not-employed men and 25% are not-employed women.

Source: Author's calculations based on the Buenos Aires TUS.

Figure 8.4 Employed women: full-minute time during the half hours of an average day

increases from 7 pm onwards. The figures also show very clearly how this productive work is distributed along gender lines, even among those employed. During all daylight hours, an important fraction of employed women's time is devoted to domestic work and care for children and/or adults for own household, while, on average, employed men devote to these activities less than half the time employed women do. Leisure time also has a slightly different composition, with employed women devoting relatively more time to social and cultural activities and employed men to mass media use at evening and night hours. Education is an important activity, particularly during evenings, for employed men and for employed women, a pattern that shows that students (particularly tertiary and university) also consistently engage in SNA work.[33]

These patterns present a striking contrast to not-employed men and women.[34] Interestingly, not-employed men engage in simultaneous

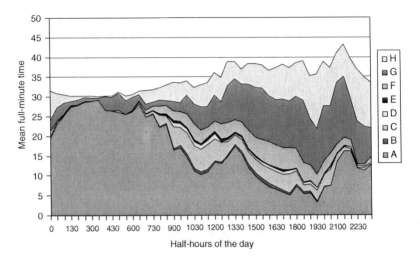

Notes:
A – Personal care activities; B – SNA work; C – Household maintenance; D – Unpaid care for children and/or adults for own household; E – Unpaid community services and help to other households (relatives, friends and neighbors); F – Education; G – Social and cultural activities; H – Mass media use activities.
The structure of total Buenos Aires TUS's population is as follows: 34% are employed men, 30% are employed women, 11% are not-employed men and 25% are not-employed women.
Source: Author's calculations based on the Buenos Aires TUS.
Figure 8.5   Not-employed men: full-minute time during the half hours of an average day

activities more often during afternoons and the evening time, while not-employed women do so more consistently along the day. Generally speaking, not-employed men are in education and not-employed women are either in education or are housewives, which is evident by the amount of domestic working time and child and adult care time they engage in. Again, it is more the time pattern of child and adult care than its amount that differs between employed and not-employed women: employed women care for children and adults increasingly over the course of the day with a peak at 11 am, and then descending during the afternoon to reach another peak at 5 pm, showing a pattern of care that has to be reconciled with paid work; on the contrary, not-employed women increase their child and adult care activity as hours pass – particularly during the afternoon – to reach a peak at 6 pm. It should also be noticed that it is among the not-employed women that unpaid community services and help to other households become significant.

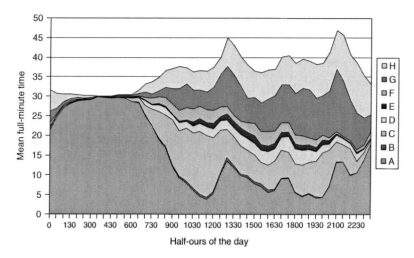

Notes:
A – Personal care activities; B – SNA work; C – Household maintenance; D – Unpaid care for children and/or adults for own household; E – Unpaid community services and help to other households (relatives, friends and neighbors); F – Education; G – Social and cultural activities; H – Mass media use activities.

The structure of total Buenos Aires TUS's population is as follows: 34% are employed men, 30% are employed women, 11% are not-employed men and 25% are not-employed women.

Source: Author's calculations based on the Buenos Aires TUS.

Figure 8.6 Not-employed women: full-minute time during the half hours of an average day

Extended possibilities for the analysis of time use when rich socioeconomic data is available

Collecting time-use data as a module of an ongoing household survey allows one to produce a comprehensive analysis of time-use data, benefiting from the existence of consistent demographic and socioeconomic information both for the individual *and* her/his household. This can partly compensate for the use of the individual as the unit of analysis, since individuals carry with them not only their own, but also all household members', characteristics. Indeed, the Buenos Aires TUS does allow to link the time use of respondents with their individual characteristics (sex, age in years, education in years, household member type – head, spouse, daughter/son or other, labor market status – inactive, unemployed or employed, earnings and so on) *and* household characteristics (household structure, employed members and dependency

Table 8.4 Buenos Aires city, 2005: participation rates and time by participant on an average day devoted to household maintenance and unpaid care for children and/or adults for own household, by sex and presence of children

	Women			Men		
	24-hour time by participant	Full-minute time by participant	Participation rate (%)	24-hour by participant	Full-minute time by participant	Participation rate (%)
Household maintenance						
Total	03:18	03:51	93	01:40	01:53	66
In households with:						
At least one child 5 or under	03:12	03:58	93	01:31	01:44	60
Children between 6 and 13	03:44	04:14	95	01:38	01:45	62
Adolescents (14–17)	03:08	03:39	92	02:11	02:26	58
Neither children nor adolescents	03:16	03:45	92	01:38	01:52	70
Unpaid care for children and/or adults for own household						
Total	03:07	04:07	31	01:52	02:30	20
In households with:						
At least one child 5 or under	03:44	05:06	91	02:01	02:33	72
Children between 6 and 13	02:41	03:25	62	01:35	02:14	41
Adolescents (14–17)	01:49	02:03	22	00:39	00:53	9
Neither children nor adolescents (*)	02:22	02:50	5	02:29	04:00	3

Note: There is no overlap in the categories 'households with at least one child five or under,' 'households with children 6–13' and 'households with adolescents (14–17).'

Source: Author's calculations, based on the Buenos Aires TUS.

* Households with neither children nor adolescents in which women/men participated in unpaid care for children and/or adults for own household. These are divorced mothers/(mostly) fathers in whose households the children do not live most of the week and of which they are therefore technically not members. The Buenos Aires TUS considered this unpaid childcare as 'for own household.'

Table 8.5 Buenos Aires city, 2005: participation rates and full-minute time by participant on an average day devoted to unpaid childcare for own household's children, by sex, household type and presence of children

	Total		Women		Men	
	Participation rate %	Full-minute time by participant	Participation rate %	Full-minute time by participant	Participation rate %	Full-minute time by participant
Persons providing unpaid childcare for own household's children	23	03:41	27	04:17	18	02:34
In households with						
Complete nuclear-family households						
At least one child 5 or under	90	04:24	92	05:50	86	02:30
Children between 6 and 13	56	03:05	62	03:41	47	02:06
Adolescents (14–17)	12	01:15	19	01:24	4	00:28
Extended families						
At least one child 5 or under	59	03:17	80	03:21	32	03:02
Children between 6 and 13	41	02:22	46	02:13	34	02:39
Adolescents (14–17)	22	02:32	22	02:52	24	01:30

Note: There is no overlap in the categories 'households with at least one child 5 or under,' 'households with children 6–13' and 'households with adolescents (14–17).' Participation rates are calculated over total population living in households with children in each different household type. Complete nuclear households with at least one child 17 or under account for 30% of population while extended families account for 8% of total population (other omitted household types with children account for another 4% of total population).
Source: Author's calculations, based on the Buenos Aires TUS.

rates, household income, presence and age of children, children's school attendance and so on).

Among the many refinements that the Buenos Aires TUS allows, the analysis of unpaid care work and its relation to the presence of children has proved to be particularly crucial in understanding care burdens and gender differences in total working time.[35]

Time devoted to child and adult care for own household's members, as well as participation rates, are highly correlated with the presence of children and decrease as the age of the child or children increases. Amounts peak at 5:06 hours among women and 2:33 hours among men (full-minute time) living in households with at least one child five-years of age or younger. It is in these households that the rate of participation in child and adult care is also the highest (91 per cent for women and 72 per cent for men). The difference between the time devoted by participating men and participating women (approximately 50 per cent) persists as childcare needs decrease with children's increasing age.

On the other hand, neither the time devoted to household maintenance nor the participation rates in it are sensitive to the age of own household children. Among women who participate, the most time is dedicated to household maintenance in households with children between the ages 6 and 13 (4:14 hours, full-minute time), while the peak for participating men is in households with adolescents (2:26 hours, full-minute time). It is in these latter households, however, that men's participation rate is the lowest (58 per cent).

Pushing the analysis further, participation in unpaid childcare and the amount of time devoted to it are highly correlated with children's ages, showing that adult care is relatively less important, particularly in households where there are children and no majors (complete nuclear families with children). Ninety-three per cent of women and 86 per cent of men (almost all mothers and fathers[36]) in nuclear households with at least one child five or under participate in caregiving. The number of hours devoted to caring for children 5 or under by participants is, in all cases, high and is above the average number of unpaid childcare hours for the overall population – 5:50 hours for the 92 per cent of women who provide unpaid childcare in nuclear households and 2:30 hours for the 86 per cent of men who do so.

Men's participation in care, when there are children five or under, drops sharply in extended households as a result of the greater number of potential caregivers and the greater likelihood that the survey interviewed a member who was not the children's father.

Concluding remarks

The main lesson to be derived from the Buenos Aires TUS is that an unprejudiced, yet meticulous, approach to time-use collection in second- (or third- or more!) best scenarios can prove fruitful. Abandoning the idealized stand-alone time-use data collection approach was a first good step. Carefully thinking about trade-offs and documenting compromises made all along the way has also helped to frame data analysis and recognize its strengths and limits.

As mentioned, designing a TUS module in an ongoing household survey implied accepting all core survey characteristics as given. Among the many limits this imposed on the TUS is the lack of seasonality measuring, the impediments to probing labor force participation due to differences in reference periods and the nonfeasibility of surveying all household members due to extensive interview times. I believe, however, that only the latter is relevant, since it made the individual (not the household) the unit of analysis.[37] This feature, which constrains distributive analysis within households, is partly overcome by having extensive information on household characteristics. Other limitations of the survey result from conscious decisions taken at design stages, based on the belief that there is no 'one-size-fits-all' TUS. This is particularly the case with respect to some difficult issues, like child labor. Only if children respond freely by themselves to the time-use questionnaires – with no interference from parents, either explicit or implicit – could a survey like this be used to accurately identify different forms of child labor. However, this could not be guaranteed, even in the context of the highly literate, relatively middle-class Buenos Aires population, and measuring child labor as one of the TUS objectives was dismissed from the outset.[38]

A future round of the Buenos Aires TUS should include the populations of pensions and shanty towns. Probing questions could possibly be restricted to childcare, given the little incidence of the other two probing questions. Additional questions on daily childcare hours received by children five-years of age or younger and on hours of paid domestic help – keeping 'yesterday' as a reference time – should be added, at least to use them as controls in multivariate analysis. A larger sample size (for example, extending the module to more than two tranches and/or selecting more household members) could eventually improve the statistical significance of the measures of activity times.

The Buenos Aires TUS has also paved the path for future, nationwide time-use data collection as a module of ongoing household surveys, possibly the EPH (Encuesta Permanente de Hogares) collected by INDEC.

The EPH shares many characteristics with the Buenos Aires Annual Household Survey and has the advantage of being collected in all major Argentine urban areas.

Advocacy, planning, funding and further collaboration among statistical offices and academia are all required for time-use data collection to become a reality at the national level in the Argentinean context. Using Buenos Aires time-use data to promote gender-aware policy analysis will help to move in this direction.

Notes

* I would like to thank Debbie Budlender, Marzia Fontana, Corina Rodríguez Enríquez and Ana Laura Fernández for engaging with me in reflecting on some of the issues covered by this chapter and reading and commenting on previous versions. All remaining errors are my responsibility.

1. There was a short module (only yes/no questions to ten tasks plus time allocated to perform them all) attached to the 2001 Living Conditions Survey. See Esquivel (2006) for further reference. Also, in 1998, a TUS was collected in the City of Buenos Aires as part of a National Women's Council research project, but only women older than 14 years of age were interviewed (see Rupnik and Colombo, 2006).

2. At the time, the Buenos Aires Directorate-General of Statistics and Census held a group of outstanding professionals, both for their credentials and their experience in household survey collection, who were all instrumental in bringing about the Buenos Aires TUS as an integral part of the 2005 Buenos Aires Annual Household Survey.

3. Strictly speaking, the Annual Household Survey is representative of the Buenos Aires city population living in residential households.

4. INDEC, Instituto Nacional de Estadísticas y Censos is the Argentine National Statistical Office.

5. The household 'head' (she/he who is recognized as such by other household members) is the Annual Household Survey preferred respondent for the household and dwelling questionnaire. Each individual questionnaire contains household members' personal information and is expected to be provided by the respondent in person, except for children (below 15 years of age). However, if the household head was not present, any adult (15 years old or over) could eventually answer on household information; if household members were not present and could not be contacted, their individual questionnaires could be answered by another adult household member (18 years old or over). Irrespective of the designated respondent, individual information for all household members should be collected before considering a household interview complete (DGEyC, 2005a:33).

6. When a selected member could not be contacted, the replacement was randomly selected again (DGEyC, 2005b:3).

7. During the pilot test, an alternative time schedule with moving starting and ending hours (based on the time of the interview) was tried. As it did not

improve recall quality and was thought to increase fieldworkers' burden and eventually their errors, it was abandoned.

8. See Budlender (2007) for a comparison.

9. A similar question is also included in the 2000 Cuban TUS (ONE, 2002).

10. Clearly, the Buenos Aires TUS did not have among its objectives to better measure the size of the labor force and took employment status as given. As the reference periods for the identification of labor force status and that of the TUS differed (last week for labor force information, 'yesterday' for the activity diary) there is no way of performing exact consistency checks between the two sources of information and none is considered superior. Indeed, it could be possible that someone was unemployed or inactive last week, but working for pay yesterday. These cases were hardly significant: only 3.3 per cent of those who reported doing paid work were either inactive or unemployed according to their employment status.

11. For a comparison between the Buenos Aires Activity Classification System and that of the 2000 South African TUS, see Budlender (2007:13).

12. Which would allow for up to six activities in a given half an hour if there is a 'main' and a 'secondary' activity in each of them.

13. A frequent error at the outset was to read each of the lines of the 30-minute time slots as if they were 10-minute time slots (with no simultaneous activities). This was detected during training – when prospect fieldworkers had to fill in their own diaries – and in the first week of fieldwork, and corrected on the spot.

14. The pilot test showed that prospects respondents asked about interview length before opting in/out of the survey. Answering to official surveys is protected by the Statistical Secret Law, and is neither compulsory nor paid for in Argentina.

15. Strata corresponded to the 16 Centros de Gestión y Participación (Centers to deal with Administrative and Participatory Matters, decentralized municipal offices that, at the time, roughly corresponded to neighborhoods).

16. Out of the 3 million people that lived in the City of Buenos Aires in 2005, 2.4 million people were between the ages of 15 and 74. Among those, 260.000 persons were not represented because they were room tenants in hotels/pensions or lived in shanty-towns.

17. The presence of three activities in the same time slot complicates the analysis, since the activities may be entirely simultaneous, successive, two simultaneous during only a portion of the time slot while a third takes place successively and so on. All of the possible combinations were considered in assigning full-minute time to each activity. See Time Assignation Chart in the Appendix.

18. These checks were performed comparing the Buenos Aires TUS population to that of the Annual Household Survey population between the ages of 15 and 74.

19. Typically, respondents differentiate what they consider 'proper' (paid) work from very informal/irregular alternatives which nevertheless generate an income. However, the Buenos Aires TUS shows this phenomenon to be marginal.

20. As in the case of some living-in paid domestic workers whose activities were initially coded as household maintenance and unpaid care work.

21. Equating activity diaries to self-administered diaries is a 'developed-country' bias, sometimes supported by developing countries' time-use experts (see, for

example, Milosavljevic and Tacla, 2007). It implies that developing countries cannot collect information based on activity diaries because of their population characteristics (for example, rural and illiterate populations) and misses the chance of seriously considering whether it is feasible to follow the 24-hour recall activity diary.

22. The difference in hours in an average day calculated using 24-hour time and full-minute time is the average simultaneity recorded in each activity category.

23. Averages were computed as follows: for total population – total time divided total population; for women only – women's total time divided by female population; for men only – men's total time divided by male population.

24. I am following the UNIFEM (2005:24) definition, which is the equivalent of non-SNA work. Unpaid care work is '"unpaid" meaning that the person doing the activity does not receive a wage for it; [is] "care" meaning that the activity serves people and their well-being; [and is] "work" meaning that the activity has a cost in terms of time and energy and arises out of social or contractual obligation, such as marriage or less formal societal relationships.'

25. Technically, tests for statistically significant mean difference can be performed.

26. In particular, identifying the difference between 'socializing with family' and 'childcare' posed a challenge to fieldworkers, according to children's ages and who else was present. Typically, a dinner at home with family and young children could involve both.

27. Of the total population 88 per cent engages in social and cultural activities during weekdays and 91 percent do so during weekends.

28. These participation rates are lower than the average employed population between 15 and 74 years of age (55 per cent among women, 76 per cent among men), since in any average day, some employed persons may not engage in SNA work (weekends, holidays, leaves and so on).

29. It should be noted that according to the Activity Classification System, traveling time is added to the activity originating the need for transportation. Therefore, SNA work includes time to get to and come back from paid work.

30. For example, total time divided by total subpopulation under analysis.

31. These graphs differ from standard daily rhythm graphs in the sense that each half-hour is not equal to any other (the graph is not respecting the 24-hour cap). An alternative to this presentation using full-minute time is normalizing to 100 per cent of time in each half-hour, as it has been done in DGEyC (2007b).

32. Note that employed men account for 11 per cent of total population, 2 percentage points are unemployed men and 9 percentage points are inactive men. Not much of this time-use pattern should therefore been accrued to 'forced idleness.'

33. Indeed, 46 per cent of those who engaged in educational activities were employed.

34. Out of the 25 per cent of total population not-employed women account for, 3 percentage points are unemployed women and 22 percentage points are inactive women.

35. Tobit regressions show that the presence of at least one child five-years of age or younger is the strongest household factor to influence time devoted

to unpaid care work and child and/or adult care (both for own household and for own and other households), over household structure and income variables. In Buenos Aires, 17.1 per cent of the population between 15 and 74 years of age lives in households with at least one child five-years of age or younger. Among income related variables, only poverty (and not per capita income quintile) was significant to explain time devoted to unpaid care work and childcare. The (absolute) poverty rate for Buenos Aires in 2005 was 5.9 per cent (Esquivel, 2008b).

36. It may happen that the respondent to the module is a sibling over 14. However, the crosstab between the type of member and type of household shows that these cases are marginal in the age bracket consisting of households with children five and under (only 4 percent of the total cases in the sample).
37. It is worth noting that most TUS share this constraint with the Buenos Aires TUS.
38. By that time, a specific survey on child labor, funded by the ILO Buenos Aires Office and the Ministry of Labor had just been collected (OIT, 2006).

References

Budlender, D. (2007) 'A Critical Review of Selected Time Use Surveys,' Programme Paper No. 2 (Geneva: United Nations Research Institute for Social Development – UNRISD).

Budlender, D., N. Chobokoane and Y. Mpetsheni. (2001) *A Survey of Time Use: How South African Women and Men Spend Their Time* (Pretoria: Statistics South Africa).

Consejo Nacional de la Mujer (2006) *Decir mujer es decir trabajo. Metodologías para la medición del uso del tiempo con perspectiva de género* (Buenos Aires: Consejo Nacional de la Mujer).

Dirección General de Estadística y Censos, G.C.B.A. (DGEyC) (2005a) *Encuesta Anual de Hogares 2005. Manual del Encuestador* (Buenos Aires: DGEyC).

Dirección General de Estadística y Censos, G.C.B.A. (DGEyC) (2005b) *Encuesta Anual de Hogares 2005. Encuesta de Uso del Tiempo. Manual del Encuestador,* http://estatico.buenosaires.gov.ar/areas/hacienda/sis_estadistico/2005/manual_enc.pdf

Dirección General de Estadística y Censos, G.C.B.A. (DGEyC) (2005c) *Encuesta Anual de Hogares 2005. Encuesta de Uso del Tiempo. Diario de Actividades,* http://estatico.buenosaires.gov.ar/areas/hacienda/sis_estadistico/2005/diario_actividades.pdf

Dirección General de Estadística y Censos, G.C.B.A. (DGEyC) (2006) *Encuesta Anual de Hogares de la Ciudad de Buenos Aires 2005. Síntesis Metodológic* (Buenos Aires: DGEyC).

Dirección General de Estadística y Censos, G.C.B.A. (DGEyC) (2007a) 'Encuesta Anual de Hogares 2005, Encuesta de Uso del Tiempo, El tiempo de trabajo total. Mujeres y varones en la Ciudad de Buenos Aires', Informe de Resultados No. 328, September, http://www.buenosaires.gov.ar/areas/hacienda/sis_estadistico/informe_328_encuesta_de_uso_del_tiempo.pdf

Dirección General de Estadística y Censos, G.C.B.A. (DGEyC) (2007b) 'Encuesta Anual de Hogares 2005, Encuesta de Uso del Tiempo, La utilización del tiempo de las mujeres y los varones', Informe de Resultados No. 329, September, http://

www.buenosaires.gov.ar/areas/hacienda/sis_estadistico/informe_329_encuesta_de_uso_del_tiempo.pdf

Esquivel, V. (2006) 'What else do we have to cope with? Gender, paid and unpaid work during Argentina's last crisis,' Working Paper Series 06-6 (CITY?: The International Working Group on Gender, Macroeconomics, and International Economics).

Esquivel, V. (2008a) 'Time Use Surveys in Latin America' in *Explorations: Time Use Surveys in the South*, Feminist Economics, April–June.

Esquivel, V. (2008b) 'An Analysis of Time-Use Data on Work/Care Arrangements and Macro Data on the Care Diamond,' Research Report 2 Argentina, The Political and Social Economy of Care Project, UNRISD.

Milosavljevic, V. and O. Tacla. (2007) 'Incorporando un módulo de uso del tiempo a las encuestas de hogares: restricciones y potencialidades,' Serie Mujer y Desarrollo N° 83, Unidad Mujer y Desarrollo (Santiago: ECLAC).

Oficina Internacional del Trabajo (OIT) (2006) *Infancia y adolescencia: trabajo y otras actividades económicas. Primera encuesta. Análisis de resultados en cuatro subregiones de la Argentina* (Buenos Aires: OIT).

Oficina Nacional de Estadísticas, Cuba (ONE) (2002) *Encuesta sobre el Uso del Tiempo*, La Habana, http://www.one.cu/publicaciones/enfoquegenero/tiempo/UsoTiempo.rar

Rupnik, A. and P. Colombo (2006) 'Las Mujeres cuentan, contemos el trabajo de las Mujeres. Investigación sobre distribución del uso del tiempo entre las mujeres de la Ciudad de Buenos Aires' in Consejo Nacional de la Mujer (2006), pp. 109–156.

United Nations Development Fund for Women (UNIFEM) (2005) *Progress of the World's Women 2005, 'Women, Work and Poverty'*, prepared by M. Chen, J. Vanek, F. Lund and J. Heintz, with R. Jhabvala and C. Bonner (New York: UNIFEM).

United Nations Statistics Division (UNISTAT) (2005) *Guide to Producing Statistics on Time Use: Measuring Paid and Unpaid Work* (New York; UNISTAT).

Appendix: Time assignation chart

Table 8A.1 shows times accrued to each activity depending on whether the activity was unique/appeared with one other activity or with two other activities in a given time slot; and whether it was simultaneous (occurred at the same time of another activity and got a code '1') or consecutive (did not occur at the same time of another activity and got a code '2') in a pair-wise comparison with each of the other activities reported in the same time slot.

Table 8A.1 Time assignation chart

Activities in each time slot	At the same time as...			
	First activity	*Second activity*	*24-hour time*	*Full-minute time*
Activity 1			30	30
Activity 1			15	30
Activity 2	1		15	30
Activity 1			10	30
Activity 2	1		10	30
Activity 3	1	1	10	30
Activity 1			10	30
Activity 2	1		10	15
Activity 3	1	2	10	15
Activity 1			10	15
Activity 2	1		10	30
Activity 3	2	1	10	15
Activity 1			10	20
Activity 2	1		10	20
Activity 3	2	2	10	10
Activity 1			15	15
Activity 2	2		15	15
Activity 1			10	15
Activity 2	2		10	15
Activity 3	1	1	10	30

(Continued)

Table 8A.1   Continued

Activities in each time slot	At the same time as...		24-hour time	Full-minute time
	First activity	*Second activity*		
Activity 1			10	20
Activity 2	2		10	10
Activity 3	1	2	10	20
Activity 1			10	10
Activity 2	2		10	20
Activity 3	2	1	10	20
Activity 1			10	10
Activity 2	2		10	10
Activity 3	2	2	10	10

9
Issues in Time-Use Measurement and Valuation: Lessons from African Experience on Technical and Analytical Issues

Jacques Charmes

Introduction

Since the mid-1990s, several TUS have been carried out in developing countries, especially in Africa; several are presently on-going. Methodological issues have been raised and experience has been gained from these various surveys, although this type of survey was originally designed for developed countries.

Based on field experience in Benin and Madagascar, as well as on various studies at the local level, this chapter addresses some technical issues arising from the implementation of TUS in rural traditional societies such as the notion of time, seasonality, simultaneous activities and sampling procedures, among others.

Also, in the present period, when time poverty reveals itself more and more as a crucial dimension of poverty, especially for women, the chapter stresses the weak use that is made of TUS results, from an analytical point of view, as well as from a political point of view. Potential correlation between time-use patterns and income or poverty groups, the health status of household members or the proximity of infrastructure has not really been investigated. As to the use of the TUS results for policy purposes, it has too often remained circumscribed to the international institutions that fund and support them, without any real impact on policy makers at national levels.

TUS carried out at national level have, for a long time, been confined to industrialized countries where they were designed to measure the transformation towards a society and an economy of leisure. More recently their results were used to show the changing roles of men and women in domestic activities. But it is, of course, the measurement of domestic activities and of the care economy that always was their major objective, as well as the measurement of their transformation with the massive entry of women into the labor market and the rise of the elderly and the disabled in the population.

Nonetheless, developing countries, especially sub-Saharan African countries, are not lacking experience in this domain. Since the 1960s and the 1970s TUS have been carried out at the local level. Although these surveys were often limited to the measurement of time spent at work (and especially in subsistence activities), activity patterns and energy expenditure, and confined to village studies or very small and often nonrepresentative samples, the experience gained from them is highly valuable. It is only recently that nationwide surveys have been implemented in Africa, with the support of UNDP programs and the UN statistics division. In Africa, Benin was the first country to embark on the implementation of this type of survey in 1998, with the direct aim of providing data for the national human development report dedicated to gender issues. It was followed by a pilot survey in Nigeria (1999), a national study in Morocco (1998–99), then in South Africa (2000), Madagascar (2001) and, more recently, Mauritius (2003) conducted such surveys. Moreover, a national TUS has been carried out in Tunisia over an entire year (2005–2006). In the meantime, however, some living standards surveys (especially in Ghana) included a time-use section in their questionnaire in order to capture the main domestic or nonmarket activities.

Also, to further a program on 'Mainstreaming Gender in Poverty Reduction Strategies: National Accounts, National Budgets and TUS' by the African Centre for Gender and Development (ACGD) of the United Nations Economic Commission for Africa (UNECA), a program on 'Time-Use Continuous Household Survey' has been launched in four African countries, namely South Africa, Uganda, Cameroon and Djibouti. The survey in Djibouti was supposed to be implemented in 2006 with the support of UNECA.

In the context of developing countries, one of the major aims of TUS is to assess the underestimation of male and (mainly) female participation to the labor force. In particular, they aim at giving an estimate of their contribution to the industrial sectors where they are often engaged in secondary activities that are not recorded by regular labor-force surveys (especially in the processing of agricultural and food products, and also in textiles/clothing activities). Moreover, results from TUS were of great help in the implementation of the 1993 SNA in countries where non-market production for own consumption (including fetching water and wood) or own capital formation is widespread. But they are also used for measurement of domestic services (unpaid, non-SNA activities) in these countries as well and the UNECA program just mentioned intends to build satellite accounts of household production. More recently, TUS have contributed to illustrating another dimension of poverty – lack of time due to multiple timetables (domestic work, care work, nonmarket economic activity and volunteer work) resulting in time poverty and low monetary income.

Tables 9.1 and 9.2 provide a summary of results from four national TUS in Africa.

Keeping in mind that the figures presented in Tables 9.1 and 9.2 cover the whole population, including the youth, pupils and students, the elderly, the active and the inactive, it is interesting to note that a woman's working day (in its broad sense) lasts from 5 hours and 43 minutes in South Africa to 7 hours and 52 minutes in Benin, while a man's day lasts from 4 hours and 25 minutes in South Africa to 6 hours and 9 minutes in Mauritius. It is also interesting to note that the total work put in by a man and a woman, on average, varies from 13 hours and 41 minutes in Madagascar to 10 hours and 8 minutes in South Africa.

In all cases, at national level (as well as at urban or rural level), a woman's working day is longer than a man's (from 7 per cent in Mauritius and 13 per cent in rural Madagascar to 41 per cent in Benin and 46 per cent in rural Benin). That is, female work time as a percentage of male work time is highest in Benin and lowest in Mauritius.

On average, the share of SNA activities (activities which are accounted for in the GDP) in total work is 59 per cent, but it drops down to 43 per cent for women and rises up to 80 per cent for men (Figure 9.2); yet in these figures, water and wood fetching are accounted for in SNA activities (for a detailed presentation of the definitions of work and SNA activities, see Charmes and Unni, 2004 and Charmes, 2006). What is important to note is that there does not seem to be any strong relationship between men's share in SNA work and women's share in non-SNA work in the sense that women's SNA work does not seem to increase with men's share in non-SNA work. This could be because women's SNA and non-SNA work is determined more by cultural norms than by sharing of work.

After this introduction, this chapter is divided into two sections. The first section will address some general or specific issues regarding the concepts, techniques and methodologies used for data collection. The second section points out some of the reasons why TUS have remained so much underanalyzed and underused in the African context.

Table 9.1 Time devoted to economic activity and to work, by gender in various countries (hours(h) and minutes(m) per day)

	Benin (1998)			South Africa (2000)			Madagascar (2001)			Mauritius (2003)		
	Women	Men	Women/ Men(%)	Women	Men	Women/ Men (%)	Women	Men	Women/ Men (%)	Women	Men	Women/ Men (%)
SNA production	4 h 37 m	4 h 26 m	104	1 h 55 m	3 h 10 m	61	3 h 42 m	5 h 40 m	65	1 h 56 m	4 h 56 m	39
Extended SNA production: domestic activities, carework	3 h 15 m	1 h 4 m	308	3 h 48 m	1 h 15 m	304	3 h 35 m	44 m	489	4 h 37 m	1 h 13 m	379
Total work	7 h 52 m	5 h 30 m	143	5 h 43 m	4 h 25 m	129	7 h 17 m	6 h 24 m	114	6 h 33 m	6 h 9 m	106
% SNA in work	58.7%	80.6%	72.8	33.5%	71.7%	47.0	50.8%	88.5%	57.4	29.5%	80.2%	36.8

Table 9.2   Gender, work and time allocation

	Year	Total work time (minutes per day) Women	Total work time (minutes per day) Men	Female work time (% of male)	Total work time (%) SNA activities	Total work time (%) Non-SNA activities	Time spent by women SNA activities	Time spent by women Non-SNA activities	Time spent by men SNA activities	Time spent by men Non-SNA activities
National										
Benin	1998	478	339	141	67	33	58	42	81	19
Madagascar	2001	437	383	114	68	32	51	49	88	12
Mauritius	2003	393	369	107	54	46	30	70	80	20
South Africa	2000	343	265	129	47	53	34	66	72	28
Urban										
Benin	1998	428	323	133	64	36	55	45	79	21
Madagascar	2001	400	344	116	61	39	44	56	84	16
Rural										
Benin	1998	508	348	146	69	31	61	39	82	18
Madagascar	2001	451	398	113	70	30	53	47	90	10

Sources: Table elaborated on basis of the results of national TUS: INSAE/PNUD (1998), Enquête emploi du temps au Bénin, Méthodologie et résultats, Cotonou, 32p. + 156 p. annexes; Statistics South Africa (2001), How South African Women and Men spend their time, A survey of time use, Pretoria, 118p,; INSTAT- DSM/PNUD-MAG/97/007: EPM 2001 – Module Emploi du Temps, Antananarivo; Republic of Mauritius, Central Statistics Office (2004), Continuous Multi-Purpose Household Survey 2003, Main results of the time-use study, 14pp.

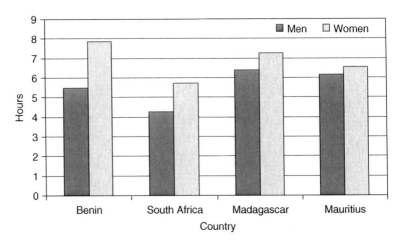

Figure 9.1   Total work time by gender (hours)

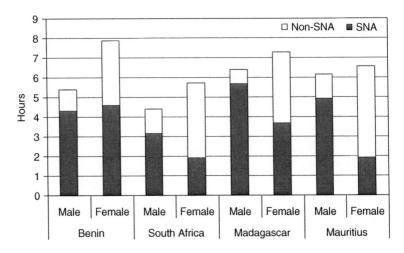

Figure 9.2   SNA/non-SNA work performed by gender (hours)

Technical issues in conducting TUS in Africa

The main technical issues to be solved in conducting TUS among the still-illiterate populations living in rural areas where the majority are subsistence farmers – as are most rural populations in sub-Saharan Africa – deal with the notion of time and seasonality. Self-completion of the diaries is, of course, excluded in Africa, except for some segments of

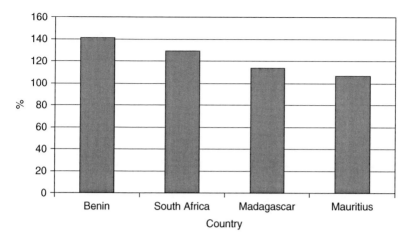

Figure 9.3 Female work time as a % of male work time

the urban population; therefore, interviewers have to ask a set of questions that were designed for the survey. In survey methodology there are two ways of designing the questions to be asked the respondents. The first way gives no freedom to the interviewer: the question must be asked as it is worded on the questionnaire. The second way is open and the quality of the data will depend on the ability of the interviewer to give the appropriate wording and to record the appropriate translation of the response. This is typically the case for a diary where the hours of the day are listed and the interviewer just has to ask what was done by the respondent at these various hours of the day. Whatever the content of the interviewer's manual, the details and the examples provided in it or during the training, the reality of the field survey is always unique and the interviewer's skills are of primary importance. In particular, how does the interviewer deal with the notion of time?

The notion of time in rural societies

Usual diaries employed in developing countries divide time into slots of 10 minutes, 15 minutes or half an hour. Therefore, how do we proceed where life is not ruled by clocks and watches? Of course, every society has its own way of dividing the day and the year. Table 9.3 shows how the Soussou of Guinea divide the day.

When the interviewer asks the question 'at what time did you wake up yesterday?' or 'what have you done after?' it will be answered through a reference to one of these major divides. The best solution for them will

Table 9.3   The divides of the day among the Soussou of Guinea

Divides of the Day	
Toxè singé raté	The first cockcrow
Toxé firindé raté	The second cockcrow
Subaha	On very early morning
Kuè yalan béré	At the time when the night is cured
Waliha	Work hour (6 O'clock)
Sogé xono	When the sun is at its zenith in the middle of the day (noon)
Sogé xono yanyi ra	When the sun is at its zenith in the middle of the day (noon)
Sèli fana	The prayer (2 O'clock)
Laxansara	The frog hour
Fitiri	The decline of the day
Sarafu	The time when one play music (9 O'clock)
Sa tèmui	The time to go to bed
Kuè tègi	The middle of the night

Source: Geslin Ph. (1997).

be to list all the activities performed all day long or at least between two successive divides so that they may try to estimate the length of each activity between two divides.

The interviewing of all household members is facilitated by the comparisons between the members for wake up, breakfast, meals and so on, and this is an argument for choosing the selection of all members (more than six-years old) of the selected household rather than one or two.

The call for prayer at the mosque, the ring of the bell at the church, the bus stop and so on, can also be landmarks.

Certainly, the urbanization process has dramatically changed rural habits and behaviors, and in urban areas time is marked by school hours, work hours, prayer hours or meal hours so that the interviewer records the list of activities undertaken by the household's member during these time periods.

Once the interviewer has established the list of activities, they still have to impute a specific duration for each of them. For those activities where length is notable, such as work in the fields, walking to the health center and so on, the interviewer will be able to put it in the diary with relatively reliable precision as far as the response makes sure that they lasted from one divide to another. But what if the activity lasted less than an interval between two divides?

With experience and observation, the interviewer comes to know how long 'washing and dressing' or preparing breakfast or meals last. The risk, however, is that the interviewer comes to apply to all household members in all households the same duration, by contagion, in a way. Studies on energy expenditures, which have measured with a high precision (with activity monitors and stopwatches) the time dedicated to each activity of a day, can be used as a control, but they are rare (see Pasquet and Koppert, 1993 for Cameroon; Benefice and Cames, 1999 or Ndiaye, 2004 for Senegal). They generally cover only a segment of the population (the active adults in the case of Cameroon or the rural adolescent girls of a region in the case of Senegal).

That means that we must accept realistically that these estimates are only approximate.

Seasonality and sampling procedures

In most African countries, agriculture and stock farming are activities that continue to occupy the majority of the population, especially in rural areas, and represent the most influential segments of economic production. These activities influence other activities, such as manufacturing (food processing and the transformation of agricultural products), trade and transport. They have an impact on time spent at work, but also on consumption expenditures and on the search of monetary activities by household members. Economic activity in general is therefore tightly linked to the variations of agricultural activities, which are seasonal.

Just as for the divides of the day, rural populations have precise notions of the calendar of the seasons. Generally there are more than two seasons, the agricultural season and the nonagricultural season (for instance, there can be a short rainy season and a long rainy season, and the same for dry seasons). This means that a survey repeated with two periods in the year may not be enough to capture changes in the time use of the population.

Comparisons between countries, which are carried out by one-spot surveys, and those which used two or more observations in the year do not appear to make substantial differences in time budgets. However, the best method is the one used in budget-consumption surveys: a rotating sample all the year round which scatters a subsample across the country for each month of the year. The aggregation of the subsamples provides seasonally adjusted time budgets. The method is costly and can be justified if the time-use section is attached to a budget-consumption (or income-expenditures) survey, as it was done in Tunisia (2005–2006). In fact, as time poverty reveals itself to be the most operative concept to theorize the 'feminization' of poverty, the systematic inclusion of a time-use section in budget-consumption surveys is probably the best approach to be recommended. It allows comparisons of individual time budgets between very poor, poor and nonpoor households.

Simultaneous activities

When recording the activities of an entire day, it appears that many of them occur simultaneously: for instance, 'socializing' can take place while working, commuting or preparing meals; 'caring for children' can take place while working for market activities or for domestic activities, as well as while socializing. An African woman has her baby on her back all day long; a radio can be switched on all day long, too. As a result, such activities are very often underreported because the interviewer does not systematically repeat the question. Questionnaire design must therefore include a systematic question on simultaneous activities. However, this is not usually enough. The South African TUS distinguishes between time spent in activities 'spontaneously declared' and time spent in 'prompted' activities in its classification of activities. However this makes the interviewer's task even more complex. The recent concern for the increased burden of HIV/AIDS epidemic borne by the households (and by women in particular) at the expense of their other caring activities does not find much support in the surveys' results. The average time dedicated to care, although three times higher in South Africa compared to Benin for instance, is only of a few minutes per day (it is of course higher for the persons participating in the activity).

Caring usually requires a specific question separate from the diary itself, such as: 'how many hours a day children are "in your care"?' or 'how many hours a day the sick members of the family are "in your care"?'

Simultaneous activities lead to having days with more than 24 hours and the issue of weighting and evaluating is then raised. If the objective is to build a satellite account of household production, then how should we evaluate simultaneous activities? Should we only take the main activity into account, in which case caring for household's members other than children counts only for two minutes a day? Or should we also impute a value to simultaneous activities and, if so, with which weight and which value?

Although some of these issues have been addressed in the literature, the proposed solutions are far from being accepted by national accountants for the compilation of GDP, even in its extended definition.

Political and analytical issues raised by TUS in Africa

Despite recent developments and methodological innovations, African TUS have remained underutilized by economists and analysts, and widely ignored by policy makers. Such weak use and treatment in a time when this type of survey began to emerge on a continent, which is usually characterized by its backwardness in statistical data collection, deserve to be tentatively explained. In a first approach, it may be argued that the weak analytical developments of TUS in Africa are mainly due to an insufficient and unconvinced commitment of policy makers regarding the usefulness and the necessity of time-use data. Consequently, it is necessary to understand why and how such surveys have been funded and implemented in a context of relative scarcity of financial and human resources in the statistical arena.

Policy issues that lie behind the weak use of time-use surveys in Africa

Generally, TUS and time-use analyses in Africa remained inter–UN agency exercises. In Benin and Madagascar, for instance, the surveys have been conducted for the purpose of providing data for the National Human Development Reports, which focused on gender (a chapter of these national reports was devoted to gender and time use). But a few years later, the next issue (2003) of the National Human Development Report in Benin, which stressed that gender-sensitive policies were lacking and needed to address the question of women's work burden and domestic chores, referred to international literature and totally missed – by ignorance – the national data collected only five years earlier. So did the 2002 Country Common Assessment and the Poverty Reduction Strategic Paper. It suggests a lack of national ownership of the TUS (Brunnich and Vacarr, 2005). An assessment of the main causes that led to such a failure could stress the following points:

- The surveys were carried out with the support of the national statistical institutes for sampling selection and field work, but the tabulation and analyses were prepared by UNDP projects and consultants in order to provide timely results to be used in the National Human Development Reports. Therefore, capacity building was oriented towards national gender specialists rather than statisticians and prevented the ad hoc TUS from being repeated or becoming a regular module of a permanent multipurpose household survey. One of the rare – if not the only one – TUS to have been conducted as a module of a budget-consumption survey (Tunisia 2005–2006) is at risk of remaining underutilized and underanalyzed for the same reasons: statisticians have been in charge of sampling and field work, but are not associated with the analyses that are made by the Ministry of Women Affairs. The combination of household income and expenditures could remain totally neglected and it is well-known that it is always difficult to proceed with such analyses and combinations if they are not done immediately after data collection.

- National gender specialists were not sensitized to time-use data nor trained in their use. Their awareness of time use and women's burden led them to believe that the gap between women and men regarding time use in economic activities and domestic and care activities should be more than double, so that they were disappointed to realize that the gap was only 141 per cent in Benin, for instance (a gap which is, however, one of the highest by international standards: see Table 28 in UNDP, 2006). As a matter of fact, Benin and Madagascar are two countries where women's contribution to the labor force and economic activities is commonly recognized.

- Although several dissemination seminars were held in various places, the survey results were not put on the website of the national statistical institutions so that no effort was made toward a better ownership by national statisticians and economists.

- Finally, the results of the surveys remained at the preliminary or descriptive stage of the main findings of a survey report, which left policy makers unaware of the potential usefulness of time-use analyses.

Analytical issues for a better use of time-use surveys in Africa

Generally, only preliminary and descriptive survey reports have been made available. Therefore, time-use analyses have remained limited to common tabulation, with ordinary cross-classification of the variables: by age group and sex, by urban and rural areas (except in South Africa), by matrimonial status (not married, married, married to a polygamous), by activity status (active, inactive) or by employment status (own-account worker, wage-earner, family worker). Such results have only been used to illustrate UN gender or human development reports. Their insistence on care activities does not meet the needs of policy makers who are more concerned with poverty-reduction strategies and employment-creation policies than with the care economy. TUS should not be confined to gender issues, but rather extended to the crucial questions about the measurement of the labor force, informal employment and multiple jobs (pluriactivity), as well as poverty, especially time poverty.

Further analyses should be processed by the socioeconomic status of the household head, by income group of the household, by educational level of the individual, by health status of the individual and by type of access to infrastructures (health, education, water, sanitation, market). In this respect, it must be stressed that TUS should cover all members of the sampled households, rather than one or two members randomly selected, because it is important to be able to correlate data collected on the household with data collected on individuals, especially where time use is a module of an income-expenditure (or budget-consumption) survey. This is one of the limitations of the South African TUS. Tunisia's survey could constitute the best opportunity for analyses on time poverty, provided that the survey is fully exploited.

Conclusion

Five countries in Africa have conducted national TUS in the last decade – Benin, South Africa, Madagascar, Mauritius and Morocco – but this experience has been characterized by an underuse of the survey results by policy makers and even UN agencies. Together with the multiplication and repetition of such surveys, improving the awareness and interest of national institutions in the use of TUS is therefore a major objective.

To this aim it is important to:

(i) make further analyses of existing surveys that would fit with policy makers' concerns (poverty, inequality, employment);

(ii) plan new surveys as modules of existing household income and expenditures surveys;

(iii) give a particular emphasis to the final stages of tabulation and analysis, as well as dissemination of results and data, with free access to researchers;

(iv) identify from the very beginning the policy makers to be targeted in order to provide them with the type of findings they are looking for;

(v) design adequate programs of appropriation and capacity building for training national economists and statisticians in the analysis and use of time-use data and their integration in the elaboration of gender-sensitive policies and resource allocation mechanisms; and

(vi) design similar programs within the UN system in order to avoid a situation in which international or national reports prepared by UN agencies (and too often by consultants) continue to make weak use of data collected in this field, particularly in Francophone countries.

References

Benefice, E. and C. Cames (1999) 'Physical activity patterns of rural Senegalese adolescent girls during the dry and rainy seasons measured by movement registration and direct observation methods,' *European Journal of Clinical Nutrition,* 53, 636–43.

Brunnich, G. and D. Vacarr (2005) 'The challenges in integrating unpaid work into economic policy in lower and middle-income countries,' Conference on *'Unpaid Work and the Economy: Gender, Poverty, and the Millennium Development Goals,'* 1–3 October (Annandale-on-Hudson, NY: The Levy Economics Institute of Bard College).

Charmes, J. (2000) *African Women in Food Processing: a Major, But Still Underestimated Sector of Their Contribution to the National Economy* (Ottawa and Nairobi: IDRC).

Charmes, J. (2003a) 'Application of Time Use to Assess the Contribution of Women to GDP and to Monitor Impacts of National Budget on Women's Time Use,' Expert Group Meeting on *'Gender-Aware Macroeconomic Model to Evaluate Impacts of Policies on Poverty Reduction,'* 7–9 May (Addis Ababa: United Nations Economic Commission for Africa African Centre for Gender and Development).

Charmes, J. (2003b) *Easy Reference Guide on Tools for Mainstreaming Gender in Poverty Reduction Strategies: National Accounts, National Budgets an Time Use Studies* (Addis Ababa: United Nations Economic Commission for Africa, African Centre for Gender and Development [ACGD]).

Charmes, J. (2005) 'Femmes africaines, activités économiques et travail: de l'invisibilité à la reconnaissance (African Women, Economic Activity and Work: From Invisibility to Recognition),' *Revue Tiers Monde,* XLVI, 182(April–June), 255–79.

Charmes, J. (2006) 'Gender and time poverty in Sub-Saharan Africa, A review of empirical evidence,' in Blackden M. and Woodon Q. (eds), *Working Paper 73: Gender, time-use and poverty in sub-Saharan Africa* (Washington, DC: The World Bank)

Charmes, J. and J. Unni (2004) 'Measurement of work,' in G. Standing and M. Chen (eds), *Reconceptualising Work* (Geneva: ILO).

Geslin Ph. (1997) 'L'innovation et le temps. Une approche ethnographique de la réallocation du temps de travail agricole chez les Soussou de Guinée' (Innovation and Time. An ethnographic approach of the re-allocation of agricultural work-time among the Soussou of Guinea),' in Ch. Blanc-Pamard and J. Boutrais (eds), *Dynamique des systèmes agraires. Nouvelles recherches rurales au Sud* (Paris: ORSTOM, colloques et seminaries).

Ghana Statistical Service (1995) *Ghana Living Standards Survey, Report of the 3rd Round (GLSS 3), September 1991–September 1992* (Accra: Ghana Statistical Service).

Ghana Statistical Service (2000) *Ghana Living Standards Survey, Report of the 4th Round (GLSS 4)* (Accra: Ghana Statistical Service).

Institut Nacional de la Statistique et de l'Analyse Economique (INSAE) and UNDP (PNUD) (1998) *Enquête emploi du temps au Bénin, Méthodologie et résultats,* Cotonou, 32pp. + 156pp. annexes.

Institut de la Statistique of Madagascar (INSTAT) (2002) *EPM 2001. Module Emploi du Temps,* Antananarivo, INSTAT- DSM/PNUD-MAG/97/007.

Leplaideur, A. (1978) *Les travaux agricoles chez les paysans du Centre-Sud Cameroun, les techniques utilisées et les temps nécessaires (Agricultural works among the farmers of Centre-South Cameroon, techniques used and required time)* (Paris: IRAT).

Ndiaye, G. (2004) *Etude de l'activité physique habituelle d'adolescentes rurales sénégalaises. Effets sur la croissance et l'état nutritionnel (Study of the usual physical activity among rural Senegalese adolescent girls. Impact on their development and nutritional status)*, Thèse de doctorat (Dakar: Université Cheikh Anta Diop).

Pasquet, P. and G. Koppert (1993) 'Activity patterns and energy expenditure in Cameroonian tropical forest populations,' in C.M. Hladik, A. Hladik, O.F. Linares, H. Pagezy, A. Semple and M. Hadley (eds), *Tropical Forests, People and Food. Biocultural Interactions and Applications to Development*, Man and the Biosphere Series, 13 (Paris, UNESCO and Carnforth: The Parthenon Publishing Group).

Pasquet, P. and G. Koppert (1996) 'Budget-temps et dépense énergétique chez les essarteurs forestiers du Cameroun,' in C.M. Hladik, A. Hladik, H. Pagezy, O.F. Linares, G. Koppert and A. Froment (eds), *L'alimentation en forêt tropicale: Interactions bioculturelles et perspectives de développement* (Paris: L'Homme et la Biosphère, Editions UNESCO).

Republic of Mauritius, Central Statistics Office (2004) *Continuous Multi-Purpose Household Survey 2003: Main Results of the Time-use Study* (Port Louis: Republic of Mauritius, Central Statistics Office).

SNA (1993) *System of National Accounts*, Commission of the European Communities, IMF, OECD, UN, WB.

Statistics South Africa (2001) *A Survey of Time-use: How South African Women and Men Spend Their Time* (Pretoria: Statistics South Africa).

United Nations Economic Commission for Africa (2005) *A Guidebook for Mainstreaming Gender Perspectives and Household Production into National Statistics, Budgets and Policies in Africa* (Addis Ababa: African Centre for Gender and Development).

UNDP (2006) *Human Development Report 2006: Beyond Scarcity: Power, Poverty and the Global Water Crisis* (New York: Oxford University Press).

Whittington, D., M. Winming and R. Roche (1990) 'Calculating the Value of Time Spent Collecting Water: Some Estimates for Ukunda, Kenya,' *World Development*, 18(2), 269–80.

10
Removing the Cloak of Invisibility: Integrating Unpaid Household Services in National Economic Accounts – the Philippines Experience

Solita Collas-Monsod*

> One of the defining movements of the 20th century has been the relentless struggle for gender equality, led mostly by women, but supported by growing numbers of men. When this struggle finally succeeds – as it must – it will mark a great milestone in human progress. And along the way it will change most of today's premises for social, economic and political life.
>
> (UNDP Human Development Report, 1995)

UN inconsistencies and the invisible woman

The UN system is at the forefront of efforts towards gender equality, the elimination of discrimination against women and 'mainstreaming' them. There are the Commission on the Status of Women (CSW), going on its 53rd Session; the Committee on the Elimination of Discrimination Against Women (CEDAW Committee), going on its 45th session; the Division for the Advancement of Women (DAW) in the Department of Economic and Social Affairs; and there are several global organizations involved in these tasks: UNDP, INSTRAW, UNIFEM, ILO, to name a few.

The UN has also organized four World Conferences of Women starting in 1975, where the need to measure and value women's unpaid work was recognized, with the clamor reaching its peak at the Third World Conference of Women in 1985 – with the Nairobi Forward Looking Strategies, as endorsed by the UN Economic and Social Council, recommending that the value of household goods and services be included in GDP:

> The remunerated and, in particular, the unremunerated contributions of women to all aspects and sectors of development should be recognized, and appropriate efforts should be made to measure and reflect these contributions in national accounts and economic statistics and in the gross national product. Concrete steps should be taken to quantify the unremunerated contribution of women to agriculture, food production, reproduction and household activities.

(para. 120, Report of the World Conference to Review and Appraise the Achievements of the United Nations Decade for Women: Equality, Development and Peace, Nairobi, 1985)

Then there are also the Millennium Development Goals, the third of which is to 'promote gender equality and empower women.'

Ironically, all these efforts are being undermined in another part of the UN System – the Statistics Division (also part of the Department of Economic and Social Affairs), with their System of National Accounts (SNA) that give the guidelines and procedures for estimating a country's gross domestic product and national income. Introduced in 1947, this national accounting system was 'based essentially on the model of an advanced industrial economy in which transactions in money are dominant' (Bos, 2005).

Since then, three major revisions have taken place in this UN-SNA, in 1953, in 1968 and in 1993. There is one constant element in all the revisions. As Bos (2005) has put it, 'They all exclude unpaid household services, do-it-yourself activities, voluntary work and the services of consumer durables. These types of production are ignored despite the existence of paid counterparts that are counted as production.'

Thus have the economic contributions of women in households been rendered invisible by a statistical cloak provided by the SNA, which is supremely ironic, because 'economics' is derived from the Greek 'oikonomia' which means: the management of family and household. Thus have the efforts of the Dr Jekylls in the UN system been negated by the Mr Hydes in the same schizophrenic system. What follows is an examination of the narrow, inadequate, erroneous definitions and concepts that are used to weave that cloak of invisibility and ultimately lay the basis for a hidden and, therefore, even more virulent type of discrimination against women. The subsequent section discusses what is needed to remove the cloak of invisibility and the Philippine experience in that regard. The last section deals with the road ahead.

The SNA: warts and all

Originally, not only the value of services, but also the value of goods produced for own consumption at home were excluded from the so-called production boundary of the SNA. Slowly, exceptions were made for certain kinds of goods (primary products and their processing), and in 1993, all goods produced for home consumption were finally allowed to enter the national accounts. But the exclusion of services – household members producing household and personal services for own consumption (cleaning, meal preparation, caring and instruction of children, caring for the sick) and volunteer workers in nonprofit institutions serving households – has remained, as mentioned above, constant nonmarket, therefore noneconomic. The articulated reasons for their non-inclusion are as follows: large nonmonetary flows of this type would obscure what is happening in the market and thus reduce the usefulness of SNA; the inclusion of the production of personal services by household members for their own final consumption would imply that such persons were self-employed, thus making unemployment virtually impossible by definition; the activities have a limited impact on the rest of the economy; it is difficult to obtain market prices to value these services; and there are differences in their economic significance for analytical purposes.

All the above are used to highlight the need to 'confine the production boundary in the SNA and other related statistical systems to market activities or fairly close substitutes for market activities' (1993 SNA para 1.22).

I have been teaching economics for almost forty years and never once have I come across a definition of economics which equates it with markets. There are command economies, there are nonmarket economies. The basic aim of economics, through the centuries has been the study of production, distribution and reproduction of systems through which people have sustained themselves. Even in contemporary neoclassical approaches, the key issue in economics is scarcity, not markets. The SNA's dictum that only what is marketed is economic (which is more descriptive of developed countries), this exclusion of the household economy from the total economy has not only distorted the macroeconomic picture (at best giving only a partial one), particularly in developing countries not far removed from the subsistence level; but the nonrecognition of the contribution of women to the economy and society in the national statistics have also implicitly perpetuated gender inequalities.

> Official non-recognition of contributions to the national as much as to the household economy obviously leads to non-recognition in policy making, planning, allocation of resources, the provision of

support services and information, and of course in the distribution of the benefits of development. The failure to recognize much of the work which women do is therefore a failure to take women into account in all these areas.

(APCAS/94/9)

Producers of nonmarketed services are therefore, not 'economically active'. There is a devastating corollary; since nonmarketed services are invisible in GDP, the efforts that went into producing these goods perforce became invisible as well. How? Again by definition: According to ILO, to be a member of the labor force, or to be 'economically active,' one does not only have to be above a specified age (working age), but must be engaged in the production of economic goods and services – as defined by the SNA. Since the SNA-defined economic services exclude those produced for home consumption, those involved in the latter's production – mostly women – are automatically excluded from the labor force. They are considered economically inactive – which is the greatest irony, since it is the work they do at home and in the community that makes it possible for husbands and children to participate in the economy as consumers and producers (now and in the future). Arguably, it is this labor that allows the rest of the economy to function, yet those who are doing it are considered to be at leisure, or 'dependents.'

The SNA reasoning in a nutshell

Reduced to its simplest terms, here is what the SNA would have us accept: If a service is not marketed, it is not economic. If it is not economic, then their producers cannot be considered economically active (namely, they cannot be part of the labor force). This is much the best solution, because the alternative would be to classify them as self-employed – which would render unemployment 'virtually impossible' – and that is a no-no. In other words, for the high priests of the SNA, it is better to make unpaid labor services in the home invisible then to have to rethink our employment concepts. This is clearly a case of the tail wagging the dog!

The 'unemployment virtually impossible' card

Let us examine this assertion a little more closely. Assume a conventional labor force of 100, with 90 employed and 10 unemployed, resulting in an unemployment rate of 10 per cent. Now assume that the inclusion of unpaid household services will increase the labor force by 50 (or 50 per cent). The unemployment rate certainly will decrease (to 6.7 per cent), but the number of unemployed remain the same, unless it is further assumed that all those who were considered unemployed under the conventional system (those not working, but seeking work) are all producing household services.

In this 'worst case' scenario, attention will perforce shift from unemployment to employment in general and underemployment (those working, but seeking more work), in particular, which, given the present realities, is what should be done in the first place.

For example, the present protocol considers one to be employed if she has spent at least one hour in the past week in 'productive' work, like feeding the chickens, but considers her not even in the labor force if she has spent 40 hours in the past week in 'reproductive' work, like feeding and caring for her children.

As regards underemployment

Looking at the statistics on poverty and employment, it becomes clear that it is not the quantity so much as the quality of employment that is important. The general view is that unemployment and poverty are closely connected. That is a myth. In a country like the Philippines, the poor cannot afford to be unemployed. Family poverty incidence in the Philippines was 26.9 per cent (in 2006, using national standards). Poverty incidence of families where the head was self-employed (using ILO norms) was 34.3 per cent, while poverty incidence among households where the head of household was unemployed was a much lower (11.6 per cent). The self-employed group, by the way, makes up over half of the total number of poor families in the Philippines. It is they, the self-employed, who deserve at least as much attention as the unemployed.

If they now include those who labor without pay to produce goods, there should be every reason to also include those who labor without pay to produce services that are so necessary for basic survival and quality of life. In any case, because of the kind of thinking behind the SNA, we are left with trying to justify why, when we pay for child care and house-cleaning, when we eat out, when we buy milk for our babies, these add to the gross domestic product and count toward economic growth and progress, but when we cook our own meals, clean our own house, breastfeed our babies, look after our own children, tune up our own cars, fix our own leaking faucets, these have no value in our current measures of progress.

Informal activities

The irony is that sometimes statisticians will go to great lengths to try to measure illegal activities in the economy as in the following

> Countries should try to make estimates from both the value added and expenditure sides, of all the economic activities covered in the SNA

production boundary. These include both informal and illegal activities where these are considered to be significant. Where an informal activity is known to be going on at a significant level, the worst estimate is zero but this is implicitly the estimate that is being made if the informal activity is simply ignored. Even a very crude estimate will improve the accuracy of the accounts.

(International Comparison Program for Asia and the Pacific Regional Inception Workshop, National Accounts Workshop, Bangkok, Thailand, 28 July–1 August 2005)

Thus, we are urged to include illegal activities (since they are within the SNA production boundary), but we are not allowed to include the nurturing services that shape our very future.

Table 10.1 Paid/unpaid hours by various studies

Reference			Average total hours of paid work/day		Average total hours of unpaid work/day		Ratio of unpaid & paid work	
			W	M	W	M	W	M
Lingsom[1]	1975–85		2.4	4.9	4.5	2.1	0.65	0.30
Canada[2]	1992		2.7	4.5	4.5	2.6	0.63	0.37
Japan[3]	1991		3.0	5.8	4.0	0.5	0.57	0.08
Miralao[4]	1979	Single	8.0	6.4	3.0	1.7	0.28	0.21
		Married	7.0	7.4	7.9	2.6	0.53	0.26
NEDA[5]	1984	Employed	5.6	–	4.3	–	0.44	–
		Unemployed	–	–	–	–	–	–
		Outside the labor force	–	–	–	–	–	–
IPC/ IIIO6	1985–90		3.7	5.3	6.6	1.9	0.64	0.26

Notes
1. Coverage: Denmark, Norway, United Kingdom, the Netherlands, Hungary, US and Canada; Unpaid House Work (UHW) = cooking, shopping, child care, odd jobs around the home and travel time related to these activities
2. UHW = cooking, housekeeping, maintenance/repair, shopping, childcare, volunteer and others.
3. UHW = housekeeping, elderly care, nursing and shopping
4. Coverage: Municipality of Candelaria and Sta. Cruz in Zambales Province and Barangay Sto. Nino, Marikina, Metro Manila; UHW = marketing, washing clothes, ironing clothes, cleaning house/yard, cooking, washing dishes, fetching water, gathering/chopping firewood, sewing/mending clothes and childcare.
5. Studied women whose UHW = marketing, laundry, cleaning house, cooking, washing dishes gardening and home beautician, baby sitting and caring for the children, other unpaid HH duties.
6. Coverage: Rural Women and Men in Bicol (1985, 1987, 1990) and Mindanao (1990); UHW = total home production time.

Another irony is that as the household economy shifts to the market economy, this is registered as growth in the GDP, even as no additional production is actually performed. This does not really make much sense.

Is a satellite account the answer?

No. In what is considered by many to be a major step forward, the 1993 UN-SNA recommended the use of special satellite accounts that can be linked to, but are separate from, the SNA accounts, in recognition of the limitations of the central framework in addressing specific aspects of economic life important to a specific country. They 'expand the analytical capacity of national accounting for selected areas of social concern in a flexible manner, without overburdening or disrupting the central system' [1993 SNA para.21.4] – thus the terms 'augmented,' 'expanded' and 'enhanced' GDP. It has been regarded by many as a 'realistic' compromise between the advantages of tradition and the adaptation of new economic, social and political requirements.

Certainly, including unpaid household services in a satellite account is better than excluding them completely, but there are disadvantages to this. First, relegating women's contribution to GDP to an adjunct, supplemental position violates the concept of gender equality – if men and women are to be treated equally, they should be equally visible in the national accounts. An augmented, expanded and enhanced GDP – such patronizing terms – is not what is needed. What is needed is an accurate picture that reflects the reality on the ground. Why should women not be included in the 'central system'? Second, insisting on a truncated GDP – and it is truncated, as we all know from various estimates (Table 10.1) just how much unpaid work contributes to the economy – and then 'enhancing' it is like amputating a person's leg and then throwing her a stick!

Third, the reference to the 'advantages' of tradition vs. new economic, social and political requirements may be misplaced. The cavalier treatment of women's caring services in the home, one should not be surprised to learn, has not always been the norm. Over 200 years ago, in the censuses of population in both England and the United States, housewives – or, more accurately, women whose work consisted largely of caring for their families – were considered to be productive/gainful workers. Unfortunately, over time, that view of the role of women slowly changed, so that by 1900 housewives were no longer considered productive workers – they were formally relegated to the census category of 'dependents' (which included infants, young children, the sick and the elderly) – mouths, rather than hands. This situation, I am sorry to say, was partly due to the influence of Alfred Marshall, the greatest economist of his time (Folbre, 1991).

Fourth, as mentioned previously, 'economic' and 'market' are not, never have been and never should be interchangeable. Certainly, first-world economies are market economies, but imposing that first world reality as a criterion for the developing world makes no sense. We should remind ourselves that GDP is the measure of the market value of all final goods and services produced in a country during a year; it is not the market value of only those final goods and services that are bought and sold in a market. Using the latter definition for fear of being overburdened is, to borrow an analogy, like looking for one's car keys one block away from where one lost them – simply because the light is better in the new location. It is more convenient, but you won't find the keys.

Undoubtedly, the valuation of unpaid work is difficult – but experiencing difficulties is par for the course in national income accounting, or, for that matter, in any endeavor where measurement is involved. I recall that prior to its publication (come to that, it is still being criticized), Mahbub Ul Haq's *Human Development Index* (HDI) was the subject of savage criticism and he was advised not to use it until the problems were ironed out. If he had followed that advice, the HDI would still be unpublished today and the world would be the poorer for it. Instead, he took the plunge – with the HDI being constantly fine-tuned and is still a work in progress. What was important was that the methodology used was transparent, the need for improvement was recognized and constructive criticism was welcome. Following the UNDP lead, many countries are now estimating intranational HDIs.

More to the point, it is not as if unpaid work in the national accounts is uncharted territory. The Norwegian national accounts for the period 1935–43 and 1946–49 included estimates of the value of unpaid household work, as apparently did other Scandinavian countries (Aslaksen and Koren, 1996). The question raises itself – if it could be done sixty and seventy years ago, why not now?

In sum, the SNA cloaks the contribution of women to the economy with invisibility by using narrow and, at the very least, inadequate definitions. That cloak should and can be removed. Including their contribution in satellite accounts should not be considered a final and permanent solution, but rather a preliminary and temporary one.

Removing the invisibility: time use → valuation → satellite accounts → full integration – the Philippines experience

If it is indisputable that women's contributions to the economy are statistically invisible, it is at least arguable that time-use data (either from full

TUS or from time-use questions included in regular household surveys) are a sine qua non in counting paid and unpaid work of men and women, which, in turn, is a necessary first step in removing that cloak of invisibility. The second step would be to use the time-use data to create monetary measures of the value of nonmarket production to facilitate their integration into the GDP figures – in the current environment through the use of satellite accounts.

The third step would be to create the satellite accounts and to institutionalize them (in the sense of not being one-shot deals). And the final step would of course be the full integration of unpaid labor into the country's national accounts.

Much work has already been done with regard to the first step. A 1999 Report (Horrigan *et al*, 1999) lists over 57 TUS undertaken by 38 countries starting from 1924 (USSR) up to 1999. The United Nations Statistics Division website features a map and a list of countries and areas – twenty in all – that conducted TUS between 1990 and 2004, seven from the developed and thirteen from the developing world. A UN Ecosoc report shows that as of February 2004, 95 TUS had been undertaken in 19 countries of the United Nations Economic and Social Commission for Asia and the Pacific (ESCAP) region (58 country membership) since 1960; of these, 44 had been conducted in the last 14 years and 8 since 2000. It also reports that at the world level, 82 countries have carried out at least one TUS. The US seems to be making up for lost time in a big way; only one TUS is listed under its name (1965–66) until 2003 when it started undertaking monthly TUS. And of course along the way, many conceptual, methodological and measurement problems have been ironed out, and many lessons have been learned.

Slow progress, but if anywhere up to 82 countries have undertaken at least one TUS, not as many have used the data gathered to value the time spent on unpaid household labor. Even fewer countries have started or developed household satellite accounts. And none, with the possible exception of Australia and Germany, have institutionalized it and are doing it on a regular basis. Table 10.1 gives a partial listing of countries that have valued unpaid work together with notations on whether they have developed satellite accounts.

Why does there seem to be, for the greater number of countries, not much follow-through, as it were, in integrating unpaid work into the country's national accounts? One reason could be that the learning curve is a deep one, notwithstanding the enormous research and training efforts on the part of organizations like United Nations Research

Table 10.2 Per capita income, human development index and gender empowerment measure, selected countries, 2004

Country	Per capita GDP (pppus$)	HDI (rank)	GEM (rank)
Malaysia	10,276	0.804 (61)	0.506 (55)
Thailand	8,090	0.784 (74)	0.486 (60)
South Korea	20,499	0.912 (26)	0.502 (53)
Philippines	4,614	0.763 (84)	0.533 (45)

Source: Virola and de Perio, 'The Contribution of Women to the Economy', (1998).

and Training Institute for the Advancement of Women (INSTRAW) and ESCAP, not to mention national institutions.

Then there are the usual problems related to lack of financial resources, particularly in developing countries.

But resolving the technical problems involved in TUS and valuation of the unpaid work that it generates are still not sufficient to achieve the goal of integrating unpaid work into the national accounts and macroeconomic policy. The support of policy makers and stakeholders has to be mobilized, which requires that they are made aware of the benefits derived from such an integration. Without that support, the valuable data gathered and analyzed may end up as a matter only of academic interest, or worse, moldering in library shelves.

The Philippine experience

In this regard, the Philippine experience may be instructive. As far as gender empowerment goes (and it doesn't go very far), the Philippines has been shown to be better off than countries in east and southeast Asia which boast of higher per capita incomes and a higher HDI. This can be seen from the data in Table 10.2, where the Philippines has the lowest GDP per capita and the lowest HDI, but the highest gender empowerment measure (GEM), a measure which focuses on the participation of women in political and economic decision-making, as well as power over economic resources (UNDP, 2006).

At the same time, the country is one of four (with Canada, Ghana and India) cited as good-practice case studies in the development of gender-sensitive indicators in a reference manual for governments and other stakeholders prepared for the Commonwealth Secretariat in 1999 (Beck, 1999). It is not coincidental that a majority of the high-level personnel in the Philippine Statistical System are women. In short, if ever there were a list of developing countries that could be in the forefront of women's visibility-raising activities, the Philippines would have to be included in it.

The effects of the International Conferences on Women

It must be said that much of the success the country has had at advancing the status of women and moving toward gender equality is owed in no small part to the galvanizing effects of the preparations for and the aftermaths of the International Conferences on Women starting in 1975. It is not coincidental that the National Commission on the Role of Filipino Women (NCRFW), the first national machinery of women in Asia, was established by presidential decree at the beginning of 1975, in time for the First International Women's Conference in Mexico. The Nairobi conference caused another flurry of activity, this time focused on mainstreaming women's concerns in policy-making, planning and programming of all government agencies. This led to the launching of the Philippine Development Plan for Women (PDPW) 1989–92, (which may have been the first of its kind) and a successful lobby for legislation ensuring women equal rights in all areas (Women in Nation – Building Act). In the wake of the Beijing conference came the Philippine Plan for Gender-responsive Development (PPGD), 1995–2025, a 30-year perspective plan officially adopted as the country's main vehicle for implementing the platform of action that outlines the policies, strategies, programs and projects that the government must adopt to enable women to participate in and benefit from national development. Under Executive Order 273, the PPGD was adopted as the country's main vehicle for implementing the 1995 PFA, adopted at the UN's Fourth World Conference on Women in 1995.

The numbers to support all the great words were provided by the work of an interagency committee on women and statistics, which published the first edition of 'Statistics on Filipino Women.' The crowning glory to such efforts was to have been to empirically measure the contribution of women to the economy – their contribution to the SNA-type GDP, but, more importantly, their share in a GDP that more accurately reflected all productive activities in the economy.

The National Statistical Coordination Board (NSCB) of the Philippines took initiative in this respect. Scarcely two years after the Beijing conference, it proposed to construct satellite accounts which, first, identified the distribution (by sex) of the economy in accordance with the SNA production boundary. It then identified, measured and included unpaid housework services of those in the labor force, also by sex, and finally included the unpaid work of those not in the labor force – those not considered economically active in the SNA.

Of course, there were problems that would have discouraged the faint-hearted. The proposed national TUS project, the first nationwide TUS to be conducted in the country, whose results were to be the used in the NSCB's valuation attempts, fell by the wayside – victim to the change in the executive directorship of the NCRFW and an accompanying change in priorities (in favor of an all-out push for programs and projects to eliminate violence against women). The attempt to distinguish the contributions of males and females to the 'conventional' GDP also met up with problems, for example, GDP by employment reflects only the number of employed persons by sex, but not by labor input (and the one-hour per week definition of employment complicates matters); there was also the underestimation problem presented by the fact that unpaid housework is also done by persons younger than 15 years of age.

All these aside from the problems associated with classification and valuation of the different types of unpaid labor (it is noteworthy that the value that was assigned to unpaid labor was assumed to be equal to the compensation of janitors – using the so-called generalist approach).

Nothing daunted, the NSCB decided to make a first pass anyway, using data generated from previous TUS. This in itself posed some challenges: the need to validate the data from these sources, the shortcomings of the data themselves – e.g. surveys were not nationwide, volunteer work and travel related to unpaid work not included in any previous TUS.

Still and all, the effort was an excellent start toward removing the cloak of invisibility of unpaid labor as far as the economy was concerned. The work was completed in 1998; the results, covering the years 1990–97, and subsequently updated to 1998, are summarized in Tables 10.2–10.6.

Women in the Philippine economy

Though the data generated by NSCB are not perfect, they are good as a starting point. Some of the observations emerging from these data are summarized below.

Distribution of GDP by sex

Table 10.3 presents the shares of men and women in the conventional GDP (including only SNA activities), where GDP is measured by employment and by hours of work, valued at the current prices. The table shows that the values range from 60 per cent to 63 per cent for men and between 35 per cent and 39 per cent for women. This indicates that though women contribute less to the GDP than men, their contribution to GDP is significant.

Contribution of unpaid non-SNA work

However, when unpaid non-SNA work (mainly unpaid domestic services) is added to calculate what NSCB calls 'adjusted GDP' and 'adjusted GNP,' the shares of men and women change considerably. Table 10.4 presents the shares of men and women in the national GDP and GNP using hours of work put in by men and women – employed in the labor market, unemployed and not in the labor market – by using opportunity cost (at current prices) for valuation. The table shows that the shares of men and women are almost equal. For the entire period of 1990–98, the shares of women are 49.90 per cent in GNP and 50.60 per cent in GDP. It is to be noted that women's contribution varies between 47.27 and 51.95 per cent in GDP and between 47.31 and 51.70 per cent in GNP.

Table 10.5 presents the values of conventional, as well as adjusted, GDP and GNP for the national economy of the Philippines for the years 1990–98. It shows that the adjusted values are much higher – by 26 per cent to almost 40 per cent – than the conventional values of GDP and GNP. What is important to note is that over the years, the excess of the adjusted values has increased, indicating an increasing share of unpaid domestic services in the national GDP and GNP.

The following charts show the values for men and women.

The tables show that the gap between the conventional GDP and adjusted GDP is much larger for women than for men.

Table 10.3   % Distribution of GDP by sex, 1990–98 (at current prices)

Year	Men		Women	
	Employment	*Hours of work*	*Employment*	*Hours of work*
1990	63.47	63.18	36.53	36.85
1991	62.75	62.26	37.25	37.74
1992	62.74	63.06	37.06	36.94
1993	61.90	62.33	38.10	37.67
1994	61.54	62.33	38.46	37.67
1995	61.81	61.78	38.19	38.22
1996	61.67	62.54	38.33	37.46
1997	61.55	61.44	38.45	38.56
1998	64.53	60.52	35.47	39.48
1990–98	62.46	62.16	37.54	37.84

Source: Virola and de Perio, 'The Contribution of Women to the Economy', (1998).

Table 10.4   % Distribution of GDP and GNP, adjusted for unpaid domestic services by sex, using hours of work for employed, unemployed and not in the labor market (at current prices)

Year	GDP Adjusted			GNP Adjusted		
	Total	Men	Women	Total	Men	Women
1990	100	51.95	48.05	100	52.69	47.31
1991	100	49.31	50.69	100	50.14	49.86
1992	100	48.45	51.55	100	49.30	50.70
1993	100	49.54	50.46	100	50.29	49.71
1994	100	49.04	50.96	100	49.71	50.29
1995	100	49.77	50.23	100	50.33	49.67
1996	100	50.21	49.79	100	50.97	49.03
1997	100	48.68	51.32	100	49.50	50.50
1998	100	47.27	52.73	100	48.30	51.70
1990–98	100	49.40	50.60	100	50.10	49.90

Source: Virola and de Perio, 'The Contribution of Women to the Economy', (1998).

Table 10.5   Values of conventional GDP and GNP and of adjusted GDP and GNP (including unpaid domestic services) 1990–98 (at constant prices)

Year	GDP	Adjusted GDP	% GDP	GNP	Adjusted GNP	% GNP
1990	720,690	913,002	126.68	716,929	909,241	126.82
1991	716,522	951,573	132.80	720,218	955,269	132.64
1992	718,941	984,727	136.97	731,396	997,183	136.34
1993	734,156	972,618	132.48	746,921	985,383	131.93
1994	766,368	1,029,654	134.36	786,136	1,049,422	133.49
1995	802,224	1,046,542	130.46	824,525	1,068,843	129.63
1996	849,121	1,110,373	130.77	884,226	1,145,478	129.55
1997	892,860	1,187,830	133.04	930,363	1,225,333	131.70
1998	888,075	1,242,643	139.93	931,127	1,285,695	138.08

Source: Virola and de Perio, 'The Contribution of Women to the Economy', (1998).

Sharing of unpaid domestic non-SNA work

The unpaid non-SNA work, mainly unpaid domestic services, is shared in a highly unequal manner by men and women in Philippines as in most other countries.

Table 10.6 presents the data on sharing of unpaid non-SNA work by men and women when women are employed, unemployed or are not in the labor market. The sharing is presented in terms of the time spent by men and women. In the cases when women are employed, men

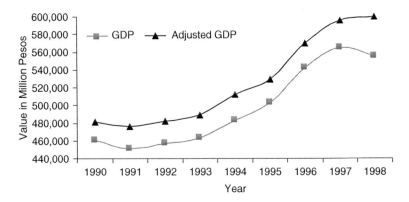

Figure 10.1   GDP and adjusted GDP: men

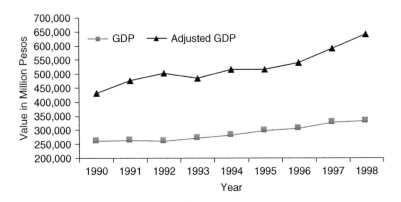

Figure 10.2   GDP and adjusted GDP: women

share about 27 per cent of the unpaid domestic work, while women per-form the other 73 per cent of the work. When women are unemployed (for example, are looking for work or are willing to work), men share 26 per cent of the unpaid domestic work and women perform 74 per cent of the work. When women are not in the labor market, men share less than 10 per cent of the unpaid domestic work (namely, they spend less than 10 per cent of the total time spent on unpaid domestic work), while women share 90 per cent of the work. On an average, women share 90 per cent of the total unpaid domestic work time. The table shows that the pattern of sharing has remained more or less the same during 1990–98.

It needs to be noted that the share of men in unpaid domestic work time in the Philippines is much less than some of the industrialized countries. For example, in Canada, men's share in the unpaid domestic work time is 65 per cent to 68 per cent almost during the same period. Table 10.6 also indicates that the contribution of women to unpaid hours of work in the sectors like agriculture, fishery and forestry; manufacturing, wholesale and retail trade; financing, insurance, real estate and business services; and community, social and personal services – sectors which comprise about 80 per cent of GDP – is greater than that of men.

These results were presented nationally at the National Conference of Statistics and internationally at the International Statistical Institute biennial meetings in 1999 (where it was the only paper dealing with the contribution of women to the economy).

No effect

While the paper was no doubt of interest to the professionals in the field, it made no dent whatsoever in the public consciousness, much less in the consciousness of the policy-makers and Filipino women. Actually, it never reached them at all. The results were as invisible as the unpaid work that was being measured and therefore could not have made a difference.

And they remained in limbo until very recently. The same fate was initially met by a TUS conducted in 2000 by the National Statistics Office. In spite of all the methodological and conceptual advances both in time-use and valuation processes, there seemed to be no felt need for a national TUS survey in the Philippines, so the proposal was scaled down to 'pilot' status covering only two areas – one urban and one rural. Even then, the results did not seem to have captured the attention of, nor made any impression on, the major stakeholders, although they were used by the NSCB to update the 'adjusted' GDP figures for 1999 and 2000.

No further work was done from 2001 to 2007 on measuring women's contribution to the economy and the integration of unpaid labor into the national accounts. In 2007 though, efforts were renewed in the aftermath of a meeting in Casablanca organized by Devaki Jain.

The Casablanca dream

One of the conclusions at Casablanca was that unless women's contributions to the economy were recognized and accepted, we would continue to be second-class citizens with all its negative implications. And nobody else could be relied to push for that recognition and acceptance but we ourselves. It was this that spurred me to contact the Secretary General of the NSCB, Dr Romeo Virola, to get a better feel of what it would take to pursue the goal of integrating women's unpaid labor into the macro-economic picture provided by our national accounts, and hopefully

Table 10.6 % Distribution of total unpaid hours of work (housework services) by sex, employed, unemployed and not in the labor force (thousands)

	1990		1991		1992		1993		1994		1995		1996		1997		1998		Average 1990–98	
	Male	Female	Male	Female	Male	Female	Male	Female	Male	Female	Male	Female	Male	Female	Male	Female	Male	Female	Male	Female
A. Employed	27.50	72.54	27.30	72.70	28.00	72.02	27.3	72.74	27.10	72.92	27.00	73.00	27.00	72.99	26.40	73.58	25.80	74.19	27.00	73.01
Agriculture, fishery and forestry	13.10	14.97	13.40	14.63	13.60	16.19	13.00	15.75	12.80	14.47	12.40	15.19	11.50	14.01	11.00	13.19	10.70	13.22	12.30	14.56
Mining and quarrying	0.24	0.09	0.27	0.10	0.26	0.09	0.22	0.08	0.17	0.04	0.15	0.04	0.17	0.09	0.19	0.07	0.17	0.03	0.20	0.07
Manufacturing	2.44	8.90	2.60	9.72	2.79	9.98	2.59	9.27	2.60	9.54	2.51	9.43	2.65	8.83	2.50	9.05	2.40	8.78	2.56	9.26
Electricity, gas and water	0.15	0.16	0.17	0.14	0.15	0.11	0.17	0.13	0.15	0.15	0.15	0.15	0.18	0.12	0.19	0.16	0.19	0.16	0.17	0.14
Construction	1.92	0.17	2.00	0.22	1.98	0.20	2.03	0.20	2.08	0.18	2.29	0.17	2.56	0.17	2.62	0.27	2.27	0.24	2.21	0.20
Wholesale and retail trade	2.57	22.12	2.23	23.15	2.31	23.3	2.40	23.12	2.39	23.75	2.46	23.86	2.55	23.86	2.62	24.40	2.53	24.42	2.46	23.60
Transportation, communication and storage	2.47	0.40	2.44	0.13	2.57	0.52	2.76	0.52	2.75	0.50	2.85	0.57	2.94	0.61	3.03	0.67	3.10	0.74	2.79	0.56
Finance, Ins., real estate and business service	0.61	1.66	0.57	1.51	0.58	1.54	0.60	1.72	0.57	1.64	0.63	1.81	0.76	2.01	0.68	1.97	0.71	2.01	0.64	1.78
Community, social and personal services	3.91	24.09	3.65	22.80	3.74	20.10	3.49	21.94	3.60	22.65	3.60	21.77	3.72	23.30	3.64	23.79	3.74	24.60	3.68	22.84
B. Unemployed	26.00	74.02	27.40	72.65	27.90	72.07	28.00	71.60	28.9	71.09	28.10	71.90	29.00	70.98	29.40	70.59	31.40	68.64	28.60	71.40
C. Not in the Labor Force	8.93	91.07	8.44	91.56	8.53	91.47	8.94	91.06	8.99	91.01	9.10	90.90	8.81	91.19	8.80	91.2	11.20	88.76	9.14	90.86
Total	10.50	89.51	10.10	89.86	10.30	89.74	10.60	89.36	10.60	89.36	10.80	89.21	10.50	89.55	10.50	89.53	12.80	87.21	10.80	89.20

Source: Virola and de Perio, 'The Contribution of Women to the Economy', (1998).

even set a time frame for achieving this goal. He was totally supportive of the idea, and welcomed my concern, and then recounted to me the efforts he had already made (recounted above) – and abandoned – in this regard. But he assured me that he and his staff would be eager to resume those efforts – if there was a demand for it.

In subsequent discussions, Dr Virola expounded on this point. In his opinion, although many conceptual technical, methodological and measurement problems still have to be ironed out, he did not agree with the conventional (UN-SNA) thinking that these constituted the main obstacle to estimating women's contributions to the economy, in general, and the integration of unpaid work into the national accounts, in particular. These could be overcome and, to a certain extent, the results of their earlier efforts demonstrated this.

The constraint that caused him to abandon his efforts was a lack of demand – as he said, 'How can we continue to produce statistics that are not being asked for, or used, when there are calls for other data to be generated?' And what is behind this lack of demand? There may be a lack of understanding of how the statistics can be used for more effective decision-making (on the part of the policy-makers) or how they can be used as tools in influencing these decisions (on the part of the policy advocates). To overcome this, what is needed, according to Dr Virola, is 'capacity-building of the users of the statistics.'

But the demand constraint, it would seem, may arise not only because of a lack of ability on the part of the 'consumers', but because of a lack of desire or willingness on their part as well. This point was made clear by Lourdes Beneria (2001). There are some experts who believe that it is worth neither the time nor the effort to measure unpaid labor. However, they do not see how such information could be of use to the poor, exploited woman who is the subject of such information or who feel that resources would be better spent on other activities that would benefit her directly. These views, held as they are by some feminists, cannot but weaken the efforts to integrate unpaid labor into the macroeconomy. And they could be used to explain, in the case of the Philippines, why the NCRFW leadership shifted focus from unpaid labor to violence against women. It must also be pointed out, however, that there may be another reason (though never articulated) for the unwillingness to pursue the issue of integrating unpaid labor into the macroeconomy: the preservation of the status quo, where women remain invisible, exploitable and unable to widen the choices open to them.

Renewed efforts

In any case, Dr Virola and the NSCB gave the effort a second go attempt – and have updated the conventional and 'accurate' GDP accounts up to 2006, based on the 2001 TUS, presented again in the 2007 National Convention on Statistics at the end of last year (2007 updates will be ready in the near future). According to the latest results, unpaid work adds 66 per cent to the GDP; women's share in conventional GDP that was at 39 per cent rose to 47 per cent when adjusted for the unpaid work; women account for 60 per cent of all unpaid work; and over 55 per cent of this contribution was performed by women not in the labor force.

Unfortunately, aside from the statisticians, very few people either know or care that the data are available, although Dr Virola reports that his plan of integrating women in the national accounts was received enthusiastically by the NCRFW. Such enthusiasm notwithstanding, the hard fact is that thirteen years after Beijing and eleven years after the proposal to create satellite accounts measuring the contribution of unpaid family work to the economy, it is still not a reality, even as the Philippines has already constructed satellite accounts for environment and tourism – which were suggested much later. This is because, according to Dr Virola, in the case of environment and tourism, there are joint international efforts to come up with a methodological framework; for environment, there is a 'City Group' created by the UN (the London Group) that comes up with recommendations on how the accounts will be compiled and for tourism, the UN WTO is spearheading the work on methodological studies (and has, in fact, come up with a revised framework for tourism satellite accounts). No similar efforts seem to have been undertaken for unpaid work, other than a guide to producing time-use statistics (by the UN Statistics Division).

The way forward: towards a tipping point

What conclusions can be drawn from the foregoing?

First, it is the SNA that threw a cloak of invisibility over women's contributions to the economy, by using narrow and, at the very least, inadequate definitions. That cloak can and should be removed. Segregating these contributions in satellite accounts should not be considered a final and permanent solution, but rather a preliminary and temporary one.

Second, the full integration of unpaid work into the macroeconomy which has been established to be done mostly by women, can be accomplished, given the present SNA reality, as a sequence of steps – gathering time-use data, then valuing that unpaid work, then creating the satellite accounts, then institutionalizing them (estimating them regularly) and then fully integrating them as part of the national accounts' 'central system.' To date, to the best of my knowledge, less than half of the UN system has gathered time-use data; at most, half of that half have begun valuing unpaid work (mostly developed countries), less again are creating satellite accounts and, at most, one or two have begun institutionalizing them. Progress has indeed been slow in removing the cloak of invisibility.

Third, the slowness of this progress is not just a problem of technical supply constraints, but also one of demand – either a lack of ability, a lack of willingness or a combination of both, to carry it forward on the part of potential users or even the potential beneficiaries themselves. This is not to belittle the supply constraints – and our statistical system must be supported, particularly financially, in their attempts to push the envelope further in identifying and integrating the contribution of women in our national accounts. But the demand side, like the second blade in a pair of scissors, has to be addressed as well.

It is the third point to which we must now address ourselves. What can be done to increase, or even create, the demand for the data that will allow women's contributions to be visible? Here we have to reach out to other disciplines and other professions for help and guidance. In a nutshell, what is required is a series of consciousness-raising or awareness-increasing activities. It is not enough that data are produced and that the producers of the data know that they have a gold mine. It is not enough that the user capacity should be increased. The public should be on the side of the angels. They should also want that data to be produced in the first place, and want to know the results, and want their leaders to make use of those results, because it is the public that can exert the pressure on reluctant policymakers, technocrats, organizations or anybody else who is in the way.

In other words, the effort to integrate unpaid work into the macroeconomy must include not only TUS and valuation processes and satellite accounts until the final goal is reached, it must include a proactive effort to get the public interested in what is being done or should be done. Not only should the public demand that data, but preferably the nature of that demand should reach epidemic proportions so that the only possible outcome is the desired outcome.

How did epidemics get into the picture? This is explained in a fascinating book (Gladwell, 2000) that may not cross the path of economists and statisticians. The author, Malcolm Gladwell, posits that ideas, messages and behavior spread like viruses do – in epidemics. And an epidemic has three characteristics: it is very contagious, little causes have big effects and tipping points.

How a tipping point is reached is also explained. Three factors are involved – starting with The Law of the Few, which says that the success of epidemics depends on the degree of involvement of a few people with a particular and rare set of social gifts. Connectors, who are at the hub of a large network of people from different walks of life and can connect these people with each other; mavens, who are to information what connectors are to people; and salesmen, who can sell ideas or products because they somehow can communicate that they believe in these ideas or products.

The second factor is the Stickiness Factor, which ensures that once a person gets infected (buys the message), she stays infected. What is involved in making something sticky is to find a way of packaging information that, under the right circumstances, will make it irresistible.

In this connection, a communications expert (woman, naturally), asked for top-of-the-head suggestions, came up with the following: Hot on MAMA (Measure and Account for Mother's Accomplishments, or Movement to Account for Mom's Accomplishments); Mothering: a 24/7 Job Without Pay; HOME. Homemaker Output Measurement in the Economy); and even one in the vernacular, playing on the double meaning of the word KITA (to see and salary) – Kawawang Ina, Di Nakikita, Di Kumikita (Poor Mothers. Unseen. Unpaid). One can only imagine what she and others could do when asked to really put their minds to a national or international campaign.

The third factor is the Power of Context, which posits that people's behavior is affected by circumstance rather than any innate set of values. Gladwell illustrated it by recalling the so-called Stanford Prison Experiment, where 24 normal, ordinary students turned into either sadists or nervous wrecks depending on whether the role randomly assigned to them was to be a guard or a prisoner (the experiment had to be stopped after only six days).

Clearly, the integration of unpaid work into macroeconomics has not yet reached that tipping point. What is needed to achieve this are people – whether researchers, economists, statisticians or feminists, who have the talents to be either connectors, mavens, or salesmen – with a message that will not be forgotten (here is where the talents of advertising and marketing agencies can be tapped, as above illustrated, and where it is clear that research budgets should include a component for information and education) and an environment that will shape the behavior of people in a large way.

Unless these requirements are met, integrating unpaid work into the macroeconomy, thereby removing the invisibility of women's contributions to the economy from their homes, will remain an idea whose time has not yet come. But we can all take heart from the last lines of the Gladwell (2000) book: 'Look at the world around you. It may seem like an immovable, implacable place. It is not. With the slightest push – in just the right place – it can be tipped.'

Note

* The author wishes to acknowledge the invaluable contributions of Dr Romulo Virola and Jessamyn Encarnacion of the National Statistical Coordination Board, Philippines. All mistakes are mine.

References

Aslaksen, I. and C. Koren (1996) 'Unpaid Household Work and the Distribution of Extended Income: The Norwegian Experience,' *Feminist Economics* 2(3), 65–80.

Beck, T. (1999) *Using Gender-Sensitive Indicators: A Reference Manual for Governments and Other Stakeholders* (London: Commonwealth Secretariat).

Beneria, L. (2001) 'The Enduring Debate over Unpaid Labor,' in M. Loutfi (ed.), *Women, Gender and Work* (Geneva: International Labour Organization).

Bos, F. (1993) 'Standard National Accounting Concepts, Economic Theory and Data Compilation Issues; on Constancy and Change in the UN Manuals on National Accounting (1947, 1953, 1968, 1993),' National Accounts Occasional Paper No. 61 (The Hague: Statistics Netherlands).

Folbre, N. (1991) 'The Unproductive Housewife: Her Evolution in Nineteenth Century Economic Thought,' *Signs* 16(2), 463–84.

Gladwell, M. (2000) *The Tipping Point: How Little Things Can Make a Big Difference* (London: Little, Brown Book Group).

Horrigan, M. *et al.* (1999) 'A Report on the Feasibility of Conducting a TUS,' Prepared for IATUR Time Use Conference, University of Essex, 6–8 October.

INSTRAW (1996) 'Valuation of Household Production and Satellite Accounts' (Geneva: The United Nations).

INSTRAW (1995) 'Measurement and Valuation of Unpaid Contribution: Accounting through Time and Output' (Santo Domingo, Dominican Republic: INSTRAW).

UNDP (1995) *Human Development Report* (New York and Oxford: Oxford University Press).

UNDP (2006) *Human Development Report* (Basingstoke: Palgrave Macmillian).

UN-ESCAP (2003) *Guidebook for Integrating Unpaid Work into National Policies* (New York: The United Nations).

Virola, Romeo and de Perio (1998) 'The Contribution of Women to the Economy,' NSCB, Manila.

11
Time-Use Surveys in Developing Countries: An Assessment

Indira Hirway

Introduction

It is now widely accepted that unpaid work, both SNA and non-SNA, is an integral part of the economy and society. That is, it is difficult to understand the functioning of an economy or a society comprehensively without understanding the role of unpaid work. Unpaid work is also a key to understanding the dynamics of gender inequalities and an important input to designing of gender-equality policies. It is necessary therefore to estimate the size of paid and unpaid economies and to understand their characteristics, including their interlinkages, in order to understand the functioning of the total economy. Unpaid work, or the work that does not receive direct remuneration, is significant in both developed and developing countries. However it holds special importance in developing countries because one observes significant unpaid work in these countries within the purview of SNA work (for example, work covered under the production boundary of the UN-SNA) as well as non-SNA work (for example, work falling within the general production boundary). As a result, the total size of unpaid work is usually much higher in developing countries compared to that in developed countries. Some of the major concerns of developing countries, such as poverty, low human development, informal labor, gender inequalities and so on, can be understood well only if one understands the nature and characteristics of unpaid work in these economies.

The need for inclusion of unpaid work in policy formulation and policy analysis calls for collection of statistics on unpaid work in a systematic manner. TUS are very important here, as they collect comprehensive information on human activities and provide the details of an individual's life with a combination of specificity and comprehensiveness not achieved in any other type of survey (Gershuny, 2000). Reliable, comprehensive and periodically available time-use data can throw useful light on the size and characteristics of unpaid work on the one hand and, with other sets of data, can help in understanding the complexities of a variety of socioeconomic issues, including gender inequalities, on the other hand.

This chapter intends to assess the status of TUS in developing countries with a view to understanding how far these surveys have helped in estimating and comprehending unpaid work in these economies. This has been done by reviewing about 56 TUS in Asia, Africa and Latin America. The chapter is divided into three sections: the first section presents the approach and scope of the chapter; the next assesses the status of TUS in the selected countries; while the final section discusses the use made of the data and the issues related to the mainstreaming these surveys in the national statistical systems, as well as the cross-country comparability of these data. It also makes suggestions about the future course of action.

Scope and approach of assessment

What are time-use statistics?

Time-use statistics provide detailed information on how individuals spend their time, on a daily or weekly basis, on SNA activities that fall within the purview of the system of national accounts,[1] non-SNA activities that fall outside SNA but within the general production boundary[2] and personal services that are personal, nondelegable activities.[3] In other words, time-use statistics are quantitative summaries of how individuals allocate their time over a specified time period – typically over 24 hours of a day or over the seven days of a week on different activities and how much time they spend on each of these activities. As the UN Statistical Commission 1979 described in its report, *Status of Work on Time-Use Statistics*, time-use statistics provide data not otherwise obtainable on human activities in the various fields of social, demographic and related economic statistics (UN, 2005). Time-use statistics have three major components: (1) information on major socioeconomic characteristics of households and individuals (for whom data are collected) through a background schedule or through the main schedule in case the TUS is a module in a major survey; (2) time spent by individuals on different activities, such as SNA and non-SNA activities and personal services; and (3) the context in which activities are carried out.[4] This opens up immense possibilities for understanding the total economy consisting of paid and unpaid work, as well as the time spent by men and women on personal activities such as human capital formation, social networking and social capital formation, leisure, as well as understanding the kinds of time stress people experience.

Brief history

Time-use statistics were first produced in the early decades of the 1900s in social surveys reporting on the living conditions of working class families. The long working hours and short leisure hours of industrial workers was a concern of organized labor, who wanted to advocate for reduction in working hours. The Bureau of Home Economics of the US Department of Agriculture conducted a TUS in the 1920s to understand the effect of new technology on the time use of farm homemakers. Later on, TUS were carried out in different countries with a variety of objectives, such as understanding the problem of commuting and the length of commuting time, use of mass media by a population, leisure time and its use by different socioeconomic groups and so on. With the emerging interest in women's unpaid work and gender inequalities in the 1970s, and the World Conferences on Women thereafter, time-use data are seen as a major input in estimating and valuing unpaid work of women and women's contribution to the national well-being. With the emergence of developing countries on the scene, TUS acquired a new focus. These countries saw several additional uses of these surveys, such as netting SNA work of the poor, particularly those engaged in informal and subsistence work, and thereby improving workforce statistics; improving estimates of national income by getting improved data on the workforce and by including subsistence production in national income statistics; and drawing policy guidelines for poverty reduction, employment generation, promotion of welfare and so on (Hirway, 2000a). Scholars in several developing countries conducted small-scale TUS in the 1970s and 1980s, covering a few villages/urban centers or a few households to illustrate the above uses of these surveys. Since the 1990s and thereafter many developing countries have conducted large or national TUS.

An interesting aspect of time-use data thus is that over the years newer uses of the data have been discovered. In the initial stages the data were used for understanding the lifestyle of people; in the 1960s and 1970s the data were used by broadcasting companies to design the timings of their programs, for planning for transportation and so on; since the mid-1970s the data are also seen to be useful in estimating the contribution of women's unpaid work to national well-being and for designing policies for gender equality. In the 1990s and thereafter developing countries have seen these data as a means of improving workforce estimates, particularly for informal labor, as well as for understanding issues related to poverty, human development and so on. In the recent years, the data were used by a few scholars to understand the total economy that constitutes paid (SNA) and unpaid (non-SNA) work.

TUS in developing countries

As per the information available from different websites and sources, so far (2007–2008) more than 100 countries in the world have conducted small or big TUS. Of these, about 40 are developed countries or transitional economies of Europe and former USSR. The rest are developing countries located in Asia, Africa and in Latin America, which are covered in this chapter. These are 18 countries from Asia, 24 countries from Africa and 14 countries from Latin America. A few countries like Panama, Vietnam and so on are not included for want of the detailed data (Table 11A.1).

Before assessing the TUS in the developing economies in the Global South, it will be useful to note that TUS are relatively new and are not yet fully established, even in developed countries. For example, about ten developed countries (such as Greece, Luxembourg, New Zealand, South Korea, Ireland, Lithuania, Slovac Republic, Estonia and so on) did not conduct any TUS before 1990 (Mrkic, 2006). Also, only about 22 developed countries have so far conducted two or more TUS and not all of them have institutionalized it in the sense of conducting these surveys regularly and periodically. It is also interesting to add that so far only 15 developed countries have undertaken valuation of unpaid work in separate accounts and, of these, only two or three countries (Canada and Australia) have institutionalized these accounts (Collas-Monsod, 2008). In short, TUS are not yet fully institutionalized, even in all developed countries.

Some of the earlier surveys in developing countries were conducted by research scholars, university teachers or others. These surveys were conducted in Gambia (1952), Burkina Faso (1967), Nepal (1976–77), India (1976–77), Cameroon (1976), Israel (1970), Kenya (1970s and 1988), Peru (1966) and so on. In all, 12 countries conducted such surveys during the 1970s (Table 11A.1). A few more countries conducted small TUS (also in the 1980s). These surveys were small, independent surveys designed for limited sectors/regions/households with specific objectives. In the 1990s, however, one observes many more countries entering the field either by conducting a systematic pilot survey, a national survey or a large-scale survey that represented large regions. Between 2000 and 2007–08 several new countries, particularly from Latin America, entered this field, raising the total number of developing countries with a TUS to more than 56.[5] Out of these 56 countries, less than half of the countries (27) have conducted a national survey. The rest of the countries have conducted either a small or a large survey or a pilot survey. Of these 27 countries, only four countries – Morocco, Mexico, Nicaragua and Ecuador – have conducted more than one national TUS. Countries like Bhutan, Mongolia, China and Turkey conducted a pilot survey before they conducted their respective national/large TUS. In short, TUS in developing countries are still in the exploratory stage. These surveys are far from mainstreamed in their respective national statistical systems.

Many of the surveys have been sponsored and supported financially and/or technically by UN agencies, including its regional offices (ESCAP, ECA, ECLAC), and by other global organizations and donor agencies. The UN regional offices have brought out guidebooks and guidelines to help their respective members to carry out TUS.[6] UNDP has supported TUS in sub-Saharan African countries, such as Benin, Madagascar, Mauritius, South Africa, Ghana and so on; the World Bank sponsored TUS as a module of the Living Standards Measurement Survey (LSMS) in Malawi, Sierra Leone, Mauritania, Guinea and other countries; UNIFEM/UNDP were instrumental in conducting TUS in Mexico, Cuba, Argentina, Chile, Ecuador, El Salvador, Guatemala, Nicaragua and others in Latin America and in Botswana, Mozambique and Zimbabwe in Africa; while FAO promoted, in collaboration with national statistical agencies, TUS in rural areas of countries like Malaysia, Pakistan and Indonesia. UNIFEM also helped Tanzania and Palestine in conducting TUS. A few countries, like India, conducted their survey without any financial or technical support from outside.

Scope of this chapter

TUS in developing countries have been reviewed and assessed by several scholars in the past. These reviews include small-scale reviews in selected regions, such as TUS in Pacific Islands organized by the regional UNDP office,[7] a review of UN-sponsored TUS in Africa by Jacques Charmes (2005) and a review for the ILO by Srdjan Mrkic, *Report on Time-Use Statistics in the Context of Social Statistics* (2006), as well as 'explorations' of selected TUS in Africa, Latin America and Asia by Valeria Esquivel, Nancy Folbre, Debbie Budlender and Indira Hirway (Esquivel *et al.*, 2008), respectively. In addition, there are larger reviews done by scholars like Debbie Budlender (2007), Indira Hirway (2007) and Nadeem Ilahi (2000). Debbie Budlender has reviewed critically some selected TUS as a part of the UNRISD research project *The Political and Social Economy of Care in a Development Context* (UNRISD, 2007). The focus of the review is on unpaid care work and it was done as a part of the process of selecting countries for inclusion in the project. The purpose of the review was to critically review selected TUS in order to assess their quality. This review paper covers 11 countries that have conducted large or national TUS[8] and assesses design of the surveys, scope of the surveys, information covered and the quality of data, as well as the weaknesses in data and methodology. Indira Hirway reviewed TUS in the Global South in order to understand their implications for employment guarantee programs. This review, or 'stock-taking paper' (Hirway, 2007), aimed at understanding the implications of time use of people, particularly their unpaid work, for the designing of public employment programs. This review of TUS covers 24 countries from the developing world.[9] The areas of assessment are adequacy of TUS in providing quality data on SNA and non-SNA unpaid work, the survey design (including sampling design, time sample, data collection and the like) and the problems faced and resolved while conducting the surveys.

This chapter is more comprehensive than the earlier reviews in terms of content and coverage. It intends to assess the status of TUS in developing countries with a view to understanding how far these surveys have helped in estimating and comprehending unpaid work in these economies. This has been done through an in-depth review of about 56 TUS in the areas of their objectives, survey design, data collection, classification and so on, as well as analysis of the time-use data collected through the TUS.

Methodology of assessment

This assessment is based on the desk research on the available literature on time-use studies on the one hand and the rich first-hand practical experience of the author on the other. The author has been involved with conducting TUS and analyzing time-use data of different countries, as well as discussing the issues related to time-use methodologies and data analysis at different national and international forums. At the national level in India, the author headed the Technical Advisory Committee that was set up by the government of India to design the first pilot TUS, as well as the scheme of analysis of the time-use data. She was also associated later on with the revision of the time-use activity classification at the all-India level.[10] Recently, the author has prepared the proposal for mainstreaming TUS in the national statistical system in India (Hirway, 2009).

At the international level, as a member of the Regional Resource Group on Integrating Paid and Unpaid Work into National Policies, the author has studied TUS in different countries and has contributed towards preparing the guidebook on integrating paid and unpaid work into national policies (UN, 2003).[11] As a member of several expert group meetings at UNSD[12] and UNDP, [13] the author discussed the issues related to TUS methodologies and contributed towards developing global time-use activity classification. In addition, as a resource person on training programs on time-use studies,[14] as well as in developing courses on time-use studies, the author has examined different methodological issues in conducting time-use studies.[15] And finally, as a researcher, the author has analyzed Indian, as well as cross-country, time-use data and assessed the strengths and weaknesses of the data.[16]

The developing countries that conducted small-scale TUS during the 1970s and 1980s covering a small number of villages, households and/or one or two urban centers, used a simple questionnaire based on the usual survey techniques and focused on one or two selected issues, such as assessing agricultural work of women, estimating women's informal work or measuring women's unpaid work. However, when these countries started conducting national and large-scale surveys, they needed standard methodologies and classifications to meet their specific needs and constraints. These were not available, firstly because the available methods and classifications were designed for developed countries and did not suit them fully and secondly because no standard global methodologies of conducting TUS were (and are) developed to meet their needs and constraints. The developing countries therefore had to design their methods and classifications adapting from the available ones.

There were/are several constraints faced by developing countries in conducting TUS and these have put constraints on their methodological choices. First of all, the low level of literacy in many developing countries has made it difficult for them to use self-reporting 24-hour time diaries with 10–15 minute time slots. These countries therefore have to use alternative methods, such as the observation method or the face-to-face interview method to record time use in 24-hour time diaries, or the methods based on stylized questions to collect data on the time use of people. Secondly, the limited use of timepieces/clocks in remote and backward areas in many of these countries does not allow detailed reporting of the time use. They have to depend on alternative ways, like linking the time use to major common events (such as office time, school time, timings of TV/radio programs) to help recall of time use and using bigger time slots (for example, thirty-minute to one-hour time slots). And thirdly, being predominantly agricultural countries, these countries need seasonal data on the time use to reflect seasonal variations in the time use. This being expensive, many countries have done single day/period TUS and failed to provide seasonal variations in the data.

In addition, the other two constraints faced by several developing countries are lack of funds and lack of the required expertise. Poor appreciation of the utility of time-use data has added to these constraints. Since conducting a TUS is time consuming and expensive, developing countries are not very enthusiastic about spending their own funds on conducting such a survey. Most TUS are therefore conducted with the support from donor agencies/global UN organizations. Therefore there is always a tendency to minimize the costs. As a consequence, many developed countries face difficult trade-offs and end up with making several 'pragmatic' compromises in sample size and coverage, survey design, data collection methods and so on. This pragmatic approach is reflected in reduced sample size, small time sample (skipping, for example, multi-season data collection), simpler methods of data collection, short list of time-use activities and so on. Our study will throw light on these compromises and short cuts.

The relevant question however is whether, despite the compromises, the data are of good quality and are usable, and whether they are actually used. Our framework of assessment basically includes the following questions:

- What are the objectives of the survey? Do they cover the major issues related to unpaid work of men and women?
- Do the surveys represent the entire country or a significant part of the country? Is the sample big enough to represent the time use in the countries?
- Is the reference period relevant to the time-use pattern of the country's population? Is the time sample representative of the total time of the population?
- Are the methods of data collection sound? Do they address the constraints and problems faced by these countries adequately?
- How good is the overall quality of the time-use data? Are the data accurate and reliable?
- Are the data analyzed well to reflect the unpaid work in the economy? Are they used in relevant policy-making?

Assessment of TUS

Objectives of TUS

There are clear differences in the objectives of conducting TUS in developed and developing countries. In developed countries, where it is assumed that conventional surveys are able to provide reliable estimates of the labor force,[17] time-use data are found useful in estimating non-SNA work, such as estimating and valuing unpaid work in satellite accounts, and in understanding a number of socioeconomic issues, such as gender inequalities, transportation, balancing family and work, loneliness of the old, social capital and so on. The main objective of the survey here is frequently stated as 'to collect data on the time people spend on doing various activities, ranging from child care and paid work to community work and socializing' (USA, Eurostat, UK). In some cases, a few major objectives are specifically mentioned: In the case of Japan and the Republic of Korea, for example, 'valuation of unpaid work to compile satellite accounts' is mentioned as one of the important objectives or in the case of New Zealand 'measuring gender inequality in time use' is mentioned as an important objective.

In the case of developing countries, however, a major objective of TUS is to collect data on SNA work, particularly informal work (including home-based work and subsistence work). This is because it is believed that the conventional labor-force surveys fail to capture the uncertain, unstable and scattered informal work and exclude most of the subsistence work, including collection of fuel wood and water in these economies (Hirway and Charmes, 2008). Since TUS collect comprehensive data on how people spend their time, they are able to capture this work easily.

The most common objective of the TUS in 56 developing countries is 'to improve workforce estimates' in the country by getting improved estimates of informal work (employment) and subsistence work (Table 11A.2). Out of these, more than 35 countries (62.5 per cent) want to get improved estimate of SNA work and workers through TUS. It is important to note that all African countries, 14 of the 18 Asian countries and 10 of the 16 Latin American countries have put this as a major objective of their time-use studies. This objective has been presented in different ways by different countries. While some countries have put this in a direct manner, others have used different words: The Lao PDR survey has stated this objective as 'to measure women's (and men's) participation in agriculture and in small-scale business in informal sectors'; Guinea and Madagascar have stated it as 'to estimate time spent on collection of fuel wood and water'; Indonesia and Malaysia have put it as 'to estimate women's agrarian labor'; Brazil and Zimbabawe have put it as 'to understand women's role in the economy and society'; Guatemala and Nicargua have put it as 'to explore labor behavior of men and women to design employment policies'; while some African countries have stated it as 'to get better estimation and better understanding of child labor'. This objective is relatively more important in Asian and African countries compared to Latin American countries. The second major objective is to get accurate estimates of 'all forms of work of men and women,' including unpaid domestic work and community services. Several countries have also put valuation of unpaid domestic work and unpaid care in satellite accounts as an important objective of the survey. Estimating and understanding gender inequalities in the economy and the society is also stated as an important objective of the TUS.

The other objectives are: 'to understand quality of life of people' (China); 'to study status of poverty and human development of the people' (Nepal, Nicargua, India); 'to collect information on the time-use patterns of different socioeconomic groups residing in different regions' (Palestine); 'to measure happiness of people' (Bhutan); 'to promote better provision of people infected by HIV/AIDS' (Botswana, Mozambique and Zimbabawe); to estimate contribution of voluntary work and so on. One more objective is 'to plan for infrastructure' (Guatemala, Malawi and Guinea), as the data show how the poor spend their time on drudgery, low paid work and so on.

Several countries have made their statistical objectives explicit. These objectives have been stated as: 'to develop sound methods for the future TUS' (India); 'to test alternative methods of data collection on time use' (Pakistan, Malaysia); or 'to develop globally comparable time use data' (Thailand).

To sum up, the objectives of the TUS are very much in line with the major needs of the developing countries. There is a clear realization that the conventional labor-force surveys are not adequate to capture informal employment and subsistence employment prevailing in these economies, and that there is a need to estimate unpaid non-SNA work of men and women to measure and address gender inequalities.

Types of TUS

TUS are basically of two types: Independent TUS (or standalone surveys) and non-independent surveys (for example, surveys conducted as a part or module of a major survey). An independent TUS collects comprehensive information on the time use of the reference population without missing out on any details. It has three components, namely, a background schedule that collects background information of the responding household and the respondent; the time-use schedule/diary that collects data on the time use of the reference 24 hours; and context variables, which provide information on the context of the time-use activities. TUS started out as independent surveys, largely because they collected information that was not collected through other surveys. Most developed countries at present conduct independent TUS. A few developing countries also have conducted an independent survey.

A number of developing countries have adopted modular TUS. In fact, out of the total 35 large and national surveys in developing countries, 22 surveys (63 per cent) are modular surveys. It is interesting to note that modular TUS are more common in Latin America (9 out of 11 surveys are modular) and in Africa (9 out of 12 surveys are modular). As Table 11A.1 in the Appendix shows, eight modular surveys are attached to LSMS surveys, four are to labor-force surveys, five to national income and expenditure surveys and three to national household surveys. One is attached to a national happiness survey (Bhutan).

There are several advantages of a modular TUS. First, a modular survey is less costly as compared to an independent survey. Secondly, it needs less effort, as it is a part of a major survey. And thirdly, it is easy to institutionalize the TUS under a large national survey. As against this, the start-up costs of an independent survey are usually large, and, therefore, not easy to institutionalize in the national database. Also, irregular survey operations make it difficult to accumulate and absorb the knowledge and experience to achieve efficient and reliable survey results. They also limit the opportunity to develop independent technical and field staff well-trained in time-use methods.

A TUS module in a survey, however, has a limited scope for data collection on time use. To start with, the module cannot be a very large module that can collect comprehensive data, as it is a part of a major national survey. The module tends to collect information that is related to the main survey, as its scope is restricted by the main survey. The collected information may not be adequate enough to understand the time use of men and women in a comprehensive manner. For example, a time-use module in a labor-force survey may not provide the data needed to compile satellite accounts of unpaid work, or a time-use module in an income and expenditure survey may not provide the data needed to estimate and understand the informal and subsistence economy. Also, most modular surveys have to use stylized questions, that ask 'how much time did you spend on activities during the reference day/week' for data collection. As we shall soon see, this method has severe constraints in terms of getting good data. On the other hand, an independent TUS collects comprehensive information on how people spend their time without missing out on any time or any activity.

There is no need to take any strong view about the superiority of independent verses modular TUS. However, one can say that an independent TUS can collect comprehensive data on the time use, which has multiple uses in formulating and monitoring policies and programs in a large number of areas.

It will not be out of place here to mention the utility of small region specific or issue specific time-use surveys. Small scale rigorous time-use surveys can contribute significantly towards understanding specific issues or problems, such as the impact of the financial crisis on the workers and their households in an industry, impact of a reduction in social expenditure on paid and unpaid work for women/poor in a region, or impact of a macropolicy on specific socioeconomic groups, etc.

Sampling under TUS

Though small-scale anthropological/sociological TUS throw light on microlevel situations, policy formulation requires representative data at the national or subnational/regional level. However, out of the 56 countries, only 18 countries have conducted a national TUS. The rest are either small-sample surveys (exploratory, anthropological, covering a few villages or an urban center or two), pilot surveys or large surveys covering a region or a part of the country. They are not representative at the national level and therefore the data cannot be treated as national level data. These data cannot be analyzed to compile reliable national-level estimates. This does not at all mean that the data have no use at all. The data do throw useful light on the nature of the issues related to paid and unpaid work and gender inequalities.

The sample size of national TUS – stand alone, as well as module-based surveys – is usually small, as the surveys are time consuming and expensive. Time-use samples are observed to be smaller than the national surveys, frequently reducing the sample size to an unacceptable level. This tends to raise sampling errors on the one hand and limits the possibility for disaggregated analysis on the other. Both these factors tend to reduce the utility of the data. The sample size of a TUS can, however, be raised by: (1) increasing the number of persons in the survey; and (2) increasing the number of days of each person selected for the survey. In this context, selecting all members of the selected households (above a certain age) is a useful strategy. In fact, selecting all the members of a household also helps in understanding the intrahousehold division of work and the intrahousehold dynamics of sharing of work.

Out of the countries that have conducted large or national surveys (for whom the issue of representative sample is relevant), one country (Morocco)[18] selected only women in the sample; two countries (Lao PDR and Argentina) selected only one person per household, while two countries (Palestine and South Africa) selected two persons at random from each of the selected households. Mongolia selected three persons from each of the selected households. The reasons for selecting a small number of persons, according to these countries, are: (1) to reduce the cost of investigation; and (2) to reduce the survey fatigue on selected households. However, as Jacques Charmes has put it, this was a missed opportunity to raise the sample size and reduce the sampling error (Charmes, 2005).

Selecting more than one day per person is another way of raising the sample size. Our study shows that most countries have selected one day ('yesterday') per person, frequently distributed equally across the reference week to cover weekly variant day as well as to arrive at weekly estimates of the time use. A few countries have used more than one day. Five countries (Argentina, Bolivia, Cuba, Ecuador and Turkey) have selected two days in a week – one week day and one weekend day. Mongolia and India have selected two or three days (if the day of the reporting is an abnormal day, a normal weekend or a week-end day is selected). Chile has selected three days in a week. Two countries, Guinea and Nigeria, have selected seven days for data collection. This is, however, too long a period and, as observed in the Nigerian case, many respondents left the survey after two or three days (Ajayi, 2000), as the investigator was expected to visit each person for one week to collect the data on the time spent the previous day. In the case of Guinea, information on the past seven days is seen as a major hurdle in data collection. In short, the sample size can be increased by increasing the number of diary days, but the number should not go beyond two. There is a need to balance between the need to increase the sample size and the probability of getting reliable data.

It will not be out of place here to mention that there are wide variations in the reference population selected for the survey. The minimum age for the sample varies from 4 years in Malawi, 5 years in Tanzania and Ecuador to 15 years in 15 countries. In fact, the minimum age for the sample is 4, 5, 6, 7, 8, 9, 10, 12 and 15 years in different countries! There are countries where there is a maximum limit also, varying from 60, 64, 65, 70, 74 and 75. Clearly there are no standard age groups for the survey. One can think of fixing the minimum age keeping in mind the prevalence of child labor in these countries.

Reference period and time sample

The reference period or the time sample of a TUS has to be representative of the total time of the population so that the estimates are stable and reliable. For example, time-use estimates for one day in a year may not be adequate to reflect the general time use of the population.

However our study shows that the time-use estimates for majority of the countries are only for one period in a year (Table 11A.3). Out of the 48 countries for which we have this data, 40 countries (83 per cent) have time-use data only for one point of time – usually one day in a year. That is, except for eight countries, no country has collected seasonal data. Of these, a few countries have collected data for one season or for four to six months. These data are far from adequate to reflect the average time use of the respective populations in these countries. They fail to provide stable and reliable estimates on the time-use pattern of people.

Neglecting seasonal or annual variations in time use is thus is also a major limitation in developing countries, which still have a majority of their workforce employed in the primary sector. For example, the rural TUS in Benin was undertaken during off-season months, with the result that the results are of limited use (Charmes, 2005). In short, extremely small and nonrepresentative time samples in many countries seem to have affected the quality of time-use data adversely.

Background schedule

The background schedule is an important component of a TUS, as the time-use data is usually analyzed with reference to the information in the background schedule. The background schedule is designed keeping in mind the objectives of the TUS. This schedule is therefore expected to collect all the data required to analyze the time-use data in the context of the objectives of the survey. For example, if an objective of the survey is to value unpaid non-SNA work, it is necessary that the background collects data on equipments and assets of the household; technologies used in cooking, cleaning, washing and so on; prevailing wages in the locality; the presence of children, old, disabled in the household; market prices of the goods produced at home and so on. If the objective is also to estimate gender inequalities, the background schedule should collect information on asset ownership by men and women, decision making by men and women and so on.

There are two sets of background schedules used in developing countries: In the case of modular TUS, the main survey can be treated as the background schedule, while in the case of independent stand-alone surveys, a background schedule is designed specifically keeping in mind the objectives of the survey. In the former case, the background schedule is determined by the main objectives of the main survey (such as labor-force survey, income and expenditure survey, living standard measurement survey or any other household survey), which may not accommodate the specific objectives of the TUS. For example, a time-use module in a labor-force survey will have different background data from that used in an income and expenditure survey. The subject of the main survey thus is likely to restrict the analysis of time-use data. A labor-force survey may not help in compiling household satellite accounts or estimate the care economy; an income and expenditure survey may not provide the required data on estimating informal and subsistence employment. The selection of the main survey to latch on a TUS module needs to be done carefully.

The background schedule for an independent TUS also needs to be designed carefully, keeping in mind the objectives of the survey. The literature has brought out several inadequacies of the background schedule in this context. Frequently, this schedule is designed casually without keeping in mind the data needed for valuation of unpaid work, for compilation of satellite accounts or estimating the informal and subsistence workforce. In the case of India, for example, there are no data on household assets to compile satellite accounts, in the case of Mongolia there are not enough background data to estimate informal employment or in the case of Nepal there are no data to determine unpaid household SNA work. In short, developing countries have to learn to pay careful attention to background data.

Methods for data collection

Getting the correct and detailed response from respondents is an important part of data collection. The developed countries use self-reported 24-hour time diaries with a ten-minute time slot for collecting information on how people spend their time. This method is not practical in many developing countries where the literacy levels are low and, in some cases (mainly in remote backward areas), people do not use timepieces to report their exact time use. Consequently, these countries have to work out their strategy for data collection carefully.

As regards methods of data collection, they have three choices: (1) to use the observation method, under which investigators observe the time behavior of the population and record it; (2) to use the one-day recall method and let investigators fill in 24-hour time diaries by interviewing respondents; or (3) to use stylized questions, for example, list the time-use activities and let investigators ask respondents to report their time use on these activities.

The observation method

The experiences with the participant observation methods in India, Nepal and Morocco have shown that this method has several problems.

It makes respondents conscious and leads them to behave differently. Also, if an investigator has to travel with the respondent or follow him everywhere, a full-time investigator will be needed for each of the respondents, which may not be feasible. If the investigator has to observe the entire household, she may find it difficult do so. Again, this method can work only during a limited period, say from 7–8 am to 7–8 pm. It may not be feasible to observe the respondents beyond this time. This method is the least-used method at present.

The method based on stylized questions

Under the method based on stylized questions, investigators present a list of activities and ask respondents to report how much time they spent on each of those activities during the reference day (usually the previous day) or the reference week. This list can be a short list of the activities of specific interest or a long list covering all possible activities. It would be difficult to manage a long, exhaustive list and check that the total time adds up to 24 hours because the respondents usually do not reply keeping in mind the total time. Also, when simultaneous activities are included, it becomes almost impossible to keep the total time to 24 hours. In practice, therefore, one observes a short or (slightly long) list, but not an exhaustive list consisting of all activities.

The stylized questions are used largely when a time-use module is added to a national survey and time-use data are collected about the time use on selected activities. This is because this is a method similar to the one used in the data collection of the main survey. This method is popular also because it is easy to operate and it avoids elaborate chronological reporting. However, there are several problems with this approach. To start with, it has been observed in some postsurvey reviews (Madagascar, Malawi) that the listed activities missed several relevant activities, as the list is predetermined and it is not always exhaustive. Also, this method does not give information on the total time use, for 24 hours.

Questions have been raised in the literature about the quality of the data collected through stylized questions. The UN guide has observed that stylized questions tend to produce results with a high degree of error (UNSD, 2005). This is because respondents underreport the time spent on the activities that are less important or less desirable and overreport the time on the activities of high importance or of high interest. Also, respondents may find it difficult to report the time spent on intermittent or scattered activities. Bonke (2002) and Kan (2006) have compared the performance of both these methods (time diaries based on one-day recall and stylized questions) at the field level. They have observed that there are clear errors emerging from the stylized questions. The studies have shown that the error comes not only from the problems of recall, but also from social desirability of the activities. Kan (2006) observes that the error varies across different socioeconomic groups also. Bonke (2002) also found that the gap in the results of both the methods is larger in the case of women than in the case of men.

Another limitation of stylized questions is that they do not provide the time of the day when the activity was performed.

Two other limitations of the stylized questions are that: (1) one cannot collect time-use data on simultaneous activities accurately under this approach; and (2) it is also not easy to use context variables efficiently under this method. The data on simultaneous activities cannot be collected satisfactorily because the respondents find it difficult to provide these data, as they are not able to identify these activities and the time spent on them correctly. Similarly, respondents also find it difficult to respond to context variables, such as for whom, with whom and so on, while responding to stylized questions.

Recall can be a serious problem with stylized questions when the reference period is more than one day. The one-week reference period in the TUS in Nepal and Guinea is seen as a serious problem. This issue has affected the quality of time-use data profoundly in both countries, and as a result the existing information can be used only as a rough approximation.

One-day recall time diary

Under the one-day-recall based recording of the time use for the past 24 hours, interviewers ask how respondents spent their time the previous day and record all their activities comprehensively in chronological order in a time diary. This method avoids many of the problems of the stylized questions. However the role of the interviewer is critical in this approach (Hirway, 2003). He/she has to get the right response without asking leading questions. He has to collect the right data without any biases. Intensive training is absolutely essential, along with a well-drafted instruction manual. In the absence of these, many countries are likely to produce low-quality time-use data.

Lite diary versus full diary

Under the diary approach, some surveys provide a predetermined list of activities and ask the respondent to choose from these activities while filling in the diary (for example, lite diary). On the other hand, some countries do not provide a list and ask respondent to describe his/her activities. Codes to these activities are assigned later on by investigators (for example, full diary). The full-diary approach is observed to be giving better results, as there is no pressure on the respondent to select an activity from the given list. However, the full diary calls for lot more work on the part of coders/analysts. If the analysts/interviewers are trained to perform this task, the full diary method is a better alternative.

Poor sense of time

An absence of the sense of time (absence of clocks/timepieces) is another challenge in data collection. Though this challenge may not be big in most countries, some countries definitely face this challenge. This leads to approximation of the time use in rounded figures and in the widening of the time slots for data collection. Many countries therefore use one-hour or half-hour time slot instead of the ten-minute time slot used in developed countries.

Recall for one day and one week

In addition, there is a problem of recall. Though one-day recall may be an acceptable recall, recall for one week is not likely to be reliable. Those countries that collect time-use data for the past week tend to compromise on the quality of data.

In short, the time-diary approach – self-reported or recorded through interviewers – is definitely a better approach of data collection under TUS. This approach gives more reliable results, provides comprehensive information on time use, is amenable to the use of context variables and can collect data on simultaneous activities. Though its initial costs are high, the costs decline substantially after it is institutionalized.

Data collection in selected countries

Our analysis of the 56 countries shows that the problem of a low level of literacy is indeed a serious problem, as only four countries (Chile, Cuba, Turkey and Occupied Palestine) could use self-reported diaries. China, Palestine and Thailand also used self-reported time diaries, but illiterates were helped either by other members of the household or pictograms in the diary. The latter created a problem as the list of pictures could not be very long. All the remaining countries used face-to-face interviews, either to record a time-use diary for the past 24 hours (13 countries) or to record the time spent on the listed activities. Six countries, namely, Israel, Oman, Philippines (pilot), Brazil (small survey) and Nigeria (pilot), used self-reported diaries for literate population and face-to-face on-day recall diary for illiterate population.

Most of the countries that have employed a time-use module in an ongoing survey, have utilized stylized questions, as it was a method similar to the one used in the data collection of the main survey. In addition, many small surveys have also used stylized questions in data collection. In fact, this is emerging as a predominant method of data collection in TUS in the developing countries. However, as seen above, there is a good amount of subjectivity in the answers to these questions, as the response to stylized questions is determined not only by 'recall,' but also by social desirability or perception of respondents.

Collection of time-use data by recording the time use chronologically through a face-to-face interview also is not fully satisfactory. Recall could be a problem here, as the respondent may not be able to remember the exact time spent on different activities. Most countries have therefore used longer time slots – up to half an hour to one hour, instead of the ten-minute slot used in self-reported time diaries. It is likely that the data are not fully accurate, though broadly correct. In addition, as seen above, the role of the interviewer is very critical, as they are expected to help the respondent and not lead them to increase or reduce the time spent.

The role of the interviewer becomes even more important when people are not used to watches or timepieces. In this context: (1) intensive training of investigators; (2) compilation of a detailed instruction manual for them; and (3) strong supervision and follow up are very important. Our review of, as well as discussions with, concerned officials shows that not many countries have paid enough attention to these aspects. This was particularly true in the case of the countries that conducted the TUS mainly because UN/donor agencies were willing to finance the survey.

The observation method has been used mainly in small surveys conducted by private researchers and scholars. The use of the participant-observation method in some of the early TUS was a part of the anthropological approach. Though this method was used in earlier small surveys carried out in Nepal, Brazil, India and so on, it is no longer popular at the national level. Only Morocco seems to be using this method as a supplementary method (to face-to-face interview for 24-hour time diary) at the national level.

In short, designing a suitable approach for data collection, given the constraints of developing countries, is a major challenge in data collection. It appears that the developing countries under our review face several problems with respect to ensuring good quality time-use data.

Treatment of simultaneous activities

Simultaneous activities are important in developing countries for the poor and women, who undertake such activities many times during a day. Information on simultaneous activities is important to design interventions for reducing time stress of the poor, particularly poor women. However, it is not difficult to collect these data, as it requires special efforts (people do not provide this information easily) and also hard to analyze since it needs good analytical tools. A key challenge pertains to deciding how to split the time spent on simultaneous activities into different activities so as to reach the total of 24 hours. One practice is to first determine primary, secondary and tertiary activities from the simultaneous activities, and to allocate the time spent on simultaneous activities among these activities according to their importance. However, it is not always clear to respondents or to interviewers as to which activity is primary, secondary or tertiary and they tend to take arbitrary decisions. The second approach is divide the total time equally between simultaneous activities without worrying about their importance. In both cases, however, there is a loss of time for activities covered. An acceptable approach could be developing time grids for simultaneous activities and/or letting the total time go beyond 24 hours. This area, however, has not received much attention in developing countries.

Our review has shown that, in order to avoid complications, most countries do not collect data on simultaneous activities. Though we do not have complete record on this,[19] the available data show that only 21 countries (less than 40 per cent) have collected information on simultaneous activities. Except for three countries, all of them have collected data only on one secondary/parallel activity. The colleted data have been analyzed poorly by these countries: About half of them have not analyzed these data and a few of them that have analyzed the data have not done it well. For example, the Indian TUS collected the data, but divided the time spent on simultaneous activities equally among the relevant activities to make the total time equal to 24 hours. On the other hand, South Africa and Argentina have analyzed these data well to estimate the time stress experienced by respondents, particularly women.

The absence of reliable data on simultaneous activities is a hurdle in estimating and understanding the time stress of women.

Time-use activity classifications

Classification of time-use activities is an important component of TUS, as it organizes the information on the time use in a systematic manner. Along with context variables, it provides rich information on how people use their time on different activities, with reference to the objectives of TUS.

There are certain well-established norms of good classification of activities. These are applicable to time-use activity classification also. First, the classification should be comprehensive and inclusive of all activities performed by men and women. Secondly, it should be hierarchical, reflecting the different levels of activities in different digits (for example, the first digit represents the major group, the second digit represents the subgroup and so on). Thirdly, it should be compatible with other relevant classifications (in this case, with the classifications of labor-force statistics). Fourthly, it should be simple, easy to understand and clear. And lastly, it should facilitate valuation of unpaid work and compilation of satellite accounts of household work, as well as help in estimating informal and subsistence work.

Since time-use studies developed first in industrialized countries, there is a well-developed set of classifications of time-use activities designed in the context of the needs of these countries. This classification divides time-use activities into four broad categories: contracted time, necessary time, committed time and free time.[20] These four broad categories are then divided into: (1) personal care activities; (2) employment-related activities; (3) education activities; (4) domestic activities; (5) childcare activities; (6) purchasing goods and services; (7) voluntary work and care activities; (8) social and community interaction; and (9) recreation and leisure. These subgroups are again divided into subgroups and into activities. The classifications developed by Australia, Canada, Eurostat (as well as several European countries) and the United States have many similarities, though there is no strictly harmonized classification, even for industrialized countries. These classifications, however, do not meet the needs of developing countries for several reasons. First, industrialized countries did not give much importance to economic activities because they assume that they get adequate information on economic activities of people through their labor-force surveys and other conventional sources. In the case of developing countries, however, one of the objectives of conducting TUS is to get improved estimates of the workforce, particularly those engaged in the informal economy. The classifications developed by industrialized countries for economic activities therefore do not meet the needs of developing countries.

Secondly, developing countries need detailed information on subsistence economic activities, including activities like collection of fuel wood, fodder and fetching water, as well as subsistence-crop cultivation and other primary activities. Since these activities are missing in the classifications of industrialized countries, developing countries need a different classification. Thirdly, details of activities in the noneconomic sector required by developing countries also differ in some ways from those of developed countries. Developing countries therefore felt the need to modify the established classifications of developed countries for their TUS.

The United Nations Statistical Division (UNSD) organized an Expert Group Meeting (EGM) in 1997 to design a global time-use classification that would meet the needs of both developed and developing countries. It developed a trial classification called the International Classification of Activities for Time-Use Statistics (ICATUS), which had ten major groups and eighty subgroup activities. Countries were required to prepare their own list of activities at the three-digit level (Bediako and Vanek, 2000). This classification is based on the SNA framework, dividing time-use activities into SNA activities (one to three major groups), non-SNA activities (four to six major groups) and personal care and services (seven to ten major groups).[21] This classification, however, had some conceptual problems and was not universally accepted. UNSD made another attempt in 2000 to develop an elaborate classification. This revised classification was developed further during 2000–2003. It has 15 major categories[22] and 54 subgroups, followed by a large number of three- and four-digit activities (UNSD, 2005). However, while the 1997 classification is used by many countries, this new classification has not been used by any country so far.

This revised classification developed by UNSD can be made comparable with the classifications developed by Canada, Australia and Eurostat (UNSD, 2005), though this requires some adjustments. The United States has developed a new classification recently,[23] which differs in some ways from the classifications developed by Eurostat, Canada, Australia and so on. An expert committee in India has also developed a classification keeping in mind the needs of India and developing countries, particularly in the areas of informal employment, subsistence work and also other activities.

In short, the task of developing a global time-use activity classification is still unfinished.

On the empirical side our review of developing countries shows that there is a wide variety of classifications used in developing countries. In the case of small surveys, researchers have developed their own classification. Scholars and researchers who conducted small-scale TUS that covered a few villages or a small number of households developed their own listing of activities depending on the objective of TUS. These lists varied from 9 to 90 activities. For example, in Brazil, where a number of small-scale surveys have been done by sociologists and anthropologists, Aguiar-Cebotarev (1984) and Aguiar (1998 and 2001) have designed several short listings of activities (Aguiar, 2005). Cebotarev divided total activities into nine major groups as follows: (1) meal preparation; (2) house/kitchen cleaning; (3) clothes-cleaning, sewing and repairing; (4) childcare; (5) garden and animal care; (6) fetching wood and water; (7) household industry/commerce; (8) remunerative work; and (9) resting, visiting and so on. Scholars in India and Nepal have also developed their own classifications when they conducted small-scale surveys. These classifications primarily depend on the objectives of the survey, regions (rural or urban) and the socioeconomic groups covered under the surveys.

Most of the national surveys, which used stylized questions, developed their own list of activities, though a few of them did use the UN Classification 1997 (with or without modifications). In all, 15 countries that conducted large and national surveys have used the UN Classification 1997. In fact, this classification has emerged as a popular classification in the developing world. The rest of the large and national surveys developed their own classifications. Thailand used two classifications: the UN 1997 classification, as well as the classification used in Eurostat surveys. This is because Thailand wanted to produce internationally comparable time-use data.

A few large and national surveys have adapted from the available classifications in developed countries. This is particularly the case when the consultants are from the North.

A major limitation of the UN Classification 1997 is that it is not compatible with the established workforce classification. If a major objective of TUS in developing countries is to get improved estimates of the workforce and to understand the characteristics of the workforce, it is important that the TUS classification is compatible with the workforce classification, for example, the industry classification. The 1997 classification does not permit this. Some countries (like India) did not agree with the main framework of the classification and argued that the first three groups of the classification – which used 'establishments' to divide work in the formal and informal sectors – failed to accurately capture the information they were looking for, since 'establishments' did not determine the formality of work and the term 'establishment' was too vague to be used in classifying activities. India therefore changed the first three major groups to meet its requirements. It also made changes in the other major groups to suit its needs[24] and developed a detailed three-digit classification system to include all activities performed by Indians. It developed suitably detailed classification for: (a) collecting goods like water, fuel wood, fodder and raw material for manufacturing from common lands and forests; (b) child and other care; (c) agricultural operations; and (d) traveling for different purposes.

One major observation emerging from the review is that most developing countries have used noncomprehensive classification. This observation is in line with the observation made by Margaret Guerrero (2005, 2008). This implies that the time-use data do not provide comprehensive information on the time use of men and women in these countries. The other observation is that these surveys do not provide enough visibility to all forms of work, particularly unpaid work of men and women. The use of stylized questions, lite diaries and short activity lists (as well as small samples) seems to be responsible for this. And lastly, the use of multiple classifications has reduced the cross-country comparability of time-use data to an extent, though some common categories do help in meaningful comparability.

Context variables

Context variables are very important in TUS, as their proper use can enhance the value of time-use data considerably. They provide critical information across all categories of activities and thereby reduce the number of total activities to a manageable level. Major context variables are broadly related to: (1) *Location of activities*: for example, whether the activity is carried out within or outside home; (2) *For whom or for what purpose*: for whom the activity is carried out, or whether the activity – production – is for self-consumption or for sale, or whether the activity is for government, private corporation/company, public undertaking, partnership or for household sector, voluntary sector and so on; (3) *With whom*: for example, whether the activity is performed with children/ adults or with household member/nonhousehold member and so on; and (4) *Type of activities*: whether the activity is paid or unpaid or whether the activity is main or secondary for the performer and so on.

Context variables can help in determining whether production is: subsistence or not (for sale or for own consumption); whether the production is for the formal (for example, government, corporate sector/ private sector, corporation) or the informal sector (household units, nonprofit sector, tiny sector, and so on); or whether an activity is paid (for example, directly remunerated) or unpaid (for example, nonremunerated).

Our review of the TUS in developing countries shows that the potential of these variables is not really tapped in many countries: Most small surveys do not use any context variable. Also, most modular TUS have not used any context variable, as it is not manageable. The countries that have used context variables are among those that have an independent TUS using a 24-hour time dairy – either self-reported and recorded through a face-to-face interview. In all, therefore, only 12 countries (less than 40 per cent of countries) have used context variables. All of them have conducted large or national and independent TUS. The data are collected in time diaries with relevant context variables. The most common context variables are meant to identify, first, the location where the activity takes place; second, whether it is paid or unpaid; and, third, who the person is with while performing the activity. The context variables like 'for whom' are used by Morocco for SNA activities and 'for what purpose' have been used by South Africa.

Limited use of context variables is a serious drawback, as it is a missed opportunity to add rich information to the time-use data.

Response rate in TUS

The data on the response rates are available only for some countries (20 countries) partly because the response rates are not calculated (particularly in the case of small-scale surveys) and partly because these rates are not reported in the documents/papers/material that is available. Out of these 20 countries, the response rate in 15 countries is more than 90 per cent, reaching 99 per cent in India, 96 per cent in Palestine, 95 per cent in Oman and Morocco and 90 per cent in Nicaragua. The rate in the rest of the countries has been above 80 per cent, except in Chile where the rate was 78 per cent.

As against this, the rate of response has been low in most developed countries. The rate is 66 per cent in Australia and New Zealand and 77 per cent in Canada. One main reason for the high response in developing countries appears to be the use of face-to-face interviews in these countries. It is not easy to not respond when the interviewer is available to record information. In the case of self-reported time diaries, however, people tend to avoid recording their time use. And secondly, interviewers substitute the nonavailable person with the available person (in a systematic manner) in personal interview methods. In this regard, it seems that the interview method has a clear advantage over the self-reported diary method.

Trade-offs faced and quality of time-use statistics

Since it is not feasible to assess the quality of time-use data produced in different developing countries directly (as data is not widely accessible), this review has tried to assess the quality based on the soundness of the survey design and methods of data collection, classification of time-use data, and content and coverage of the data with reference to the objectives of conducting the TUS. That is, it has made this assessment based on the likely sources of poor quality.

In this context it is extremely important to study what are the trade-offs faced by developing countries with respect to choice of methodologies of TUS and how they have faced these trade-offs. A major challenge in front of developing countries is to face the trade-offs and manage the quality of time-use data. The main reasons why developing countries have 'to make adjustments in methodology,' 'to take pragmatic decisions about conducting TUS' or 'to choose second best methods' are the constraints and problems they face in different areas.

Facing low literacy and poor use of timepieces

Since the level of literacy is low in the country and the use of clock/ timepieces is not widespread, developing countries have to use: (1) face-to-face interview methods for data collection; (2) to use large time slots while recording time-use data; and (3) to devise ways to enable respondents to report the time they spent in different activities. In some cases pictures are used to help the self-reporting of time diaries. These adjustments are inevitable. However, they are likely to affect the quality of the data to an extent. One can therefore say that time-use statistics in developing countries are not 'point estimates' (accurate to the point) and are 'range (through narrow) estimates.' It will be relevant to quote the observation by Kitterod and Lyngstad (2005), made on the basis of a comparative study of self-reported diary and interview-based diary, that the self-reported diary gives more accurate results. This is because: (1) there is a problem of recall in the interview method (respondents are not able to give accurate data); (2) sometimes biases get into responses; and (3) frequently very short breaks are missed out. However, the paper observes that there are no major differences in the time-use patterns under the two approaches.

Lack of adequate funds

The lack of adequate funds to spend on this new, time-consuming and expensive survey is another major constraint. UN bodies and other international organizations have given funds to developing countries for this purpose. It is observed, however, that many developing countries have adopted cost-cutting strategies to reduce the cost of conducting a survey. These strategies include: (1) small sample size in terms of coverage of regions, households and number of persons per household; (2) small time sample, frequently providing an unstable and nonrepresentative time period; (3) use of modular TUS attached to an ongoing national survey (with a smaller sample); (4) use of stylized questions that cannot provide comprehensive data on time use and cannot provide data on simultaneous equations and context variables; (5) short activity classifications; and (6) frequently low investment in training and in preparing instruction manuals for conducting field surveys. All these choices are likely to affect the quality of time-use data adversely.

Limited capacity of national statistics offices (NSOs)

The limited capacity of NSOs to conduct such a survey and to analyze the data meaningfully is one more constraint of developing countries. International bodies have tried to help developing countries through consultants from the developed and developing world. This is not found to be very satisfactory in many cases. As a result, there is a problem of the quality of time-use data arising from the limited capacity of the NSOs.

Poor appreciation of the utility of time-use data

And lastly, the absence of proper appreciation of the utility of time-use data is also a constraint faced in many countries. Many NSOs are therefore not very enthusiastic about conducting national surveys (for example, the Philippines and Brazil) or about mainstreaming these surveys in the national systems (almost all developing countries).

In short, the constraints have encouraged most of the countries to compromise on the quality of time-use statistics. A particular development in Latin America and Africa is worth mentioning in this context: There is a new model emerging in some of these developing countries, which Neuma Aguar calls 'the Latin American Time-use Research Model.'[25] It is argued by the funders that the European model of conducting TUS is too expensive (and has a bad response rate). There is therefore a need to develop a less expensive model that consists of adding a module to ongoing surveys, using stylized questions and restricting sample size and reference period (time sample). Since research costs are a matter of deep concern to donors (and national governments), 'pragmatic compromises' are suggested. However, these are likely to affect the quality of the data and, therefore, the utility of the data adversely.

It can be argued that these compromises are made because full-fledged, sound surveys are not feasible in these countries given the constraints mentioned above. These 'pragmatic surveys' can pave a way for the future, as they may establish the utility of the data and may help in building expertise in this area. We believe that this could be a good short-term strategy if one is aware that: (1) the compromises do not allow the data to be used for meeting the main objectives of the survey; and (2) there is a need to move to improved methodologies in the long run. It is possible that this short-term strategy will help in policy advocacy to raise the demand for TUS in these countries. And this, in turn, may result in sound TUS in the medium and long run. One reason why countries like the Philippines, Nigeria or Brazil have not moved beyond the pilot stage is that there is not enough demand for these data from stakeholders (Collas-Monsod, 2008).

To sum up

Our assessment shows that there were quite a few achievements made by developing countries in the field of TUS during the past few decades, particularly from 1990 onwards. One finds rapidly growing awareness about the need to collect time-use data to estimate the paid and unpaid work of men and women in the economy and to measure and address gender inequalities prevailing in the society. TUS, which began as small-scale surveys in several developing countries in the 1970s and 1980s, are now increasingly graduating into large and national surveys. Though the specific objectives of conducting TUS differ to an extent, the broad objectives do not differ drastically. There is a rising awareness about the need to collect time-use data to estimate and understand paid and unpaid work ('all forms of work') of men and women.

Given the constraints arising from the specific problems faced by these countries while conducting TUS, each country has designed surveys in specific ways. They have made difficult choices, within the constraints and the trade-offs arising from the constraints, with respect to survey design, sampling, data collection and field operations, classification of time-use activities and analysis of time-use data. There is no one solution, but multiple solutions, emerging from different countries. These solutions are frequently emerging from 'learning by doing' in these countries (Esquivel *et al.*, 2008).

In spite of the limitations of the concepts, definitions, data collection, data analysis, classification and so on, concrete data have emerged in a large number of countries on unequal sharing of paid and unpaid work by men and women in the economy. A new understanding is emerging on the nature and extent of gender inequalities prevailing in these economies (Esquivel *et al.*, 2008). This dynamism indicates that these countries will be able to face the remaining challenges in the coming years.

In spite of these achievements, however, these countries have a long way to go to conduct systematic TUS to collect reliable data. Some of the major limitations of the TUS in developing countries can be listed as follows: To start with, a large number of developing countries have conducted only small-scale, isolated TUS, usually conducted by private researchers, scholars, and frequently conducted by official agencies. More than 50 per cent of countries have not yet conducted a national survey, either as an independent or a modular survey. Except for four countries, no country has conducted more than one survey so far. In short, these surveys are far from being a part of the national statistical systems in these countries.

There are serious methodological problems with respect to survey design, sampling, data collection methods and classification of activities and so on: the sample is usually small and not representative at the national level; the reference period and the time sample are frequently small and unstable to represent the time use of people; the methods of data collection selected are not always likely to give accurate estimates; there are serious limitations with respect to the treatment of simultaneous activities and use of context variables; and there are issues related to the classifications of time-use activities used by many countries. It appears that these countries have compromised on the quality of the survey in the process of addressing the difficult trade-offs.

Assessment and inferences for the future

Analysis and use of time-use statistics

Looking to the general objectives of TUS in developing countries, one would expect that time-use data would be analyzed to (a) reveal all forms of work performed by men and women and the time spent by them on this work, as well as to measure unequal sharing of paid and particularly unpaid work; (b) to compile valuation of unpaid non-SNA work in household satellite accounts; (c) to estimate national workforce and understand the characteristics of the workforce; (d) to analyze intra-household gender inequalities; and (e) to understand some important issues such as poverty, human development, child labor, well-being and so on. One would also expect that the time-use data are used in national human development reports, in assessments and analysis of poverty, in gender reports and studies on gender inequalities and in employment planning, particularly in policy formulation for informal workers and so on.

The empirical evidence shows, however, that there has been limited analysis of time-use statistics in developing countries and poor use (or almost non-use) of these data in official reports or in policy-making. It appears that many national statistical agencies (which are usually associated with conducting TUS), with a few exceptions, have compiled this report with some minimum tables drawn form the time-use statistics, and dumped it in a corner and is outside the purview of policy-making. An interesting use of time-use statistics has been made in Bhutan. This country has used time-use data to estimate national happiness. It is argued that the number of working hours and the degree of time stress it involves, the time spent on socialization and community participation, the time spent on leisure and sports, on religious activities, have a significant influence on the status of happiness of people; time-use data in this case have been used to compile Happiness Index for its population.

Corner (2003) and Charmes (2005) have carefully examined the issue of the low use of time-use data in policy-making in developing countries. Based on the evaluation of UNIFEM's work on gender statistics in South Asia, Southeast Asia and East Asia, Corner observes that there has been very little use of the data generated through national surveys/reports on gender in general and on TUS in particular. The major reasons for the underuse of time-use statistics in these countries are: (1) low capacity of national statistical offices to analyze and use these data; and (2) low level of interest of policy-makers in the issues of intrahousehold inequalities and household economies and their links with the macroeconomics. Corner also blames poor policy advocacy for the use of the data from other stakeholders, such as researchers and civil society organizations. Jacques Charmes (2005) also observes that the time-use data in the selected African countries are not used well in the national level reports like Human Development Reports, Poverty Reduction Strategy Papers and Gender Reports and so on. Though these data can be very useful in shaping these reports, as well as in policy-making in these areas, national governments do not seem to be interested in using them. According to Charmes, the major reasons for this are the lack of funds and inadequate capacity in the national governments to use these data as well as the fact that many of these surveys are undertaken due to the pressure (and the funds) from donor agencies. Our review, as well as personal experience with several developing countries also confirms the above observations. It seems that the main reason why developing countries have been able to make only a limited use of time-use data are: (1) the statistical offices and policy makers have not been able to appreciate the utility of time-use data; (2) the data are not recognized as usable data because there are serious problems with the quality of the data; and (3) the data are not backed by harmonized concepts and methods.

Several UN agencies, international organizations and private researchers/scholars at research institutions and universities, however, have used these data in some ways. INSTRAW made one of the first efforts to compile the value of unpaid work in six countries, namely, Canada, Hungary, Nepal, Dominican Republic, Tanzania and Venezuela. It brought out a publication entitled 'Measurement and Valuation of Unpaid Contribution: Accounting through Time and Output' in 1995. This volume showed that women contribute a significant portion of the national GDP through their unpaid work (INSTRAW, 1995). Researchers at the World Bank, for example, estimated time poverty of men and women in African countries, like Benin, Burkina Faso, Madagascar, Ghana, Guinea, Malawi, South Africa, Mauritius, Kenya and others (Blackden and Wodon, 2005). These scholars have developed a concept of time poverty and estimated it for men and particularly women in sub-Saharan Africa. UNDP also has used time-use data in their global HDR, particularly in HDR 1995 and HDR 2007–08. They have used these data to compile value of GDI and GEM in some countries. Researchers and scholars from universities and research institutions have also used these data – though in a very limited way. International organizations on time-use research such as IATUR, CTUR, ATUS, RNTU, TURP (which are largely involved with the issues and analysis of time-use data in developed countries) have encouraged a few scholars to analyze time-use statistics from developing countries. Private scholars have also used these data in some countries and produced research papers – though in a very small number.[26] The total number of scholars using time-use data from developing countries is not very large. Also, these papers have made a limited (if any) impact on policy-making at the national level.

Our review of the literature shows that there are two major problems with respect to the use of the data in policy-making. The first is about the 'poor respect' given to the data due to its less than satisfactory quality and/or due to the use of nonstandard (not harmonized at the global level) methods of data collection; the other problem is that the collected data are frequently not capable of giving sound estimates. That is, the data are not adequate to undertake these tasks.

Our experience shows that almost no national government has officially revised their workforce estimates based on the time-use statistics so far or officially estimated the size of the informal workforce, including subsistence workforce, using time-use statistics. Again, no developing country has so far compiled systematic household satellite accounts of unpaid work. Though simple estimates have been made of the value of the unpaid work (by multiplying the time spent on this work by relevant wage rates) in a few countries like the Philippines, South Africa, India, Nepal and so on, the estimates are not validated by the official agencies. For example, the NSO of the Philippines estimated women's contribution to GDP through their SNA and non-SNA work using the results of the pilot Philippino TUS 2000. The estimates indicated that women's contribution to GDP through paid work is between 39–47 per cent, while their contribution through unpaid work is about 60 per cent of the GDP. These estimates, however, are not officially recognized and accepted (Collas-Monsod, 2008). Similarly, the CSO in India calculated the workforce participation rates of men and women using time-use statistics and also compiled the value of the unpaid work of women. The analysis showed that the WPRs based on the TUS were much higher than the rates given by the conventional surveys (Saha, 2003) and the unpaid domestic work contributed 19 to 34 per cent of the state domestic product (SDP) (Nath, 2003). However these estimates have not been recognized in official statistics. In the case of Nepal, Meena Acharya compiled the value of GDP using informal and subsistence work of men and women in Nepal, but the estimates are not a part of the official data (Acharya, 2003). Debbie Budlender has also stated how the official agencies were upset when the TUS data showed a substantial rise in the national GDP (Esquivel *et al.*, 2008).

Similarly, there are some problems with the data that do not allow their sound use. For example, a major objective of many developing economies is to estimate the informal and subsistence workforce in the economy and to estimate the time spent by them on this work. The simple tables generated in several countries, such as India, Nepal, Laos PDR, Thailand, Benin, Madagascar, South Africa, Morocco, Mexico, Indonesia, Nicaragua and so on, do give larger estimates of the workforce, indicating that a large number of men and particularly women are engaged in informal work, as well as in collection of fuel wood and water, agriculture, animal husbandry and so on. That is, they provide enough evidence to show that conventional surveys underreport the workforce in an economy and that TUS are able to get improved estimates of the workforce, intermittent, scattered and short-term informal work. TUS can also capture voluntary work performed by men and women.

However, these conjectures are not adequate for estimating the exact size of the informal and subsistence workforce not for understanding their characteristics. In order to arrive at exact estimates of the workforce in the different sectors and activities, we need additional data as follows (Hirway, 2004; Hirway and Charmes, 2008):

- We need appropriate context variables to determine if the work performed is formal, informal or subsistence. These variables will be: (1) for whom the work is done (for example, for government/ public sector organization, private companies, cooperative unit, small-scale unit, household unit, voluntary service unit); (2) where the work is done (for example, inside/outside home, whether it is home-based); and (3) for what purpose (paid/unpaid or for sale or self-consumption);

- We need suitable classification of time-use activities to determine in which industry/sector the activity is performed. This list will have to be compatible with the standard industry classification;
- We will also need a representative sample in terms of its geographical and household coverage; and
- The time sample will have to be large enough to give stable and reliable information on employment. It should also provide data on seasonal variations.

In short, although TUS provide improved estimates of the workforce much more needs to be done to accurately determine the size and characteristics, as well as the value of the contribution by the informal and subsistence workforce. It is not surprising therefore that so far hardly any country has produced national-level estimates of informal employment and subsistence employment as per their activities and value of output (Hirway and Charmes, 2008).

Cross-country comparability of time-use statistics and need for harmonization at the global level

Like statistics on national income, human development and the labor force, time-use statistics also should be comparable across countries. Cross-country comparability of these data will help in comparing these data across countries and in explaining the variations across countries in order to design policies, particularly in the areas of gender inequality, well-being, poverty and so on. The comparability will particularly help in designing global-level policies in these areas.

Cross-country comparability of time-use data depends on several factors: (1) the comparability in the basic concepts and design of the surveys and in the methods of data collection across countries (lack of comparability here can produce totally different data sets, which cannot be compared across countries); (2) the differences in the quality of investigators/interviewers or in field operations (large differences here may reduce the comparability of the data across countries); and (3) the comparability in the manner in which the data are analyzed, tabulated and presented. The first set of factors is a serious obstacle in comparing time-use data because here the nature of the differences in the data could be fundamental. The second and third set of factors are important, but are not fundamental, because the second set of factors will always be there and though the differences can be reduced, they cannot perhaps be eliminated; the third set of factors can be addressed by reprocessing of the data.[27]

Our assessment of the TUS indicates that the comparability of the time-use data is adversely affected primarily by the basic differences in the survey design, sampling (including time sample) and data collection methods. To start with, there are basic differences among developing countries with respect to the survey design: some surveys are independent and national, while others are modular and small. Again, there are differences in data collection methods, with some using chronological recording and covering all 24 hours, while others are stylized questions on listed activities. The geographical and household samples also differ widely, with some surveys focusing on agriculture or rural areas, while others cover one or a few urban centers only. In addition, time samples also differ widely. Some surveys produce the time-use information of the population based on only one day in a year or one week in the year, which provide nonrepresentative time samples. Some countries, on the other hand, have included the entire year as a reference period. Some countries include simultaneous activities, while others do not bother about this. In short, the data are basically different and cannot be compared across countries.

Indira Hirway's (2004) study of three developing countries (India, Thailand and Mongolia) observes that in the absence of harmonized methods at the global level, each of these countries has developed their own survey – design, sampling data collection methods and classifications. These data are not comparable because of the basic differences in the survey design, sampling, reference period and so on, as well as the other differences in the details of the analysis of the data. She suggests that there is a need to harmonize at least the basic concepts and methods to ensure basic comparability of the data.

It is frequently argued that one should not worry about the comparability of time-use data at this initial stage of development of time-use studies in developing countries. What is important at this stage is to see that time-use data *are* generated and that more countries are entering into this field. One should not worry if different countries are coming out with different survey designs, sampling and classifications. This argument is acceptable only as long as the soundness of the survey methodology is not compromised. We believe that it is important that statistically sound methodologies are used in developing economies in spite of the trade-offs.

The noncomparability arising from different levels of efficiency and capacity of statistical staffs in different countries needs to be addressed mainly by capacity building. Considering the fact that most countries depend on face-to-face interviews for data collection in which the interviewer is a key figure, (1) intensive training of the staff; (2) compilation of detailed instruction manuals; and (3) strong supervision and follow-up have to be important components of TUS. As seen earlier, this is one of the weak points of developing countries and it needs to be addressed effectively. The noncomparability arising from the differences in analysis and presentation of time-use data is also not that serious. This can be managed easily if one intends to generate comparable data for different countries. Steps such as standardization of the age groups covered, standardization of classification of activities and so on will also help in enhancing the comparability.

Harmonization of concepts and methods

The above discussion finally brings us to the issue of harmonization of basic concepts, methods and classifications at the global level. This will not only enhance cross-country comparability of time-use data, but it will also improve the basic quality of time-use data in developing countries. Several efforts have been made in this area by UNSD and several regional offices of the UN, for example, ESCAP, ECA and ECLAC. These organizations have produced guidebooks for conducting TUS. In addition, efforts have been made by the ILO and other UN agencies, such as UNDP, UNIFEM, FAO and so on. For developed countries, Eurostat has taken a major step by formulating Harmonized Methodology for conducting TUS in European Countries.[28] Recently IATUR has taken a major step by organizing a special workshop on time-use studies in developing countries.[29] To borrow a quotation from Szalai, there is a need to resolve unresolved methodological issues in the collection and analysis of time-use data (Szalai, 1972).

There is an urgent need to coordinate these efforts and take the process of harmonization further. We believe that global agencies like UNSD and the ILO should take a lead in this process. This is an international responsibility and these organizations must take it up.

Mainstreaming TUS in national statistical system

Mainstreaming TUS means that: (1) a national TUS is conducted at a regular interval; (2) the results are analyzed keeping in mind the objectives of the survey and are published and accessible; and (3) there is a commitment to the data in the sense that the data are used in all major national documents, such as national human development reports, poverty assessment, reports on status of women and so on, as well as in policy-making and policy monitoring (Hirway, 2009). Mainstreaming of TUS provides ample opportunities to use time series data to analyze changes and monitor developments in gender inequalities, economic changes and social changes.

Our review of the time-use studies in 56 developing countries, however, has shown that, except for four countries, no country has conducted more than one national TUS. Even the four countries that have conducted more than one national survey, have not necessarily mainstreamed the survey in their respective national statistical system. Still mainstreaming of this survey is a goal (a distant goal in some cases) in all developing countries. It will be useful to discuss how it can be achieved. Though there are no clear-cut steps available, the successful and unsuccessful experiences in some countries do provide some points. It will be useful to refer to the long struggles in India and the Philippines in this context.

In the case of India, the pilot (large) TUS was conducted in six major states in 1998–99. The survey report was brought out in 2000. The results of the survey, as well as papers based on the analysis of the data and the methodological issues, were discussed in two international seminars.[30] Based on the experiences of the seminars and the lessons learned from the survey, a third international seminar, entitled 'Towards Mainstreaming TUS in the National Statistical System' was organized in 2001. After in-depth discussions on the uses and methodological issues, a paper consisting of the proposal for mainstreaming of the TUS in India was submitted in 2008, ten years after the pilot survey was conducted. The outcome of this proposal is awaited (Hirway, 2009).

The case of the Philippines is somewhat similar (Collas-Monsod, 2008). The Philippines have been one of the more gender-sensitive countries in the region, as their high GDI and GEM attest to. The country was the first in Asia to set up a National Commission on the Role of Filipino Women (NCRFW) in 1975. The country also was the first in Asia to design a gender-responsive development plan (1995–2025). The national statistical office conducted a pilot TUS in 2000 and used these data to compile the value of women's SNA contribution to national GDP (in SNA) and non-SNA contribution in national well-being. These estimates were of course not recognized, as these were based on a small pilot survey and many approximations. In spite of these developments, however, no national TUS have been conducted in the country. And the main reason for this, according to Solita Collas-Monsod and the head of the NSO, is 'the lack of demand' for time-use statistics. There is not enough evidence in the county to show how critical the data are for national policy-making. It is therefore argued that there is a need to undertake strong lobbying for the survey along with showing the utility of the data.

On the basis of these experiences, one can say that the first important step towards mainstreaming TUS is to establish the utility of time-use data in addressing major national concerns such as poverty and human development, informal sector and household workers, gender inequality, care and so on. No statistical agency will collect time-use data just to collect information on how men and women spend their time. The objective has to be linked with national concerns. An important strategy here will be to use the available data to show how they address these concerns. Establishing a dialogue between the data producers and data users could be a very useful second step. It will be important to ensure 'respectability' to the time-use data by giving an objective critique of the available data on the one hand and recommending clear measures to ensure a sound quality of data on the other.

It needs to be noted that 'funds' may not be a major constraint once the utility of the data is established and the sound quality of data is ensured.

Concluding observations

Developing countries in Asia, Africa and Latin America have made very good progress in the field of TUS in the past few decades, particularly in the past decade and a half. TUS, which began as small-scale surveys in 1970s and 1980s, are now increasingly graduating into large and national surveys. There is a growing awareness about the importance of unpaid (SNA and non-SNA) work in these countries and the urgent need to collect time-use data to address wide gender inequalities.

In spite of these achievements, however, there are serious problems with respect to the survey design, sampling and data collection, as well as classifications, of TUS. Several countries seem to have made compromises in the methodology to face the trade-offs that they have to confront in this area, frequently adversely affecting the quality of the data. It is not easy to decide whether these compromises should be allowed given the constraints of developing countries or if efforts should be made to look for sound methodologies right from the beginning. One can only say that the compromises are fine as long as there is full awareness about the limitations of the data and about the need to shift to sound survey methodologies in the future. Though there need not be a one-size-fit-all model for these countries, there is a need to focus on shifting to better and more reliable methods of data collection in the coming years.

What is needed urgently at present is to analyze the available time-use data, because more often than not, they are the only source of information in addressing some of the critical concerns on economies. Harmonization of concepts and methods are important in this context not only to enhance cross-country comparability of the data, but also to ensure the quality of the data.

Notes

1. SNA activities are those activities that fall within the Production Boundary of the UN-SNA. These activities constitute the activities which are included in national income accounts.
2. Non-SNA activities are not included in national accounts, but are covered under the General Production Boundary. They include all delegable production of services not covered under the national income accounts.
3. Personal services are nondelegable services, for example, the services that cannot be delegated to others, such as sleeping or watching TV.
4. The context variables in time-use statistics usually refer to the location where the activity took place (where), the presence of other people when the activity took place (with whom), the beneficiary, person or institution of the activity (for whom the activity was carried out), the motivation of the activity (for example, whether the activity was paid or unpaid) and so on.
5. This is not an exhaustive list, as there are a few countries, such as Panama and Vietnam, for which we do not have much information and are not covered in this chapter.
6. These guide books brought out by UN agencies include *Guide to Producing Statistics on Time Use* by UNSD, *Integrating Unpaid Work into National Policies* by UN-ESCAP and *Why Should we Count Unpaid Work* by UN-ECA.
7. Small TUS are also conducted in many other countries not listed in Appendix 1. For example, a stock-taking research paper by UNDP Pacifica Center has shown that several pacific islands have conducted (largely by research scholars/university department) small TUS. However, some such surveys are not included in our list in the appendixes. Refer to Suki Beavers and Ferdinal Strobel (2008) in E-discussion Gender Net, UNDP 2008–2009.
8. These countries include Argentina, Brazil, Mexico and Nicaragua from Latin America; Bangladesh, India and Korea from Asia; and Chad, Mali, Tanzania and South Africa in Africa.
9. The countries covered include Argentina, Mexico, Chile, Brazil and Nicaragua in Latin America; Benin, Guinea, Mali, Malawi, Madagascar, Mauritius, Morocco, South Africa, Kenya, Chad in Africa; and India, Nepal, Bangladesh, Thailand, Mongolia, Sri Lanka, Lao PDR and South Korea in Asia.

10. This author was a member of the expert committee to design time-use methodology and particularly a time-use activity classification that would meet the specific needs of the country. The committee has now designed a full-fledged time-use activity classification for India.
11. The author was involved in the drafting of this guidebook.
12. UNSD organized two EGMs for designing on time-use methodology and particularly a time-use activity classification in 1997 and 2000. The author was a member of both these EGMs.
13. The author was a member of two recent EGMs, namely EGM 'Equal sharing of responsibilities between men and women, including care-giving in the context of HIV/AIDS' set up by United Nations Division for the Advancement of Women, and Member Expert Group Meeting (EGM) on 'Unpaid Work, Economic Development and Human Well-being,' UNDP, 16–17 November 2008, New York.
14. These training programs have been organized at UNIFEM/UNESCAP Bangkok, IWG GEM at University of Utah and in India by CSO, Government of India. The author has also been involved with designing a virtual course on TUS–SAM–CGE at IWG-GEM.
15. The author has also been involved with designing a virtual course on TUS–SAM–CGE at IWG-GEM.
16. Please refer to the references at the end of this chapter.
17. This assumption is not fully acceptable, as the informal sector is emerging in these economies also. Again, the details of different work-time arrangements and what people do at the workplace is not revealed by the conventional surveys in these countries.
18. Indonesia, which has conducted a small TUS, also covered only women in the sample.
19. All country reports have not mentioned explicitly whether the data on simultaneous activities are collected in the survey.
20. In the 1978 Hoybraten Dagfinn developed a classification that was widely used by several countries from the 1970s to 1990s. According to this framework, time spent by human beings is basically of four types, namely, necessary time (time spent on necessary activities for survival), contracted time (time that human beings spend to fulfill the contracts that they have made), committed time (time committed to fulfill social responsibilities) and free time (the residual time left after performing contracted, committed and necessary time).
21. The major groups are: (1) employment for establishments (seven subgroups); (2) primary production activities not for establishments (eight subgroups); (3) services for income and other production of goods not for establishments (nine subgroups); (4) household maintenance and shopping for own households (nine subgroups); (5) care for children, the sick, elderly and disabled for own household (eight subgroups); (6) community services and help to other households (nine subgroups); (7) learning (six subgroups); (8) social, cultural and recreational activities (nine subgroups); (9) mass media use (seven subgroups); and (10) personal care and self-maintenance (eight subgroups).
22. ICATUS major divisions: SNA Work is divided into: (1) work for corporations, quasicorporations, government and NPIs; (2) primary production activities; (3) nonprimary production activities; (4) construction activities; (5) providing services for income and non-SNA work. Non-SNA work is

divided into: (6) providing unpaid domestic services for own final use within household; (7) providing unpaid caregiving services to household members; (8) providing community services and help to other households; (9) learning; (10) socializing and community participation; (11) attending/ visiting cultural, entertainment and sports events/venues; (12) engaging in hobbies, games and other pastime activities; (13) indoor and outdoor sports participation; (14) use of mass media and (15) personal care and maintenance.
23. This classification has 17 major groups: (1) personal care; (2) household activities; (3) caring for and helping household members; (4) caring for and helping non-HH members; (5) working and work-related activities; (6) education; (7) consumer purchases; (8) professional and personal care services; (9) HH services; (10) government services and civic obligations; (11) eating and drinking; (12) socializing, relaxation and leisure; (13) sports, exercise and recreation; (14) religion and spiritual activities; (15) voluntary activities; (16) telephone calls and (17) traveling.
24. The Indian time-use classification developed the following major groups: (1) primary production activities (six subgroups); (2) secondary activities (two subgroups); (3) trade, business and services (two subgroups); (4) household maintenance, management and shopping for own household; (5) care of children, sick, elderly and disabled for own household; (6) community services and help to other households; (7) learning; (8) social and cultural activities, mass media and so on; and (9) personal care and self-maintenance.
25. This term has been taken from the discussion on time-use studies in Latin America. Neuma Aguar has quoted this term in this discussion.
26. Scholars like Debbie Budlender, Valeria Equivel, Marcelo Medeiros, Neuma Aguar and others are worth naming. In the case of India, for example, research papers have been produced by scholars from research institutions using the time-use data (Yadav, 2007; Chakraborty, 2008; Hirway and Jose, 2008; Maitra and Rai, 2008; Rastogi, 2008; Hirway *et al.* and others).
27. This has been attempted at the Center for Time Use Research (CTUR) at Oxford University under the Multi Country Time Use Surveys (MTUS) program.
28. Eurostat formulated harmonized guidelines in 2000 to cover all the countries under the EU.
29. IATUR (2008) has examined time-use data of 24 countries here. Refer to references at the end of the chapter.
30. The first seminar was organized in December 1999 in Ahmedabad by the Ministry of Statistics Government of India in collaboration with UNDP and UNIFEM at Bangkok and CFDA, Ahmedabad. The report of the seminar was published by the Government of India. The second seminar was organized in 2003 on 'Application of Time Use Statistics' by the Government of India in collaboration with UNIFEM and UNDP Regional Office, New Delhi. The report of the seminar was also published by the Government of India. Please refer to references.

Bibliography

Acharya, M. (1997) 'Time Budget Studies for Measurement of Human Welfare,' submitted to UNDP for Presentation in the Workshop of Integrating Paid and Unpaid Work into National Policies, Seoul, 28–30 May.

Acharya, M. (2003) 'Time Budget Studies and Its Policy Relevance – The Case of Nepal,' in *Applications of Time Use Statistics* (New Delhi: Central Statistical Organization, Government of India).

Aguiar, N. (1998) *A Mulher na Forca Time Use Survey* (Brazil: Federal University of Minas Gerais) Available at www.undp.org

Aguiar, N. (1999) 'Time Use Analysis in Brazil: How Far Will Time Use Studies Have Advanced in Brazil by the Year 2000?,' paper presented at the Conference at the International Association for Time Use Research, Colchester, 6–8 October.

Aguiar, N. (2001) *Belo Horizonte Time Use Survey* (Brazil: Federal University of Minas Gerais) Available at www.undp.org

Aguiar, N. (2005) 'Time Use and Household Inequality: Behavioural and Perceptual Data,' paper presented at the Annual Meeting of the International Association for Time Use Research, Halifax, Canada, 2–4 November.

Ajayi, O.O. (2000) 'Conducting the TUS – Nigerian Experience,' paper prepared for Expert Group Meeting on Time Use Survey, New York, 23–27 October.

Akarro, R. (2002) 'Does Time Use Differentials Contribute to Differences in Poverty Levels in Tanzania? A Case Study of Regions in the Eastern and Northern Zones of Tanzania,' University of Dar es Salaam, Tanzania.

Asi, S. (2000) 'Report: Palestine Time Use Survey – A Palestinian Example,' paper presented at the United Nations Expert Group Meeting on Methods of Conducting Time Use Surveys, New York, 23–27 October.

Anxinli, An (2008) 'TUS in China,' IATUR 30th conference in Sydney, Australia, 4 December.

Apps, P. (2002) 'Gender, Time User and Models of the Household,' Policy Research Working Paper 3233 (Washington, DC: The World Bank).

Arboleda, H. (2001) 'Time Use Data and Valuation of Unpaid Work,' unpublished document, ESCAP, Bangkok.

Bardasi, E., and Q. Wodon (2000) 'Measuring Time Poverty and Analyzing Its Determinants: Concepts and Application to Guinea,' *World Bank Economics Bulletin*, 10(10), 1–7.

Bayudan, C.G. (2006) 'Wives time allocation and intra household power: evidence from the Philippines,' *Applied Economics* 38(7), 789–804.

Bediako, G., and J. Vanek (1998) 'Trial International Classification of Activities for Time-use Statistics,' paper presented at the International Conference on Time Use, University of Luneberg, 22–25 April.

Bediako, G., and J. Vanek (2000) 'Trial International Classification of Activities For Time Use Studies,' in *Proceedings of the International Seminar on Time Use Studies* (Delhi: Central Statistical Organizations, Government of India).

Bittman, M. (2008) 'Methodological Issues in Conducting Time Use Survey at the Global Level and Emerging Lessons,' in *Mainstreaming Time Use Surveys in National Statistical System in India* (New Delhi: Ministry of Women and Child Development, Government of India).

Blackden, C.M., and Q. Wodon (2005) 'Gender, Time Use, and Poverty in Sub-Saharan Africa,' World Bank Working Paper No. 73 (Washington, DC: World Bank).

Blanke, K.M. (1993) 'The With Whom Coding,' paper presented at the International Association for Time Use Research Conference, Amsterdam, Netherlands.

Bonke, J. (2002) 'Paid Work and Unpaid Work: Diary Information Versus Questionnaire Information,' paper presented at the Conference of the International Association for Time Use Research, Lisbon, 16–18 October.

Bonke, J., and J. Mcintosh (2005) 'Household Time Allocation – Theoretical and Empirical Results from Denmark,' *Electronic Journal of International Association of Time Use Research* (EIJTUR), No. 2 University of Oxford, UK.

Budlender, D. (2000a) 'Major Issues in Developing the South African Time Use Classification,' Expert Group Meeting on Methods for Conducting TUS, New York, 23–27 October.

Budlender, D. (2000b) 'The Policy Implications of the Time Use Survey in South Africa,' in *Proceedings of the International Seminar on Time Use Studies* (New Delhi: Central Statistical Organization, Government of India).

Budlender, D. (2007) 'A Critical Review of Selected Time Use Suvreys,' Gender and Development Paper No. 2 (Geneva: United Nations Research Institute for Social Devlopment, UNRISD).

Budlender, D., and D. Bosch (2002) 'South Africa Child Domestic Workers: A National Report' (Geneva: ILO and IPEC) May 2002.

Budlender, D., and A.L. Brathaug (2002) 'Calculating the Value of Unpaid Labour: A Discussion Document,' Working Paper 2002/1 (Pretoria: Statistics South Africa).

Bureau of Labour Statistics (2003) *American Time Use Survey Activity Lexicon* (Washington, DC: BLS). Available at: http://www.bls.gov/tus/lexiconnoex0307.pdf

Ceborarev, E. (1984) 'Timing of Organization of Domestic and Non-domestic Activities of Peasant Women in Latin America (Brazil, Venezuela and Mexico),' in N. Aguair (ed.), *Time Use Analysis in Brazil* (Brazil: Federal University of Minas Gerais).

Central Statistical Organization (2000) *Report of the Time Use Survey* (New Delhi: Ministry of Statistics and Programme Implementation, Government of India).

Central Statistical Organization (2002) *Proceedings of the National Seminar on Applications of Time Use Statistics* (New Delhi: Central Statistical Organization, Government of India).

Chakraborty, L. (2008) 'Statistical Invisibility of Care Economy in India: Evidence from Time Use Data,' in *Mainstreaming Time Use Surveys in National Statistical System in India* (New Delhi: Ministry of Women and Child Development, Government of India).

Charmes, J. (1999) 'Results and Lessons of a National Time Use Survey in Benin, and Consequences on Re-estimation of Women's Participation in the Labour Force and Contribution to GDP,' paper presented at the Conference of the International Association for Time Use Research, Colchester, 6–8 October.

Charmes, J. (2005) 'A Review of the Empirical Evidence on Time Use in Africa,' in 'Gender, Time Use and Poverty in Sub-Saharan Africa', Working Paper 73. (Washington, DC: The World Bank).

Charmes, J. and I. Hirway (2006) 'Estimating and Understanding the Informal Employment through Time Use Studies,' paper presented at Expert Group on Informal Sector Statistics (Delhi Group), 11–12 May.

Collas-Monsod, S. (2008) 'Integrating Unpaid Work into Macroeconomics Some Indian Experiences,' in *Mainstreaming Time Use Surveys in National Statistical*

System in India (New Delhi: Ministry of Women and Child Development, Government of India).

Corner, L. (2003) 'Use of Time Use Data for Policy Advocacy and Analysis,' in *Applications of Time Use Statistics* (New Delhi: Central Statistical Organization, Government of India).

Dedecca, C.S. (2005) 'On Times and Gender in Brazilian Society,' paper presented at the Conference of the International Association for Time Use Research, Tours, 18–23 July.

Delittman, M. (2000) 'Issues in the Design of TUS for Collecting Data on Paid and Unpaid Work,' paper presented at the United Nations, Expert Group Meeting on Methods for Conducting TUS, New York, 23–27 October.

Dhital, R. (2000) 'Time Use Survey in Nepal,' in *Proceedings of the International Seminar on Time Use Studies* (New Delhi: Central Statistical Organization, Government of India).

Economic Commission for Latin America and the Caribbean (2002–2003) *Poverty and Inequality from a Gender Perspective* (Santiago, Chile: Economic Commission for Latin America and the Caribbean–ECLAC).

Economic Commission for Latin America and the Caribbean (2004) *Family Structures, Household Work and Well-being in Latin America* (Santiago, Chile: Economic Commission for Latin America and the Caribbean–ECLAC).

Eivind, H. and A.M. Greenwood (2000) 'Statistics on Working Time Arrangements: Issues and the Role of Time Use Surveys,' paper presented at Expert Group Meeting on Methods for Conducting TUS, New York, October 23–27. www.ilo.org.

Elson, D. (2000) 'Progress of the World's Women, 2000,' in *Biennial Report* (New York: United Nations Development Fund for Women).

Esim, S. (2000) 'Impact of Government Budgets on Poverty and Gender Equality,' paper prepared for the Inter-Agency Workshop on Improving the Effectiveness of Integrating Gender in to Government Budgets Commonwealth Secretariat, Malborough House, (ICRW), London, 26–27 April.

Esquivel, V. (2006) 'What Else Do We Have To Cope With? Gender, Paid and Unpaid Work During Argentina's Last Crisis,' Working Paper 06-6 (July) (Salt Lake City, UT: International Working Group on Gender Macroeconomics, and International Economics).

Esquivel, V., D. Budlender, N. Folbre and I. Hirway (2008) 'Explorations: Time Use Surveys in the South,' *Feminist Economics*, July, 107–52.

EUROSTAT (1999) *Proposal for a Satellite Account for Household Production* (Luxembourg: Office for Official Publications of the European Communities).

EUROSTAT (2000a) *Guidelines on Harmonized European Time Use Surveys* (Luxembourg: Office for Official Publications of the European Communities).

EUROSTAT (2000b) 'Methodological Guidelines on Harmonized European Time Use Surveys: With Reference to Experiences of the European Time Use Pilot Surveys,' paper presented at the Expert Group Meeting on Methods for Conducting Time Use-Surveys, New York, 23–27 October, New York.

EUROSTAT (2003a) 'Household Production and Consumption Proposal for a Methodology of Household Satellite Accounts,' Task force report for Eurostat, Unit E1, Working Paper (Luxembourg: Office for Official Publications of the European Communities).

EUROSTAT (2003b) 'Proposal for a Satellite Account of Household Production,' Working Paper 9/1999/A4/11 (Luxembourg: Office for Official Publications of the European Communities).

Fisher, K., J. Gershunu, A. Gauthier and C. Victorino (2000) 'Exploring New Ground for Using the Multinational Time Use Study,' paper presented at the International Sociological Association RC33 Conference on Social Science Methodology, Universitat zu Koln, 3–6 October.

Floro, M. (1995) 'Economic restructuring, gender and the allocation of time,' *World Development*, 23, 1913–29.

Galay, K. (2007) 'Patterns of Time Use and Happiness in Bhutan: Is There a Relationship Between the Two?,' Working Paper, No. 432. (Chiba, Japan: Institute of Developing Economies, Japan External Trade Organization).

Gershuny, J. (2000) *Changing Times: Work and Leisure in Postindustrial Society* (Oxford: Oxford University Press).

Government of India (1999) *Proceedings of the International Seminar on Time Use Studies* (New Delhi: Central Statistical Organization, Ministry of Statistics and Programme Implementation, Government of India).

Government of India (2000) 'Report of the Time Use Survey' (New Delhi: Central Statistical Organization, Ministry of Statistics and Programme Implementation, Government of India).

Government of India (2008) *Report of the International Seminar 'Towards Mainstreaming Time Use Surveys in National Statistical System in India'* (New Delhi: Ministry of Women and Child Development, Government of India and UNDP)

Government of Morocco (1999) *Women's Time-use in Morocco, in 1997/98 National Survey on Women's Time Budge, Volume 2*, Directorate of Statistics, Government of Morocco, Kabat, Morocco.

Government of Thailand (2008) Gender-Disaggregated Statistics, Office of Women's Affairs and Family Development, Ministry of Social Development and Human Security, Bangkok.

Grosh, M. and P. Glewwe (eds) (2000) *Designing Household Survey Questionnaires for Developing Countries: Lessons from Fifteen Years of LSMS Experience* (Washington, DC: World Bank).

Guerreo, M. (2005) 'Module One: Collecting Time Use Data,' in *Integrating Unpaid Work into National Policies* (New York: United Nations/UN-ESCAP).

Guerreo, M. (2008) 'Presentation on Activity Classification under Time Use Surveys,' in *Report of the International Seminar 'Towards Mainstreaming Time Use Surveys in the National Statistical System in India* (New Delhi: Ministry of Women and Child Development, Government of India).

Harvey, A.S. (1999) 'Time Use Research: The Roots to the Future,' in J. Merz and M. Ehling (eds), *Time Use: Research, Data and Policy: Contributions from the International Conference on Time Use* (Baden-Baden, Germany: FFB-Schriftenreihe Band).

Harvey, A.S. (2000) 'Time Use,' in M. Grosh and P. Glewwe (eds), *Designing Household Survey Questionnaires for Developing Countries; Lessons from Fifteen Years of LSMS Experience* (Washington, DC: World Bank).

Harvey, A.S. (2003) 'Time Use Research: Past, Present and Future,' in *Applications of Time Use Statistics* (New Delhi: Central Statistical Organization, Government of India).

Harvey, A.S. and M.E. Taylor (1999) 'Activity Settings and Travel Behaviour: A Social Contract Perspective,' *Transportation* 27, 53–73.

Hirway, I. (2000a) 'Conceptual and Methodological Issues of Time Use Studies in India,' in *Proceedings of the International Seminar on Time Use Studies* (New Delhi: Central Statistical Organization, Government of India).

Hirway, I. (2000b) 'Estimating Workforce Using Time Use Results and Its Implications for Employment Policy in India,' in *Proceedings of the International Seminar on Time Use Studies* (New Delhi: Central Statistical Organization, Government of India).

Hirway, I. (2000c) 'Tabulation and Analysis of the Indian Time Use Survey Data for Improving Measurement of Paid and Unpaid Work,' paper presented at Expert Group Meeting on Methods for Conducting TUS, New York, 23–27 October.

Hirway, I. (2002) 'Gender Approach to the Collection and Use of Data: The Time Allocation Component,' UNIFEM, Bangkok.

Hirway, I. (2003) 'Indian Experience in Time Use Survey,' in *Proceedings of the International Seminar on Application of Time Use Statistics* (New Delhi: Central Statistical Organization, Government of India).

Hirway, I. (2004) 'Issues in Collection and Analysis of Cross National Time Use data: With Reference to Developing Countries,' paper presented for Sixth International Conference on Social Science Methodology: Recent Developments and Application in Social Science Methodology, Amsterdam, 16–20 August.

Hirway, I. (2007) 'Implications of Time Use Patterns for Public Employment Guarantee Programmes in Global South,' Stock Taking Paper March–April. Prepared for The Levy Economics Institute of Bard College.

Hirway, I. (2008a) 'Conceptual and Methodological Issues in Conducting Time Use Surveys in Developing Countries,' in *Mainstreaming Time Use Surveys in National Statistical System in India* (New Delhi: Ministry of Women and Child Development, Government of India).

Hirway, I. (2008b) 'Multiple Uses of Time Use Statistics in Developing Countries,' in *Mainstreaming Time Use Surveys in National Statistical System in India* (New Delhi: Ministry of Women and Child Development, Government of India).

Hirway, I. (2009) ' Mainstreaming Time Use Surveys in the National Statistical System in India,' *Economic and Political Weekly* XLIV(12).

Hirway, I. and J. Charmes (2008) 'Estimating and Understanding Informal Employment, Through Time Use Studies,' in *Mainstreaming Time Use Surveys in National Statistical System in India* (New Delhi: Ministry of Women and Child Development, Government of India).

Hirway, I. and Sunny Jose (2010) 'Understanding Women's SNA Work Using Time-Use Statistics: The Case of India,' *Feminist Economics*, Forthcoming.

Hirway, I., and R.N. Pandey (2000) 'Gender Issues in the Measurement of Paid and Unpaid Work,' paper for the Expert Group Meeting on Time Use Survey, New York, 23–27 October.

Hirway, I., M.R. Saluja and Bhupesh Yadav (2009) 'Assessing Impact of NREGA Works in a Village Based on SAM,' in *The National Rural employment Guarantee Act: Design, Process and Impact* (New Delhi: Ministry of Rural Development, Government of India).

Hook, J. (2005) 'The Difference a State Makes: Women's Allocation of Unpaid Work in the 50 States,' Poster Session at the American Time Use Survey Early Results Conference, Washington, DC.

Hunter, D. (2008) 'International Labour Statistics and Their Place in Defining the Scope, Content and Overall Framework for Social Statistics,' Department of Economic and Social Affairs, United Nations Expert Group Meeting on The Scope and Content of Social Statistics, 9–12 September.

ICATUS (2003) 'Background Paper on the Trial International Classification of Activities for Time-Use Statistics,' paper prepared for the Expert Group Meeting on International Economic and Social Classifications, New York, NY, 8–10 December.

Ilahi, N. (2000) 'The Intra-household allocation of time and tasks: what have we learned from the empirical literature?,' Policy Research Report on Gender and Development, WP Series, No. 13 (Washington, DC: World Bank).

INSTRAW (1995) *Time Use Pilot Survey for the Measurement and Evaluation of Work: Paid and Unpaid: Guidelines for Interviewers*, Advancement of Women, International Research and Training Institute for the Advancement of Women, Sante Domingo. Dominican Republic, DominicanRep/sourcedom95d.pdf. http://unstats.un.org/unsd/demographic/sconcerns/tuse/

INSTRAW (1997) 'Measurement of Women and Men's Contribution To Development Through Time-Use: The Case Of Dominican Republic.'

Ironmonger, D. (2008) 'Multiple Uses of Time Use Statistics in Developed Countries,' in *Mainstreaming Time Use Surveys in National Statistical System in India* (New Delhi: Ministry of Women and Child Development, Government of India).

Judd, K., M. Durano, and H. Cueva-Beteta (2006) 'UNIFEM's Role As a User of Statistics,' Inter-Agency and Expert Group Meeting on the Development of Gender Statistics, United Nations, New York, 12–14 December.

Juster, F.T. (1985) 'The Validity and Quality of Time Use Estimates Obtained from Recall Diaries,' in F.T. Juster and F.P. Stafford (eds), *Time Goods and Well Being* (Ann Arbor, MI: Institute for Social Research, Survey Research Center, University of Michigan).

Kalton, G. (1985) 'Sample Design Issues in Time Diary Studies,' in F.T. Juster and F.P. Stafford (eds), *Time, Goods and Well-Being* (Ann Arbor, MI: Institute for Social Research, University of Michigan).

Kan, M.Y. (2006) 'Measuring Housework Participation: The Gap between '"Stylized" Questionnaire Estimates and Diary-based Estimates,' Working Paper 2006–11 (Essex, UK: Institute for Social and Economic Research, University of Essex).

Kes, A. and H. Swaminathan (2005) 'Gender, Time Use, and Poverty in Sub-Saharan Africa,' in *Gender, Time Use and Poverty is Sub-Saharan* (Washington, DC: IBRD).

Kitterod, R.H. and T.H. Lyngstad (2005) 'Diary vs. Questionnaire Information on Time Spent on Housework: The Case of Norway,' *Electronic International Journal of Time Use Research* 2. Available at: www. eijtur.org

Latigo, A. (2003) 'Pro-Poor Growth Strategies in Africa: A Proposed Easy Reference Guide (ERG) to Engender National Accounts and National Budget,' paper presented at Expert Group Meeting, Kampala, Uganda, 23–24 June.

Lloyd, C.B., M. Grant and A. Ritchie (2008) 'Gender Differences in Time Use Among Adolescents in Developing Countries: Implications of Rising School Enrollment Rates,' *Journal of Research on Adolescence* 18(1), 99–120.

Lopreite, C.D. (2005) 'Gender and path-shifting changes in "hybrid" welfare regime: Argentina in comparative perspective,' paper submitted to RC-19 Annual Meeting, Chicago, 8–10 September.

Maitra, Pushkar and Ranjan Ray (2006) 'Is There a Gender Bias in the Household's Time Allocation In a Developing Country? The Indian Experience,' Department of Economics, Monash University, Australia.

Meinzen-Dick, R., L. Pandolfelli, S. Dohrn, and J. Athens (2005) 'Gender and Collective Action: A Conceptual Framework for Analysis,' International Research Workshop on Gender and Collective Action, Chiang Mai, Thailand, 17–21 October.

Motiram, S. and L. Osberg (2008) 'Demand or Supply for Schooling in Rural India?,' in *Mainstreaming Time Use Surveys in National Statistical System in India* (New Delhi: Ministry of Women and Child Development, Government of India).

Mpetsheni, Y. and D. Budlender (2000) 'Country Report: South Africa Time Use Survey 2000,' paper prepared for Expert Group Meeting on Time Use Survey, New York, 23–27 October.

Mrkic, S. (2006) *Report on Time-Use Statistics in the Context of Social Statistics, Time Use Paper* (New York: UNSD).

Mussa, A.S. (2003) 'Probing Time Use by Gender on Socio-Economic Activities,' mimeo. University of Dar Es Salaam, Tanzania.

Nath, S.K. (2003) 'Valuation of Unpaid Household Work and Community Services Using Time Use Statistics,' in *Applications of Time Use Statistics* (New Delhi: Central Statistical Organization, Government of India).

Noov, Y. (2000) 'Country Report: Mongolia: Time Use Survey 2000,' paper prepared for the Expert Group Meeting On Time Use Survey, New York, 23–27 October.

Ongley, P. (2001) 'Gender and Unpaid Work: Findings from the Time Use Survey,' available at www.stats.govt.nz.

Pandey, R.N. (2000a) 'Operational Issues in Conducting the Pilot Time Use Survey in India,' in *Proceedings of the International Seminar on Time Use Studies* (New Delhi: Central Statistical Organization, Government of India).

Pandey, R.N. (2000b) 'Sampling Issues in Time Use Survey-Indian Experience,' paper prepared for Expert Group Meeting on Time Use Survey, New York, 23–27 October.

Pandey, R.N. (2008) 'Lessons from the Pilot Mainstreaming Time Use Survey: Surveys in India,' in *Mainstreaming Time Use Surveys in National Statistical System in India* (New Delhi: Ministry of Women and Child Development, Government of India).

Pandey, R.N. and I. Hirway (2000) 'Conducting the Time Use Surveys – Indian Experience,' paper prepared by for the Expert Group Meeting on Conducting TUS, New York, 23–27 October.

Paton, D. (2000) 'Collecting Time-Use Data, Including Context Variables and Simultaneous Activities, at Statistics Canada,' paper prepared for Expert Group Meeting on Time Use Survey, New York, 23–27 October.

Patricia, M.C. (2000) 'Country Report: Mexico,' paper prepared for Expert Group Meeting on Time Use Survey, New York, 23–27 October.

Rastogi, P. (2008) 'Rural Child Work, Labour and Daily Practices: Time Use Survey Based Analysis,' in *Mainstreaming Time Use Surveys in National Statistical System in India* (New Delhi: Ministry of Women and Child Development, Government of India).

Rego, C. and M. Sicat (2005) 'Asia-Pacific Millennium Development Goals AP-MDG-Social Community of Practice: Understanding the Female Face of Poverty,' UNESCAP.

Report of the Secretary General (2001) 'Progress of a project on gender issues in the measurement of paid and unpaid work,' Statistical Commission, Thirty-second Session, 6–9, March.

Robinson, J. (1985) 'The validity and reliability of diaries versus alternative time use measures,' in F.T. Juster and F.P. Stafford (eds), *Time, Goods and Well-Being* (Ann Arbor, MI: Institute for Social Research, Survey Research Center, University of Michigan).

Ruger, Y. and J. Varjonen (2008) 'Value of Household Production in Finland and Germany: Analysis and Recalculation of the Household Satellite Account System in Both Countries,' Working Paper 112 (Helsinki: National Consumer Research Center).

Saha, V. (2003) 'Estimation of Workforce Using Time Use Statistics,' in *Applications of Time Use Statistics* (New Delhi: Central Statistical Organization, Government of India).

Szalai, A. (1972) 'The Use of Time: Daily Activities of Urban and Suburban Populations in Twelve Countries' as referenced in *Guide to Producing Statistics on Time Use: Measuring Paid and Unpaid Work* (New York: The United Nations/UNSD).

Srdjan, M. (2000) 'Time Use Statistics in the Context of Social Statistics,' Website of UN Statistical Division, UN, New York.

Strobel, F. and S. Beavers (2008) 'E-Discussion on Unpaid Work, Gender and the Care Economy – Phase 2: Data, Analysis, and Methodology,' ILO Regional Office, Arab States, as presented on UNDP Website, UN, New York.

Su-hao, T. (2000) 'Measuring Farm Women's Time Spent on Unpaid Work: Diary versus Stylized Estimates' EJTUR, IATUR Website.

TUIDC (2008) 'Time Use in Developing Countries (TUIDC) Workshop,' International Association for Time Use Research Australian Time Use Research Group, 4 December.

United Nations (2003) *Integrating Unpaid Work into National Policies, Economic and Social Commission for Asia and Pacific (UN-ESCAP)* (New York: United Nations Publications).

United Nations (2005) *Guide to Producing Statistics on Time Use: Measuring Paid and Unpaid Work* (New York: United Nations Publications).

United Nations Development Programme (UNDP) (1999) *Project Document on Gender Equality in the Asia-Pacific Region*, UN-ESCAP, Bangkok.

United Nations Research Institute for Social Development (UNRISD) (2007) *The Political and Social Economy of Care in a Development Context: Conceptual Issues, Research Questions and Policy Options* (Geneva: UNRISD)

United Nations Statistics Division (UNSD) (1999) 'Towards International Guidelines in Time Use Surveys: Objectives and Methods of National Time Use Surveys in Developing Countries,' paper presented at the International Seminar on Time Use Studies, United Nations Economic and Social Commission for Asia and the Pacific, Ahmedabad, 7–10 December.

——(2000) 'International Classification of Activities for Time Use Statistics,' paper prepared for Expert Group Meeting on Methods for Conducting TUS, New York, 23–27 October.

Väisänen, P. (2004) 'Guidelines on Harmonized European Time Use Surveys, Annex I Directions for the Survey Forms,' EUROSTAT Working Paper, Luxembourg.

Varojen, J. and K. Aalto (2006) *Household Production and Consumption in Finland, 2001* (Helsinki: National Consumer Research Center).

Varojen, J. and K. Aalto (2007) 'Combining time and money for family well-being – life cycle perspective,' Proceedings of the Nordic Consumer Policy Research Conference 2007, Helsinki, Finland.

World Bank (1996) 'A Manual for Planning and Implementing the Living Standards Measurement Study Survey,' Working Paper No. 126, The World Bank, Washington, DC.

Yung, K.C. (1995) 'The World's Women, 1995: Trends and Statistics, Social Statistics and Indicators,' No. 12, UNIFEM, New York.

Yung, K.C. (1996) *Report of the Fourth World Conference on Women* (New York: World Bank).

Yung, K.C. (1997) 'Concept Paper', presented at the Expert Group Meeting on the Trial International Classification of Activities for Time Use Statistics, 11 November.

Yung, K.C. (2000) 'Report of the Expert Group Meeting on Methods for Conducting Time Use Surveys,' paper prepared for Expert Group Meeting on Time Use Survey, New York, 23–27 October.

Yung, K.C. (2001) 'Changes in Korean People's Use of Time during 1981–2000', paper presented at International Association of Time Use Research (IATUR) 2001 Conference, Oslo, Norway, 3–5 October.

Appendix

Table 11A.1 Preliminary information on TUS in developing countries

No.	Continent/ country	Year	Name and type of survey	Size (pilot/small/ large/ national)	Organization conducting TUS
	Asia				
1	Bangladesh	1984–85	Labor Force Survey	Small	National Statistical Agency
		1990–91	Labor Force Survey	Small	National Statistical Agency
		2005	TUS (I)	Small	Dhaka University
2	Bhutan	2006–2007	National Happiness Survey	Pilot (small)	Center for Bhutan Studies
		2007–2008	National Happiness Survey	National	Center for Bhutan Studies
3	China	2005	Pilot TUS	Small pilot	National Bureau of Statistics
		2008	National	National	National Bureau of Statistics
4	India	1976–77	TUS (Pilot)	Small	ISST (Research Institute)
		1980s	Small surveys	Small	Private Researchers
		1998–99	Indian TUS	Large/national	Central Statistical Organization (CSO)
5	Indonesia	1998–99 (2 times)	Pilot Study on TUS (Small)	Pilot (100 villages)	B.P.S. – Statistics, Indonesia
6	Israel	1970	Time Use in Israel	Small	Private researchers
		1990	Time Use in Israel	Large	The Guttmann Center
		1991–92	Time Use in Israel Time Budget Survey	National	Ministry of Labour and Social Welfare, Ministry of Tourism, the National Insurance Institute
7	Lao PDR	1997–98	Expenditure and Consumption Survey 1997–98	National	National Statistical Office

(Continued)

Table 11A.1 Continued

No.	Continent/country	Year	Name and type of survey	Size (pilot/small/ large/ national)	Organization conducting TUS
8	Malaysia	1990–91	Use of Time by Women and Men	Small survey	FAO/UN Malaysia's Ministry of Women, Family & Community Development (MWFCD), in collaboration with the Department of Statistics
9	Mongolia	2000	Pilot TUS	Pilot	National Statistical Office
		2007	TUS	National	National Statistical Office
10	Nepal	1976–77 1992 1993–94	Small TUS	Small	Women's Department and other government departments and scholars
		1998–99	National Labor Force Surveys	National	National Statistical Office
11	Oman	1999	Household Expenditure and Income Survey	National	Ministry of National Economics
12	Pakistan	1990–91	Use of Time by Women and Men	Small survey	FAO/ UN
13	Palestine	1990–2000	TUS 1999–2000	National	Central Bureau of Statistics
14	Palestine (Occupied Territory)	1999–2000	TUS 1999–2000	National	National Statistical Office
15	Philippines	2000	Pilot TUS (one rural and one urban area)	Pilot	National Statistical Office
16	Saudi Arabia	1980s	Small survey	Small	Private researchers
17	Thailand	2000–2001	TUS	National	National Statistical Office
18	Turkey	1996	EU Harmonized Pilot	Pilot – Small	EU
		2003	TUS in Rural Areas : A Case-Study in Turkey	Small survey	Economic Research Center, MET University
		2006	TUS	National	Turkish Statistical Institute

Africa

19	Benin	1998	1. Annual Household Survey (Urban) 2. Living Conditions of Household Survey (Rural)	Large	National Institute of Statistics and Economic Analysis
20	Botswana	2005	Small surveys	Small	Scholars/government department (by UNIFEM)
21	Burkina Faso	1967	Small survey	Small	Private Researchers
22	Cameroon	1976, 1993 1996	Small surveys	Small	Private Researchers
23	Chad	1995	Time Use Study (a part of nine-country time-use study)	Small	National Institute of Statistics and Economic Development Studies
24	Gambia	1952	Small	Small	Private Researchers
25	Ghana	1991–92 1998–99 2003–2005	Ghana Living Standards Survey	National	Ghana Statistical Agency
26	Guinea	2002–2003	Living Standards Measurement Survey	National	Ministry of Planning
27	Kenya	1970s 1988		Small	Private Researchers
28	Madagascar	2001	Parallel Sample of Continuous Living Standards Measurement Survey	National	National Statistical Agency
29	Malawi	2003–2004	Living Standards Measurement Survey	National	Tango International
		2004	National Household Survey	National	National Statistical Agency

(Continued)

304

Table 11A.1 Continued

No.	Continent/country	Year	Name and type of survey	Size (pilot/small/ large/national)	Organization conducting TUS
30	Mali	1994	Small survey (A part of a country TUS)	Small	National Statistical Agency
31	Mauritius	2003	Multi Purpose Household Survey	National	National Statistical Agency
32	Morocco	1997–98	National Survey on Women's Time Budget	National	National Statistical Agency
		2003–2004	National Survey on Women's Time Budget	National	National Statistical Office
33	Mozambique	2005	Small surveys	Small	Scholars / Government department (by UNIFEM).
34	Nigeria	1992	TUS (small)	Small	National Statistical Agency
		1998	TUS (pilot)	Small pilot	National Statistical Agency
35	Papua New Guinea	1962		Small	Private Researchers
36	Rwanda	1976	TUS (small)	Small	Private Researchers
37	Sierra Leone	2003	Living Standards Measurement Survey	National	National Statistical Agency
38	South Africa	2000	TUS	National	Statistics South Africa
39	Tanzania	2004	TUS	National	Department of Statistics
		2006	Integrated Labour Force Survey	National	National Bureau of Statistics
40	Tunisia	2005	Budget Consumption Household Survey	National	National statistical agency
41	Uganda	1976	Small TUS	Small	Private Researchers
42	Zimbabwe	1933–34	Small	Small	Private Researchers

	Latin America				
43	Argentina	2001	Nacional Living Conditions Survey	Large	National Statistical Agency
44	Bolivia	2005	Buenos Aires TUS	Large	National Statistical Agency
		2001	Continous Household Survey 2001 (Labour Force Survey)	Large	National Statistical Office
45	Brazil	1990–2001	TUS (Small)	Small	Private Researchers
		1998	TUS (Small)	Small	Neuma Aguair (Federal University of Minas Gerais)
		2001	TUS	Small	Neuma Aguair (Federal University of Minas Gerais)
46	Chile	1999	TUS (small)	Small (Santiago)	Department of Sociology, University of Chile
47	Costa Rica	2004	Continuous Household Survey 2001 (Labour Force Survey)	Small	National Government Agency
48	Cuba	2001	Cubans TUS 2001	Santiago	National Statistical Agency
49	Dominican Republic	1995	National TUS 1995	National	National Statistical Agency
50	Ecuador	2003–2004	Labor Force Survey Since 2003–04 (Permanent)	National	National Statistical Agency
		2005	Labour Force Survey 2005	National	National Statistical Agency
51	El Salvador	2004	National Environment and TUS	National	National Statistical Agency
52	Guatemala	2000	Living Standards Measurement Survey 2000	National	National Statistical Office – supported by the World Bank

(Continued)

306

Table 11A.1 Continued

No.	Continent/country	Year	Name and type of survey	Size (pilot/small/ large/ national)	Organization conducting TUS
53	Mexico	1996	Income and Expenditure Survey	National	National Statistical Office
		1998	Income and Expenditure Survey	National	National Statistical Office
		2002–2006	Income and Expenditure Survey	Large/national	National Statistical Office
54	Nicaragua	1995–96	National TUS	National	FIDEG (Independent Research Center)
		1998	Living Standards Measurement Survey	National	INEC (National Statistical Agency)
55	Peru	1974		Small	Private Researchers
		1966		Small	Private Researchers
56	Uruguay	2003	Montevideo TUS	Urban/suburban	National Statistical Agency

Table 11A.2 Objectives of TUS in developing countries

No.	Continent/ country	Objectives
	Asia	
1	Bangladesh	*For 1984–85 and 1990–91 surveys* • To estimate informal and subsistence work of men and women. • To understand gender inequalities in the time spent on paid and unpaid work. *For 2005 survey* • To understand and estimate all forms of work done by men and women. • To understand gender inequalities in sharing of different categories of work.
2	Bhutan	*For both surveys* • To use time-use studies to measure Gross National Happiness Index. • To understand how people spend their time on different activities to determine their happiness. • To study time spent on unpaid work (household work, care and so on) and linked with socioeconomic characteristics of respondents.
3	China	• To measure quality of life in time-use aspects. • To improve methodology on women's contribution to national income and social development. • To develop new measurement on women's unremunerated work. • To enlarge social statistics to meet increasing demand from governments, NGOs and other civil society.
4	India	• To collect and analyze time-use patterns of men and women to understand the time spent on marketed and nonmarketed economic activities. • To generate a more reliable estimate of workforce. • To estimate and value unpaid work. • To develop a conceptual framework and a suitable methodology for designing and conducting time-use studies in India.
5	Indonesia	• To estimate contribution of parents (fathers and mothers) and youth to domestic work, particularly in caring of children. • To record total time in reported economic activities and domestic work.
6	Israel	*All TUS* • To collect comprehensive information on different socioeconomic groups located in different regions (non-residents, immigrants, locals, etc.) in the country.

(Continued)

Table 11A.2 Continued

No.	Continent/ country	Objectives
		• To collect detailed information on personal activities, such as religious activities and other activities.
7	Lao PDR	• To measure productivity in farming, mainly rice cultivation. • To measure labor input work in small-scale business and informal sector.
8	Malaysia	• To determine what unpaid work men and women do and how much they do (share). • To test eight methods of time-use data collection to assess which method yields the most accurate data on women's agrarian labor. • To understand work performed by men and women in agricultural and related activities.
9	Mongolia	*For both surveys* • To collect data on employment and informal sector to come up with realistic assessment of employment. • To collect data on gender inequality and women's paid and unpaid work. • To determine what unpaid work men and women do and how much they do (share).
10	Nepal	*Small surveys* • To improve GDP estimates by incorporating subsistence and informal work. • To measure all forms of work of women. • To measure children's work as well as voluntary work. • To collect comprehensive statistics on employment, unemployment and underemployment, and to collect data on characteristics of workers in the formal and the informal sectors of the economy. • To estimate paid and unpaid work of men and women more accurately. • To formulate more realistic employment policy and employment planning.
11	Oman	• To measure an individual's use of time for social and economic analysis, namely, productivity, informal sector size and women's economic activity. • To estimate time spent on care, leisure and information on hidden economy.
12	Pakistan	• To test eight methods of time-use data collection to assess which method yields the most accurate data on women's agrarian labor.

(Continued)

Table 11A.2 Continued

No.	Continent/ country	Objectives
		• To understand work performed by men and women in agriculture and related activities.
13	Palestine (Occupied Territory)	• To provide data on time spent by people on different activities for policy-making and decision-making (time spent on paid and unpaid work, time spent by unemployed on searching for job, leisure, care of children and elderly, hidden economy and so on).
14	Palestine	• To collect information on all activities practiced by the Palestinians and to estimate all time spent by people on different activities. • To understand the social environment in which different activities are practiced. • To collect information on unpaid work and women's activities – TUS to be the main source of information on women in the country. • To estimate the time spent on leisure and social activities and in traveling.
15	Philippines	• To collect data on all the forms of work performed by men and women. • To estimate women's contribution to GDP and to total well-being of the population. • To learn from this pilot study to organize national TUS.
16	Saudi Arabia	N/A (small survey in 1980s)
17	Thailand	*Earlier surveys (1985, 1990, 1995)* • To understand the participation of people in cultural and custom-related activities. *2000/2001 survey* • To get comprehensive knowledge on how people over ten years of age spend their time on different paid and unpaid work. • To understand gender differences in paid and unpaid work. • To provide data to markedly improve the estimates of labor contribution to GDP. • To provide internationally comparable time-use data for the country.
18	Turkey	*1996 survey* • The harmonized pilot survey aimed to collect information on household production, human capital, caring, personal development, voluntary work and travel done by men and women in rural and urban areas.

Table 11A.2 Continued

No.	Continent/ country	Objectives
		2003 survey • To highlight the roles that women play in agricultural production and related production activities. • To collect information on the time use in three different agricultural seasons. **2006 survey** • To collect comprehensive data on paid and unpaid work of men and women in rural and urban areas in Turkey.
	Africa	
19	Benin	• To assess women's work in informal home-based and subsistence activities. • To estimate women's domestic work. • To obtain information on gender difference in time use.
20	Botswana	*UNIFEM regional office commissioned TUS* • To encourage development of gender-sensitive policies and budgets. • To encourage the development of satellite accounts to measure contribution of unpaid care to the economy. • To promote recognition of women's contribution to the economy and society. • To promote better provision for people infected and affected by HIV and AIDS.
21	Burkina Faso	N/A (small survey in 1967)
22	Cameroon	N/A (small survey in 1967)
23	Chad	• To investigate male and female participation in the labor force, including informal and subsistence work.
24	Gambia	N/A (small survey in 1967)
25	Ghana	• To collect information on living standards of people in Ghana. • To collect statistics on the work performed by men and women in Ghana.
26	Guinea	• To collect information on the time spent by men and women on paid and unpaid work. • To estimate the time spent by men women on informal work, including the collection of fuel, agriculture and so on.
27	Kenya	N/A (small survey in 1967)
28	Madagascar	• To understand sharing of paid and unpaid work by men and women. • To estimate time spent on subsistence and informal work by men and women.

(*Continued*)

Table 11A.2 Continued

No.	Continent/ country	Objectives
29	Malawi	• To collect information on the time spent by men and women on household work, collection of fuel, agricultural activities, fishing and so on. • To estimate unpaid domestic work performed by men and women.
30	Mali	• To investigate male and female participation in the labor force, including informal and subsistence work.
31	Mauritius	• To understand sharing of paid and unpaid work by men and women. • To estimate time spent on subsistence and informal work by men and women.
32	Morocco	• To examine how women participate in economic life. • To understand how sociocultural norms and practices constrain women's participation in work. • To quantify and describe the different tasks of women. • To determine the factors that influence women's contribution to development. • To find an adequate methodology to estimate women's conditions and their contribution to economic and social development.
33	Mozambique	*UNIFEM regional office commissioned TUS:* • To encourage development of gender-sensitive policies and budgets. • To encourage the development of satellite accounts to measure contribution of unpaid care to the economy. • To promote recognition of women's contribution to the economy and society. • To promote better provision for people infected and affected by HIV/AIDS.
34	Nigeria	*For both surveys* • To measures women's unpaid work, to understand the division of labor within the household, to estimate the incidence of the child labor and to collect data for compiling household satellite accounts. • To determine methods for collecting data on time use for analysis of social and economic issues such as division of labor in the households, women's unpaid work, changes in allocation of time to do activities and so on.
35	Papua New Guinea	N/A (small survey in 1962)

(Continued)

312

Table 11A.2 Continued

No.	Continent/ country	Objectives
36	Rwanda	N/A (small survey in 1962)
37	Sierra Leone	N/A (small survey in 1962)
38	South Africa	• To measure and analyze time spent by men and women. • To provide new information on division of paid and unpaid work by men and women. • To incorporate unpaid work in satellite accounts. • To gain more insight on the reproductive and leisure activities by household members. • To gain more understanding of productive activities such as subsistence work, casual work and work in the informal sector.
39	Tanzania	• To estimate workforce employed in paid work, including informal work. • To collect data on time spent by men and women in unpaid work.
40	Tunisia	N/A
41	Uganda	N/A (small survey in 1976)
42	Zimbabwe	*UNIFEM regional office commissioned TUS:* • To encourage development of gender-sensitive policies and budgets. • To encourage the development of satellite accounts to measure contribution of unpaid care to the economy. • To promote recognition of women's contribution to the economy and society. • To promote better provision for people infected and affected by HIV/AIDS.
	Latin America	
43	Argentina	• To quantify unpaid care work performed by women and men in the household. • To use the data to promote policies focused on enhancing the living conditions of women and on the equitable integration of women and men into society.
44	Bolivia	• To collect information on informal work done by men and women, and to collect data on unpaid care work/ voluntary work performed by men and women.
45	Brazil	*All surveys* • To understand and estimate unpaid domestic work of women and men. • To understand gender inequalities in the economy and society.

(Continued)

Table 11A.2 Continued

No.	Continent/ country	Objectives
46	Chile	• To understand time spent on paid and unpaid work by men and women in Santiago.
47	Costa Rica	• To collect statistics and estimate unpaid work performed by men and women in the economy. • To collect data on all the forms of work of men and women.
48	Cuba	• To have statistics on the use of time in various population groups. This purpose is related to gender equality in paid/unpaid work. • To get statistics on individual and household levels. The second purpose is related to work division inside the house.
49	Dominican Republic	• To evaluate the magnitude of unpaid work. • To analyze the participation of women and men in unpaid work. • To identify the variables related to unpaid work.
50	Ecuador	• To collect information on the time spent on unpaid care by men and women and informal/subsistence work.
51	El Salvador	• To measure the economy of care by measuring unpaid domestic work. • To design policy for care.
52	Guatemala	• To provide policy-relevant data on living conditions to design a poverty alleviation strategy. • To explore issues of labor behavior more fully. • To understand how government policies can be developed for employment, infrastructure and so on.
53	Mexico	• To understand the different activities men and women perform. • To measure how much time they spend on these activities during the day.
54	Nicaragua	• To provide policy-relevant data on living conditions to design poverty alleviation strategy. • To explore labor behavior more fully so that government can design employment policies, infrastructure and so on.
55	Peru	• To understand the time-use pattern of men and women in paid and unpaid work. • To understand gender inequalities in the distribution of total work.
56	Uruguay	• To collect comprehensive information on unpaid work of men and women.

Table 11A.3 Survey design of TUS in developing countries

No.	Continent/ country	Sample size	Surveyed population	Reference period	Method of data collection	Context variables
	Asia					
1	Bangladesh	Small sample	6 years and older all HH members	Yesterday – single period	Face-to-face interview – stylized questions	
		Small sample 1000 HH (R + U)	6 years and older all HH members	Yesterday – single period	Face-to-face interview – stylized questions	
2	Bhutan	Pilot – small 350 respondents	All selected HH	Pilot survey 5 months	Face-to-face interview one-day recall time diary	
		National 950 respondents	All selected HH	Four months	Face-to-face interview one-day recall time diary	
3	China	Pilot small sample (R + U)	15 to 74 years all HH members	One day – single period	Self-reported 24-hour time diaries (illiterates were helped)	
		National (10 provinces) 16661 HH and 37142 members	15 to 74 years all HH members	One day (May 2008) – single period	Self-reported 24-hour time diaries (illiterates were helped)	
4	India	Small	6 years +	One day	Observation	None
		Small	6 years +	One day	Observation and recall	None
		18600 HH		2 days in a week – one year	Face-to-face interview one-day recall time diary	Paid/unpaid, inside/outside home
5	Indonesia	Small – 100 Villages – 1200 HH	15–49 years women HH	One day – single period	Time diaries – recall	None

	Country	Sample	Population/age	Time period	Method	Activity details
6	Israel	Small survey National 951 diaries	20 years + all HH members New residents, migrants, old residents etc	One day – single period	Face-to-face one-day recall 24-hour diary	None
		National 4843	14 years + all HH members New residents, migrants, old residents etc	One year	Face-to-face one-day recall interview and self-reported time diaries	None
7	Lao PDR	National 8882 persons	10 years + 1 person from each HH	One year	One-day recall interview – time diary	None
8	Malaysia	Small rural sample	15–64 years	Agri season in the year	Stylized questions	None
		National sample 32000 respondents		Single time period		None
9	Mongolia	Pilot	12 years and older – 3 persons from each HH	2–3 days in a week April 2000 – single time period	Self-reported 24-hour time diary and face-to-face one-day recall	Where, with whom, paid/unpaid, what transport
		3135 HH	12 years and older all HH members	Four quarters – one year	Self-reported 24-hour time diary and face-to-face one-day recall	Where, with whom, paid/unpaid, what purpose
10	Nepal	Small surveys (3) – 192 HH – 24 HH and 420 HH	6 years + all HH members	Carried out in different seasons	Observation methods – random observations from morning to evening	None
11	Oman	National	5 years + all HH members	Last week – one year	Face-to-face interview – stylized questions	None
		National	15 years + all HH members	One year	Self-reported 24-hour time diaries and one-day recall interview (time diary)	None

(Continued)

Table 11A.3 Continued

No.	Continent/ country	Sample size	Surveyed population	Reference period	Method of data collection	Context variables
12	Pakistan	Small women agricultural laborers		One day – single period	8 methods tried out	None
13	Palestine	National 4019 HH	10 years + two members (M + W) from each HH	One year	Self-reported 24-hour time diaries and family members helped when illiterate members	Paid/unpaid, where, with whom
14	Palestine (Occupied Territory)	National 4019 HH	10 years + all HH members	One year	Self-reported 24-hour diary	Paid/unpaid, with whom, where, location and transport
15	Philippines	Pilot survey (1 rural, 1 urban area)		One day – single time period	Self-reported 24-hour time diary and face-to-face one-day recall interview	N/A
16	Saudi Arabia					
17	Thailand	National 27000 HH	10 years +	One day (August 2001)	Self-reported 24-hour time diary	Where, with whom, for whom and paid/unpaid
18	Turkey	Small sample 86 urban and 31 rural HH	12 years + all HH members	One day – single period	Self-reported 24-hour time diaries	
		Small – 57 HH	12 years + all HH members	Two days in the reference week. Three different months to get seasonality	Self-reported 24-hour time diaries	Paid/unpaid

	National 5070 HH	12 years + all HH members	One year	Self-reported 24-hour time diaries	
Africa					
19 Benin	National 1787 HH – U, 1419 HH – R	6–65 years	March–April – Single time period	Yesterday – face-to-face recall interview (diary)	None
20 Botswana	Small surveys	N/A	Single time period	Face-to-face interview	N/A
21 Burkina Faso	Small survey		One point period	Face-to-face interview	
22 Cameroon	Small surveys			Face-to-face interview – stylized questions	
23 Chad	Small survey			Face-to-face interview – stylized questions	
24 Gambia	Small survey		One point period	Face-to-face interview – stylized questions	
25 Ghana	National 5998 HH	7 years + all HH members	Seasonality included	Face-to-face interview – stylized questions – time spent in selected HH activities in the last seven days.	
26 Guinea	National	15 years + all HH members except disabled and sick.	One week – single period	Face-to-face interview – stylized questions and one week recall	
27 Kenya	Small study	All HH members	Yesterday – single time period	Face-to-face one-day recall interview	
28 Madagascar	National 2663 HH	6–65 years all HH members	October–November One day in a year – single time period	Face-to-face interview – stylized questions	

(Continued)

Table 11A.3 Continued

No.	Continent/ country	Sample size	Surveyed population	Reference period	Method of data collection	Context variables
29	Malawi	Large survey	4 years + all HH members	Sample spread over one year – monthly time use available	Face-to-face interview – stylized questions	
		National 11280 HH	4 years + all HH members	Yesterday – 13-month survey	Face-to-face interview – stylized questions	
30	Mali	Small survey – 12 villages	12 years + all HH members	Yesterday – single period	Face-to-face interview – stylized questions	
31	Mauritius	National 6480 HH	10 years + all HH members	Once in a year – single time period	Face-to-face interview – one-day recall	
32	Morocco	National – 2776 Women	Women 15–70 years	Sample spread over one year	One-day recall interview and observation method	Where, for whom / purpose
		National	Women 15–70 years (only women covered)	Sample spread over one year	One-day recall interview and observation method	Where, for whom / purpose
33	Mozambique					
34	Nigeria	Small pilot (R + U)	10 years +	One day (during reference week) – single time period	Self reported 24-hour time diary and face-to-face one-day recall time diary	None
		Small pilot (R + U)	10 years +	One day (during reference week) – single time period	Self reported 24-hour time diary and face-to-face one-day recall time diary	None
35	Papua New Guinea					

No.	Country	Coverage	Population/Age	Time period	Method	Notes
36	Rwanda	N/A	N/A	N/A	N/A	
37	Sierra Leone				Face-to-face interview – stylized questions	Where, purpose of travel
38	South Africa	National 10800 dwelling units	10 years + 2 members from each HH (randomly selected)	Feb.–Oct. 2000	Face-to-face recall interview (Time Diary)	
39	Tanzania	National	5 years + all HH members	Yesterday for seven continous days – single time period	Face-to-face one-day recall interview	
40	Tunisia	National	10 + years	Yesterday single time period	Face-to-face interview stylized questions	N/A
41	Uganda	Small study			Face-to-face interview – stylized questions	
42	Zimbabwe	Small study		One point period		
	Latin America					
43	Argentina	1425 HH (Sub sample of the main survey)	15 to 75 years – all HH members	Last week – weekday and weekend day Single period (Oct.–Dec. 2005)	Face-to-face interview – Stylized questions	None
		Bueaneous Aries – 1 Urban Center	15 to 75 years – (one randomly selected HH members)	Yesterday – 24 hours	Face-to-face recall interview (Time Diary)	
44	Bolivia	Large Sample	7 years + all HH members	Last week (weekday and weekend day)	Module on unpaid domestic work – face-to-face interview – stylized questions	

(Continued)

Table 11A.3 Continued

No.	Continent/ country	Sample size	Surveyed population	Reference period	Method of data collection	Context variables
45	Brazil	Small	Men and Women	One day – single period	24 hour self reported diaries	None
		Small	Men and Women	Three days – single period	24 hour self reported diaries	None
		Small Size 376 HH	8 years + all HH members	One day (weekly estimates)	Self reported 24 hour time diary and picot grams for illiterates	None
46	Chile	2300 HH	15 years + all members of HH	Three days in a week (one Sunday) – single period	Self reported 24 hour time diaries	Inside/ outside home, inside/ outside sentiago, or with whom
47	Costa Rica	National	12 years + all HH members	Yesterday	Face-to-face interview – stylized questions	
48	Cuba	National 1125 HH	15 years + all HH members	Predefined days – two diary days	Self reported 24 hour time diary	Where, for whom, with whom, paid / unpaid
49	Dominican Republic	National	9 years + all HH members	Yesterday June–Dec. 95 (seven months) – one diary day	Combination face-to-face recall interview and direct observation	Where, for what purpose, paid/unpaid

No.	Country	Coverage	Population	Reference period	Method	Context
50	Ecuador	National	5 years + all HH members	Last week – annual	Face-to-face interview – stylized questions	
		National	12 years + all HH members	Last week (weekday + weekend day) – single period	Face-to-face recall interview	
51	El Salvador	National			Face-to-face interview stylized questions	
52	Guatemala	National	7 years + all HH members	One day (single period)	Face-to-face recall interview – stylized questions	None
53	Mexico	National 12000 HH	8 years + all HH members	Single period (yesterday)	Face-to-face recall interview – Time Diary	Where, with whom
		National 12000 HH	8 years + all HH members	Single period (yesterday)	Face-to-face recall interview – Time Diary	Where, with whom
		National 12000 HH	8 years + all HH members	Single period (yesterday)	Face-to-face recall interview – Time Diary	Where, with whom
54	Nicaragua	National	15–60 years	Yesterday – single period	Face-to-face recall interview – Time Diary	None
		National	6 years + all HH members	Yesterday – single period	Face-to-face interview – stylized questions	None
55	Peru	Small study				
56	Uruguay	Montevideo city and suburban areas	Unpaid domestic workers in the HH	Last week – single period	Face-to-face interview – stylized questions	

322

Table 11A.4 Simultaneous activities, classification used and analysis of TUS data

No.	Continent/ country	Treatment to simultaneous activities	Classification used
	Asia		
1	Bangladesh	No data collected	Short activity list
		No data collected	Short activity list
		No data collected	Short activity list
2	Bhutan	Data collected	Own classification based on Indian classification (18 major groups) including travel and waiting.
		Data collected	Own classification
3	China	Data collected	N/A
		Data collected	N/A
4	India	No data collected	Own classification
		No data collected	Own classification
		Data collected	Indian classification – 1998–99
5	Indonesia	No data collected	Own classification
6	Israel	No data collected	Own classification
		No data collected	Own classification
		No data collected	Own classification
7	Lao PDR	No data collected	Own classification (21 activities)
8	Malaysia	No data collected	Own classification
9	Mongolia	Secondary activity recorded	Adapted UN trial classification – 1997
		Secondary activity recorded	Adapted UN trial classification – 1997
10	Nepal	Data collected	Own classification
		No data collected	Own list of activities
11	Oman	Data not collected	Own classification time-use activity classification 1999 (23 activities)
12	Pakistan	No data collected	Own classification
13	Palestine	No data collected	Adapted classification (Norway – EUROSTAT) and UN trial classification
14	Palestine (Occupied Territory)	No data collected	UN trial classification – 1997 (10 major groups)
15	Philippines	Data collected	Adapted UN trial classification
16	Saudi Arabia		N/A

(*Continued*)

Table 11A.4 Continued

No.	Continent/ country	Treatment to simultaneous activities	Classification used
17	Thailand	No data collected	UN trial classification 1997 and EUROSTAT classification
18	Turkey	Data collected	EUROSTAT classification
		Data collected	EUROSTAT classification
		Data collected	EUROSTAT classification
	Africa		
19	Benin	Data collected	Own classification (8 groups and 63 activities)
20	Botswana		N/A (small survey)
21	Burkina Faso	No data collected	Own classification
22	Cameroon	No data collected	Own classification
23	Chad	No data collected	Own classification
24	Gambia	Data not collected	Own classification
25	Ghana	Data collected	Own classification
26	Guinea	Data not collected	Adapted UN Classification
27	Kenya	Data not collected	Own classification
28	Madagascar	Data not collected	Own classification (8 groups and 63 activities)
29	Malawi	No data collected	Own classification – Adopted list of activities
30	Mali	Data not collected	Own classification
31	Mauritius	Data collected	Adapted UN trial classification 1997
32	Morocco	Data collected on parallel activity	Classification of activities by women 1998 (4-digit classification 9 major groups)
		Data collected on parallel activity	Classification of activities by women 1998 (4-digit classification 9 major groups)
33	Mozambique		N/A
34	Nigeria	Data not collected	Own classification
		Data on parallel activity collected	UN trial classification 1997 (10 major groups)
35	Papua New Guinea	Data not collected	Own classification
36	Rwanda		N/A (small survey)
37	Siera Leone		N/A

(Continued)

No.	Continent/ country	Treatment to simultaneous activities	Classification used
38	South Africa	Data collected but no prioritization	Adapted UN Classification 1997
39	Tanzania	Data collected	Adapted UN Classification 1997
40	Tunisia		N/A
41	Uganda	No data collected	Own classification
42	Zimbabwe	Data not collected	Own classification
	Latin America		
43	Argentina	Data collected	Adapted UN trial classification 1997
		Data collected	Adapted UN trial classification 1997
44	Bolivia	Not data collected	Short list of tasks (7 housework and care)
45	Brazil	Data collected	Own classification
		Data collected	Own classification
46	Chile	Data collected on primary, secondary and tertiary activities	Own list (42 activities)
47	Costa Rica	Data collected	Own classification (15 predefined activities)
48	Cuba	Data collected	Adapted UN trial classification 1997
49	Dominican Republic	Secondary activity recorded	Classification – 1995 (117 activities)
50	Ecuador	No data collected	Short list of five tasks
		No data collected	Exhaustive activity list – 99 activities + 11 tasks
51	El Salvador	Data collected	List of six productive activities + 24 predefined activities
52	Guatemala	Yes	Guatemala classification – 2000 (22 activities)
53	Mexico	No data collected	Short list of 34 activities
		No data collected	Own classification – 14 major groups, 68 subgroups
		No data collected	Own classification – 14 major groups, 68 subgroups
54	Nicaragua	Data collected but not adequate	22 specific activities
		Data collected but not adequate	22 specific activities
55	Peru		N/A
56	Uruguay	No data collected	Short list of activities

Index

Acharya, Meena, 283
active labor market policies, *see*
  employment guarantee programs
Africa, and time-use surveys
  and aims of, 216–17
  and development of, 216
  and gender and time-use
    inequalities, 217–20
  and implementation of national
    studies, 216
  and methodological issues, 220–1;
    notion of time in rural societies,
    221–3; sampling procedures,
    223–4; seasonality, 223;
    simultaneous activities, 224;
    time-use interview, 221
  and results of, 217, 218–20
  and underuse of results, 215, 225;
    explanation of, 225–6; improving
    analytical relevance, 226–7;
    measures for improving, 225–6
  see also HIV/AIDS care
African Centre for Gender and
  Development (ACGD), 216
Aguar, Neuma, 278
antiretroviral therapy, and HIV/AIDS
  care, 126, 134
Argentina
  and *Jefes y Jefas de Hogar* program,
    169
  and time-use survey, 256; sample
    size, 263, 264
  see also Buenos Aires time-use
    survey
Australia, 238, 273, 276

Beijing World Conference on Women,
  and Platform for Action, 14
benefit incidence analysis (BIA), and
  public investment, 151
  aggregating users into groups, 152
  calculating benefit incidence,
    152–6

estimating unit cost, 151
identifying users, 152
Beneria, Lourdes, 247
Benin
  and time-use survey, 24, 216, 225,
    227, 256; reference period, 265
Beveridge, Sir William, 168
Bhutan, and time-use survey, 256;
  objectives of, 261; use of data, 281
Bolivia
  and duration and incidence of
    work, 62
  and gender and time-use
    inequalities, 72–4;
    between-group, 62–7;
    decomposing, 70–2;
    within-group, 67–70
  and gendered division of labor, 58–9
  and time-use survey: methodology,
    60–1; sample size, 264
Botswana
  and female-headed households, 116
  and HIV/AIDS care, 112, 117,
    123–4, 126; costs of water, 131;
    poverty, 121; transport costs, 130
  and time-use survey, 256; objectives
    of, 261
Brazil, and time-use survey:
    classification of activities, 273–4;
    data collection methods, 269;
    objectives
    of, 261
Budlender, Debbie, 256, 283
Buenos Aires time-use survey, 181–2
  and activity classification system,
    185–6
  and activity diary, 183, 192–3
  and advantage of modular
    approach, 191–2; use of
    socioeconomic data, 203–6
  and assigning times to activities,
    189–90
  and consistency checks, 189

325